D1117365

HENRY LEE'S
CRIME SCENE HANDBOOK

HENRY LEE'S
CRIME SCENE HANDBOOK

Henry C. Lee
Timothy M. Palmbach
Marilyn T. Miller

ACADEMIC PRESS

A Harcourt Science and Technology Company

San Diego   San Francisco   New York   Boston
London   Sydney   Tokyo

This book is printed on acid-free paper.

Copyright © 2001 by ACADEMIC PRESS

All Rights Reserved
No part of this publication may be reproduced or transmitted in any form or by any means, electronic or mechanical, including photocopying, recording, or any information storage and retrieval system, without permission in writing from the publisher.

ACADEMIC PRESS

A Harcourt Science and Technology Company
Harcourt Place, 32 Jamestown Road, London NW1 7BY, UK
http://www.academicpress.com

ACADEMIC PRESS

A Harcourt Science and Technology Company
525 B Street, Suite 1900, San Diego, California 92101-4495, USA
http://www.academicpress.com

ISBN 0-12-440830-3

Library of Congress Catalog Number: 2001090543
A catalogue record for this book is available from the British Library

Typeset by Kenneth Burnley, Wirral, Cheshire, England.

Printed and bound by CPI Group (UK) Ltd, Croydon, CR0 4YY
Transferred to Digital Print 2012

CONTENTS

PREFACE

Despite countless historical cases from which to learn and improve upon we continue to watch serious crimes go unsolved or end without justice served because of errors associated with the crime scene investigation. Virtually no jurisdiction in the United States or abroad has shed this plague. It seems ironic that while forensic science has experienced significant advances and improvements, the utilization of forensic science is still at the mercy of the crime scene investigator. If the crime scene is not properly managed, all of the technology and advances we currently possess and will possess in the future will be unable to overcome these shortcomings, and true justice will continue to be unattainable in far too many cases.

A high-quality crime scene process need not be elaborate or sophisticated; rather, the simple adherence to fundamental principles and procedures will suffice. Essential crime scene functions involve the recognition, documentation, collection, and preservation of all relevant physical evidence: pattern, conditional, transient, transfer, and associative in nature. If these elements are achieved then there is a much higher probability that the case will be resolved through a reconstruction of the events and an accurate interpretation of the available information and data.

However, there is no detailed step-by-step comprehensive plan that will direct an investigator through every necessary step to process a specific crime scene. At best, and certainly the intended objective of this book, are general recommendations and guidelines that are well-established protocols designed to provide a logical plan for crime scene investigators. As depicted in the logic trees of thinking in Chapter 7 in this text, it is possible to identify common elements and issues for certain classifications of crimes.

Being aware of these fundamental elements and how they relate to one another and the overall investigation is a key for successful crime scene investigations. We believe that as you gain experience in crime scene processing you will also become aware of the reality that a logical and systematic approach is essential; yet, each scene will likely challenge you and present unique problems and issues that can best be resolved through a team approach. Whenever possible, incorporate the advice and assistance of a diverse group of representatives from police officers, crime scene technicians, forensic scientists, medical examiners, attorneys, and academia.

Our goal is to see the day when it is no longer common for a trial or investigation to conclude abruptly or implode because of mistakes made at the crime scene. Unlike a great novel or epic movie, we have only one opportunity to conduct an original crime scene search. History is a valuable, but also expensive lesson. We hope our experiences in crime scene investigation will assist students as well as experienced investigators to learn from history and avoid making similar mistakes in crime scene investigation.

CONTRIBUTORS

HENRY C. LEE

Dr Henry C. Lee was born in China in 1938. He graduated in 1960 from the Central Police College in Taiwan, Republic of China, with a major in police science. After working in Taiwan for several years as a police captain, he came to the United States to pursue further study. In 1972, he earned his BSc degree in forensic science from John Jay College of Criminal Justice in New York. He went on to study science and biochemistry at New York University and earned his MSc degree in 1974 and PhD in biochemistry in 1975. He also holds honorary doctoral degrees conferred by the University of New Haven in Connecticut, St Joseph College in West Hartford, Connecticut, University of Bridgeport – School of Law, and Roger Williams University.

Dr Lee worked at New York University Medical Center from 1966 to 1975. In 1975 Dr Lee joined the University of New Haven as an Assistant Professor where he created the school's forensic science department. He was granted tenure as a full professor three years later. Dr Lee has served as Commissioner for the Department of Public Safety, Chief Criminalist, and Director of the Connecticut State Police Forensic Science Laboratory in Meriden, Connecticut. Currently, he is Chief Emeritus for the Connecticut Division of Scientific Services. He is also a professor of the Forensic Science program at the University of New Haven and a distinguished adjunct professor at eight other universities.

Dr Lee is the recipient of many awards including the Distinguished Service Award from Taipei Taiwan Police Headquarters in 1962; the American Academy of Forensic Sciences Criminalist Sections Distinguished Criminalists Award in 1986; and the J. Donero Award from the International Association of Identification in 1989. He has received several hundred other commendations and awards. In 1992 he was elected a Distinguished Fellow of the American Academy of Forensic Sciences. He is an editor for seven academic journals, including the Editorial Board of the *Journal of Forensic Sciences*. Dr Lee has authored or co-authored 30 books, major chapters and reports; and has published approximately 400 articles in professional journals. He has served on national and international committees in forensic science, criminal justice, education and training; and has conducted and instructed over 800 workshops and seminars.

Dr Lee has assisted law enforcement agencies and investigated over 7000 major cases around the world. He has testified over one thousand times in both criminal and civil cases. He serves as a consultant for over 900 agencies.

TIMOTHY M. PALMBACH

Timothy M. Palmbach earned a Juris Doctorate at the University of Connecticut School of Law. He graduated from University of New Haven with a Master of Science in Forensic Science – criminalistics concentration. He was awarded a Graduate Fellowship Award for his academic excellence. In addition, he earned bachelor degrees in chemistry and forensic science from the University of New Haven, West Haven, Connecticut.

In 1982 Mr Palmbach became a member of the Connecticut State Police. Currently, he holds the rank of Major and serves as the Commanding Officer for the Division of Scientific Services – Forensic Science Laboratory, Controlled Substance and Toxicology Laboratory, Computer Crime and Electronic Evidence Laboratory. Previous assignments within the State Police include Chief of Staff for the Department of Public Safety, Assistant Director at Forensic Science Laboratory, and Supervisor for the Major Crime Unit. During these assignments he has testified on numerous occasions in both Connecticut State and Federal courts, including giving expert witness testimony in the areas of crime scene processing and analysis, and blood spatter pattern interpretation.

He has worked on several high profile criminal investigations and assisted Dr Henry Lee with crime scene reconstruction of several other high profile investigations. Currently, he serves as a member of three national and international forensic investigative committees. These committees consist of world-renowned forensic experts such as Dr Henry Lee, Dr Michael Baden, Dr Cyril Wecht, Dr Peter Dean, Professor James Starr, Attorney Linda Kenney, and Judge Haskell Pitluck.

Mr Palmbach is a Practitioner in Residence at University of New Haven, Department of Forensic Sciences. He is also an adjunct professor and guest lecturer at several other universities. In addition, he is a certified law enforcement instructor, and a staff lecturer for the Institute of Forensic Science, West Haven, CT. He has presented training and provided consultation in the United States as well as several Asian countries.

Mr Palmbach is a member of the Connecticut Bar Association as well as the United States District Court of Connecticut Bar Association. He is also a member of the American Academy of Forensic Sciences and a member of the International Association of Blood Spatter Analysts. Also, the International Association of Identification have certified him as a Senior Crime Scene Analyst.

MARILYN T. MILLER

Marilyn T. Miller is a graduate of Florida Southern College with a bachelor's degree in Chemistry. She earned a master's degree in Forensic Chemistry from the University of Pittsburgh. In May 2002 she will receive an EdD for Johnson & Wales University in Post-Secondary Educational Leadership. She is an Assistant Professor and Coordinator for the Undergraduate Forensic Science program at the University of New Haven, Connecticut. Marilyn is a full member of the Criminalistics section of the American Academy of Forensic Science, the Southern Association of Forensic Scientists, and the American Chemical Society. As a post-secondary educator she teaches a wide variety of forensic science and crime scene investigation classes to both forensic science and criminal justice majors at the undergraduate and graduate levels. She is a faculty member of the Henry Lee Institute of Forensic Science. She has presented and taught as part of hundreds of forensic seminars across the United States.

For over 15 years she worked as a supervisor and forensic scientist for law enforcement agencies in North Carolina, Pennsylvania, and Florida. She has testified over 350 times in county, state, and federal courts of law as an expert witness in the field of forensic sciences and crime scene reconstruction. Marilyn designed, opened and operated forensic laboratories on the West Coast of Florida. She has participated in hundreds of crime scene investigations, both as an active investigator and recently, as a consultant for both state and defense attorneys. In addition to expertise in forensic science, other areas of emphasis are scientific crime scene investigation and reconstruction and bloodstain pattern analysis.

Marilyn relates that her biggest accomplishment has been to prepare objective, ethnical, and eager forensic science and criminal justice students for the real world of forensic investigations.

CHAPTER 1

GENERAL CRIME SCENE CONSIDERATIONS

INTRODUCTION

Crime scene investigation is more than the processing or documentation of crime scenes, nor is it just the collection or packaging of physical evidence. It is the first step and the *most crucial step* of any forensic investigation of a possible criminal act. The foundation of all forensic investigations is based on the ability of the crime scene investigator to recognize the potential and importance of physical evidence, large and small, at the crime scene. The subsequent identification of the physical evidence along with determination of the possible source or origin of the evidence, that is, its individualization, are the next steps in the investigation. Finally, proper crime scene investigation is the starting point for the process of establishing what occurred – in other words, it is the initiation of

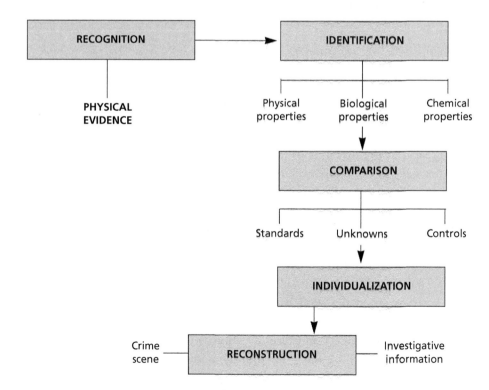

Figure 1.1
Forensic examinations.

the crime scene reconstruction. Of course, careful processing, documentation, and collection of physical evidence are integral parts of the 'investigation process' and crime scene investigation.

Contrary to the way it is portrayed in popular television programs or mystery movies, crime scene investigation is not glamorous or accomplished in an easy or lackadaisical manner. It is an organized, methodical, systematic, and logical process. If done properly, it requires not only adequate training, current and ongoing, and experience on the part of the investigator, but necessitates a managed and coordinated team effort. Crime scene investigation must never restrict the flow of information from the scene, it must provide for an opening of communication between scene investigators and all other law enforcement personnel. *Communication and team effort* are integral parts of any crime scene investigation. Figure 1.2 illustrates the coordinated effort necessary for crime scene investigations.

TYPES OF CRIME SCENES

There are many ways to classify a crime scene. One classification can be based on the original location at which the crime was committed, another is based on the boundary of the scene, and the activities at the scene; and finally, the classification of the scene can be based on the size or condition of the crime scene. The following are some common classification categories.

PRIMARY AND SECONDARY

This is a classification based on original location where the crime occurred.

On 22 November 1999, the Midpoint Police Department responds to a call to investigate a suspicious death. Upon arrival at the scene, the officer finds a woman's partially clothed body in a dilapidated garage. There appear to be tire tread marks in the dirt next to the body in the garage. The victim's clothing appears to have large clumps of fibrous material adhering to it and the body has been partially wrapped in drapery material. Several small diameter, white cord materials are used as ligatures to tie the victim. Is this the location where the crime was originally committed or just the location where the body was just dumped? Are there other areas that might be part of the crime scene too? In this case, the suspect lured the victim from her home to his home, where the woman was tied up and eventually strangled. The suspect then, using his own vehicle, transported the body to the abandoned garage. The result – many crime scenes will be identified and associated with this investigation. Careful crime scene investigation and forensic testing of physical evidence from this case, including matching the cord from the body to the drapery cords in the suspect's house and matching the clumps of fibers on the victim's clothes to the carpet fibers in the suspect's house, will be done to solve this crime. Physical evidence from all the scenes will be necessary for a successful conclusion.

Historically or traditionally, the definition of this homicide scene is the area where her body was found. However, by now we have learned through experience that any area, for example the suspect's house, victim's house, suspect's vehicle, and the road to the garage, are connected to the homicide. Therefore, the crime scene can be and often is more than one location. The victim's home, the victim's place of business, the victim's car, the suspect's home, the suspect's place of business, the suspect's car, the road they travel, and the site where the victim's body was found – can and should all be considered possible crime scenes. In an attempt to further delineate and even organize the crime scenes, the term *primary scene* is often used to refer to where the original or first criminal act occurred and any subsequent scene(s) is considered to be a *secondary scene(s)*, as shown in Photo 1.1.

Consider another example. The Four Corner National Bank is held up in Riverton, Wyoming. Two masked, armed robbers enter the bank. Waiting for them in the getaway car is a female accomplice/driver. After jumping the counter to retrieve the money, one of the robbers enters the vault area and attempts to retrieve additional cash. Shortly, the two robbers exit the bank, dropping one of their bags as they jump into the car. Later, a uniformed patrol officer finds the getaway car abandoned at a location several miles from the bank. What is the primary crime scene? And the secondary scene(s)?

Photo 1.1

Secondary crime scene: an outdoor secondary scene depicting a location where the victim's body was deposited in the wood after she was murdered.

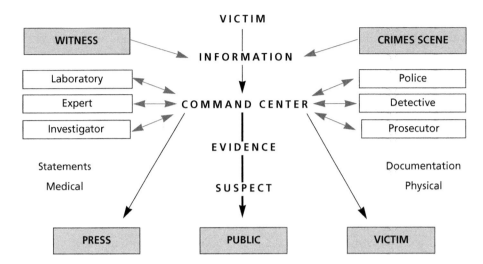

Figure 1.2

Role of crime scenes in criminal investigations.

MACROSCOPIC AND MICROSCOPIC

This is a classification based on size.

A crime scene may additionally be defined from macroscopic and microscopic points of view. The macroscopic point of view of the crime scene above would include not just a location, but the victim's body, the suspect's body, the houses, and the vehicle involved. Essentially this definition is looking at variously sized crime scenes within a crime scene – all are important and should be treated and investigated as crime scenes. The microscopic definition of a crime scene is any specific object or piece of physical evidence related to the crime being investigated. In the example case, bitemarks found on the body, ligatures, fibers/hairs, fingernails, cigarette butts, any impressions and the cording are considered microscopic 'crime scenes' and would be individually investigated as crime scenes.

Every case investigated will contain many of these macroscopic and microscopic crime scenes, as shown in Photos 1.2 and 1.3. The interrelations between macroscopic and microscopic definitions of the crime scene should be considered. They can each potentially yield information useful for the entire criminal investigation and ultimate solution of the crime.

OTHER CRIME SCENE DEFINITIONS

Classifications other than those above can be based on type of crime (homicide, assault, robbery, etc.); classification based on location (indoor or outdoor); classification based on scene condition (organized or disorganized); or classification based on criminal activity (active or passive).

The crime scene can be further classified using many different classifications.

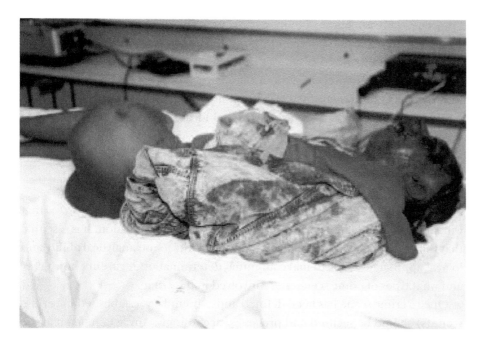

Photo 1.2

Unidentified body was found in an alleyway in Boston, MA. A body should be considered a crime scene unto itself, as it may contain many types of evidence.

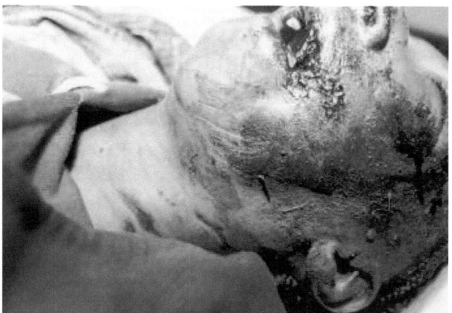

Photo 1.3

Close-up view of a homicide victim's face, depicting vegetative soil debris, physiological material, and pattern evidence.

Scenes can be classified according to the type of crime commited, such as a homicide scene, a sexual assault scene, or a burglary scene can classify the crime scene. Classifications of scenes can be based on physical location, such as indoor scenes or outdoor scenes. An elaboration of this classification would be to include the location of any potential bodies or physical evidence, such as buried or under-water scenes. Another classification of a crime scene is based on the location of the scene, such as a house, a train, a bank, or a car. Another classification of the crime scene is based upon the condition or apparent condition of a scene, such as organized or disorganized crime scenes. The use of this crime scene classification has gained popularity recently, given the increasing use of criminal profiling in investigations. Additionally, the classification of crime scenes as being 'active vs passive', 'organized vs disorganized', gives an idea of the condition at the crime scene.

SUMMARY

It is important to keep in mind that there is *no one, single classification method* that will satisfy all the elements of the crime scene and its investigation. It is essential that the crime scene investigator develop the ability to use analytical ability and logical approaches so as to make an initial determination regarding how many and what types of crime scenes were involved in the crime.

Once a crime scene has been defined and a 'boundary' established the crime scene(s) should be secured and processed accordingly. Any action taken at the crime scene should meet all legal and scientific standards and requirements. While exacting and precise boundaries of a crime scene are not always well defined and are often adjusted according to the ongoing investigation, it is essential for the crime scene investigator to understand the concept that many potential and various crime scenes could exist. Once the locations are determined, the proper sequence of events of the crime can be established, and physical evidence can be recognized from each of the scenes. The crime scene investigation and the forensic process will begin.

PHYSICAL EVIDENCE IN A CRIMINAL INVESTIGATION

INTRODUCTORY COMMENTS

Physical evidence can be classified according to its physical state, by the type of crime, by the nature of the evidence, by its composition, or by the types of question to be resolved, etc. Each of these classifications is useful for offering conceptual ideas and practical means in the crime scene search and any other investigational assistance. These classifications of physical evidence will be discussed in greater detail in subsequent chapters. It is important for the crime scene investigator to understand the value of physical evidence as well as the limitations of physical evidence; to appreciate the interaction of various definitions or classifications of crime scenes; the theory of evidence transfer; and the proper methodologies for locating microscopic crime scenes within the more obvious macroscopic crime scenes. Most of the clues that lead to the solution of the crime are at the crime scene in the form of physical evidence. In the previously described investigation, the recognition that the beige fibrous material on the victim and its subsequent identification and individualization as a Monsanto carpet fiber found in the suspect's house were instrumental in the solution of the crime. Therefore, crime scene investigators must use their knowledge of physical evidence as part of the total investigation – to recognize, classify, and define the crime scene. The experienced crime scene investigator also knows to expect the unexpected, and that classifying and defining crime scenes is the guiding procedure for proper investigations. It is from the analysis of the crime scene that the crime scene investigator can determine what type of physical evidence will most likely be found at a particular type of crime scene, where to find the physical evidence at a particular type of crime scene, how to recognize, collect, preserve, and process the physical evidence, and based upon the evidence examination in the laboratory combined with the scene appearance, reconstruct the crime scene.

The objectives of crime scene investigation are to recognize, to collect, to interpret, and to reconstruct all the relevant physical evidence at the crime scene. The major objective of the examination of physical evidence is to provide useful information for the criminal investigator in solving cases. It is the interaction of these objectives of crime scene investigation and physical evidence examination that is the basis of 'scientific crime scene investigation'.

USES OF PHYSICAL EVIDENCE

The following are examples of crime scene analysis and physical evidence examination interaction and the value of the interaction in criminal investigations.

Information on the corpus delicti

Corpus delicti is not just the body in a death investigation, as the literal translation from the Latin would indicate, but is the determination of the essential facts that will show that a crime has occurred. The essential facts are the physical evidence, patterns of evidence at the scene, and any lab results of testing of the physical evidence. Broken window glass, ransacked rooms (see Photo 1.4), disturbed cash-drawers or metal shavings outside safes would be examples of physical evidence that would be important in establishing a burglary. Likewise, bloodstains in the middle of a highway would indicate a possible vehicle hit-and-run accident has occurred, but the laboratory results showing the presence of bovine blood will further inform the investigator as to the exact type of accident that has happened. Similarly, the location of a victim's blood found on floorboards as opposed to being found at shoulder height provides for information with regards to bloodshed locations that may be significant in the reconstruction of an assault case.

Photo 1.4

View of a ransacked room located within a crime scene.

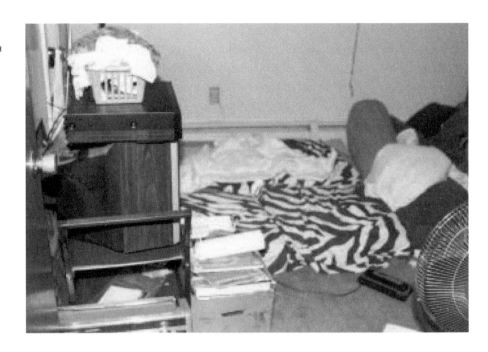

Information on the modus operandi

Most experienced criminal investigators know that many criminals have a particular method of operation or *modus operandi* (MO) which is their personal or signature/characteristic way of committing a crime. The physical evidence found at the crime scene can be very instrumental in identifying or establishing a pattern of MO (Photo 1.5). In burglaries involving breaking into a safe, the method of entry into the safe and the resulting physical evidence are all-important characteristics to establish the criminal's *modus operandi*. In bombing cases, the ignition device used, the main charge's composition, and debris found after the explosion are physical evidence examples that help to establish the pattern or signature of a bomber. Cases that are seemingly unrelated can be connected by careful crime scene investigation of similar MOs. Connection of cases by use of the physical evidence or MO is especially important in serial case investigations.

Linkage of persons to other persons, objects, or scenes

Linking a suspect to a victim is the most common and important type of linkage that the use of physical evidence can help establish (Figure 1.3). Linkage of this type is especially significant in the investigation of violent crimes. The linking of physical evidence between persons, like suspects to victim, is also directional. That is, it is important to think of linking by finding physical evidence from the suspect on the victim but it is equally important and probable to find physical evidence from the victim on the suspect (if identified and found within a reasonable time period to the crime): for example, the identification/individualization

Photo 1.5

A rash of burglaries occurred in a residential area. In all cases the point of entry was through a first-floor kitchen window. Recognition of this common element helped define the modus operandi, *and ultimately identify a suspect. Dr Lee working with FBI agents assigned to Evidence Response Team.*

of the suspect's semen on the victim's body by the matching of DNA profiles, or the identification of victim's blood, hairs, clothing fibers, or cosmetics on a suspect's clothing. Other obvious linkage between suspects and victims can be finding the victim's personal items in the suspect's possession, for example the victim's credit cards. Sometimes the exchanged physical evidence is of such a small size, referred to as 'trace', it can often be overlooked or contaminated. Therefore, it is important that all physical evidence be treated carefully and separately to avoid secondary cross-contaminations or loss of evidence.

Additionally, the linkage of a person (a suspect, a victim, or even a witness) to a crime scene is accomplished by crime scene investigation and physical evidence analysis. The identification of an individual's fingerprints at the crime scene is a direct link between the individual and a particular scene. With the advent of newer laboratory techniques now commonly being used in forensic laboratories, biological evidence such as blood, semen, hairs, and saliva can be used for the direct linking of persons to crime scenes. Indirect linkage between persons and crime scenes by the use of physical evidence can also be done. Evidence of physical objects found at the scene like footwear impressions, tire tread marks, toolmarks, or items belonging to persons found at the scene can be an indirect link. The directional, indirect linkage of the physical evidence is demonstrated by the fact that objects can be taken from the scene too. For example, the soil or vegetation of a certain scene may end up in a suspect's pant cuff or in a suspect's car. Fibers or debris from a suspect's home maight be deposited on the victim's body or on a crime scene.

Finally, another type of linkage that might occur between persons, objects, and crime scenes is the linking of an object to a particular crime. The discovery of physical evidence at a location or on a person can often link a scene or person to a specific criminal act: for example, a firearm with an obliterated serial number found at a scene. The forensic laboratory restores the serial number, the number is traced, and the owner of the firearm is identified and linked to the crime. A more specific example of linking an object to a crime occurred in the investigation of the bombing of the World Trade Building in 1985 (Photo 1.6). In the debris of the parking garage at the World Trade Center, the remains of a truck chassis with an intact vehicle identification number was found. That VIN identified the truck and the owner. Subsequent investigation led to the identification of an individual who rented the truck and reported it stolen. Hence, an object found at the crime scene linked to a crime (and a person in this case).

Figure 1.3
Linkage theory.

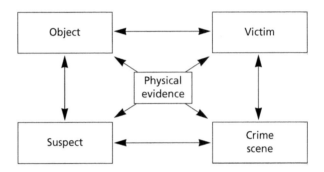

Photo 1.6

Overall view of the devastating bombing of the World Trade Center in New York City. (Courtesy of Charles Walsh, FBI.)

Disproving or supporting witness statements or testimony

The proper crime scene investigation and analysis of physical evidence can often assist with the determination of the creditability of victims', eye witnesses' or even suspects' statements or testimony. An example would be the investigation of a person believed to be the driver of a hit-and-run vehicle. An examination of the car might reveal traces of blood on the underside of the bumper or fender area. The driver explains that the blood and other damage done to the car are the result of running into a dog. Laboratory analysis on the blood reveal if it is dog or human blood, therefore, proving or disproving the driver's statement.

Crime scene patterns or patterned physical evidence are especially useful for the determination of credibility of statements. For instance, the size, shape, and distribution of gunshot residue on the shirt of a shooting victim can be used to determine the range of firing for the firearm used in a shooting. If eye witnesses differ in their statements regarding how far away a shooting victim is from the shooter, a series of test firings of the firearm and ammunition in question will facilitate the determination of eyewitness credibility (Photo 1.7). Bloodstain patterns are also an example of patterned evidence that can be used to prove or disprove statements. If a suspect explains that the victim's blood is on their clothing because the victim was held, this statement can be easily proved by identification of the bloodstain pattern type.

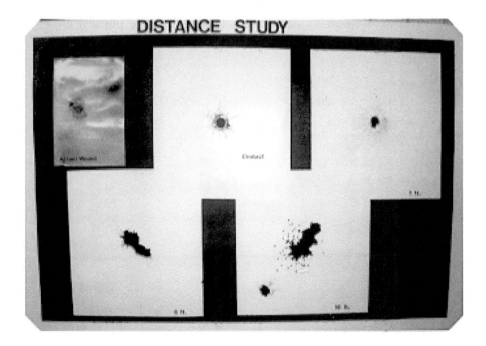

Photo 1.7

Firearms evidence distance study: upper left photograph illustrates the actual wound. The remaining targets represent test firings that confirm eyewitness statements that the victim was shot by the suspect with a shotgun and that they were 4–5 feet apart.

Identification of a suspect

The forensic examination process follows a basic sequence of steps: recognition, identification, individualization and reconstruction. The identification of a suspect by the use of physical evidence found at a crime scene uses the first three steps of this process. Physical evidence is individualized in order to identify the origin or source of the evidence after it is recognized (and collected) at the crime scene and identified at the forensic laboratory. Many types of physical evidence are individualized by examination and comparison. The best example of this individualization for the identification of a suspect is the use of fingerprint evidence (Photo 1.8). A fingerprint found at the crime scene can be searched against the AFIS (Automatic Fingerprint Identification System) fingerprint database and identified as belonging to a particular person.

Other types of physical evidence found at the crime scene that can be used to identify suspects include the identification of bitemarks and the DNA profile match of a semen sample with a suspect's known blood sample. With the current use of CODIS databases, unidentified semen and DNA samples can be 'cold' searched and suspects can be identified if their known DNA records are in the database. Figure 1.4 illustrates the use of DNA databases.

Providing investigative leads

Physical evidence recognition and laboratory analysis can be helpful in directing an investigation along a productive path. Not all physical evidence will be directly linked to or can identify a suspect. However, the physical evidence could provide indirect investigative information or leads to the solution of the crime. This is the most important and significant use of physical evidence

Photo 1.8

Fingerprint latent-to-known comparison. Latent print on the left was found at a crime scene, and was matched to the suspect's known prints (courtesy of the Sarasota Sheriff's Office).

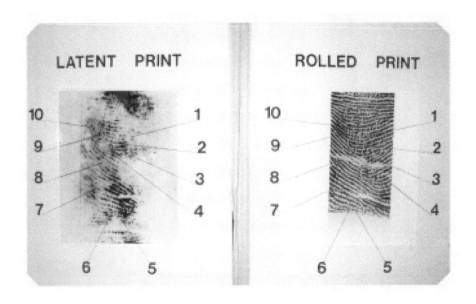

(a)

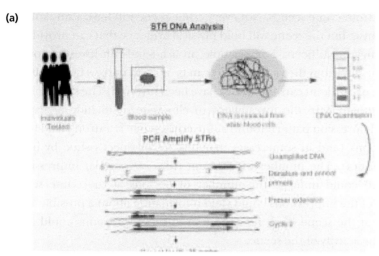

(b)

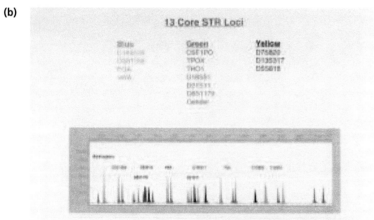

(c)

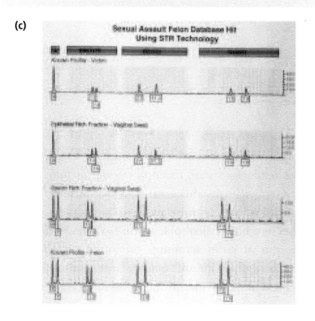

Figure 1.4

(a) STR DNA analysis.

(b) Thirteen core STR loci used in STR DNA analysis.

(c) Sexual assault felon database hit using STR DNA analysis.

(Courtesy of Dr Carl Ladd and Dr Michael Burke, CT Forensic Lab.)

collected from crime scenes. Not every crime scene will have a smoking gun or an eyewitness, but the scene will hold physical evidence that can provide help to the investigating officers. For example, in a hit-and-run investigation, a five-layer paint chip from the victim's body can be used to narrow down the number and kinds of different cars that could have been involved. The size of a footwear impression can help the investigator to eliminate or include a suspect; the footwear impression pattern found at the crime scene is a strong lead for future investigations (and in some cases may link to a suspect's shoe by individual characteristics). The number of different types of footwear impressions (see Photo 1.9) could indicate the number of persons at the crime scene, the locations of the impressions could yield information about a possible sequence of events at the scene, and the condition of the impressions could also help identify the activity of the scene.

Photo 1.9

Several footwear impression patterns observed in the snow, with blood-like stains also present.

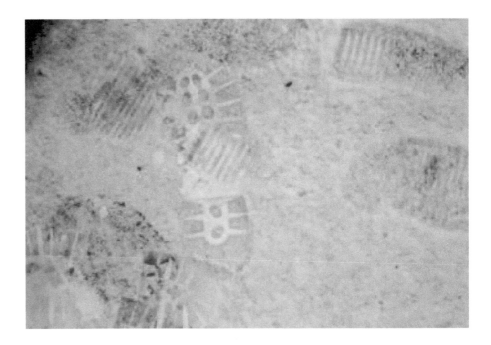

Identification of unknown substances

Another common use of physical evidence found at crime scenes is to identify the substance or chemical present. Examples would include the identification of suspected controlled substances or poisons. Additional examples of substance identification are identification of accelerants in fire debris at suspected arson scenes, blood alcohol levels or toxicology of blood specimens, and the examination of paint scrapings can often provide information of chemical composition so as to identify manufacturers or model years of suspect vehicles. Another example of identifying substances at crime scenes is the identification of chemical substance precursors at clandestine laboratories in order to identify the controlled substance being manufactured by the lab, even if the finished product is not present at the lab.

Reconstruction of a crime

This use of the physical evidence from crime scenes and their subsequent laboratory testing is also a basic step in the forensic process. In many crime scene investigations the identity and individualization of physical evidence is not in question. It is of more importance to the investigator to determine how the evidence was created and in doing so determine how the crime scene came to exist. This type of information received from the physical evidence is using the physical evidence as it was found at the crime scene to reconstruct how the crime occurred. For example, at a crime scene where only one person is bleeding, the victim, individualization of the blood on the wall next to the victim's body in the victim's bedroom is not as significant as knowing that the bloodstain pattern is consistent with blunt force trauma. The blood of course will be individualized to confirm the match to the victim but the location, number of blows inflicted, and other subsequent movements of the victim will provide information as to how the crime progressed that is especially informative for investigation and eventual prosecution. Photo 1.10 illustrates how the bloodstain evidence reconstruction indicates a sequence of events of a homicide scene.

Photo 1.10

Crime scene photograph depicting an area with multiple deposits of medium velocity impact spatter. The trashcan was moved after the blood spatter was deposited.

SCIENTIFIC CRIME SCENE INVESTIGATION

Most of the textbooks currently in the field limit crime scene investigation to the documentation of the crime scene and the subsequent collection of the physical evidence. The role of the crime scene investigator has been unfortunately defined as a crime scene technician who is only involved in crime scene security, documentation of the crime scene, and the collection and preservation of physical evidence from the crime scene. Documentation of the crime scene and the collection of physical evidence are important aspects of the crime scene investigation and must be properly done. However, these activities are purely mechanical tasks. Any investigator with minimum training might be able to perform them correctly. The completion of these crime scene tasks is essential for the integrity of the physical evidence and the ultimate conclusion of criminal investigation. These tasks are extremely important, but however have limited direct value on the solution of the crime.

Scientific crime scene investigation, as shown in Figure 1.5, is a process which not only includes the above mechanical aspects of scene security, documentation of the crime scene, and the collection and preservation of the physical evidence. It also demands and expects more dynamic approaches like scene survey, scene definition or analysis, development of the link between physical evidence and persons, and the reconstruction of the crime scene. These more dynamic aspects of the crime scene investigation play an extremely important role in the identification of the suspect(s) and the solution of the crime.

Scientific crime scene investigation is based on scientific method. That means that the investigation of the crime scene is a systematic and methodical approach. It begins with the initial response to a crime scene and continues through the scene security, the crime scene survey, documentation of the crime scene, recognition of physical evidence, development of physical evidence, collection, packaging, and preservation of physical evidence, examination of the physical evidence, crime scene analysis and profile, to, finally, the reconstruction of the crime scene. Systematic crime scene investigation is further based on the principles of transfer theory (the Locard Exchange Principle), basic logical analysis, and the utilization of scientific knowledge with forensic techniques of physical evidence examination to generate investigative leads that will ultimately solve the crime.

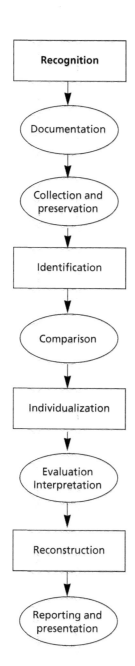

Figure 1.5
Forensic investigation
process.

CHAPTER 2

ELEMENTS OF CRIME SCENE MANAGEMENT

INTRODUCTION

In the earlier parts of this century criminal investigations were dependent on the ability of law enforcement officials to obtain information from witnesses and suspects, or on the use of informants or undercover operations. If interviews or interrogations failed to provide the needed investigative information, or no informants were available, often the cases remained unsolved.

Contemporary law enforcement has greatly expanded its ability to solve crimes by the adoption of techniques and procedures that recognize the importance of the combined powers of crime scenes, physical evidence, records, and witnesses in successful criminal investigations. Today's crimes are most often solved by a system that focuses on teamwork, advanced investigative skills, and the ability to process a crime scene properly, recognizing, collecting and preserving all relevant physical evidence and information.

However, numerous routine and high profile cases have demonstrated the harsh reality that, despite available current crime scene technologies and specialized personnel, the effectiveness of crime scene functions are only as good as the management system that supports those functions.

COMPONENTS OF AN EFFECTIVE CRIME SCENE MANAGEMENT SYSTEM

Successful crime scene management requires four separate but interconnected sub-components: information management, manpower management, technology management, and management of logistics. A deficiency in any one of these areas, or an over-emphasis on one component and neglect of another, will result in a system that is out of balance and that will jeopardize the overall crime scene investigation process.

INFORMATION MANAGEMENT

For centuries, crimes have been solved traditionally through the effective gathering of investigative leads by investigators. However, since the early 1970s many court decisions have severely constrained police and fire investigators in their use of traditional interrogation techniques. With new developments in crime scene technology the investigator has realized that the crime scene contains a tremendous amount of information. This information can often link a suspect to a crime scene, prove or disprove an alibi, or develop investigative leads. Information can be in oral form, written statements or documents, or in the form of pattern evidence. Information can be derived from individuals at the scene, forensic evidence located or remarked absent from the scene, or pattern evidence located within the scene. The sooner information can be recognized, analyzed, collected, and preserved, the better chance that the case will be solved.

There are various types of information which can be used for solving crimes, as described below.

INFORMATION FROM VICTIM

In most cases a comprehensive victim background investigation can provide valuable investigative leads. Essentially, this background investigation can be subdivided into two components. First, investigators should conduct an inquiry into the actions and whereabouts of the victim and his or her belongings during the 24-hour period preceding death. In the days and weeks to follow, investigators can commit the necessary resources and time to expand on the 24-hour period and develop a comprehensive background on the victim. Figures 2.1 and 2.2 are two examples used by law enforcement agencies in the US.

Twenty-four hour background

Once a victim has been identified, a preliminary inquiry should be made to locate the victim's family, friends and associates, to establish a 24-hour period time line, and to determine how the victim arrived at that location and what if any history the victim has with that specific scene location. The more remote the connection between the victim and that scene, the more likely someone else was involved with bringing the victim to that location. Good investigative practices include a check with motor vehicle registry files to determine what cars were available to the victim or his known close associates. Efforts should be made to locate and account for each of these vehicles. If one or more of these vehicles is suspected of being at the scene near or about the time of the incident the vehicle should be considered as a potential evidentiary source and properly preserved.

Figure 2.1 (opposite) Victim background checking form.

In addition, all of the victim's belongings, such as a purse, wallet, credit cards, safe deposit keys, or jewelry should be accounted for as soon as possible. Descriptions or photographs of missing items can be extremely valuable for solving cases.

	ASSIST	TOWN
CASE #		
VICTIM - NAME		
	ASSIGNED	DATE OF REPORT
Background		
Criminal History		
Medical Records		
Death Certificate		
Birth Certificate		
Photo		
Interview		
Written Statement		
Re-Interview		
Other		

VICTIM CHARACTERIZATIONS

Name of victim (last, first, middle)						Address No. Street, Town, State
Birth date	Age			Height	Weight	Where Employed

DAY OF WEEK OF CRIME
- a Sunday
- b Monday
- c Tuesday
- d Wednesday
- e Thursday
- f Friday
- g Saturday

WAS CRIME REPORTED
- a Within 24 hours
- b 24 - 48 hours
- c 48 hours to week
- d One week to one month later
- e More than one month later

NUMBER OF TIMES SEXUALLY ATTACKED BY ASSAILANT(S)
- a Once
- b Twice
- c More than twice

VICTIM'S SEX
- a Male
- b Female

VICTIM'S RACE
- a White
- b Black
- c Hispanic/light, med.
- d Hispanic/dark
- e Oriental
- f Other ____
- g Unknown

VICTIM'S MARITAL STATUS
- a Married
- b Single
- c Separated
- d Divorced
- e Widow (er)

VICTIM'S OCCUPATION
- a Clerical, Office
- b Entertainer
- c Factory worker
- d Food service worker (cook, waitress, etc.)
- e Foreman
- f Health services
- g Housewife
- h Laborer (unskilled)
- i Laborer (skilled)
- j Manager, Administrator
- k Mechanic, Repairman
- l Police, Fire
- m Professional and Technical
- n Prostitute (known or admitted)
- o Salesperson
- p Service worker (custodian, etc.)
- q Stewardess
- r Student
- s Teacher
- t Telephone operator
- u Truck driver
- v Writer/Artist
- w Unemployed
- x Other ____

VICTIM RESIDES WITH
- a Parents
- b Spouse
- c Family, other than above
- d Alone
- e Roommate—male
- f Roommate—female
- g Children and other family
- h Children only

MEDICAL ASSISTANCE
- a Refused medical assistance
- b Treated and released
- c Private doctor
- d Injured/outpatient
- e Serious injury/hospitalized
- f Homicide

VICTIM'S RESISTANCE
- a No resistance
- b Physical resistance—successful
- c Physical resistance—unsuccessful
- d Verbal resistance—successful
- e Verbal resistance—unsuccessful
- f Used weapon on attacker
- g Other ____
- h Multiple—specify ____

VICTIM'S RESISTANCE OVERCOME
- a By threat
- b By slight force
- c By great force

MEANS EMPLOYED BY ASSAILANT
- a Hand gun
- b Alleged gun
- c Knife
- d Oral threat
- e Physical force
- f Chemical or drugs
- g Toy gun
- h Rifle/shotgun
- i Blunt instrument
- j Cutting instrument
- k Multiple weapons
- l Other ____

RELATIONSHIP OF ASSAILANT TO VICTIM
- a Date
- b Pick up
- c Hitchhiker
- d Friend/Social acquaintance
- e Babysitter
- f Relative (immediate family) (father, brother, etc.)
- g Relative (uncle, cousin)
- h Boyfriend/Girlfriend
- i Business relationship
- j Same school
- k Neighbor
- l Has seen in the neighborhood
- m Nickname known
- n Full name known
- o Name and address known
- p Co-worker
- q Landlord
- r Total stranger
- s Unknown - no information

PREMISES ACCOSTED
- a Abandoned building
- b Alleyway
- c Apartment
- d Automobile
- e Backyard
- f Bar/Inn/Tavern
- g Basement
- h Beach
- i Bus
- j Bushes
- k Church
- l Clubhouse
- m Day Care Center
- n Driveway

- o Dwelling
- p Elevator
- q Factory
- r Garage
- s Hallway
- t Hospital
- u Hotel/Motel
- v Laundry room
- w Loading platform
- x Loft
- y Massage parlor
- z Movie theater

- a Office/Business
- b Park/Sports arena
- c Prison
- d Parking lot
- e Restaurant
- f Rest room
- g Roof landing/top
- h School/premises
- i Shed
- j Stairwell
- k Store
- l Street
- m Subway
- n Subway station
- o Taxi
- p Truck
- q Train/Bus depot
- r Vacant lot
- s Wooded area
- t Unknown
- u Other ____

INSIDE/OUTSIDE
- a Inside
- b Outside
- c Accosted IPS, taken outside
- d Accosted outside, taken inside
- e Accosted inside, taken outside
- f Accosted IPS, taken inside (note: IPS-Interior Public Space)

CRIME
- a Rape
- b Rape and burglary
- c Rape and Robbery
- d Rape and Sodomy
- e Rape, Burglary and Sodomy
- f Rape, Robbery and Sodomy
- g Attempt Rape
- h Attempt Rape and Burglary
- i Attempt Rape and Robbery
- j Attempt Rape, Robbery and Sodomy
- k Attempt Rape, Burglary and Sodomy
- l Attempt Rape and Sodomy
- m Anal Sodomy
- n Attempt Anal Sodomy
- o Multiple Sodomy (Anal and Oral)
- p Oral Sodomy (Cunnilingus)
- q Oral Sodomy (Fellatio)
- r Attempt Oral Sodomy
- s Multiple Sodomy (Cunnilingus and Fellatio)
- t Sodomy and Burglary
- u Sodomy and Robbery
- v Sexual Abuse (contact)
- w Sexual Abuse and Attempted Rape

NUMBER OF ASSAILANTS OF THIS CRIME ____

VEHICLE TYPE (Used in crime)
- a Auto
- b Bus
- c Large Truck
- d Small Truck/Camper/Van
- e Motorcycle
- f Taxi
- g Bicycle
- h Other
- i Unknown

VEHICLE MAKE
- a GM
- b Ford
- c Chrysler
- d American Motors
- e Foreign
- f Other ____
- g Unknown

VEHICLE BODY COLOR
- a White/Cream/Light
- b Grey/Silver
- c Gold/Yellow
- d Red/Maroon
- e Brown/Beige/Tan
- f Black/Dark
- g Green
- h Blue
- i Other ____
- j Unknown

VEHICLE BODY STYLE
- a Four-door
- b Two-door
- c Convertible
- d Station Wagon
- e Compact
- f Sports Car
- g Other ____
- h Unknown

WEATHER CONDITIONS
- a Seasonal, No Precipitation
- b Rain
- c Snow
- d Exceptionally Hot
- e Exceptionally Cold
- f Foggy

VICTIM'S COMMENTS (IF ANY) ADDITIONAL INFO (IF ANY)

_____
_____
_____
_____
_____
_____
_____
_____

As witnesses or associates are identified and located, initial questions should be focused on witnesses' interactions with the victim as close as possible to the suspected time of death. Seemingly basic information, such as what did they last see the victim wearing or what was the last food consumed by the victim, may be crucial. During autopsy, examination of the stomach contents may be used in conjunction with a known eating event to help determine the approximate time of death, based on food articles and degree of digestion. Also, critical information can be obtained from the victim during other phases of the autopsy, such as the presence of trace material, foreign biological material, or drugs on or within the victim.

Extended victim background

As soon as possible, investigators should conduct a comprehensive background investigation. Any and all business, family, and personal associates should be identified and interviewed. In addition to gleaning information relevant to the relationship between the victim and associate, the associate should be questioned as to other factors concerning the victim that may provide investigative leads. For example, it would be beneficial to know any habitual behavior that the victim demonstrated, such as stopping at a particular local bar every Friday night after work.

Depending upon the particular case it may be appropriate to conduct a separate but related investigation into an associate of the victim whom you suspect may be involved in the victim's death or disappearance.

Investigation into the business and financial affairs of the victim can be a tedious but informative process. Any unusual transactions or dealings contemporaneous with the time of death should be very carefully scrutinized. In several instances the accused parties continue to utilize the victim's credit cards or bank accounts even after the victim's demise. Therefore, credit and bank traces and monitoring should be requested as soon as possible. Also, telephone call records, pager messages, postal and electronic mail, and any other variety of messages should be thoroughly checked.

Finally, with the assistance of a family member or close associate the victim's residence and personal belongings should be inventoried and examined to detect any missing articles or anything out of the 'norm' for the victim.

INFORMATION FROM WITNESSES

Witnesses come from a wide variety of sources; therefore, a potential witness source should not be overlooked or ignored. However, history has shown that all too often an individual's perception of a particular act or event they witness by one or more of their five senses is not totally consistent with reality. Thus, as

Figure 2.2 (opposite)
Victim characterizations checking form.

the old axiom warns, one must takes another's word with a grain of salt. Yet, there are certain truths in even grossly exaggerated or distorted personal recitations of observed events.

Since even under the best of circumstances crime scene processing is difficult and challenging, any information which may help illuminate the underlying facts or sequence of events should not be overlooked. The information obtained from these individuals should not determine the scope of crime scene functions. Yet, one of the objectives of the process should be to try and find physical evidence or corroborating facts, which either tend to prove or disprove witness's statements. Further, crime scene personnel may want to take a few photographs or make notations recording the scene from the physical perspective of a witness. It would be very beneficial to document the existing lighting conditions or obstructions that may affect a witness's ability to see or hear accurately a critical event. Listed below are some potential witnesses an investigator should interview as soon as possible.

Direct witness

Any witness that actually perceived some portion of an incident with any of these senses should be questioned in great detail. A witness's ability to relate minute details which can be only corroborated through physical evidence helps to bolster the credibility of that witness. One form of veracity check is to inquire if the location or manner in which the witness alleges to have witnessed the events could realistically have resulted in his or her observations. For example, was there sufficient ambient light for a witness to observe what he claimed to observe?

Another consideration is to determine what actions that witness may have taken that could have damaged or altered the crime scene.

First responding officer

Often the initial police officer or firefighter arriving at a scene of a crime has an opportunity to observe and note information that will not be available at a later time, even after the arrival of seasoned crime scene investigators. Witnesses and potential suspects may still be at or contemporaneous to the scene, but may elect to leave as soon as a police presence is detected. Any information that may help later identify these individuals may be invaluable. First responders should also be aware of any transient or conditional evidence that may be present. Subsequent movement or entries into the scene can easily alter many forms of conditional evidence, such as the position of a door or the on/off status of a light switch. Transient evidence by its very nature will quickly change or dissipate, thus the first responder may be the only trained individual present during the existence of transient evidence.

General public

While caution must be exercised to prevent discrete details about a crime from becoming public knowledge, there are occasions when a general plea to the public for information proves very fruitful. A recent example involved a double homicide case where a broken watch was located at the scene and was believed to have been torn from the perpetrator during the struggle. A close-up photograph of the watch was given to the local television stations that aired the photographs. Subsequently, a TV viewer contacted the police with the name of an individual who owned such a watch and exhibited additional characteristics that made this witness suspicious. This tip resulted in the arrest of the named watch owner and initiated a successful murder investigation.

Informants

Throughout the years informants have proved to be a valuable asset for investigators. However, as observed in countless examples, the reliability of informants can and often should be questioned. Thus, informant information should be corroborated and carefully evaluated for veracity. One means to conduct this analysis is to try and determine why the particular informant chose to provide the information. It may be that the informant merely provided information to help eliminate the competition in a lucrative drug trade, or to reduce their own criminal liability or exposure in a current prosecution.

INFORMATION FROM THE CRIME SCENE/EVIDENCE

Many cases have been ultimately solved not by a lengthily scientific analysis, but rather by the properly documented, seemingly insignificant detail located or observed at the crime scene. Quality documentation includes photographs, videotaping, preparation of sketch maps, and other forms of written or audio/visual recording formats.

Information located at a scene comes in different forms requiring different methods to properly recognize, collect and preserve such information. Photo 2.1 shows an investigation searching physical evidence by utilizing forensic light source.

Some of the information obtained at the crime scene is in the form of physical evidence. Physical evidence is what we generally perceive to be as the forensic evidence, such as the murder weapon or bullet casing. However, in any given case any particular object may prove to be the crucial piece of physical evidence necessary to solve the case. Thus, physical evidence can be best described as any evidence that can provide useful information for investigators in solving cases.

Photo 2.1

Investigator uses a forensic light source to search for trace and other evidence during the examination of an exhumed body. (courtesy of Gaetan Cotton, Cottonphoto.com, Boston, MA).

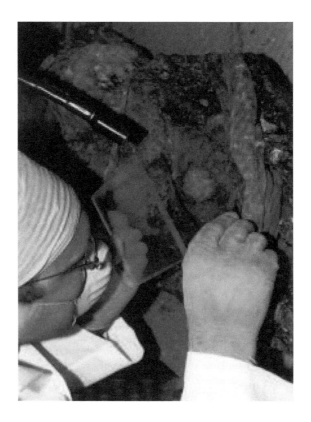

Photo 2.2

Transient evidence: color of flames and smoke will yield valuable information to arson investigators in determining the intensity of the fire.

Odors at scene	Color of flame	Temp.
• Gasoline/kerosene	• Dark red	975°F
• Material burn	• Dull red	1290°F
• Body burn	• Dull cherry red	1470°F
• Cyanide	• Full cherry red	1650°F
• Plastic	• Clear cherry red	1830°F
• Explosives	• Deep orange	2010°F
• Sulfur	• White	2370°F
• Organic solvent	• Bright white	2550°F
	• Dazzling white	2730°F

Figure 2.3
Transient evidence at fire scene.

Photo 2.3
Conditional evidence: several forms of conditional evidence can be seen in this one photo: window is open, light is on (as seen in reflection), and the closet door was open at the time of the investigators' arrival.

Transient evidence

Transient evidence is a type of evidence that is, by its very nature, temporary and can be easily changed or lost. Commonly encountered transient evidence includes odours, temperatures, temporary markings, and some biological and physical phenomena. Photo 2.2 shows a fire scene. Types of transient evidence found in fire scenes are listed in Figure 2.3.

Conditional evidence

Conditional evidence is produced by an event or an action. Similar to transient evidence, if conditional evidence is not observed and documented while at the

Photo 2.4

Pattern evidence: a glass fracture pattern observed at the point of entry at a homicide scene.

crime scene that information will be lost for ever. Examples of commonly encountered conditional evidence include lighting conditions, smoke or fire, condition of the victim's body, or precise location of specific pieces of evidence located within the scene, as shown in Photo 2.3.

Pattern evidence

There are a variety of patterns that can be found at crime scenes; most of these patterns are in the form of imprints, indentations, striations, other markings, fractures or depositions. The patterns commonly found at different crime scenes are: blood spatter or stain patterns, glass fracture patterns (as illustrated in Photo 2.4), fire burn patterns, furniture position patterns, projectile trajectory patterns, track-trail patterns, clothing or article patterns, tire or skid mark patterns, *modus operandi* patterns, powder or residue patterns.

Transfer evidence

Transfer evidence, also referred to as trace evidence, is generally produced by physical contact of persons, objects, or between persons or objects. Locard's Theory of Exchange best states this phenomenon by declaring that any time two or more surfaces some into contact with one another there is a mutual exchange of trace matter between those surfaces.

Photo 2.5
Transfer evidence: hair and fiber evidence was located on tape fragment on broken glass pane. This trace evidence was subsequently linked to the suspect.

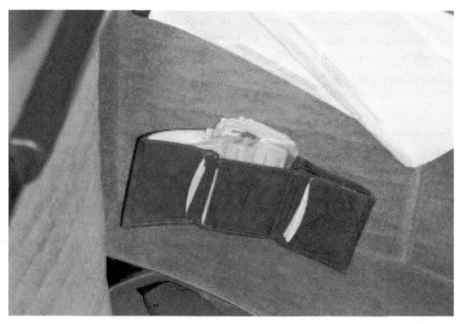

Photo 2.6
Associative evidence: during a traffic stop, followed by an investigative search, a wallet was found. This wallet belonged to a robbery homicide victim who was located 50 miles away.

Associative evidence

Specific items located at a crime scene or during an investigation may be used as evidence to associate a victim or suspect with a particular scene or to each other. Examples of associative evidence include a suspect's wallet found at the crime scene or one of the victim's personal belongings found in the suspect's possession (as shown in Photo 2.6).

INFORMATION FROM SUSPECTS

Linking the suspect to the scene, the victim, or physical evidence associated with the investigation is vital to solving the case. Traditionally, police focused their efforts regarding a suspect on obtaining a confession or incriminating statements. Recent advances in behavioral science and criminology have made apparent the significance of determining a potential suspect's motives, opportunities and *modus operandi*, or method of operation, patterns. In addition, the tremendous advances in forensic science and recent implementation of artificial intelligence and forensic databases have also expanded the potential pool of information available from a suspect.

Background information

Generally, the same basic investigative inquiries should be conducted into the suspect's background. As prescribed in investigating a victim's background, the 24-hour background is critical and needs to be thoroughly conducted as soon as possible. Moreover, a time line and comprehensive financial analysis is often beneficial. Thereafter, a more extensive background can be conducted focusing on information that would associate the suspect with the victim, or help in establishing a reasonable motive and opportunity. Also, it may be beneficial merely to place the suspect at the scene of the crime or in contact with a piece of significant physical evidence.

Modus operandi *patterns*

Behavioral science and criminal profiling research and analysis has identified specific general patterns or methods of operation that can be deduced from a systematic and thorough crime scene analysis. Once a particular *modus operandi* pattern has been identified, generalizations can be established that may help identify a limited class of likely suspects. Moreover, in cases involving serial criminals identification of these patterns may help link separate cases and associate the known previous behavior of a suspect to those cases. Typical cases where this type of analysis is beneficial are those cases involving serial killers, serial rapists, or serial arsonists. However, caution should be exercised to avoid placing too much emphasis on behavioral profiling as that may result in tunnel vision or a misguided investigation. As with any form of investigative information, *modus operandi* patterns should be evaluated in conjunction with other investigative information and physical evidence.

INFORMATION FROM DATABASES

Records pertaining to an individual's identification vary in the degree of individualization and in the accessibility to law enforcement. Until the past few years the vast majority of laboratory examinations were conducted to compare known samples to unknown samples, or merely identify some class and individual characteristics for a piece of physical evidence. However, with the advent of forensic databases, forensic laboratories are employing artificial intelligence methods that can actually identify potential suspects and link previously unconnected cases.

Current databases store and search data including DNA profiles, fingerprint identifications, and bullet and cartridge casing characteristics. Each of these systems has accomplished significant successes and helped to solve no-suspect homicides, sexual assaults, burglaries, and other criminal offenses. This ability to search no-suspect cases against offender databases has greatly enhanced the value of forensic analysis in a preponderance of criminal investigations. Some of these databases are created and maintained locally, but many jurisdictions are in the process of linking their databases to national databases, thus greatly expanding the size of the database.

DNA databases

Some of the most individualizing records are DNA profiles obtained within a sexual offender or felony database. With the discriminating power of current

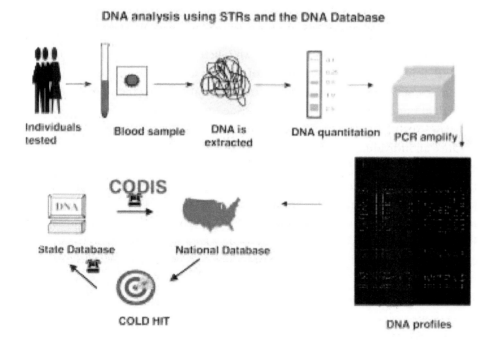

DNA analysis using STRs and the DNA Database

Individuals tested

Blood sample

DNA is extracted

DNA quantitation

PCR amplify

CODIS

State Database

National Database

COLD HIT

DNA profiles

Figure 2.4

Utilizing a national DNA database to help identify suspects whose DNA profile were obtained after their conviction of a serious offense, as prescribed by that jurisdiction's state law (courtesy of Dr Heather Coyle-Miller, Conn. State Forensic Laboratory).

DNA systems such as the short-tandom repeat (STR) multiplex system, the identification ability or discrimination index is extremely high (Figure 2.4).

Many state and federal jurisdictions have enacted legislation that allows for the collection of known blood samples from convicted offenders. These blood samples are then analyzed and DNA profiles are obtained and stored within an offender database. No-suspect cases in which suspect DNA profiles have been obtained can then be compared to the offender database profiles. This technology has solved many no-suspect rape cases, and identified several serial rapists. Yet the potential value for these databases has not been realized since most jurisdictions have only implemented their offender databases within the past five years and the relative size of these databases compared to all known offenders is still small.

In a majority of jurisdictions the law restricts the offender DNA database to felony-level sexual assault related convictions. However, several states have expanded the scope of their sex offender databases to include DNA profiles from a wide range of convicted felons.

In an effort to balance the privacy interests and concerns associated with an individual's DNA profile, many states have implemented stringent regulations concerning the accessibility to and use of the database profiles. As technologies continue to expand and become increasingly more common and accepted, the use of individualizing records, such as DNA databases, will likely expand.

Fingerprint databases

Automated fingerprint identification systems have been used to solve crimes and associate unknown fingerprints to an individual for many years. The success of these systems is mainly due to large databases. Many states have fingerprint files in the millions range, including known inked fingerprint impressions from persons arrested for a wide variety of offenses, military and government employees, special license applicants, and other various sources. Many of these individual fingerprint databases are connected to adjacent or nationally linked databases.

Once an individual's known fingerprints are entered into the automated fingerprint system, those fingerprints can be checked against a file of unidentified latent prints associated with a criminal investigation, or checked against the known file to determine if the person is using an alias or is wanted for a crime under a different name. A sketch diagram of AFIS system is shown in Figure 2.5. Photo 2.7 shows an AFIS workstation. As new technology and better trained crime scene personnel become more prevalent, more fingerprint evidence will be located and recovered from crime scenes, thus further enhancing the success rate of automated fingerprint identification systems.

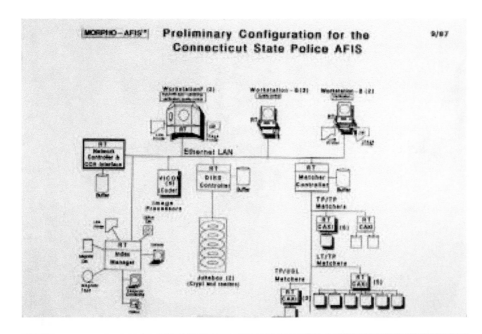

Figure 2.5
An example of an Automated Fingerprint Identification System (AFIS).

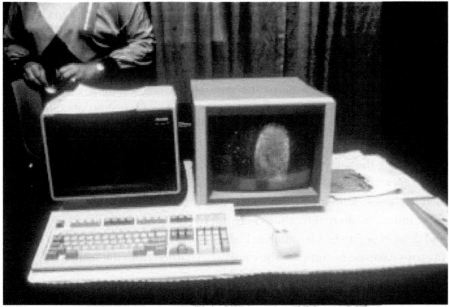

Photo 2.7
An AFIS workstation.

Casing and bullet databases

Violent crime involving the use of weapons, particularly drug related offenses, prompted the introduction of databases systems that can store individual characteristics associated with firearms evidence and help solve many of these violent crimes.

With many of the all-too-common drive-by shootings or street crimes associated with the illegal drugs trade, the only available evidence has been a few

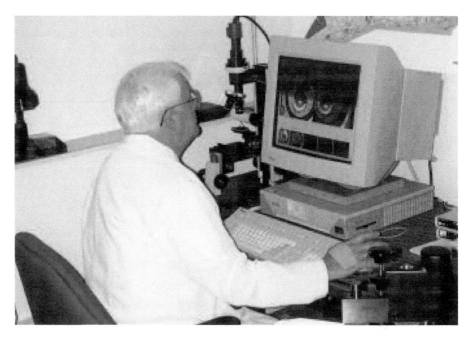

Photo 2.8

A firearms evidence system being used to compare a shell casing located on the ground at a drive-by shooting to a test-fired cartridge obtained from the suspect's gun.

cartridge cases recovered from the shooting scene. Until the advent of these databases, this evidence was of little value unless the police were able to recover the weapon used in the shooting. Currently, these databases can be used to associate cartridge cases from one crime scene to another crime scene, or associate those cases to a particular gun from which a known cartridge case sample has been obtained. Known databases consist of test shots obtained from any weapon submitted to the firearms unit of the laboratory as well as from guns seized by police and ordered to be destroyed.

Following the success of databases that stored individualizing information on casing, new databases are being developed to store and search individualizing characteristics identified on the bullets themselves. This technology is helpful in those instances where the casings were not recovered and a bullet was recovered and determined to be identifiable. Photo 2.8 shows a firearms examiner using a firearms database to compare the evidence recorded from the scene.

INFORMATION FROM RECORDS

Records and data available for investigative purposes have grown exponentially during the past decade. Many of the traditional law enforcement databases have been expanded while entirely new databases have been developed and implemented. In addition, our computer-dominated culture has spawned an entire network of personal databases that often provide invaluable information to investigators. A vast majority of that data is readily available as public records or can be located relatively easily through Internet domain searches.

```
 31/09/1980  13:58:13  ***************
NAME: Doe, Jane              NUMBER: 123456           DOB: 01/01/70
LOCATION: DISCHARGE          JURISDICTION: DISCHARGE  STATUS: ACCUSED
LOCATION ENTRY TYPE: DISCHARGED, DID NOT RETURN FROM COURT  DATE: 08/15/1997
OFFENSE: 53A117   CRIMINAL MISCHIEF, THIRD DEGREE   BM   BOND:      0
SENTENCE: MIN:   0 Y  0 M   0 D  MAX:   0 Y  0 M   0 D   DETAINERS:
RELEASE DATES:   MIN: 00/00/0000  MAX: 00/00/0000      ESTIMATED:
SPECIAL MANAGEMENT:
                            DNA   DRWN .......... CONFM ........
RACE: BLACK           SEX: FEMALE       HAIR COLOR: BLACK    EYES: BROWN
HEIGHT: 5 FT 09 IN    WEIGHT: 130 LBS   MARITAL STATUS: M    DEPENDENTS: 1
EDUCATION LEVEL: 10   VET STATUS: N     MED INSURANCE: N     MVD:
SSN: 000-01-0001      FBI #: 12345      OTHER #:             SFBI #: A1234
BIRTHPLACE:    CONNECTICUT            CITIZENSHIP: UNITED STATES
HOME ADDRESS: 10 Main Street    TOWN: Hatfield       STATE: CT  ZIP:

* * * * * * * * * * * EMERGENCY CONTACT INFORMATION * * * * * * * * * * *
NAME:   Jack Jones           RELATION: FRIEND          PH:
STREET: 10 Main Street       TOWN: Hatfield     STATE: CT ZIP: .....

PRIOR LOCATION:        FILE LOCATION:        MED FILE:
INITIAL DOC ADMISSION: 01/17/1992    LATEST DOC ADMISSION: 08/04/1997
SP35 01/17/2001 CT DEPT OF CORRECTION  = FACE SHEET DISPLAY  RT50  CSP35  END

TRANSACTION: RT50    NUMBER:
```

Figure 2.6
National Crime Information Center (NCIC) criminal history sample printout.

Criminal records

For years criminal histories were limited to basic information such as offender name, last known address, some identification numbers, and a list of criminal charges. Current criminal record files contain detailed information on the offender, including case dispositions, multiple identifiers or tracking numbers, blood types, availability of DNA profile, and some general *modus operandi* characteristics. Also, a majority of the individual state and local criminal record systems are linked through a national criminal history index. An example of a NCIC record is shown in Figure 2.6.

Firearms sale and transfer records

Responding to a recently decreasing but still significant number of gun-related deaths each year, legislatures have expanded firearms laws and regulated the sale and transfer of weapons significantly. As more states adopt these measures it will be easier for investigators to trace the history of any particular weapon, and determine if that weapon was used in any other crime throughout the country. In addition, permits and weapons check systems are being automated, thus making it more difficult for an individual with a felony criminal history or lack of proper permits to legally obtain a firearm. Figure 2.7 shows a firearms record tracking form.

Judicial and correction records

An offender spends the majority of the time outside the control and custody of the law enforcement agencies. Rather, the offender often spends years under

State of Connecticut
Department of Public Safety

Firearm Tracing & Identification

FOR NTC USE ONLY

Pursuant to Sec. 54-36n, C.GS, print or type all entries and submit completed form on date of seizure, retaining original copy in the incident file.
FAX to the Statewide Firearms Trafficking Task Force @ (203) 238-6176.

PART I TRACE INITIATION INFORMATION

1a Date of Request	1b Priority	☐ Routine	☐ Urgent (if urgent, check one or more of the following boxes):
		☐ Assault ☐ Terrorist Act	☐ Robbery ☐ Terrorist Threat	☐ Kidnapping ☐ Other: (specify)	☐ Murder/Suicide ☐ Rape/Sexual Assault

PART II – CRIME CODE INFORMATION

3a Gang Involved ? ☐ YES NAME OF GANG_____ ☐ NO	Juvenile Involved ? ☐ YES ☐ NO	Entered into NIBN/DRUGFIRE ? ☐ YES ☐ NO

PART IV – OTHER AGENCY REQUESTING TRACE (PART III WAS OMITTED)

4a. ORI Number(NCIC)	4b. Agency Contact Numbers Telephone No. FAX No.	4c. Agency Officer's Name	4d. Badge No.
4e. Agency Case No.	4f. Department/Unit	4g. Agency Mailing Address	

PART V – FIREARMS INFORMATION (verify data in 5a-5e & 5h)

5a. Serial Number ☐ Attempted to Raise ☐ Obliterated ☐ None	5b. Firearm Manufacturer	5c. Type (code letter only, see below)

5d. Caliber	5e. Model	5h. Any Additional Markings	5f. Imported By	5g. Country of Origin

PART VI – POSSESSOR IDENTIFICATION

6a. Name (last)	(first)	(middle)	(suffix)	6b. Criminal History ? ☐ YES ☐ NO
ALIAS (AKA) (last)	(first)	(middle)	(suffix)	AKA Date of Birth

6b. Height	6c. Weight	6d. Sex	6e. Race	6f. Address – Route No.
6g. Apt. No.	6h. Street No.	6i. Direction	6j. Street Name	6k. City
6l. County	6m. State	6n. Zip Code	6o. Country
6p. Date of Birth	6q. Place of Birth	6r. Possessor's ID No.	6s. ID Type/State

PART VII – ASSOCIATE INFORMATION

7a. Name (last)	(first)	(middle)	(suffix)	Criminal History ? ☐ YES ☐ NO
Alias (AKA) (last)	(first)	(middle)	(suffix)	AKA Date of Birth

7b. Height	7c. Weight	7d. Sex	7e. Race	7f. Address – Route No.
7g. Apt. No.	7h. Street No.	7i. Direction	7j. Street Name	7k. City
7l. County	7m. State	7n. Zip Code	7o. Country
7p. Date of Birth	7q. Place of Birth	7r. Associate's ID No.	7s. ID Type/State

PART VIII – FIREARM RECOVERY INFORMATION (Confirm recovery data in 8a, 8g & 8h)

8a. Recovery Date	8b. Route No.	8c. Apt. No.	8d. Street No.	8e. Direction	8f. Street Name
8g. City		8h. State	8i. Zip Code		
8j. Additional Information					

Letter Codes for Question 5c, Type, are as follows: C=Combination has both rifled & smooth bore barrels; M=Machine Gun fires more than one shot with a single trigger pull;
P=Pistol, single shot or semiautomatic handgun with integral or permanently aligned chamber & barrel; R/R=Revolver, pistol design based on cylinder rotation;
R/D=Pistol/Derringer, small handgun with hinged or pivoting barrel(s); R=Rifle, long gun with rifled barrel; S=Shotgun, long gun with smooth bore barrel(s).

DPS-258-C (New 09/00)

the control of the court, corrections, or probation and parole offices. These criminal justice agencies maintain highly detailed records that can be of great value to subsequent investigations. Many states are recognizing a need to merge all of these criminal justice data sources into a common, accessible, criminal justice information record management system. This will allow one-stop searching to obtain a very comprehensive history on any individual who has interacted with any portion of the criminal justice community.

Motor vehicle related files

State motor vehicle department files contain a significant amount of information about an individual's personal information such as address and brief description, as well as a list of vehicles registered to that person. Most states also maintain a color-photograph mug-shot file of all licensed operators. Since a majority of people depend upon the use of personal motor vehicles for their daily transportation needs, an operators' license and vehicle registration are common possessions. Even those individuals engaged in criminal activity will often maintain current and valid licenses and registrations in an effort to avoid police inquiries.

Financial records

Financial records can be obtained from a variety of sources, and often provide excellent investigative information. Banks, credit companies, investment firms, tax records, and social security deposits are examples of records that should be considered. Investigators with minimal efforts and no authorization can obtain some of these records. Other records may require written authorization from the account owner or legal representative, or court order. Family members and associates may be able to assist in identifying and locating important financial documents.

These records may be valuable information for a number of reasons. Any comprehensive background investigation should include a financial component. Many motives or intentions can be established through financial records.

For example, a recent and significant increase in an individual's life insurance coverage may be a factor supporting suicide as the manner of death. Also, a victim's credit and bank accounts should be monitored after the crime to see if the suspect is attempting to acquire the victim's funds. In addition, financial records can be used to track and locate the recent whereabouts of an individual. Very few people can survive for an extended period without the need to obtain money from some traceable account or source.

Figure 2.7 (opposite)
Firearms tracking form.

MANAGEMENT OF MANPOWER

Ideally, manpower for any criminal investigation is not an issue. However, the reality is that agencies responsible for crime scene processing and reconstruction have limited personnel resources. There are many concerns and factors involving manpower that adversely affect crime scene management.

First, are there sufficient personnel assigned specifically to crime scene functions or are they restricted by their competing responsibilities as either general investigators or laboratory scientists? Second, do these personnel have an adequate base of training and experience to properly perform their assigned functions? Finally, how much workload is placed upon the crime scene team, and can they spend the necessary amount of time at one scene before being dispatched to the next scene or other emergency assignment? If the supervisor of a crime scene unit does not have the ability to consistently draw on and depend on the necessary qualified man-hours then it is unlikely that the maximum will be obtained from every scene.

Following are some issues that should be considered in crime scene manpower management.

ALLOCATION OF PERSONNEL AND TRAINING

Every jurisdiction struggles with properly allocating limited resources during the preliminary aspects of a major investigation. There are several significant competing interests. A substantial uniformed or patrol presence is necessary to protect the scene and control traffic and public movement around the scene. As we have observed far too many times during high-profile cases, crime scenes are not given the necessary attention nor the personnel to properly and thoroughly search and document the scene. Finally, it is well established that the likelihood of bringing an investigation to a successful conclusion diminishes substantially after the first 24 hours. Thus it is prudent to assign as many personnel as possible to investigative functions during the same time period, while crime scene protection and search functions also require personnel.

It is not possible for one very experienced and multi-talented crime scene investigator to adequately process a crime scene alone. In addition, as the complexity of the case increases so do the requisite man-hours necessary to complete the many crime scene functions. In most cases, where available resources and workload permit, a versatile and functional crime scene unit should consist of at least four investigators and one supervisor.

All of these investigators and the supervisor may have certain strengths or skills, but they should strive to expand their skill bases and become generalists in scope. Obviously, some of the more technical or complex tasks such as blood spatter reconstruction or advanced latent print processing methods may be within the expertise of none or only one of the assigned unit. And if that skill level is not present it is incumbent upon the supervisor to recognize the need to obtain outside expertise before critical mistakes or oversights occur.

There are basic skills or training objectives that a crime scene investigator should possess. All aspects of scene documentation need to be fully covered at a scene. These methods include still photography in a variety of formats, video-taping, and preparation of sketch maps and diagrams. A wide variety of searching methods and techniques must be included in the available proce-dures. These include organized manual search grids and technology-based methods involving the use of metal detectors, flammable vapor detectors, and portable lasers and forensic light sources. Specialized skills in a wide variety of disciplines will often be needed to address evidence or potential evidence located at the scene.

Investigators must be proficient in recognizing, collecting and preserving fingerprints, footprints and tire tracks, bloodstains and other biological specimens, entomology specimens, trace evidence, narcotics and chemicals, firearms, explosive residues, botanical and soil samples, etc.

Finally, even if the crime scene unit does not possess the expertise to conduct a full-scale scene reconstruction, its members must be sufficiently trained so as to understand the process and basic requirements for a successful reconstruc-tion.

Regardless of the size of a particular jurisdiction, these personnel demands will be realized during a major investigation. The only truly effective method to manage these conflicting personnel demands is through the establishment of a team concept. This concept is highlighted later in this chapter as the premiere choice for crime scene management options.

TECHNOLOGY AND EQUIPMENT MANAGEMENT

Advances in technology mandate the continual acquisition of new and often expensive equipment and supplies in order to maximize the potential for effective crime scene processing. The amount of resources allocated to pur-chasing and upgrading equipment should be appropriate for the variety and volumes of crime scenes encountered by that unit.

At the minimum, a crime scene supervisor must take a detailed inventory of his unit's equipment, keep abreast of available technologies, and be aware of his unit's limitations due to a lack of equipment. In addition, personnel must be provided with adequate training to properly utilize any new technology or equipment.

The different categories of equipment are essentially:

Photo 2.9a–b

Connecticut State Police Major Crime Squad crime scene processing van.

2.9a: exterior view.

2.9b: interior view.

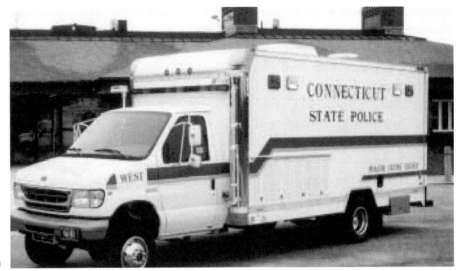

(a)

(b)

1 Support vehicles – commonly, customized cube vans specifically constructed for crime scene purposes.

2 Communications – two-way radio with channels for the police jurisdictions serviced by the crime scene unit, cellular telephones and fax machines, laptop computers with modem. Currently, teleforensics and telecommunication technologies are being developed. Teleforensics involves the use of portable instrumentation and technology that can transmit data directly to a laboratory for further analysis, while the crime scene processing is being conducted.

3 Tools and search equipment – hand tools, yard/garden tools, power saws and drills, auxiliary lighting and generators, forensic light sources, metal detectors.

4 Specialized crime scene kits – e.g. GSR collection, latent print kits, trajectory reconstruction dowels and accessories, casting kits for tool marks and footwear impressions, etc.

5 Chemicals and reagents – e.g. bloody print enhancement reagent, presumptive blood testing reagents, latent print chemical developers, etc.

6 Evidence packaging materials and related forms.

7 Portable instrumentation – e.g. portable lasers, portable gas chromatography, ground-penetrating radar, night vision equipment.

MANAGEMENT OF LOGISTICS

Logistical concerns must be properly addressed or managed to ensure that the maximum information possible is obtained from the crime scene and during the critical first 24 hours of a major investigation. Organization and efficient allocation of resources must be established early in the investigation. The following elements should be established.

COMMAND POSTS

First responders and their supervisors must do everything possible to secure the integrity of the crime scene. However, in order to maintain the integrity of that scene, crime scene managers need to establish outer perimeters and a command post.

A command post has to be outside the perimeters of the working crime scene, where evidence may be located and investigators can have the space to document the scene properly. However, the command post must be convenient enough to the crime scene to logistically support the crime scene personnel as well as provide a center for accurately and quickly disseminating relevant information to and from the crime scene. During the initial portion of the investigation, when crime scene processing is a primary function, a mobile or temporary command post is ideal as it can be located near the outer perimeter of the scene. If possible, this command post should not be the same vehicle or structure where the crime scene processing equipment and personnel are located as command post functions may interfere with the crime scene functions.

As the investigation evolves and crime scene functions diminish a longerterm command post may be established. This command post should focus on supporting the investigative personnel and provide a facility to establish a task force office or long-term investigative center.

MEDIA RELATIONS

Care should be taken to restrict access to the command post and identify a separate area for members of the public or media to gather. It is always beneficial to establish a specific media area and have a department public information officer available to the media. Whether we like it or not, the media will exercise their right to gather information and publicize the event. It is to our advantage to control this portion of a major criminal investigation. If the public information officer is constantly updated and portrays an honest and timely dissemination of information to the media, the vast majority of media representatives will gladly comply with reasonable requests to protect the scene or sensitive investigative information. The media area should be close enough to the actual crime scene so that they can obtain some file footage for their newscasts. Again, if you control the placement of that location you can be careful to protect sensitive information or views from the cameras. Periodic news conferences should be scheduled and conducted by PIO officers during major case investigations. Photo 2.10 shows a scheduled news conference during a major case investigation.

Photo 2.10

Media relations: at the successful conclusion to a multi-jurisdiction joint investigation a press conference was held by police department public information officers and agency heads.

INTER-AGENCY LIAISON

Even in large agencies with significant resources there are occasions when an investigation will involve multiple agencies. This situation may arise when the crime(s) occur in more than one jurisdiction, or when the investigating jurisdiction realizes that it lacks the necessary resources, personnel, expertise or equipment. In either scenario, the key to a successful investigation is complete cooperation and a team approach to solving the case. One way to assist in the team spirit is by establishing a formal liaison between the involved agencies.

An effective liaison relationship involves a commitment by all involved agencies to cooperate and share information and resources readily. Despite cooperation, it is necessary to establish the lead investigating agency and any chain of command within the individual agencies. The biggest obstacle often involves inadequate communication between the agency members. By assigning a liaison officer or staff a system can be established to funnel all information through the liaison in a timely manner. It is the responsibility of the liaison personnel to keep all interested parties informed of developments, problems and needs. If this model is followed, not only will the probability of success greatly increase but the future inter-agency cooperation and relations will also be enhanced.

RESOURCE ALLOCATION

Recent advances in forensic science and crime scene technology are astounding. When all of these innovative resources are properly integrated into a criminal investigation, in a timely manner, the probability for success is high.

Unfortunately, very few jurisdictions have the individual financial resources or demands to justify possessing the full array of these resources. In addition, many of these new high-tech methods or instruments require operation by specially trained personnel. Thus, it is often more beneficial for a law enforcement agency to identify the spectrum of available services within their jurisdictions and establish mutual exchange or support agreements with agencies that offer needed services. Not only will they access the availability of newer crime-solving technology, but they will also not have needlessly depleted their personnel or fiscal resources.

DEVELOPING PROCEDURES

Merely obtaining each of the aforementioned four key components is not enough to ensure that the crime scene is managed to its utmost potential. Developing organized and comprehensive procedures is imperative to any type of crime scene management system, from the most basic to a highly technical and innovative model. To a great extent this is an area lacking in many jurisdictions tasked with crime scene processing.

Most likely, the lack of a comprehensive written crime scene management procedure can be attributed to one of the following reasons.

First, a particular agency may feel that it has survived thus far relying on the expertise and guidance of a few select individuals to individually access the crime scenes. Second, those specific crime scene managers may be the dwindling few who have not endured the public disgrace and reality of a failed criminal investigation due largely to an ineffective crime scene process. Third, the importance of crime scenes in the overall success of a criminal investigation has not been identified thus the managers do not know what they do not know.

Some agencies have the benefit of a few key crime scene investigators or technicians who have accumulated sufficient training and years of experience. Despite their reliance on written guidelines or procedures, these investigators frequently conduct professional and high-quality functions based on their individual expertise. Yet even these most experienced individuals risk the possibility of making a crucial mistake or omission because they fail to realize the value of a systematic approach to crime scene processing. Moreover, these local crime scene experts can fail to realize the need to pass on their expertise and help train newly developing personnel.

In the light of the on-the-job aspect of acquiring crime scene expertise, it is too late to adequately prepare a new crime scene investigator once the experienced personnel have retired. However, if these experienced crime scene investigators and their managers commit to preparing some form of written procedures many of these potential problems can be minimized or averted altogether.

How many times must we, as professionals in the criminal investigative and forensic science community, live with the daily public scrutiny of a high profile criminal case that remains unsolved or unable to be successfully tried in court due mainly to inept or insufficient evidence and information obtained from the crime scene? Problems with many high profile cases from the past, such as Sacco or Venzetti, the John F. Kennedy assassination, were equally aggravating but far easier to accept. Clearly, investigators in those days did not have even a fraction of the technological and scientific advances available to today's crime scene personnel. Yet despite our tremendous gains we continue to see these basic critical errors occurring at the initial crime scene. Vicent Foster, O.J. Simpson and Jon Bonet Ramsey are but a few examples.

Every agency must accept the reality that it too is susceptible to these problems and embarrassments unless it adopts a philosophy that recognizes and commits to the importance of quality crime scene management.

No longer will good old-fashioned police work and a confession be the necessary and complete ingredients for the resolution of a case in today's physical evidence oriented criminal trials. Regardless of the reasons why, the reality in almost every modern legal system is that physical evidence, forensic examination of that evidence, and the crime scene analysis related to that evidence are integral and desired components of the process.

Simply, juries want to hear about and see demonstrative evidence detailing the crime scene and evidence located at that scene. Thus, an overall criminal investigation plan must incorporate a crime scene management model that is realistic for the available resources, yet effective.

SELECTING AN APPROPRIATE CRIME SCENE INVESTIGATION MODEL

Currently, there are many major crime scene investigative models available to choose as the backbone of a criminal investigative approach that recognizes the value of crime scenes in criminal investigations. Each model has its own positive and negative attributes. Selecting the appropriate model requires careful consideration of many key factors. These factors include available resources, manpower and qualifications, types of crimes, the crime rate and need for crime scene services, degree of scientific and legal system requirements of the jurisdiction, and support services available for analysis of the gathered physical evidence.

Ultimately, each jurisdiction should evaluate these criteria against the different models and select the one model or combination of several models that best suits the needs of the criminal justice system in their community.

Traditional concept

A traditional approach to crime scene management utilizes regular patrol officers and detectives from local detective units as the primary crime scene personnel. This model is beneficial in jurisdictions where there are limited law enforcement resources and the demand for crime scene processing functions is relatively low. Also, if alternative models are not available this becomes a default model, as police services will always need to be in place. Some of the negative features of this model include the use of personnel with limited scientific training and technical experience, and minimal crime scene experience. Moreover, the time commitment needed for effective crime scene processing may conflict with daily patrol, investigative and public service functions.

Crime scene technicians

This concept utilizes full-time crime scene, civilian personnel. This system allows for continuity and specialization. Often these personnel have special scientific and technical training. However, sometimes this category of crime scene personnel has minimal investigative experience.

General investigative experience is invaluable for assisting a crime scene processor in identifying and recognizing relevant evidence for a particular crime or *modus operandi*. Often, these personnel lack a global perspective to the criminal investigation, for which their role as crime scene technicians is essential.

Scene-of-the-crime/major crime squad

Scene-of-the-crime units comprise sworn officers specifically assigned to full-time crime scene processing and investigation duties. Unlike members of a traditional approach, these individuals can focus only on criminal investigations and/or crime scenes. This allows for increased experience, less distractions and an opportunity to obtain supplemental scientific and technical training.

One major drawback is the very nature of most police agencies that will transfer personnel in and out of the unit due to promotions or shifting agency priorities. While they often possess more scientific and technical skills than do most traditional personnel, they still lack many of the skills associated with the recent technological advances in forensic science. Also, using sworn personnel

Photo 2.11

Forensic scientists search for evidence of mass gravesite in Bosnia. (Courtesy of Dr Dragun Primorac, Croatia.)

to conduct the technical functions of crime scene processing may deplete resources needed to actually conduct the criminal investigation.

Laboratory crime scene scientist

Laboratory scientists usually have superior technical and scientific skills over all the previous models. These individuals, by nature of their job and exposure to the forensic academic and research communities, will also often stay more up to date with the changes that may affect crime scene technology. This model is also advantageous in that the crime scene field and laboratory examination functions are closely integrated. Some negative features of this model include personnel who have no investigative experience and are thus prone to problems with evidence recognition. In most cases the laboratory scientists lack motivation for crime scene work due to a lack of resources, therefore they respond to only a select few types of crime scenes; thus they are often somewhat limited in their experience. Finally, assigning laboratory scientists to time-consuming field assignments will deplete laboratory resources needed to analyze the seized physical evidence.

Collaborative team approach

In most cases this is the best overall crime scene investigative model. However, this model requires extensive resources in diverse areas: police, laboratory, crime scene personnel, medical examiners and prosecuting authorities. Further, the success of this model mandates a comprehensive crime scene procedure to be implemented and followed by each participating member of the cohesive team. In this model, advanced scientific, technical and investigative resources are available.

Not only are demanding crime scene responsibilities shared among the team components, but also this team approach enhances the future abilities of each individual member. As with other models there are some obstacles to overcome. The team must work together to develop and integrate a plan for crime scene processing and the recognition, collection and preservation of physical evidence. This model requires cooperation not competition. Photo 2.11 shows forensic scientists and investigators searching for explosive and firearm evidence at a mass grave scene in Bosnia.

CHAPTER 3

GENERAL CRIME SCENE PROCEDURES

INTRODUCTION

Crime scene investigation is a discovery process. The crime scene investigator seeks to discover all the aspects of the criminal activities at the crime scene – such facts as the nature of the crime, the patterns of the crime, the variety of physical evidence associated with the scene, and an even more vast assortment of other facts related to the crime and the crime scene. For example, in a death investigation, such facts would include the cause and manner of death, possible time of death, identity of the deceased, relevant medical history of the deceased, identity of suspect(s), and possibly, any sequencing of victim's behavior prior to scene discovery. Photo 3.1 shows scientists and investigators working together at a homicide scene to examine the scene for potential evidence.

The crime scene must be methodically and systematically examined. This examination will include many steps that must be done properly and have to follow a certain sequence; the omission of a step could possibly cause valuable pieces of evidence to be overlooked or to not meet the legal or scientific

Photo 3.1

Dr Lee analyzing a crime scene with detectives.

challenges. Every experienced crime scene investigator will develop the expertise to determine whether the sequence of steps should be changed in exceptional circumstances. Figure 3.1 illustrates a scene investigator applying systematic and methodical procedures to ensure the complete investigation of the crime scene. As an experienced crime scene investigator relates, 'It's all in the details.' Take the time to survey and assess. This step alone will often reveal important clues in the investigation.

The following discussions are just a brief outline of the steps to illustrate the importance of methodical crime scene investigation. A more detailed discussion of each of the steps in the sequence of crime scene investigation will be covered in subsequent chapters.

Figure 3.1
Crime scene investigator.

ROLE OF THE FIRST RESPONDING OFFICER

The first responders to a crime scene are usually police, emergency medical personnel, or fire department personnel (see Photo 3.2). Their actions at the scene are often the foundation for the successful resolution of the crime. These first responding officers are the only people to view the crime scene in its original condition. They are also in many cases some of the individuals who may, through the course of 'doing their job', inadvertently change or alter the crime scene from its original condition. They must do their job but they must always keep in mind that they will begin the process of linking the crime scene to the victim, the witnesses, and ultimately, to the suspect. Any disruption of the crime scene may prevent the link! Training, education, and experience are all necessary for any potential first responder.

The 'Basics' of the first responder's duties are to:

1 Assist the victim.

2 Arrest the suspect; search for or apprehend any suspects still on the scene or in the vicinity.

3 Detain witnesses; witnesses have valuable information about the crime scene; try to separate the witnesses to prevent discussions about the incident; and of course, the witnesses will need to be interviewed.

4 Protect the crime scene; begin the crime scene protection measures. Use barrier tape, official vehicles, or necessary measures as needed; consider any POEs (points of entry or exit); if any potential physical evidence, especially transient evidence or patterned evidence, is likely to be lost, contaminated, or altered from its original condition, it should be recorded and protected. Do not use any items or facilities at the scene (telephones, bathrooms, paper towels, water, etc.). NO EATING, DRINKING OR SMOKING within the scene itself.

5 Communicate with supervisors (see Photo 3.3).

6 All actions, observations, or changes to the crime scene by the first responder will be reported to the crime scene investigator. A reasonable attempt to avoid disturbing the scene in any way should be the guide that most first responders follow.

Any crime scene investigator and first responder must have an open and objective mind when approaching the crime scene. Mistakes made at this beginning step could jeopardize the entire investigation. It is for this reason that first responders must thoroughly document their observations of and

Photo 3.2

First responding officers arriving at a homicide scene. Note that the patrol vehicles were parked outside of the immediate crime scene area.

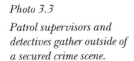

Photo 3.3

Patrol supervisors and detectives gather outside of a secured crime scene.

actions at the crime scene. Documentation in the form of audio recording notes or in combination with sketches are especially well suited for this purpose. A good guideline for first responder's documentation is to answer the questions of who?, what?, when?, where?, and how? Some specific examples are: observations about vehicles parked in or vehicles leaving the crime scene vicinity, medications located next to the victim, any persons present or that have left the scene, any disturbances or objects out of place, whether any dated materials (newspapers, letters, or notes) are observed adjacent to the victim, whether any objects have been touched, or moved.

Upon arrival at the scene, the first responding officer should always keep safety in mind – their own, the safety of the others present at the scene, and the safety of any bystanders. Determine the nature of the incident and stabilize the situation. Treat any injured parties involved in the situation. Locate the perpetrator if one may be present, then secure the crime scene as much as possible, and communicate with the departments or agencies immediately. If careful protection, documentation and preservation by the first responders has occurred, then the 'original' condition of the crime scene will be known and nothing lost or contaminated.

ASSISTING THE VICTIM

Upon arrival at the scene, the first responder or crime scene investigator should always assess the situation and secure the scene as discussed previously.

However, if an injured person(s) is found at the scene and first aid is warranted, then it is important to assist the victim and administrate first aid. Such assistance should take precedence. Careful documentation must also be made of any crime scene changes or alterations that occur while assisting the victim.

SEARCH FOR AND APPREHENSION OF ACCUSED

The apprehension of the suspect is the primary function of any law enforcement agency. However, the search for and arrest of the suspect should not include the destruction of physical evidence that can be used to link the suspect to the crime scene. For example, any suspects in a shooting investigation should never be allowed to wash their hands as that will likely destroy any gunshot residue that might be found on them. The clothing of a suspect involved in a fight where blunt or sharp force trauma was exhibited should be immediately photographed and collected. If a suspect has been apprehended away from a crime scene, that suspect should never be returned to the scene. Any victims or witnesses can identify the suspect in a more controlled environment. Most importantly by keeping the suspect away from the scene, any physical evidence found at the scene that originated from the suspect will link the suspect to the scene only at the time of the crime and not from the suspect having been returned to the scene for identification by victims or witnesses.

The 'Basics' of taking suspects into custody are to:

1   Check for weapons – if present, remember to be aware of safety and that they are evidence. Firearms will need to be recorded and unloaded (don't handle or dry fire them!).
2   Remove from scene and isolate the suspect. If necessary, stay with suspect while using any restroom facilities.
3   Do not let the suspect return to the scene.
4   Document the condition of the suspect – describe, photograph, etc. Photo 3.4 is a sequence of photographs taken when a suspect was taken into custody at a homicide scene.
5   Document the behavior of the suspect and record any spontaneous statements made by the suspect.
6   Document any injuries of the suspect and record the condition of the suspect's clothing.

SECURING THE CRIME SCENE

With the understanding that it is singularly important to make a crime scene secure to prevent possible loss of evidence, access to the crime scene must be restricted or even prevented. The use of a physical barrier is helpful to define the restricted area. There are numerous means available for this purpose. Ropes, commercially available crime scene tapes, or signage are commonly

Photo 3.4 a–e

Photographs of a suspect depicting blood-like stains on his clothing, face and hands.

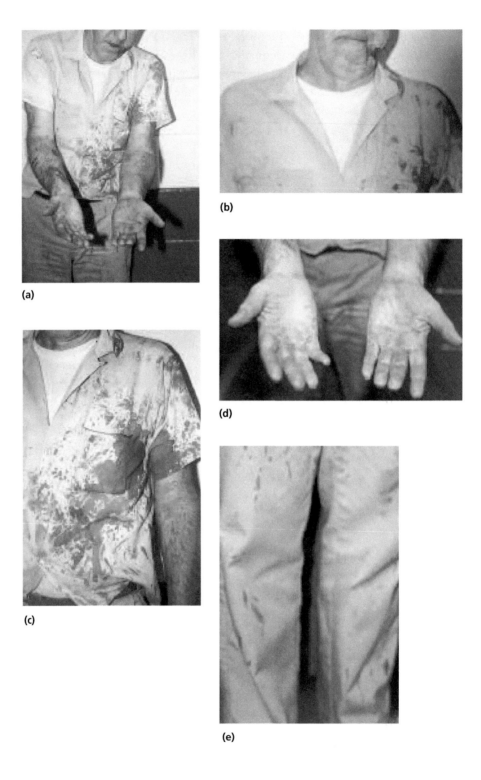

(a)

(b)

(c)

(d)

(e)

used. The official vehicles from the police or fire department can be used successfully in highway, street, or larger outdoor scenes where use of tapes is sometimes difficult (as illustrated in Photos 3.2 and 3.3). The barrier's location is significant in that it will locate the area that is to be restricted, but it should be kept in mind that this barrier is not fixed. The area defined as the crime scene is always subject to change dependent on the progress of the crime scene investigation. The changing of the barrier might mean making the area larger and smaller too, as the investigation proceeds.

A scene security officer should be assigned to intercept anyone trying to enter the general scene area. In capital cases, homicides for example, it is often times helpful to assign a second security office near the target area or body location. Restriction to the crime scene should include all non-essential personnel, including police officers or investigators, fire department personnel, witnesses, victim's relatives, neighbors, or bystanders, in addition to members of the news media. A crime scene personnel log should be kept to document *anyone* entering or leaving the crime scene. Limiting traffic through the general area of the crime scene will help to minimize the destruction or loss of physical evidence. Experienced scene investigators will admit that the concept of restricting access to the crime scene to preserve evidence is easy to understand but is the most difficult concept to enforce, especially with superior officers or higher ranking officials. The use of instant photography or videotapes will greatly assist in the handling of these types of curious officials.

Under ideal circumstances and at least with any major case investigation, a *multi-level* approach to crime scene security should be used (Figure 3.2).

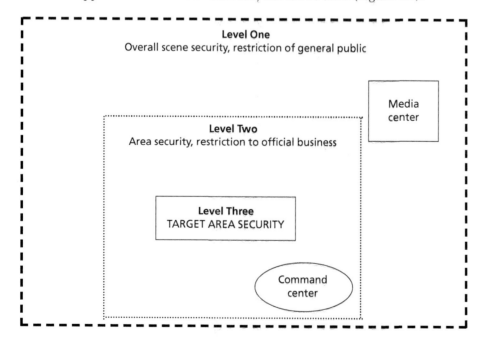

Figure 3.2

Multi-level approach to crime scene security.

Photo 3.5

Many onlookers gather at the scene where a police officer has been involved at a shooting incident.

Multi-level crime scene security

1   The first level is the outermost perimeter or the perimeter of the general crime scene area. This level is often referred to as the overall security level. A scene security officer should be positioned at a check-point location for this level. It is the job of the security officer at this location to limit the traffic through the scene and to prevent unnecessary personnel from entering. A special area within this first level may be designated for the media – such an area should not be within the next level but should be specifically for the media. By providing the media with such an area apart from the general public, a great deal of diplomacy and a resulting cooperation with the media will be established. See Photo 3.5.

2   The second level of security is set up in an area adjacent to the crime scene. Only police personnel, emergency personnel, support personnel and any official vehicles, like crime scene vehicles, should be allowed in this area. A portion of the second level can be set aside for higher ranking police and other officials. This designated area will allow them access somewhat closer to the crime scene without the chance of physical evidence contamination or loss. A command post should be set up in this level to coordinate all the crime scene activities, such as briefing the investigators, logistical support personnel, break and rest area for the scene investigators, and other relevant activities. See Photo 3.6.

3   Level three security is the crime scene target area. This area should have the strictest control and the highest limit of access. Level three should only allow access to crime scene investigators.

Photo 3.6
Multi-level crime scene
security established. The
command center is located
in the level two area (refer
to Figure 3.2).

INITIAL CRIME SCENE RESPONSE
CRIME SCENE SURVEY

Once the scene is secure, the crime scene supervisor or lead crime scene investigator with the case officer should conduct a preliminary crime scene survey.
This preliminary survey is commonly referred to as 'the walk-thru'. This survey
can be greatly facilitated if the first responder is available to accompany the
crime scene investigators. Remember that it is the first responder who has the
direct knowledge as to the original scene appearance or any changes that might
have occurred to the scene; as such, the first responder should be interviewed at
this time. The use of instant photography during the survey can be useful for
preliminary documentation purposes too.

The following is a suggested guideline listing of the tasks that should be
performed during the crime scene 'walk-thru'.

1 Mentally begin a *preliminary* reconstruction of the events that might have led to the
   facts of the crime. This step is not the act of forming a rigid or fixed theory of how the
   crime occurred; it is only a beginning point of the reconstruction. Keep in mind that
   scientific crime scene investigation is objective and systematic. To allow it to be
   otherwise risks developing a so-called 'tunnel vision' and may mislead the direction of
   the investigation.

2 Note the types of transient and conditional evidence present at the scene. Be aware of
   weather conditions (and their changeability), light switches on or off, door locks intact
   or broken, windows opened or closed, heating, ventilation or air conditioning status,

presence of odors, patterned physical evidence, etc. At this point, documentation, protection, preservation or collection of these special forms of physical evidence might be necessary.

3 Note the point of entry, point of exit, paths between them, the target area of the scene, types of damage, and any *major* issues or situations (like highway or road closures) involved in the investigation. An example of walk-through notes is shown in Figure 3.3.

4 Attempt to answer the following questions: Who? What? Where? When? Why? and How?

5 Access the type of scene, the boundary of the scene, and the personnel and equipment needed.

Figure 3.3

Sample of crime scene walk-through notes.

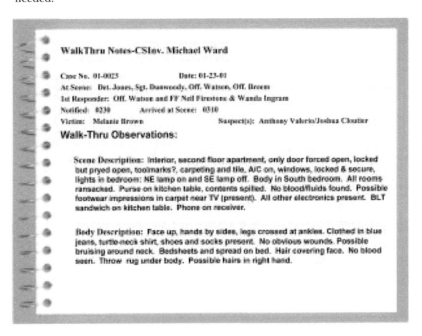

WalkThru Notes–CSInv. Michael Ward

Case No. 01-0025   Date: 01-23-01
At Scene: Det. Jones, Sgt. Dunwoody, Off. Watson, Off. Breem
1st Responder: Off. Watson and FF Neil Firestone & Wanda Ingram
Notified: 0230   Arrived at Scene: 0310
Victim: Melanie Brown   Suspect(s): Anthony Valerio/Joshua Cloutier

Walk-Thru Observations:

Scene Description: Interior, second floor apartment, only door forced open, locked but pryed open, toolmarks?, carpeting and tile, A/C on, windows, locked & secure, lights in bedroom: NE lamp on and SE lamp off. Body in South bedroom. All rooms ransacked. Purse on kitchen table, contents spilled. No blood/fluids found. Possible footwear impressions in carpet near TV (present). All other electronics present. BLT sandwich on kitchen table. Phone on receiver.

Body Description: Face up, hands by sides, legs crossed at ankles. Clothed in blue jeans, turtle-neck shirt, shoes and socks present. No obvious wounds. Possible bruising around neck. Bedsheets and spread on bed. Hair covering face. No blood seen. Throw rug under body. Possible hairs in right hand.

CRIME SCENE COMMUNICATION

At the completion of the scene survey, the crime scene investigator should communicate to other scene investigators and case investigators as to their findings and results of the survey. It is this communication of findings that begins the crime scene team concept and continues the scientific nature of crime scene investigation.

Specific crime scene responsibilities can be assigned to each team member, for example, evidence collection, still photography, videography, fingerprint processing, etc. The team concept and scene management begins with communication because all aspects of the scene investigation are vital. The actual processes of the assigned responsibilities will be discussed briefly below and in greater detail in subsequent chapters. It must be emphasized that sharing of information, findings or ideas is an essential component of scientific crime scene investigation. Without good communication vital physical evidence can be missed and proper processing of the crime scene ignored.

NOTIFICATION OF SUPERIOR OFFICERS AND OTHER AGENCIES

It is important for the first responder to notify their superior officer about the crime scene situation as soon as possible. A crime scene check-list (Figure 3.4) should become part of standard operating procedures for law enforcement agencies.

1. In accordance with departmental guidelines or practices, notify the appropriate personnel in the departmental chain of command.

2. Notify the forensic laboratory or other appropriate technical support group if necessary. The forensic sciences are expanding and changing so much in recent days, that it is difficult for law enforcement agencies to possibly keep a staff that would provide all the technical services that might be needed at a crime scene. It is therefore, common for specialists from various sources (academia, private industry, laboratories, etc.) be available for crime scene response. A current list of available experts should be maintained. Some of the specialists that may be needed for a crime scene investigation are bloodstain pattern analysts, bomb technicians, anthropologists, K-9 handlers (bomb and accelerant detection, drug detection, and body decomposition), engineers, entomologists, odontologists, surveyors, and criminalists or forensic scientists from the lab.

3. Notify the prosecutor's office when required. The usefulness of having the prosecutors at the crime scene, not necessarily in the crime scene, is two-fold. The prosecutors will be able to observe, in person, the actual crime scene thus allowing them to do their job in the courtroom better. It will also allow the prosecutor to better appreciate the duties of the crime scene investigator. The observation of the documentation, searching, and collection processes being done by the investigator at the scene by the prosecutor will provide for good communications and understanding of crime scene investigations in general.

4. In cases of unattended deaths, untimely deaths or other death investigations, notification of the medical examiner's office (MEO) and other appropriate agencies may be required. In most jurisdictions, the body is the evidence and under the control of the MEO and as such, the medical examiner or their representative must be present at the scene in order for any investigation of the body be attempted.

Figure 3.4

*General crime scene
check-list.*

General Crime Scene Check List

Case # _____   Type of Crime _____

General Information:
Location _____ Date & Time _____
Name of Victim _____
First Officer on the Scene _____ Time _____
First Detective at the Scene _____ Time _____
Weather Conditions _____
Scene Conditions _____
Lighting _____
Witness _____ Address _____
_____ Address _____
Suspect _____ Address _____

Crime Scene Logs/Records:
Security Log _____ Officer _____
Notes _____ Officer _____
Photo Log _____ Officer _____
Sketch _____ Officer _____
Video Taping _____ Officer _____
Audio Taping _____ Officer _____
Evidence Log _____ Officer _____
Survey Log _____ Officer _____

Notifications:
Detective Commander _____ Time _____
Chief of Police _____ Time _____
Major Crimes Unit _____ Time _____
Identification Unit _____ Time _____
Forensic Laboratory _____ Time _____
Medical Examiner _____ Time _____
State's Attorney _____ Time _____
Other Agencies _____ Time _____
_____ Time _____
_____ Time _____
Physical Evidence _____ Time _____
_____ Time _____
Neighborhood Check _____
_____
_____
Neighboring Vehicle _____
Signed _____

Fig 3-4

LEGAL IMPLICATIONS FOR CRIME SCENE SEARCHES

Even if the most advanced equipment and techniques are available, both to process the crime scene and subsequently analyze the evidence, there is little evidential value obtained from that evidence if those results are not admissible in a subsequent judicial proceeding. One of the most commonly used means to diminish the value of a particular piece of evidence by defense counsel is to demonstrate that the evidence was obtained illegally. If a court determines that the evidence was obtained illegally or did not follow legal or scientific requirements for collecting or preserving the evidence, then, barring a few limited exceptions, it will be deemed as inadmissible. This principle is premised on the Constitutional protections against unreasonable searches and seizures, as declared in the Fourth Amendment to the United States Constitution, as well as similar provisions in state constitutions. This Constitutional protection has been enforced through application of the Exclusionary Rule in a series of well-established cases by the United States Supreme Court, including the landmark case of *Mapp v. Ohio* 367 US 643 (1961). Further, any secondary or additional evidence derived from the inadmissible evidence may also be deemed as inadmissible through the 'Fruit of the Poisonous Tree Doctrine', *Nardone v. United States*, 308 US 338 (1939).

Legal implications regarding a crime scene search and seizure of evidence from that scene fall into two general concerns. First, is the actual search of the premises lawful? Second, is the seizure of a specific piece of evidence within the confines of a legal seizure? When evaluating the legality of conducting crime scene searches and seizing evidence there is a central court decision that dictates lawful conduct, *Mincey v. Arizona*, 437 US 385 (1978).

In *Mincey*, during a narcotics raid of the defendant's apartment an undercover police officer was shot and killed and the defendant was wounded. Homicide detectives proceeded to the scene and conducted a warrantless search of the apartment, lasting four days. During that search detectives seized hundreds of pieces of evidence, many of which were used in the defendant's trial. Upon review of this case by the United States Supreme Court, the Court held that law enforcement personnel responding to a crime scene could essentially conduct three functions legally, without consent from the owners, prior court authorization, search and seizure warrant, or other exigent circumstances.

First, officers could enter the scene to search for victims and render aid to those in need. The scope of this search is restricted to those areas in which a victim could reasonably be located. For example, it would be permissible to search under a bed, but not permissible to look in a desk drawer. Further, just because one victim is readily located, officers are not precluded from conducting a reasonable search to ascertain if additional victims may be present.

Second, first responding officers may also enter the scene to search for the perpetrator/s. As with a search for victims, the scope of this search must be reasonable and restricted to areas in which a perpetrator could be secreted. Again, locating one perpetrator within the scene does not prohibit officers from continuing their search to ensure that no additional perpetrators are present.

Third, while the officers are legally within the premises for the purpose of either of the two previously mentioned functions they may seize any evidence in plain view. There are limitations to this exception. The item to be seized must be readily determined to be of evidentiary nature. No additional manipulation is allowed.

For example, it is not permissible to pick up an item and examine the serial number, which is not readily visible, in an effort to determine if that article is stolen property, *Arizona v. Hicks*, 480 US 321 (1987). Generally, it is not recommended to seize an object under the plain view exception while searching for victims and/or perpetrators. While it may be legally permissible, it shortcuts the complete documentation and potentially proper collection and preservation of that piece of evidence. Therefore, plain view seizures conducted by first responding officers should be avoided unless there is a significant risk that the evidence may be lost, destroyed, or altered. Examples of those circumstances would be a half-eaten Popsicle with visible bite-marks located on the floor next to a ransacked refrigerator, or a fully automatic loaded gun lying on the street in the midst of 200 angry protesters. In either scenario, the greater need is to protect the evidence from destruction or disappearance.

Once these three functions are completed, any further search and seizure activities will probably be deemed illegal. Officers are allowed to secure that scene and prevent access to that area while they seek court authorization or written consent from the lawful owner to proceed with a detailed crime scene search. If the search is justified on consent, it must be determined that the consenting individual has the legal capacity to grant permission to search the desired areas. There is no stated time limit as to how long first responding officers may be on the premises before securing a search warrant or consent, but it must be reasonable based upon the prevailing circumstances.

A final legal consideration involves the scope of the search even if the actual search has been court authorized, based upon consent, or a legally recognizable exigent circumstance. In order to obtain a valid search and seizure warrant the participants need to describe specific property or types of property that they will seek during the search. The property sought must be based on articulated probable cause that those items may be present at the location that will be searched. Once the search is commenced, only items within the scope of the search warrant or by the written permission of the owner may be seized. Items falling outside the scope of the authorization may still be legally seized so long

Figure 3.5 (opposite)

Template for crime scene mere evidence search and seizure warrant – pursuant to Mincey v. Arizona (note the actual form may vary somewhat in different jurisdictions).

**AFFIDAVIT AND APPLICATION
SEARCH AND SEIZURE WARRANT**
CCP-7A REV. 3-82
GEN. STAT. 54-33a, 54-33j

STATE OF CONNECTICUT
SUPERIOR COURT
CCP-3D must be completed

A Judge of the Superior Court

The undersigned, being duly sworn, complains on oath that the undersigned has probable cause to believe that certain property, to wit:

A.

☐ is possessed, controlled, designed or intended for use as a means of committing the crime of . . .

☐ is or has been or may be used as the means of committing the crime of . . .

☐ was stolen or embezzled from . . .

☐ constitutes evidence of the following crime or that a particular person participated in the commission of the crime

B.

☐ is in the possession, custody or control of a journalist or news organization, to wit . . .

And is within or upon a certain person, place, or thing, to wit . . .

C.

: the facts establishing the grounds for issuing a Search and Seizure Warrant are the following

D.

-12-
(Over, For Continuing Affidavit; Signatures of Affiant(s); and Jurat)

"MINCEY" WARRANT APPLICATION

A. Blood, semen, saliva, physiological fluids and secretions, hair, fibers, fingerprints, palmprints, footprints, shoeprints, weapons and firearms including pistols, rifles, revolvers, shotguns, hatchets, axes, cutting instruments and cutting tools, blunt force instruments, projectiles, ammunition, bullet casings and fragments, dirt, dust and soil, paint samples, glass and plastic fragments, marks of tools used to gain access to locked premises or containers, and items containing traces of any of the above mentioned articles.

B. Constitutes evidence of an offense, or that a particular person participated in the commission of an offense, to wit: (Specify Crime).

C. Describe location of place to be searched.

D. (Add the following paragraphs to the wording of the Search Warrant Application. These paragraphs should be at the end of the Affidavit.)

   1. That the affiant, _____, is a regular member of the _____Police Department and has been a member for the past _____years. That I am presently assigned to the Detective Division's Major Crime Squad Crime Scene Processing Unit and have been so assigned for the past _____years. That I have investigated and processed numerous serious and violent crimes, including murder, and have received specialized training and experience in the collection of physical evidence, crime scene processing and the investigation of such cases. That I have personal knowledge of the facts and circumstances hereinafter related as a result of my own investigative efforts and those of brother officers who have reported their findings to me.

      (One of the two affiants should be a member of the crime scene processing unit. The second affiant should be an investigator and should use his customary paragraph of introduction.)

   2. That the affiants do believe that the offense hereinbefore stated was committed at the location to be searched, in that: (Specify circumstances indicating commission of offense at place to be searched; include information as to when crime was first reported, what first officer on scene observed, a description of the scene, etc. This information may require several paragraphs.)

   3. That the affiants have personal knowledge, based upon their experience and training, that crimes of violence involve a struggle, a break, the use of weapons and other instrumentalities, and/or the element of unpredictability. That the person or persons participating in the commission of a violent offense is in contact with physical surroundings in a forceful or otherwise detectable manner. That there is often an attempt to alter, destroy, remove, clean up, or cover up evidence of a crime. That traces may be left in the form of blood, semen, saliva, physiological fluids

and secretions, hair, fibers, fingerprints, palmprints,
footprints, shoeprints, weapons and firearms including
pistols, rifles, revolvers, shotguns, hatches, axes,
cutting instruments and cutting tools, blunt force
instruments, projectiles, ammunition, bullet casings and
fragments, dirt, dust and soil, paint samples, glass and
plastic fragments, marks of tools used to gain access to
locked premises or containers, and items containing traces
of any of the above mentioned articles. That many of the
above items are minute and/or microscopic, thus requiring
additional specialized examination by forensic laboratory
techniques.

4. That the affiants have personal knowledge based upon their
experience and training, that a crime scene, such as
described above, will contain physical evidence, hereinbefore
itemized, which will aid in establishing the identity of
the perpetrator(s), the circumstances under which the
crime was committed, and/or which in general will assist
in the discovery of the pertinent facts; and that such
evidence requires a systematic search to locate, seize,
record and process.

5. That based upon the foregoing facts and information, the
affiants have probable cause to believe and do believe
that evidence of (specify offense) will be found within
and upon (specify place to be searched).

*Mere Evidence Search Warrant Affidavit and Application pursuant
to Mincey v. Arizona, __U.S.__, 98 S.Ct. 2408 (1978)

as they are inherently items of contraband or fall within a class of other, very limited exceptions. However, if the nexus is too great the evidence may be subsequently determined to have been unlawfully seized. Further, the scope of the areas to be searched must be articulated within the search warrant or written consent document. Courts may argue that particular items were seized from areas beyond the authorized scope. Common examples include searches of vehicles located on the premises, but not listed as areas to be searched, or the search of unattached buildings or structures, also not mentioned in the affidavit. Figure 3.5 is an example of an affidavit and application for search and seizure warrant used in Connecticut.

In summary, crime scene investigators should possess the necessary legal training to properly evaluate the legality of a particular search and seizure. If questions arise, investigators should consult the district attorney or the prosecuting authorities within a particular jurisdiction. Also, beware that related provisions in state constitutions and case precedence may differ substantially from federal rulings. Investigators need to be aware of the dire consequences of seizing evidence unlawfully.

Photo 3.7

Crime scene photographer is thoroughly document- ing the scene, using step stools and tripods to get the best perspective and photograph.
(Courtesy of Micky Gura, forensic photographer.)

DOCUMENTATION OF THE CRIME SCENE

Any crime scene must be thoroughly documented or recorded by notes, pho- tography, sketching, and videotaping. Sometimes the use of audiotaping is done as part of documentation. Photography, videotaping, and sketching will provide a permanent graphic record of the appearance and position of victims, objects and physical evidence and their relationship to each other at the crime scene. Photo 3.7 illustrates an outdoor homicide scene. It shows the location of victim's body and their pick-up truck. Notes and audiotaping will provide a record and description of the scene conditions, names, directions, odors, situa- tions and other non-photographable information at the crime scene. The doc- umentation techniques not only support the testimony of the crime scene investigator as to what was found, its location, nature, and condition at the crime scene, but also will provide crucial information for possible future recon- struction, case analysis, and courtroom presentation. Documentation of crime scenes will be discussed in great detail in Chapter 4.

CRIME SCENE SEARCH

Crime scene searches involve both the surrounding area and the target area of a scene. The primary purpose of a crime scene search is the recognition and collection of physical evidence. Unless the potential physical evidence can be recognized and collected, there is no forensic testing that can be conducted. In other words, if the first step of the forensic process, recognition, is not done then the whole process is affected and the crime scene investigation may have failed, and the case will most likely remain unsolved.

The search of the area and scene should be carefully planned. There are various crime scene search models and methods that have been developed; these will be discussed in Chapter 5. Special crime scenes, such as large outdoor scenes, underwater scenes, clandestine drug labs, fire scenes, and excavations, which require extra attention to searching, documentation, and evidence collection, form part of Chapter 9.

COLLECTION, PRESERVATION, AND PACKAGING OF PHYSICAL EVIDENCE

One investigator should be assigned as the physical evidence collector. This individual will have the responsibility to collect, mark, preserve, and package the evidence found at the scene. There are many and diverse possible types of physical evidence. Physical evidence types, classifications of physical evidence, physical evidence and forensic science, and the specialties of forensic science as it relates to physical evidence will be discussed in Chapter 7. Chapter 7 will also coordinate physical evidence to specific crimes and tie them together in 'logic trees' for the reader's ease of use and recognition. The collection and preservation of various categories of physical evidence is presented in Chapter 6. As part of the collection procedures for crime scene physical evidence is the use of field tests or enhancement reagents. These on-scene techniques, recipes, and protocols will be found in Chapter 8. Special attention to crime scenes that involve deaths, bodies, excavations, and their respective physical evidence are discussed in Chapter 9.

PRELIMINARY RECONSTRUCTION

Crime scene reconstruction involves scene information analysis, interpretation of scene patterns, and the examination of the physical evidence. The crime scene should be viewed from several different angles with all possible alternatives. The scene as it exists, the physical evidence and its examination results, and the use of simple logic, both deductive and inductive, along with common sense, will tell what happened, when, where, who with and how it happened. There are various types of physical evidence that are especially well suited for use in reconstruction. For example, bloodstain patterns, glass fracture patterns, footwear impressions, and gunshot residue patterns found as part of shooting investigations are commonly used in crime scene reconstructions. Chapter 10 will look at crime scene reconstruction processes that achieve information as to how a crime scene came to exist.

RELEASING THE SCENE

The crime scene is released only when it is reasonably certain that all the facts and answers have been obtained. Be sure that all pertinent physical evidence has been documented and properly collected. Keep in mind that the collection, packaging, and preservation directly influences the success of the forensic testing to be performed on the evidence – improper collection or packaging means no laboratory results or inadmissibility in court. Communication with all investigators should help with the determination of the scene being released. It is a good practice to go back over all the team responsibilities at this point. A break, or getting away from the crime scene will assist with this reflection step. Once all the information has been processed and completed, release the crime scene.

CRIME SCENE INVESTIGATIVE TEAM

The crime scene investigation team comprises the personnel who share certain duties and responsibilities that will always be part of any major investigation. They must work as a team. In order to conduct a thorough, coordinated, and successful investigation all participants must know their duties, importance, and limitations. It is important to note that in many investigations it is not always possible to have only one person assigned to a duty and it is common that one individual will perform more than one assignment. Regardless of the number of team members and their respective duties, each team member – from first responder to the investigating detective, from the laboratory scientist to the prosecuting attorney – must work with each other to best do their part in solving the case.

There are many different crime scene investigation models, such as the local agency's crime scene technician concept; the federal, state or county major crime squad concept; and the uniformed officer/detective concept. These various concepts are widely used, but the most effective model for conducting a crime scene investigation is the team concept. In this concept the individuals of the team are assigned to specific duties, dependent upon their specific experiential training, to produce the most efficient and successful results in the crime scene investigation. For all positions on the team, training and experience are important, but interest and attitude can be significant given the human aspect of crime scene investigation. The complete criminal investigation team should consist of all of the following members:

1 First responder
2 Crime scene investigation team: team leader, photographer, videographer, sketcher, notetaker, evidence collector
3 Forensic personnel

4 Medical examiner (if required)

5 Forensic specialists – anthropologist, computer analyst, entomologist, etc.

6 Prosecutor's Office personnel

Each of the above team members and their duties will be discussed in greater detail in subsequent chapters pertaining to their particular jobs and responsibilities. The most important aspects of the team concept are cooperation, coordination, and communication. Investigators should work together with each other to avoid any 'tunnel vision' problems.

BIOHAZARDS ASSOCIATED WITH CRIME SCENES

Crime scenes are laden with hazards that every investigator and technician must be aware of any constantly protecting against. Hazards exist in many varieties and forms including, chemical, biological, explosive, and structural. Scenes with chemical hazards such as are commonly encountered in clandestine drug laboratories are discussed in Chapter 9, Special Scene Techniques. Also in Chapter 9 is a discussion on weapons of mass destruction, which can be chemical, biological, or nuclear in nature. Moreover, Chapter 9 emphasizes the need to beware of booby traps at crime scenes, and how they impact the crime scene functions. In this section we will discuss AIDS and other biohazards in crime scene processing.

While the potential for exposure to a biohazard at a crime scene has existed all along, during the last decade crime scene personnel have become at far greater risk of being infected with a pathogen while performing their basic crime scene duties. AIDS and other virus-caused diseases, such as hepatitis B, as well as tuberculosis are all too common in today's society. These blood-borne and airborne pathogens can be transmitted to crime scene personnel as easily as minimal physical contact – touching or breathing in confined spaces where the airborne pathogens are present. As troubling as this reality is to crime scene professionals, there is some good news. The probability of contracting one of these diseases is tremendously reduced by carefully adhering to a few basic universal precautions. Each agency that has personnel assigned to crime scene functions or handling physical evidence retrieved from crime scenes should develop specific procedures for the proper handling and disposition of biohazardous materials.

The primary objective for adherence to these precautionary guidelines is for the protection of crime scene personnel. However, there is an additional advantage. With the development of highly sensitive testing procedures, such as PCR and mitochondrial based DNA typing methods, the possibility of evidence contamination by investigators has greatly increased. Thus, by following these procedures, wearing gloves, protective gowns and head coverings, and surgical masks, the possibility of contamination by an investigator's own DNA or a secondary transfer between two or more objects is greatly reduced.

COMMONLY ENCOUNTERED PATHOGENS

AIDS: Acquired Immune Deficiency Syndrome

AIDS has presented a variety of manifestations ranging from asymptomatic, to some signs of illness (so-called AIDS Related Complex or ARC), to severe immunodeficiency and life-threatening secondary infections. The virus, which causes the disease, has been known by several names. It is currently referred to as Human Immunodeficiency Virus (HIV or HIV-1). The AIDS virus is a retro-virus, which invades the victim's own DNA and affects his immune system. The resulting gradual, irreversible destruction of the immune response mechanisms cause the patient to become highly susceptible to various infections. Pneumo-cytis pneumonia is a common opportunistic infection of AIDS patients. The AIDS virus has been isolated from blood, bone marrow, saliva, lymph nodes, brain tissue, semen, plasma, vaginal fluids, cervical secretions, tears and human milk. The mode of transmission generally involves direct contact of AIDS-con-taminated blood or body fluids with the bloodstream or mucous membranes. It is most frequently transmitted by direct sexual contact, or by using a needle contaminated with AIDS virus to make an IV injection. The latter route of trans-mission is common among the IV drug-abuser population. However, exposure of any open cuts, wounds, lesions, or mucous membranes to AIDS-contami-nated blood or body fluids does carry a risk of possible infection. Unfortunately, there is no cure for AIDS. Vaccines and medications are all in the experimental phase.

Hepatitis B

Hepatitis is an infectious disease of the liver. It has different forms, commonly referred to as types A, B, or C.

Hepatitis B is the so-called 'serum hepatitis' which can result in jaundice, cirrhosis, and sometimes cancer of the liver. It is caused by a virus that is trans-mitted by way of blood and body fluids in a manner very similar to HIV. The virus may be found in human blood, urine, semen, cerebrospinal fluid, saliva, and vaginal excretions. Injection into the bloodstream and sexual contact with infected persons are well-known routes of transmission. Exposure of mucous membranes to infected droplets or dust and exposure to infected body fluids through broken skin are also primary hazards. Fortunately, there is a 3-series vaccine available for protection against Hepatitis B. However, hepatitis is still considered a very serious and sometimes even fatal disease.

Tuberculosis (TB)

Tuberculosis is an airborne pathogen. Its main means of transmission is through inhalation of the TB pathogens. Commonly this would occur if an individual infected with TB were to cough on an individual, or if the TB-infected person and potential exposed person are in a confined air space. Recently, a large resurgence of infectious tuberculosis has been seen, especially among the same 'high risk' group as with AIDS and Hepatitis B. This form of TB has been shown to be highly resistant to traditional antibiotic treatments.

GENERAL PRECAUTIONARY MEASURES

Crime scene personnel should follow their agencies' specific guidelines regarding precautions against biological and chemical hazards. However, those guidelines should be based on established protocols such as those released by United States Public Health Service Centers for Disease Control for Health Care Professionals. By practicing the following guidelines investigators and technicians may perform their required duties while minimizing the risk of accidental infection.

These precautions should be enforced routinely, regardless of whether the persons or evidence involved are known to have originated from an infected individual or scene.

1 All blood and body fluids are to be considered infectious whether wet or dry.

2 All needles, syringes, razor blades, and sharp instruments should be handled with utmost caution, and placed in puncture resistant containers.

3 Good personal hygiene is the best protection against infectious diseases. Wash hands with soap and water frequently.

4 Know your skin integrity. Keep all wounds carefully bandaged while on duty. Use a bandage which provides complete impermeable 360-degree coverage. Change the bandage if it becomes soiled or dirty.

5 Latex gloves should be worn when handling blood specimens, body fluids, materials and objects that may be the source of contamination. Dispose of gloves after one use.

6 Gowns, masks, and eye protection should be worn when your clothing may be soiled by blood or body fluids or when procedures are being performed which may involve extensive exposure to blood or potentially infectious body fluids (including activities such as the transport of the victim's body, laboratory examination of specimens, post-mortem examination).

7 Avoid all hand-to-face contact, including eating, smoking, and drinking, where the possibility of transmission exists.

8 Hands and skin area must be washed immediately and thoroughly if they accidentally become contaminated with blood or body fluids.

9 Contaminated surfaces and objects should be cleaned up with a solution of one (1)

part household bleach to nine (9) parts water. An alcohol pad or soap and water can be used as a subsequent cleaning solution and to remove the odor of bleach.

10 Constantly be alert for sharp objects. When handling needles, knives, razors, broken glass, nails, broken metal, or any other sharp object bearing blood, use the utmost care to prevent a cut or puncture of the skin.

Specific Guidelines for Crime Scene Investigators

1 Wear latex gloves and coverall gowns when conducting crime scene searches.

2 Surgical masks or facemasks with the appropriate filter cartridges should be worn when aerosol or airborne pathogens may be encountered. This caution may apply to dried blood particles as well.

3 Double latex gloves, surgical masks and protective eye wear should be used when handling bodies, liquid blood, body fluids, dried blood particles, and evidence containing trace amounts of the above.

4 Latex gloves, eye-coverings, surgical masks and a gown should be worn when attending an autopsy.

5 When processing the crime scene, constantly be alert for sharp and broken objects or surfaces.

6 Do not place your hands in areas where you are unable to see when conducting a search. If you must, then wear specially designed search gloves, which can give added protection.

7 Under no circumstances should anyone at the crime scene be allowed to smoke, eat, or drink.

8 When liquid blood and body fluids are collected in bottles or glass vials, this container must be prominently labeled 'Blood Precautions' or 'Biohazards'.

9 Blood and body fluid stained clothing and objects must be dried and packaged in double bags and labeled properly. If evidence is collected from a possibly infected person or scene, the package should be labeled 'Caution – Potential AIDS (Hepatitis) Case.' However, beware of legal requirements that often protect the confidentiality of infected individuals and mandate non-disclosure of that information.

10 If practical, use only disposable items at a crime scene where infectious blood is present. All non-disposable items must be decontaminated after each use.

11 Any reports, labels or evidence tags splashed with blood should be destroyed with information duplicated on clean forms or labels.

12 After completing the search of a scene, investigators should clean their hands with diluted household bleach solution and with soap and water. Alternatively, there are some commercially available cleansing reagents, some of which are good for field use, away from water.

13 Any contaminated clothing or footwear should be properly disposed of.

CHAPTER 4

CRIME SCENE DOCUMENTATION

INTRODUCTION

Documentation is often the most time-consuming, but one of the most important, steps in a crime scene investigation. It is the step that requires the crime scene investigator to be the most systematic and organized in their procedures. At the same time it is a step that must be subjected to constant innovation, creativity, and originality by the crime scene investigator. It is the investigator's common sense, training, and experience that set the foundation for crime scene documentation. The purpose of crime scene documentation is to record and preserve the location and relationship of physical evidence in the crime scene and the condition of the crime scene. Also, proper documentation of a crime scene will allow for any subsequent re-evaluation of the scene or physical evidence found at the scene. The five processes or methods utilized in the documentation of the crime scene are: note taking, videotaping, still photography, sketching, and audiotaping. Each of the methods of crime scene documentation is in themselves important, but none is an adequate substitute for another. Ironically, the documentation methods may seem redundant but they are good checks and balances for each other. Good note taking will not replace good still photography, sketching, or videography, but notes with detailed descriptions of the scene can supplement and be relied upon when batteries or film processing equipment fail. The details of a victim's wounds may not be completely written in an investigator's notes but can often be viewed in videotape or in a still photograph. Photographs may not show brand names or labels, but a note detailing the description of medications found in a suicide victim's medicine cabinet could assist in the death investigation. The methods of crime scene documentation to be presented in the following chapter will be note-taking, videography, still photography, and sketching. A fifth method of crime scene documentation, audiotaping, is a form of note taking; therefore audiotaping is essentially an audio form of note taking, which may or may not be transcribed into written notes for the crime scene investigator or for the case file. Additionally, dependent upon the jurisdiction's discovery rules of evidence, the audiotaped notes may eventually have to be presented in written form.

DOCUMENTATION BEGINS

The exact time for the documentation starts at the moment that the investigator begins his or her involvement, of any kind, in the investigation. That beginning moment may be the receiving of a communications call while sitting in the forensic services office at the station, the receiving of a pager signal at lunch or even the abrupt telephone call at 2 a.m. while sleeping at home. All these situations 'signal' the beginning of the process of documentation as essential parts of the crime scene investigation. The documentation never stops; it may be slowed and the investigation stalled, but the documentation process is ongoing. It will stop only when the investigation is completed and the case is closed.

In this chapter the methods of crime scene documentation will be introduced and a suggested procedure for systematic completion of the documentation method will be presented. Photos 4.1a–g show a complete sequence for scene documentation. In addition, the merits of each method will be discussed.

EFFECTIVE NOTE-TAKING

The notes are the written record of all activities or all the items observed in and about the crime scene. The note taker is essentially the secretary of the crime scene. The notes reflect the 'when', the 'who', the 'what', the 'where', and the 'how' of the scene investigation. Effective notes will seek to answer all those questions. Pre-prepared forms are frequently used to facilitate the recording of notes at the scene (see Appendix II). Forms are useful but will never be able to include all the note taker's information for all scenes or scenarios. They can provide an outline or guideline but complete reliance on crime scene forms may lead to ineffectiveness on the part of the crime scene investigator. A pre-printed form is never a substitute for a detailed and complete written note.

GENERAL GUIDELINES

Photo 4.1a–g (opposite)

Faculty of University of New Haven Forensic Science Department work with students during a crime scene practical exercise, emphasizing the importance of quality notes and documentation. (Courtesy of Dr Howard Harris, UNH.)

Some basic principles for notes include making the notes permanent (by use of ink writing instruments and by not editing the notes), legible, and each page identified with sequential number, case number and note taker's name. There is no set process or procedure for crime scene investigation note taking, but some minimum requirements that should be found in the notes are:

1 Notification information:
   (a) mode;
   (b) dates and times;

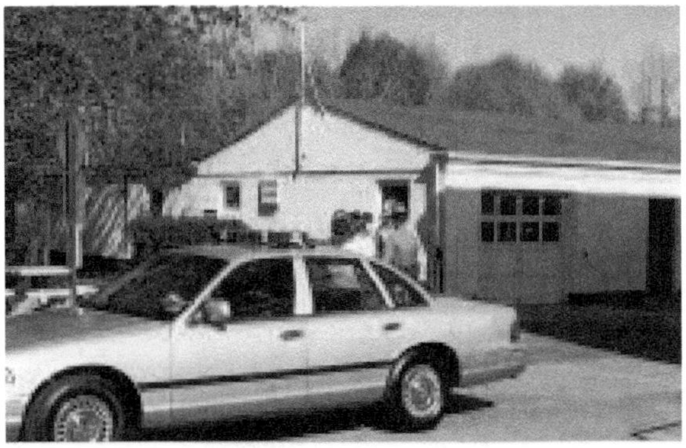
(a)

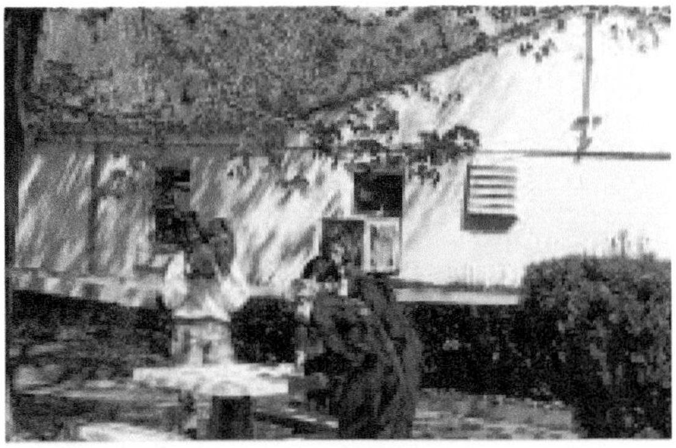
(b)

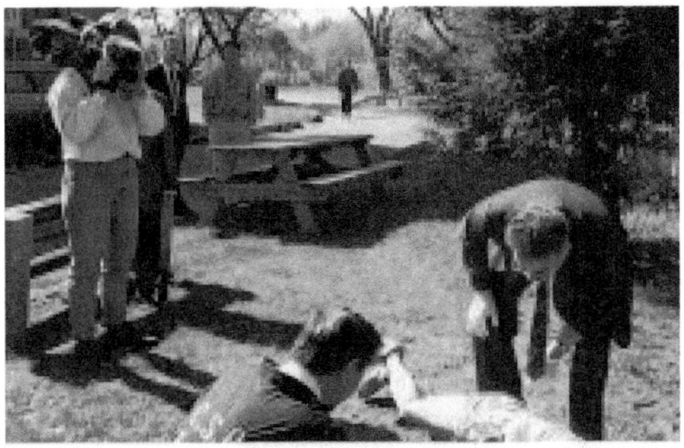
(c)

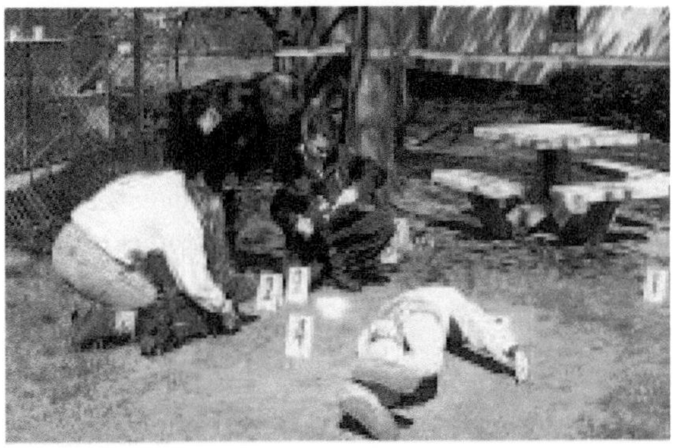
(d)

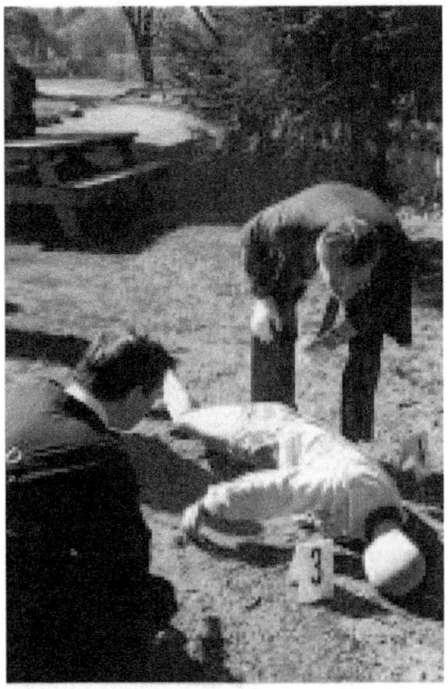
(e)

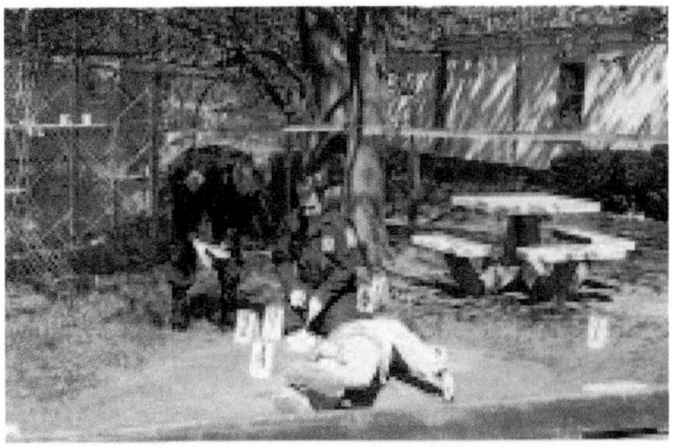
(f)

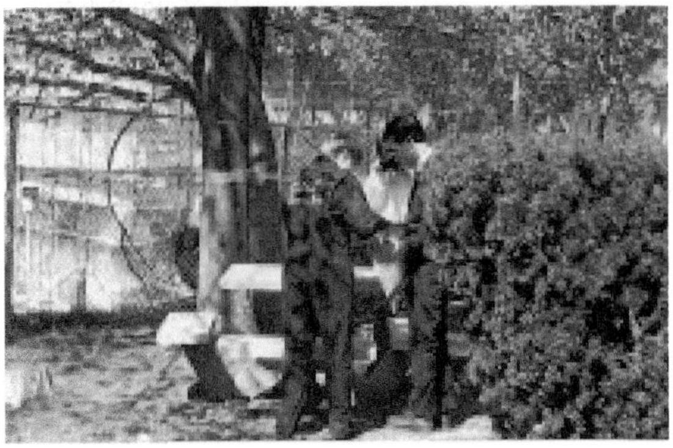
(g)

(c) information received (type of case, victim(s) if any, address, case number to be assigned, lead investigator, etc.);

(d) identity of person doing the informing (rank, position, requesting official, and other identifying information).

2   Arrival information:

(a) mode of transportation to scene location (intermediate stops, secondary scenes, etc.);

(b) date and time;

(c) address, telephone number, and other identifications;

(d) personnel already on scene (witnesses, suspects, victims, police, emergency medical personnel, etc.);

(e) notifications made or to be made – medical examiner, forensic experts (odontologists, anthropologists, etc.), fire departments (hazardous materials, search and rescue, etc.), helicopters, state or district attorneys, or other assistance that may be required.

3   Description of the scene:

(a) weather (temperature, winds, rain, etc.);

(b) location (interior/exterior, first floor/second floor, car/house, etc.);

(c) description of scene;

(d) vehicles, buildings, or other major structures or observations at the scene;

(e) evidence easily identified (prior to preliminary scene survey) and especially the transient (smells, sounds, sights) and conditional (light switches, HVAC controls) evidence.

4   Description of victim(s) – in many jurisdictions the body is the evidence of the medical examiner or coroner and as such, any movement or disruption of the body at the crime scene must be with the authorization or approval of the appropriate authority. Once given the following may be included in the notes:

(a) position or location;

(b) lividity or rigidity;

(c) wounds;

(d) clothing, footwear, jewelry, forms of identification – presence or absence, type, etc.);

(e) weapons at scene.

5   Crime scene investigation team:

(a) duty assignments – notes, video, photography, sketching, evidence collection, processing responsibilities, etc. – who, what, when, where, and how these assignments are accomplished;

(b) preliminary scene survey information – first responder's information; evidence identification – including bloodstain pattern identifications, trajectory recognition, and transient/conditional evidence (footwear impressions or tire tread marks); changes to scene; and other observations from the 'walk-thru';

(c) start and ending times for the scene duties;

(d) evidence processing, collection, packaging, and transportation/storage.

Generally, the written record of the crime scene investigation must include the investigator's overall observations, actions, descriptions of the scene and specific information of identification like name, date, telephone number, and address. The legible notes include a *detailed* description of the scene and any items of physical evidence determined to be relevant to the scene. Answering the following questions will assure a complete, detailed description of the scene and evidence: How many (quantity)? What is it (name or other identifier)? Where is it (location)? What does it look like (appearance, color, construction, size, condition)? Is it unique (serial numbers, signatures, brand or model name, etc)? Who is at the scene? Who is a potential witness?

Additionally, the documentation notes, the crime scene's written record, will be used to relate the scene to its physical evidence, the following major aspects of the crime scene deserve attention and observation at most interior scenes:

1 The location: room, walls, floors, ceilings. Remember a room is essentially a box with six surfaces that may hold evidence.
2 The points of entry/exit and paths of travel: doors, windows, ceilings, ventilation systems, carpets, floors. Record condition, open/closed, ajar, locked/unlocked, screens, movement, or footwear impressions.
3 Appliances and utilities: conditional evidence. Remember this type of evidence must be turned on/off or plugged in by the action of a person. This evidence is related to natural lighting/heating and cooling needs, too.
4 Ashtrays and trashcans: contents. Often this type of evidence will establish recent, past actions by victims and suspects.
5 Clothing: visible or disturbed presence. Indicates movements at scene by victims and suspects.
6 Furniture: described in relation to the victim, other evidence, and the overall scene.
7 Witness, suspect, victim description (age, condition, position, injury).

Any evidence, either that which is present at – or evidence that is absent from – the scene should be included in the crime scene documentation notes. Often, the absent evidence is omitted or overlooked in the notes of the crime scene investigation. Absent evidence comprises items of evidence that, based upon available information from witnesses or victims, logic, and case circumstances, are absent or missing from the crime scene – such as stereo systems or computer equipment missing from the scene that can be identified or traced at a later date. Of course, the crime scene investigator must also be aware of evidence that should be absent but is present. For example, the death investigation case where the husband reports that the murdering burglar stole only the dead wife's jewelry and none of his jewelry, or the fact that a large amount of cash was not taken by the burglar; such pieces of evidence are certainly significant to the investigator. Remember, missing evidence, as well as evidence present at a scene, can provide motive, a means for collaborating or disproving statements of witnesses, victims or suspects, and confirmation of the *corpus delecti* or body of the crime; therefore its significance must be recorded in the crime scene notes.

The effective use of notes as a component of crime scene documentation for the written record of activities, location of physical evidence, descriptions of people at the scene, and the condition of the crime scene is not only crucial for initial crime scene investigation, but is also important for subsequent investigation. Accurate crime scene reporting, valid suspect apprehension, and reliable courtroom testimony are all essential in the successful completion of an investigation and case resolution.

VIDEOGRAPHY OF THE CRIME SCENE

The use of videography at the crime scene has become a routine procedure for crime scene documentation in recent years. The use of videotapes and digital videography has widespread acceptance in the law enforcement community today. Several factors have influenced its commonplace use. For most law enforcement agencies the accepted use of videography in crime scene documentation is due to availability – in terms of the several *affordable* models of video cameras from which to choose and the increased availability of excellent optics or 'zoom lenses' on cameras that allow transitions between wide-angle and telephoto views of the crime scene and the physical evidence.

The biggest influence leading to the accepted use of videographic documentation of crime scenes comes from juries expecting videotaping of crime scenes. Most private citizens themselves have used or currently use videotaping in their own lives. They want and expect crime scene investigations to include a form of video documentation. Indeed, the crime scene investigator can use videography as a valuable tool for crime scene documentation.

Videotaping crime scenes should be the first step after the walk-thru (or preliminary scene survey) and Polaroid photos (instant photographs) have been taken. The actual process or technique for the videotaping of crime scenes is summarized below:

1 Start the videotaping with an introduction. The introduction may be auditory by the videographer or in the form of a placard without sound. The introductory information should include, at least, the case number, the date, time, location, type of crime scene/investigation and any other *objective* information deemed necessary by the videographer (weather conditions, camera used, etc.).

2 The videotaping of the entire crime scene, after the introduction, should be without

any subjective audio recording (some departmental procedures may require audio recording and, as such, should be followed). In some circumstances, the addition of comments by the videographer may be deemed subjective by the courts and can lead to omissions in the taping process. It is important to prevent added subjectivity to the crime scene documentation making sure that all law enforcement personnel are not videotaped on the scene. The video should only contain the crime scene, victims, and the physical evidence, not investigators or first responders standing around viewing the process.

3 Begin the crime scene videotaping with a general view of the areas surrounding and leading into or away from the crime scene. A general view of the crime scene should follow the initial taping of the surroundings. The use of the four compass points will insure that all general viewpoints are taped. This orientation step of the documentation is the most important and useful for subsequent viewing by investigators, witnesses, attorneys, and juries.

4 Continue taping throughout the crime scene using the wide-angle view format followed by more close-up views of the items of evidence. The videotape should illustrate the orientation or relationship of the evidence within the crime scene. It is important to retain a sense of continuity while viewing the videotape. Haphazard jumping from one item of evidence to the next produces ineffective videotape documentation. Videotaping of the crime scene has as its primary purpose the orientation of the crime scene in a graphic nature and is not intended to allow for detailed, high-quality recording of close-up views of individual items of evidence.

5 The videotaping of the crime scene should also include a view of the crime scene looking from the victim's point of view. Standing near the victim's location (if the victim is still present at the scene) and taping towards the four compass points can achieve this viewpoint and oftentimes is useful for further investigation. Do not destroy evidence or alter the victim's position when attempting this step.

6 While videotaping, use slow camera movements especially when panning or zooming. A tripod or monopod will greatly facilitate these movements. Walking, videotaping, and producing a 'smooth' videotaped product can be difficult, but practice and experience can assist in the production of the documentation product.

7 For low light or night videotaping, most cameras come equipped with lights; however, some additional lighting, like floor floodlighting, might be necessary. Fire trucks and some special police and highway construction trucks have additional lights that may be useful for these situations.

8 Videotaping of the crime scene, once completed, should never be edited or altered. The original tape should be kept as evidence and duplicate copies made for viewing.

Another advantage of videotaping in addition to the low cost of useful equipment and judicial acceptance is its ability to give a three-dimensional presentation of the scene. The minimal amount of training needed, ease of operation, the availability and declining costs of video-printers, reproducibility, and the interfacing abilities with other video and digital systems are some of the ease-of-use advantages to be found in videotaping crime scenes. One of the most useful advantages of videotaping for the crime scene investigator is the ability of the videographer to view and evaluate the videotape on the crime scene. The video cameras in use today can be examined by viewing through the viewfinder, evaluated immediately, and the entire scene re-videotaped if necessary. Another advantage of videotaping the crime scene is the ability of other investigators and interested officials to view the crime scene without actually being present on the scene and not altering or contaminating the physical evidence.

Videotaping as a documentation technique can provide a perspective of the crime scene that is more easily perceived than by notes, sketches, or still photographs. Remember, however, that it is a supplemental technique and not a replacement for the other techniques.

PHOTOGRAPHIC DOCUMENTATION

The purpose of crime scene photography is to provide a visual record of the scene and related areas; to record the initial appearance of the crime scene and physical evidence; to provide investigators and others with the permanent record subsequent analysis of the scene; and to provide the permanent record to the courts. The traditional method for the visual documentation of crime scenes and physical evidence is by the use of still photography. Numerous formats of cameras and film types have been used successfully through the years. Photo 4.2 shows some of the commonly used formats. Equipment and film changes, but the need for a 'true and accurate' record of the crime scene and the physical evidence will remain the same.

The material to be presented in this chapter is intended to provide a basic foundation for crime scene photography. This chapter is not intended to present the detailed technological components of photography. The information on photographic documentation presented will be the 'building blocks' from which the crime scene investigator may form a firm foundation or base of knowledge that will lead to the best resolution of the investigation.

GENERAL PHOTOGRAPHIC RESPONSIBILITIES

A series of poorly planned, poorly executed and poorly displayed crime scene photographs have the ability to directly affect the success of the other efforts of the crime scene investigation. For this reason, crime scene photography is one of the most important steps in the entire investigation process. As one of the primary documentation components, a systematic, organized visual record of

Photo 4.2
Evolution of cameras and
film. Upper and lower left
are 4 × 5 format: upper
and middle right are
35mm format; and lower
left represents a digital
camera.

an undisturbed crime scene must be achieved. For this reason, photographing
the crime scene is normally done immediately following videotaping of the
scene. If no videotaping is done, then the still photography of the scene begins
immediately following the preliminary scene survey. The systematic, organized
method for recording the crime scene and pertinent physical evidence is most
often achieved by following a 'progressive general to specific' guideline. Photos
4.3–4.7 show a sequence of pictures, from general to specific, of a death scene.
This process has been described as 'overall views' to 'mid-range views' to 'close-
up views'. By following this guideline process the conditions as shown in the
photographs give a 'true and accurate' representation of the crime scene. The
progressive, stepwise nature of the photographs allows for orientation of the
crime scene as a whole, the orientation of the evidence within the crime scene,
and to provide for examination quality photographs of specific items of
evidence, such as footwear impressions or tire tread marks, that may be subsequently used for laboratory examination and comparison purposes.

Any number of photographs should be taken with the idea that the cost of
the film and processing does not and should never outweigh the important
value of completeness. The crime scene investigator should never have any
doubts as to whether a photograph should be taken – whenever there is doubt
about a photograph, TAKE IT! Hindsight will not be 20/20 when a part of a
crime scene or a piece of evidence appeared to have no significance and was not

Photos 4.3 to 4.7 depict the proper general to specific method for photographing a crime scene.

Photo 4.3

An aerial overall view of a highway which was the site of a kidnapping/murder.

Photo 4.4

Intermediate range aerial photo depicting a blood trail on the highway.

photographed and then subsequently becomes immensely important at a later date. For example, a photograph of the dish of ice cream observed by the police officer in the condo in Brentwood, California would have yielded information on the time of the incident and thus provided a valuable lead in the Nicole Simpson death investigation. Since the dish of ice cream was never photographed, the correct time of the incident was not possible to reconstruct.

Photo 4.5
Ground-level overview of blood trail.

Photo 4.6
Mid-range ground-level view of specific portions of the blood trail.

Photo 4.7

Close-up view at end of blood trail.

When taking the general overall photographs of a crime scene, aerial photographs are best suited for this type of viewpoint. Photographs of the surrounding areas, roads, paths, and waterways and their proximity to the crime scene can be easily depicted in the aerial photograph. Unfortunately, not every investigative agency has immediate access to the helicopter or airplane needed for these types of photographs. However, the areas surrounding, leading into or out of a crime scene should be photographed at ground level by the scene investigator. The aerial photographs should be taken as soon as possible so as to depict a crime scene that has not been altered by time, weather or other environmental factors (natural or manmade).

Overall photographs of the outside of the crime scene should also include views of the exterior of any buildings where the crime occurred, the windows, doors, pathways/walkways, or other means of entry/exit. Any numerical displays of address or names on the exterior of buildings or structures should be included in an overall photograph of the scene. These displays include address numbers, names on doors or mail boxes and street names (see Photo 4.10). If there are any exterior balconies or stairwells, overall photographs from these structures may facilitate an aerial view of the crime scene. The value of overall photographs of a crime scene is found in the ability of the photographs to be compiled to illustrate the victim(s)' and/or suspect(s)' approach to the crime scene, entrance to the scene, commission of the crime, and finally, the exit from the crime scene.

If the crime scene involves a vehicle, the same photographic procedure will apply. Surrounding areas and structures should be photographed. Aerial

Photo 4.9a

An overall view of a shooting scene depicting blood spatter on pillow cases and wall above head board. This photo was taken by the first responding officer.

Photo 4.9b

This photo was taken at a later time by crime scene investigators. Note the altered crime scene, blood-stained pillow case placed on head board.

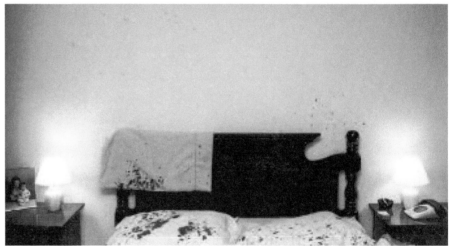

Photo 4.10

Street signs used as identification markers.

Photo 4.11a

An abandoned car located near a homicide scene. When the license plate was removed there were some decals on the front bumper.

Photo 4.11b

Close-up view of the decals which aided in identifying the owner, and ultimately solving the case.

photographs taken as soon as possible, including the vehicle, must be taken for orientation purposes. Ground level, overall photographs of each side and the four corners of the vehicle will fully document the vehicle. Be sure to include the license plate, vehicle identification number, decals/bumper stickers, and any other unique or identifying appearances on the exterior of the vehicle, as shown in Photos 4.11a and 4.11b.

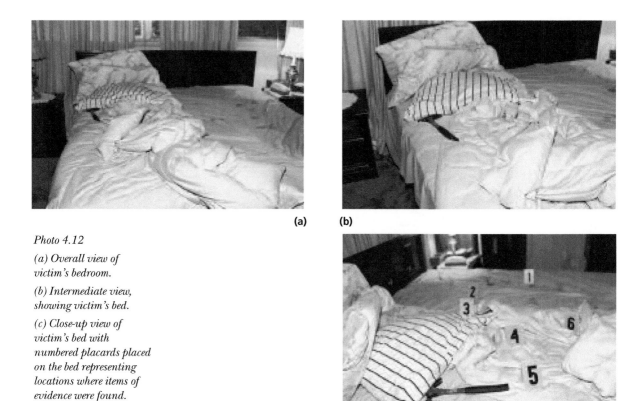

(a) (b)

(c)

Photo 4.12

(a) Overall view of victim's bedroom.

(b) Intermediate view, showing victim's bed.

(c) Close-up view of victim's bed with numbered placards placed on the bed representing locations where items of evidence were found.

The documentation of the interior of a crime scene will follow the same progressive, stepwise nature as shown in the exterior documentation photographs. Begin by photographing the entrance to the crime scene, first with an orientation, overall photographs followed by more close range photographs that for example document tool marks or other patterned evidence that may be present on the entrance. Once inside the room or interior scene, photograph the area as it appears at the entrance. An overlapping technique of photographs may assist with the total documentation of the area. As the photographer enters completely inside the interior crime scene, using the four compass points or corners will assist with achieving total recording of the scene. These photographs will depict the overall view of the scene and as the mid-range photographs are taken will focus on the items of evidence found in the scene. Any connecting rooms or adjacent areas need to be included in the overall orientation photographs.

The individual items of physical evidence need to be photographed with a mid-range photograph for orientation purposes followed by a close-up, examination quality photograph. The mid-range photograph will show how the item of evidence is related to its surroundings and the close-up photograph will document individualizing details on the item. Photo 4.12 shows a series of pictures to demonstrate this procedure. The various techniques used for pho-tographing the items of physical evidence will be presented later in this chapter. Individual items of evidence may be marked by a number of commercially available markers. Numbered markers or cones work well to 'identify' the item in the photographs. To document the size and distance relationships of the physical evidence at the scene place scales or rulers adjacent to or next to the item of evidence (never on top or within an item). Tape measures and other measuring devices are useful for both mid-range and close-up photographs. A good practice is to photograph the scene with and without (original condition) identifying markers and scales at the mid-range and close-up viewpoints.

The large number and types of photographs that are taken as part of crime scene documentation must be chronologically recorded. The common procedure used for this purpose is the maintenance of the 'photo log'. The log is the complete written record of all the photographic documentation at the crime scene. Figure 4.1 is an example of a photo log. The photo log is essentially the documentation of the photographic documentation at the scene. The log should include the following information:

1. Name of photographer and log keeper;
2. Agency case number;
3. Date of incident and date photos taken;
4. Type of investigation;
5. Time photo taken;
6. Location of the photo.

The log must also include the photography equipment documentation:

1. Make, model, and type of camera;
2. Camera serial number;
3. Lens make, model (focal length), and serial number;
4. Type of film, number of exposures/roll, speed rating (ASA or ISO);
5. Flash information (make, model, and serial number).

Every photograph taken as part of the crime scene investigation must be recorded in the log. Variables of the photographs that must be recorded are:

1. Date and time of exposure;
2. Roll number and exposure number;
3. Type of photograph taken (overall, mid-range or close-up);
4. Distance between camera and subject;
5. Camera settings (lens setting, f/stop and shutter speed);
6. Use of tripod or flash (with setting);
7. Brief description of photograph;
8. Any special filters or equipment used and whether light sources were used.

Figure 4.1
Photo log.

Photo Log

DATE TAKEN ________

INV. ______________ **CASE NO.** ______________

EQUIPMENT USED:

CAMERA ______________ **BODY SN** __________

LENS(ES) ______________ **LENS SN** __________

TYPE OF FILM __________ **NO. OF EXP** __________

ISO ________

FLASH USED __________ **FLASH SN** __________

Roll _____

Time	Exp. No.	Type*	Description*	Dist.*	Settings & Misc.*

***Type:** Overall, mid-range, specific
Description: What is being depicted in the photograph
Dist. Or Distance: Distance from camera to subject
Settings and Miscellaneous: Camera apperature, shutter speed, and any other relevant information.

The photo log and its information will assist the crime scene investigator with any identifications of the scene and its evidence, should it be necessary at a later time. Also, the film type and camera settings are necessary for the chemical processing and development of negatives and photographs. The photo log must correlate to the actual negatives and photographs from the scene investigation. No attempts to omit or destroy unusable negatives or photographs should ever be done. The log and the photographs are evidence too!

SPECIAL PHOTOGRAPHIC TECHNIQUES AND CONSIDERATIONS

Use of instant photography

Often the transient and conditional evidence found at the crime scene can be easily lost, changed or altered. In a last-chance effort to prevent its loss or if the crime scene no longer exists in its original condition, instant photography cameras or film are excellent media to supplement for videography or still photography. For example, a thunderstorm is rapidly approaching that threatens to obliterate the footwear impressions or bloodstain patterns that are present at the outdoor scene of a shooting. The first responder has a Polaroid camera with a flash. Orientation and mid-range photographs of the impressions and patterns can be taken using this camera so the evidence will not be lost. The use of instant photography can also prevent the loss or contamination of the scene and its physical evidence: overall photographs of the crime scene taken by instant photography can be shown to other investigators, officers, witnesses, or other interested parties outside the crime scene security barrier tape, thereby keeping them out of the crime scene.

Overlapping photographs

Overall photographs of a crime scene are best achieved by utilizing the four compass points with a moderate wide-angle lens, as shown in Figure 4.2. If a wide-angle lens is not available, a normal focal length lens (50–55 mm) can be

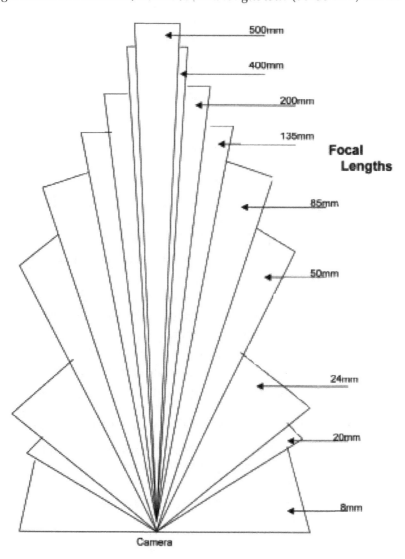

Figure 4.2

Lens focal length and field of vision chart.

Figure 4.3

Proper camera placement for general overall photographs.

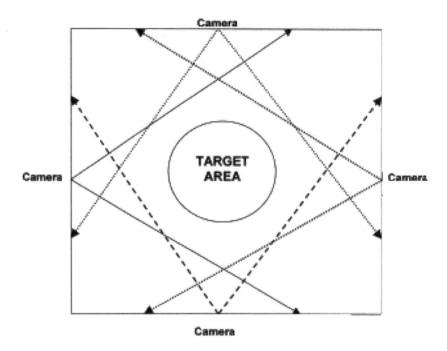

used while positioning the camera for overlapping photographs to achieve an approximate 360-degree view of the scene, as shown in Figure 4.3.

'Forensic comparison' or 'examination quality' photographs

The purpose of these photographs is to accurately record the detailed and close-up appearance of items of physical evidence found in the crime scene should subsequent laboratory examination of the evidence be necessary. Evidence of this type includes most patterned evidence like fingerprints, footwear impressions, bloodstain patterns, gunshot residue, and glass fracture patterns. Close-up photography of this type can be accomplished with a few suggested techniques and guidelines. The item to be photographed should be photographed in natural lighting and with added oblique lighting. The type of patterned evidence will determine the light source positioning (see Figure 4.4a&b). The item should be photographed both without a scale and with a scale along two axes of the plane of the item. Be sure to fill the frame of the picture with the item being photographed (see Photo 4.13). The camera and the film plane must be placed at right angles to the item being photographed. The use of a tripod and leveling device is very useful for achieving good examination quality photographs (see Figure 4.5). Examination quality photographs that will be used for subsequent laboratory examination or comparison purposes will show a greater amount of contrast and facilitate examinations if photographed using black-and-white film. In addition, close-up photographs of the item of evidence with color film should be used to document the color, trace textures or designs of the evidence.

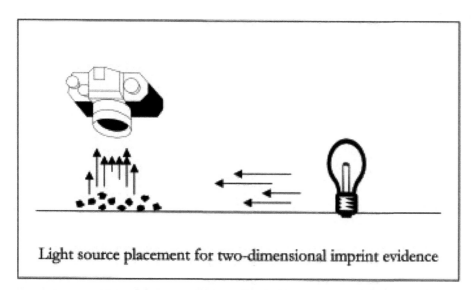

Light source placement for two-dimensional imprint evidence

Figure 4.4a

Proper light source placement for two-dimensional imprint evidence.

A. Light source is placed at the same level as the imprint evidence so that light is reflected off of the imprint residue particles.

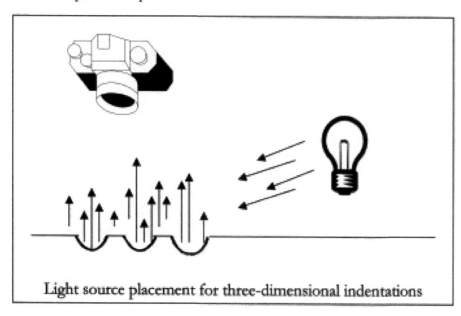

Light source placement for three-dimensional indentations

Figure 4.4b

Proper light source placement for three-dimensional indentations.

B. Light source is placed at a 45degree angle to the indentation evidence so as to create shadows for better contrast.

Photo 4.13

*Forensic examination
quality photograph of
footwear impression.*

Use of flash attachments

This technique is recommended not just for use in low light situations, but also for photographing most crime scenes in general. The flash attachment is essential for casting shadows in examination quality photographs to enhance details of patterned evidence, but it is successful for enhancing the details in mid-range orientation photographs and all items of evidence. For example, consider the scene of a suspected arson, as shown in Photo 4.14. The burned structure has no electricity for added lighting, occurred at night, and the scene is essentially a black color due to the total burn of the structure (black items of evidence with a black background). The use of flash photography is essential in the documentation of fire scenes which are low-light areas and do not have high contrasting colors present. Another use for flash photography in crime scene documentation is a technique of filling-in with flash (see Photos 4.15a&b). This technique is used in high-light situations, outdoor scenes in bright sunlight, in an attempt to illuminate evidence in dark shadows.

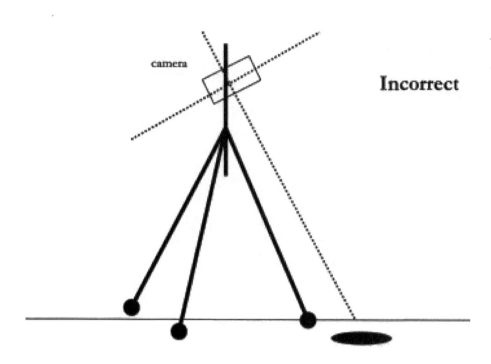

Incorrect

Figure 4.5
Tripod positions for exam-
ination photographs.

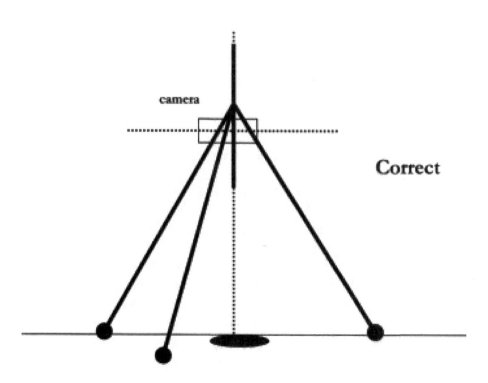

Correct

Photo 4.14

Proper illumination of badly burned homicide victims.

The technique uses the following steps:

1 Set the camera's shutter speed to the flash synchronization speed.
2 Use the camera's built-in light meter to determine the proper f/stop. Using manual controls, set the f/stop.
3 Set the flash attachment to manual control and determine the flash-to-subject distance for the f/stop set above.
4 Using the distance determined above, hold the flash at that distance from the shadowed area.
5 TTL flash attachments can be set automatically for fill-in flash capabilities.

A final useful technique with flash photography for crime scene documentation is 'painting with light'. It is essential for documentation of night-time, large outdoor crime scenes (see Photos 4.16a&b). Painting with light will produce properly exposed photographs of overall, large areas at the crime scene. This is a technique of multiple exposures of a single film frame with moving light sources (the flash attachment). A flash that is capable of illuminating up to 150 feet, a synchronization cord (or remote slave unit) for the flash, a camera with a manual or 'B' setting shutter speed, and a tripod will be the equipment necessary for this technique. A separate, rechargeable external battery for the flash is helpful because there will be many full power flash discharges within a short period of time, which is difficult with standard flash batteries. The technique uses the following steps:

Photo 4.15a

View of the underside of a vehicle. Note a small reflection in the center of the photo, which is a screwdriver.

Photo 4.15b

Fill flash technique used to remove shadows and illuminate the screwdriver located under the car.

(Courtesy Forensic Photo Unit CT State Forensic Lab.)

1 Mount the camera on the tripod and position it for documentation of the overall scene. Up to 500 feet of distance can be photographed.

2 Set the camera shutter speed to 'B' (bulb setting) and set the f/stop to a middle setting like f/11 (good depth of focus).

3 Remove all other extraneous lighting from the scene (law enforcement and other emergency vehicles) and moving objects (personnel, vehicles, etc.).

4 Trip the camera shutter (the setting will keep the shutter open until re-tripped at the conclusion of the technique).

5   Start firing the flash at the farthest point from the camera; repeat the firings at various locations, while progressively changing the angle and distances moving towards the camera. There is no need to worry about the photographer stepping into the field of view of the camera. The flash discharges will obliterate the photographer's presence in the photograph.

6   Once the photographer returns to a location near the camera, the shutter is re-tripped to close it.

Large overall photographs and mid-range photographs can be taken using this technique.

Photo 4.16a

Overall view of the scene of a fatal shooting located along a highway in the night hours.

Photo 4.16b

Painting with light technique used to illuminate a large area during night hours.

(Courtesy Det. Joe Destefano, Major Crime CT State Police.)

Changing the point of view

Most crime scene photographs are taken at a normal, eye-view height. However, due to the size-of-room constraints and other factors, a change of viewpoint can be important to the total documentation effort. Consider taking photographs from a victim's viewpoint by lowering to ground level or adjusting a tripod to a ceiling height. In some instances, a documentation photograph with a changed viewpoint may provide useful investigative information. Photo 4.17 shows two different views of homicide victim's right foot to illustrate the bloodstain patterns.

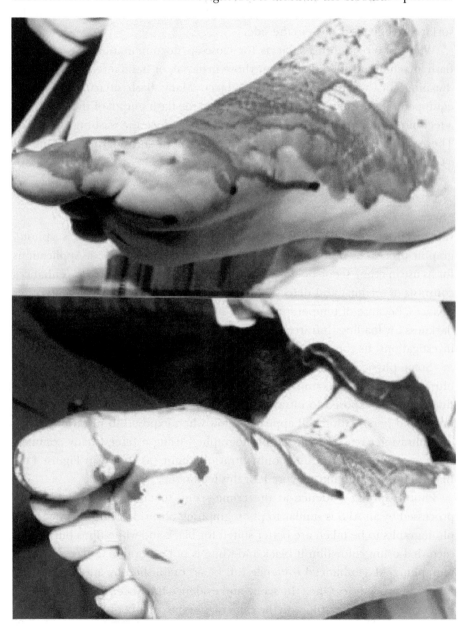

Photo 4.17

Two different photographs taken of the victim's right foot, changing the perspective in each photo.

Awareness of lighting positions

In available lighting situations be sure the light is over the photographer's shoulder so as to illuminate the front of the subject. If photographing towards the sunlight, try to shade the lens if possible or wait until the lighting conditions change. If using flash lighting, front lighting is the best and most common, unless patterned evidence details are being recorded. In those situations, side lighting from the compass points is used. Do not use front lighting for polished or reflective surfaces. Glares may result from these types of surfaces. Better results will be obtained by placing the flash unit at a 45-degree angle to the surface to reflect the flash to the side.

When photographing subjects for close-up documentation, covering the flash attachment with a tissue, pantyhose material, or handkerchief to prevent 'burning' or 'washing-out' of the subject. Many flash attachments come equipped with the ability to reduce or control the flash output of the unit. Also, a technique of 'bouncing the light' will work to reduce the washing-out effect. There are several commercial products, camera and flash attachments, available to utilize this technique.

The use of infrared, ultraviolet and alternate light source (ALS) photography

Infrared photography does have applications in law enforcement. It is a photographic process by which invisible, infrared radiation is recorded. Applications for its use in crime scene documentation include aerial photography (enhances contrasts of terrain) and detection of gunshot residues on clothing and other surfaces. Because of temperature requirements and the fact that it needs total darkness for loading, infrared photography is not useful for most crime scene investigations. Its common use at the crime scene is limited for these reasons.

Some physical evidence will absorb ultraviolet light and others will reflect ultraviolet light. For example, many fingerprint powders may be chosen that fluoresce with exposed to ultraviolet light. Physiological fluids such as semen, urine, and perspiration will appear to glow when exposed to ultraviolet light. The ultraviolet reaction can be photographed using a filter (many commercially available) that transmits only ultraviolet light (as shown in Figure 4.6). Black-and-white film must be used for this technique.

Photographing evidence at the crime scene that has been found by or processed by an ALS is similar to photographing ultraviolet fluorescence. The photographs to be taken are better suited for black-and-white films but can be recorded using color film if black-and-white is not an option. Success in photographing ALS-enhanced evidence can be accomplished by adhering to the following procedure. Once the scene and evidence have been processed, place the correct wavelength filter on the camera, put the camera on a tripod, and set

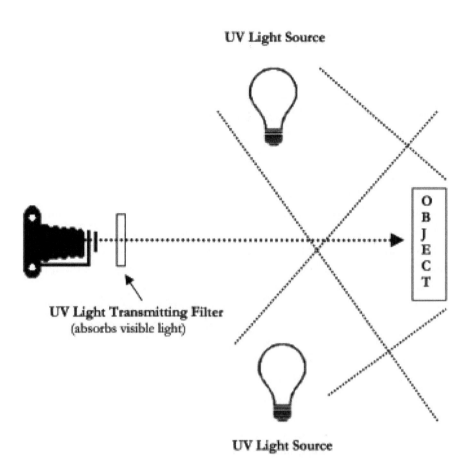

Figure 4.6
General methodology for ultra-violet photography.

the camera at a proper distance for photographing the subject. Using a light meter, the camera's through the lens light meter or the automatic exposure feature, set the f/stop and shutter speed. Take the picture. After this exposure, change either the f/stop or the shutter speed by two settings and take the picture. Repeat this process once more. This adjustment scheme is the process of bracketing. Do not move the camera from its set location while bracketing.

Digital photography

Digital image technology provides the crime scene investigator with powerful new tools for capturing, analyzing, and storing the pictorial record of the crime scene and the physical evidence. (See Photo 4.17.) These digital tools complement the traditional video and still photography used for crime scene documentation. The advantages of digital photography include instant access to the images, easy integration into existing electronic technology, and no need for film processing equipment or darkrooms. The digital camera does not utilize conventional film for recording of the subject. An image sensor located within the camera captures the subject's image, as shown in Photo 4.18. Single lens reflex and point-and-shoot digital cameras are most commonly found on the market today. The single lens reflex digital camera, like the conventional film camera, is best suited for crime scene documentation purposes. A digital camera's image sensor requires more precise determinations of exposure measurement. However, this limitation of exposure is not an issue because the investigator can view the images by direct linkage to a laptop computer at the crime scene. If the digital photograph is not usable it can be immediately retaken at the scene. Most digital cameras also provide for viewing of many images directly on the camera's viewfinder. The use of lenses, wide-angle to zoom, resolution (essentially film speed with conventional films), and lighting availability with digital cameras is similar to traditional still photography.

Conventional wisdom within the law enforcement community suggests that digital image technology can easily be integrated into crime scene documentation techniques. At this point in time, it is not suggested that one technology is chosen over the other. The two techniques provide for a successful integration of instant viewing capabilities and image management efficiency with technologies already in use, and the integration of cost saving from digital photography with the high resolution of various formats, wide exposure latitudes, and versatility of conventional film still photography. Some issues of admissibility in court have arisen because of the ease of manipulation of digital images. It is the investigator that is testifying, not the photograph or image. Any other questions relating to the manipulation of digital images can be averted by written and fully implemented policies and procedures for the use of digital photography in crime scene documentation.

Points to remember for good crime scene photographs

1 Use a tripod. Depth of field (also referred to as depth of focus) is defined as the distance from the closest clear object in a photograph to the farthest clear object in the photograph. For good depth of field keep the camera's aperture small (f/stop number is larger). This process will cause the shutter speed to be slowed down. Therefore, the likelihood for vibrations or blurry pictures will increase. To prevent blurry pictures and to keep the subject in focus always uses a tripod. (Se Figure 4.7.)

2 Remember the f/16 rule. For reasonable exposures and printable negatives, the f/16 rule is: set the camera's shutter speed near the speed of the camera (ASA 100 is close to a shutter speed of 1/125th second) and set the aperture to f/16.

3 Use the flash attachment and get it off the camera. Even in available light situations the flash attachment will bring out details of the crime scene that may be overlooked or missed.

4 Practice and be prepared. The camera and accessories are the tools of trade for the crime scene investigator; they should never be foreign or strange. When new, updated

Photo 4.18
Photograph shows digital camera, image card, and image reader for creation and storage of digital photos on a computer.

Figure 4.7
Depth of field.

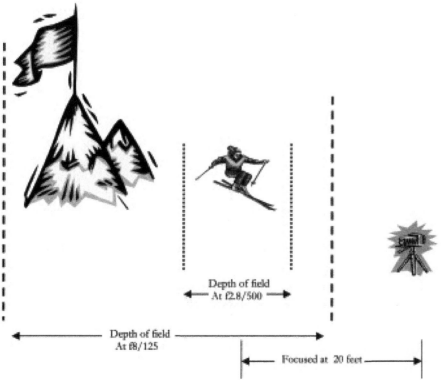

Depth of field
At f2.8/500

Depth of field
At f8/125

Focused at 20 feet

or replacement equipment is purchased, the crime scene photographer must become familiar with it. Practice by taking pictures around the office, in the parking lot, or in the laboratory. Keep the camera and accessories in good working condition. This preparation will keep maximum effectiveness and professionalism. Keep back-up batteries on hand and available. The same applies to film; it must be kept fresh and usable. The time to process a crime scene should never include running back to the office or store for new batteries or more film.

5   When in doubt . . . photograph it! It goes without repeating that still photography is an important component of crime scene documentation. The entire crime scene and its physical evidence must be recorded. The crime scene investigator must never subjectively choose to omit photographing an item of evidence because of any uncertainty. For example, the body in a death investigation is the primary piece of physical evidence. It must be photographed using the proper techniques discussed above. Extra care and attention in the form of extra photographs is understood and expected.

Table 4.1

Basic equipment for crime scene photography.

Basic kit contents	
• Camera	• Film – color and b/w
• Normal lens – 50 mm	• Owner's manuals for flash and camera
• Wide-angle lens – 28 mm or similar	• Label materials – cards, pens, etc.
• Close-up lens or accessories	• Scales or rulers
• Filters	• Flashlight
• Electronic flash	• Grey card
• Sync cord for flash	• Extra batteries
• Locking cable shutter release	• Log sheets
• Tripod	

SKETCHING THE CRIME SCENE

The final component of crime scene documentation is the preparation of the crime scene sketch or diagram. Still photography is a two-dimensional representation of three-dimensional areas and items. It, therefore, inherently will result in some distortion of the spatial relationship of objects in the photographs. For example, an overall photograph of the front entrance of the house in the crime scene will not show the actual length of the walkway leading to the entrance. These spatial distortions can interfere in the reconstruction of shooting trajectories or bloodshed points of origin. The crime scene sketch is the permanent record of the actual size and distance relationships of the crime scene and its physical evidence. The sketch must correlate and supplement the still photographs taken at the scene.

Crime scene sketches do not require artistic abilities but can require some planning and organizational skills by the crime scene investigator. The drawing of the sketch and the taking of measurements will require more than one individual working as a coordinated unit. This coordination of effort takes patience and practice on the part of the crime scene investigators.

There are two basic types of crime scene sketches as part of a crime scene investigation: a *rough sketch* and a *finished or final sketch* (see Figures 4.8, 4.9). There are two basic types of perspectives that are used for crime scene sketches: the *overhead* or 'bird's eye view' (see Figure 4.10) and the *elevation* or 'side-view' (see Figure 5.11).

A rough sketch is usually made at the crime scene before evidence collection. It shows all the evidence to be collected, major structures present in the crime scene, and other relevant structures in or near the crime scene. The rough sketch will show all the measurements taken to determine the size and distance relationships at the crime scene. A final or finished sketch, drawn to scale or not, is prepared from the rough sketch. The final sketch is normally prepared for courtroom presentation. It will show the major structures within the crime scene and all items of evidence or a number for the evidence. It should never show any measurements. It has a clean or uncluttered appearance.

A crime scene sketch is usually drawn from a looking-down or overhead perspective. This type of perspective is the most common type and is most recognizable by other investigators and juries. Where appropriate or when the crime

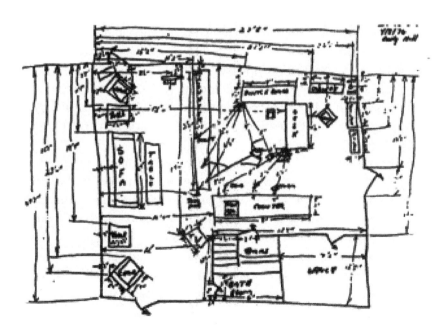

Figure 4.8
Rough crime scene sketch.

Figure 4.9

Finished (to scale) crime scene sketch.

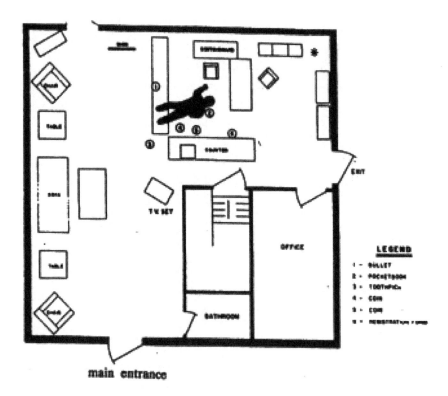

main entrance

scene presents evidence at various heights in a crime scene, a side-view or elevation sketch can be used. The elevation sketch can be used for supplementing the side-view appearance of the still photography documentation. Shooting trajectory reconstruction and bloodstain pattern documentation will oftentimes use elevation sketches. Additionally, final sketches used for courtroom presentation will often employ a combination of the elevation and overhead perspective. This combination of perspective is known as a cross-projection or exploded view sketch. For example the six surfaces of a room, four walls, a ceiling, and a floor, are laid flat or unfolded to record the crime scene and the evidence (see Figure 4.12). Three-dimensional sketching is not normally done, but measurements can be used for 3-D model construction (see Photo 4.19) and 3-D sketches where needed.

There are three techniques for taking measurements or locating the evidence at the crime scene: triangulation, polar coordinates, and rectangular coordinates (sometimes referred to as the base-line or ordinate pairs technique). All three measurement techniques (Figures 4.13, 4.14 and 4.15) are based upon the determination of fixed, or known, starting points. The fixed points should be permanent, for example, in-ground survey markers, large trees, utility poles with serial or locator numbers, corners of buildings or rooms, or other more immovable objects. If the fixed points are permanent, then the crime scene can be reconstructed at a later time.

Figure 4.10
Overhead finished sketch.

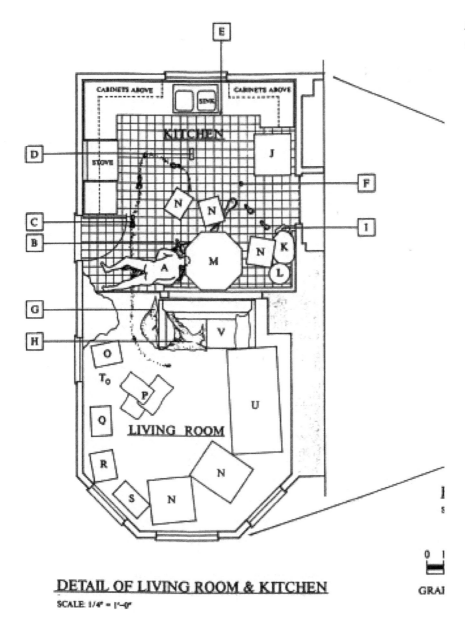

DETAIL OF LIVING ROOM & KITCHEN

SCALE: 1/4" = 1'-0"

1 Triangulation. Select two fixed points, measure the distance between them, and prepare a basic layout sketch of the scene with the points included. Every item of evidence is then measured from these two points (Figure 4.13).

2 Polar coordinates. From a fixed point, all evidence is measured for distance from the point and is measure for direction or angle. The angle is measured by the use of a pro-tractor or other survey instruments (Figure 4.14).

3 Rectangular coordinates, base-line or ordinate pairs. Establish a straight line or base-line between two fixed points. The items of evidence will be measured along the fixed

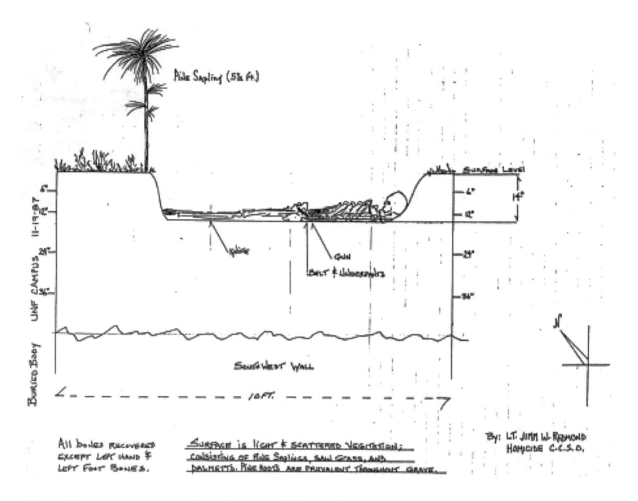

Figure 4.11
Elevation sketch.

Figure 4.12 (opposite)

Exploded sketch: this sketch depicts the hallway where a beating death occurred. Bloodstains located on three walls and the floor were depicted in this one sketch.

line and at perpendiculars to the line. A variation of this technique uses two perpendicular lines (three fixed points). The evidence is measured from these perpendicular lines (Figure 4.15).

The crime scene sketch must include not only the measurements of the crime scene and the physical evidence but also other important documentation information. The crime scene sketch should always be titled or captioned. The title information is essentially the subject of the sketch; for example: 'Rough Sketch of Scene Showing Items of Physical Evidence' or 'Finished Sketch Depicting Bloodstain Evidence'. A legend of abbreviations, symbols, numbers, or letters used should also be shown on the sketch. The crime scene sketch is a form of orientation documentation of the crime scene and as such the sketch must be oriented. For this reason, the crime scene sketch must also include a designation of a compass direction. The most commonly used direction is north. The rough sketch, drawn at the scene, is not normally drawn to scale. It has approximate proportions, therefore it should be labeled 'Not Drawn to

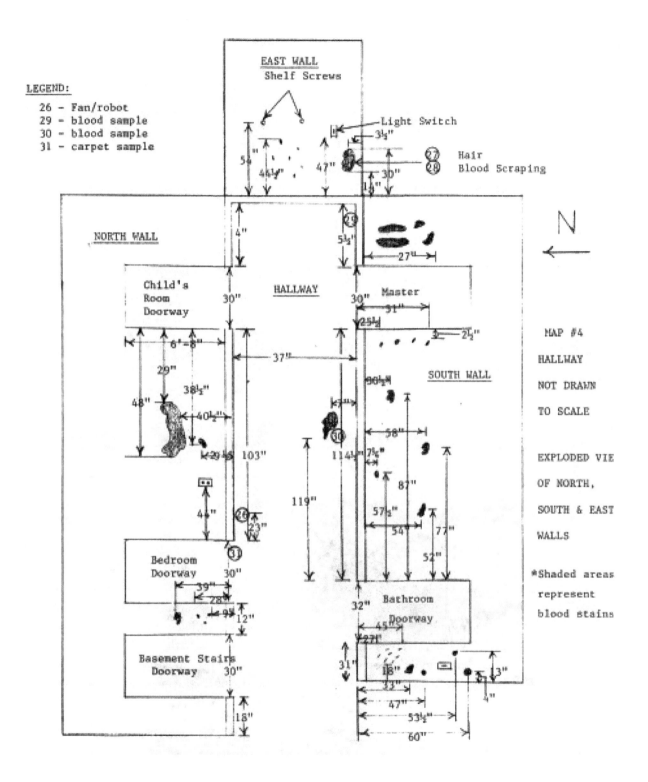

Figure 4.13
Triangulation measure-
ment method.

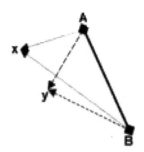

Two fixed points are selected. Measure the distance between them. Measure the distance to objects in the scene from each of these two points. A & B are fixed points and x & y are objects in the scene.

Figure 4.14
Polar coordinates
measurement method.

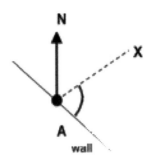

The distance and angle/direction of an object in the scene from a fixed point. Object x is 25 feet from wall A and 25 degrees north east. Transits or compasses may be used to measure angles.

Figure 4.15
Base line coordinates
measurement method.

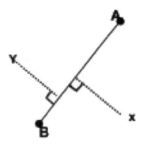

Two fixed points are selected, the objects are measured along the line between the points and at right angles to the line. Walls or tape measures along the ground work well. A & B make the fixed line and x & y are objects in the scene.

Scale'. If, however, there is a distance measurement between significant items of evidence, for example, the distance between a victim and a murder weapon, this should be placed on the sketch. Most often the final or finished sketch is drawn to scale and the scale that is used needs to be placed on the sketch. The final key element that should always be included as part of the crime scene sketch is the documentation block or area. The information to be included in this portion of the sketch is as follows:

1   Agency case number.
2   Offense or incident type (death investigation, burglary, etc.).
3   Victim(s) name(s). *Never place a suspect'(s) name on the sketch.*
4   Address or location.

5   Scene describer (Interior of House, Outdoor Area of Scene, Room 222, etc.);
     including weather and lighting conditions.

6   Date and time the sketch was begun.

7   Sketcher's name, assistant sketcher's name, or verifier's name.

8   Scale used (1 mm = 1 inch).

9   Legend (# = item of evidence) of physical evidence.

To facilitate the sketching at the crime scene some simple equipment or tools can be used. Graph paper, rulers/tape measures, compasses, pens and inks are very useful for sketching the crime scene. Additional tools are commercially available from a wide variety of companies. A recent tool added to the sketching documentation function at the crime scene is an electronic measuring and sketching system that uses computerization to replace bulky or cumbersome tapes and sketch pads. The system will generate to-scale sketches at the crime scene, allow for individualization by sketcher, and is simple and easy to use by the sketcher. The automated sketching computer system is also compatible with today's technologically advanced computer-aided design (CAD) programs, either two-dimensional or three-dimensional in nature. Figure 4.16 shows a computer-generated 2-D sketch.

CAD programs are readily available at most computer retail outlets and crime scene specialty companies. Law enforcement related computer-sketching programs are specially designed and applicable to most criminal investigations. Most law enforcement based CAD programs include a 3-D option as well as

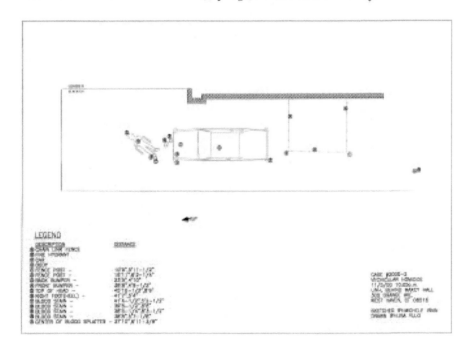

Figure 4.16
Computer-generated overhead view of crime scene.

Figure 4.17

Computer-generated three-dimensional view of crime scene.

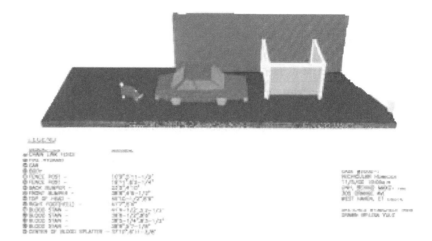

some programs that allow for animation sketching, if needed. Figure 4.17 is an example of a 3-D sketch generated by computer.

An additional form of crime scene documentation that is a direct derivative of sketching documentation is the use of to-scale crime scene models, as shown in Photo 4.19. The use of scale models necessitates the taking of many detailed measurements, is time consuming and requires the use of all photographs, drawings, and often, the use of structural blueprints. Some of the advantages for the use of scale models are that it is very beneficial for presenting important points to juries and the use of the models provides a sense of professionalism to the total crime scene investigation.

Photo 4.19

Photograph of scale model of dormitory rooms where homicide occurred. Model used during courtroom testimony of crime scene investigator.

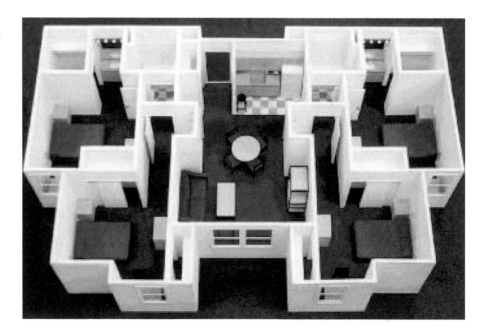

CHAPTER 5

SEARCHING FOR PHYSICAL EVIDENCE

INTRODUCTION

Physical evidence obtained from the crime scene or other segments of the investigation is often the cornerstone upon which the successful outcome of the case depends. Yet, many cases are never solved or prosecuted due to a lack of physical evidence. While it is theoretically possible that the near perfect crime was committed and the perpetrator was able to commit the crime leaving minimal physical evidence, it is more likely that the critical evidence never was found. Many investigators have obtained the necessary expertise to recognize, document, collect, and preserve a broad range of physical evidence types. However, the assumed simple task of finding that critical evidence can be the failure point of the crime scene investigation.

One common practice is to collect everything that could in any possible manner be construed as evidentiary in nature. However, if all objects at the scene are collected and submitted to a forensic laboratory for further analysis, the forensic facility will be overwhelmed, and the majority of substantial evidence might have no probative value. This type of practice is not only a waste of time and resources, but also causes legal and investigative problems. Conversely, if critical evidence is omitted or improperly preserved, the use of modern state-of-art laboratory instrumentation and technology cannot salvage the investigation. Hence, a system must be developed where the relevant physical evidence is recognized and located, while superfluous material is excluded. This will only occur when crime scene investigators understand the goals of a crime scene search, grasp the concepts and techniques for effective searching, and routinely exercise the discipline to rely on a systematic structured search process.

OBJECTIVES OF A CRIME SCENE SEARCH

The goal of a crime scene search is to locate all potentially relevant and meaningful physical evidence that could be used to link or exonerate a suspect or witness to a crime. Experience and training will assist a crime scene investigator in determining the commonly encountered evidence, but experience will also reveal that no two cases are alike, and one must expect the unexpected. An astute seasoned crime scene investigator will also possess good instincts as to where the relevant evidence will likely be located. Yet, once again there is the inevitable reality that not all evidence can nor will be located by relying on normal expectations. Thus, the very best investigators have come to the realization that a systematic and structured basic approach is often the only guarantee that they will relinquish the crime scene confident that no evidence is left behind. Underlying the search process are two general issues: where should you look for the evidence, and how should you actually conduct the search process? Before exploring these issues in depth, it would be helpful to understand the concept of linkage and the principles of transfer theory.

LINKAGE THEORY

A concept known as the four-way linkage theory explains the interrelations between a crime scene, a victim, a suspect, and physical evidence. Understanding and appreciating these connections between these components will provide guidance in determining where evidence may be located, and the need to identify evidence so that the linkages may be established. Figure 5.1 shows the basic principle of this four-way linkage theory.

Figure 5.1
Four-way linkage theory.

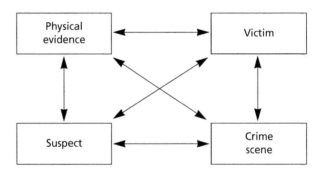

Theoretically, if associations can be established between two or more of these components – scene, victim, suspect, and physical evidence – then the case may be resolved. The more associations established, the greater the probability of successfully solving the case. For example, if the investigation and a statement from the suspect indicate that the suspect has never been at the location where the crime occurred, the scene should be carefully examined for any evidence that would prove that the suspect was present at the scene at some point in time. A suspect may have left behind fingerprints, footwear patterns, or transfers of trace evidence. At the same time, evidence such as vegetative material, soil, or glass might have been taken away from the scene. This evidence may establish a link between the suspect and that scene. Also, if a comprehensive search of the scene reveals no evidence that the suspect was at the scene it may help focus the investigation on other suspects or scenarios. However, if any credibility is to be asserted to these conclusions the investigator must be certain that the scene was properly and completely searched, and that all evidence was recovered.

If the scenario were such that the suspect resided at or frequented the scene of the crime then this type of association would be of relatively low value for developing investigative leads. A possible exception would be if the precise location of the evidence were suggestive of the suspect's involvement in the crime or if the time frame in which the evidence was deposited could be established: for example, a bloody fingerprint recovered from the homicide scene or on a victim's body. This type of assimilation could provide necessary linkage between a suspect and victim.

In many cases, family members or close associates of the victims commit violent crimes. In a wealthy rural community a couple were bludgeoned to death and their bodies set on fire. Careful examination of the entire exterior of the victim's house indicated that access was gained into the house by removal of a window air conditioning unit. On the panes of glass where the air conditioner had been removed a set of 10 latent fingerprints were located and developed. Subsequently, these latent prints were identified as belonging to the couple's estranged son. Due to their son's drug problems, the couple had asked the son to leave their home a few months earlier and had changed the locks on the house doors. Thus despite the previous presence of the son within the house the exact location and pattern of the latent prints was highly relevant and could be attributed to having been deposited during the illegal entry into the home at the time of the killings. This case demonstrates the value of systematic search for evidence, and the ability to solve a case by linking the scene, victim, suspect, and physical evidence in some meaningful fashion.

TRANSFER THEORY

Transfer evidence results whenever two surfaces come in contact with each other. The existence of this phenomenon was established in Locard's Theory of Exchange. This theory postulates that whenever two surfaces come in contact with one another there is a mutual exchange of matter across the contact boundary. Photos 5.1 and 5.2 are two examples of contact transfer of forensic evidence crossing the contact boundary. In more practical terms, when a perpetrator enters a crime scene he leaves something, and when he exits the scene he takes something with or on him. The daunting issue is whether or not we will find the transferred materials.

Photo 5.1

Close-up view of sole of suspect's shoe, depicting soil and trace material which was used to link the suspect to the crime scene.

Photo 5.2

Paint transfer on a vehicle involved in an evading traffic accident.

The obvious direct transfers, such as a bloody palm print on the doorknob, should not be – although all too often have been – overlooked during the crime scene investigation. In some instances, transfer of materials can result without direct contact, such as when gunshot residue particles are deposited on a surface, or blood spatters deposited on a suspect's clothing. Moreover, some transfers can be attributed to secondary transfers rather than direct transfers.

With secondary transfers there is some intermediate object or person responsible for the secondary transfer from the original source onto the final target surface. An example of a secondary transfer is the transfer of blood from a bloody doorknob, deposited by the perpetrator, and subsequently transferred onto a third party's hands as they touch the bloodstained doorknob.

Generally there are two types of transfer evidence; trace transfer and pattern transfer evidence. Examples of commonly encountered trace transfer evidence include fibers, glass, soil, and blood. Examples of pattern transfer evidence are imprint and impression evidence. Many times transfer evidence is a combination of trace and pattern components such as bloody shoeprints, greasy fingerprints, or fabric impressions.

Trace amount of materials are difficult to recognize, locate and collect. Trace materials can consist of biological or chemical components and exist in a wide variety of forms, presenting a broad range of detection and collection problems. This is yet another rationale for approaching the scene analytically and understanding what is the goal of your search process as well as what linkages can you possibly establish. Often trace evidence is merely suspected or anticipated as being present rather than being positively recognized at the scene. Thus the investigator must use one of the many acceptable methods for collecting trace samples from an isolated area at the crime scene. Tape lifts, vacuum sweepings, and seizure of the article containing the trace are a few of the more commonly employed methods. Collection of trace evidence is addressed in further detail in Chapter 6.

Recent analytical advances and increased sensitivities in instrumentation have further enhanced the significance of transfer evidence. For example, gas chromatography–mass spectroscopy (GC-MS) analysis is capable of detecting accelerants at fire scenes in amounts in the magnitude of a few parts per million. As a result, more advanced and sensitive accelerant detection devices have had to be developed. Ironically, despite significant advances in remote sensors, one of the most reliable and sensitive methods for detecting accelerant residues at arson scenes is by canine detection. Highly trained dogs have the capability of detecting minute amounts of a wide variety of accelerants due to their proven superior olfactory abilities.

Another area where advanced methodologies have highlighted the significance of trace amounts of materials involves DNA analysis. Current techniques involving short tandem repeats (STR) or analysis of mitochondrial-DNA are highly sensitive and able of yielding a DNA profile with minute amounts of DNA. Thus, the crime scene investigator must begin to evaluate a scene and implement search methods which take into consideration the fact that trace amounts of DNA containing material may have been deposited during the crime.

In addition to the positive attributes of Locard's Theory, which states the probability of locating relevant transfer evidence, there is a negative feature which must not be overlooked in the light of current highly sensitive analytical techniques. Sloppy crime scene processing can easily result in the destruction of valuable evidence as well as introduction of contaminants through secondary transfers. Unless precautions are taken, there can be detrimental transfers of evidence occurring during the crime scene investigation. Only by approaching a crime scene with a detailed structured plan and search method can the risk of contamination or evidence destruction be eliminated.

GENERAL CONCEPTS OF CRIME SCENE SEARCHES

Where should you look for the evidence, and how should one actually conduct the scene search process? To process a crime scene properly for physical evidence, it is necessary to view the crime scene in its entirety and not just from the perspective of the singular operation involved in evidence collection, e.g. fingerprints, blood, photography, etc. To accomplish this task, it is useful to examine areas that you are normally not accustomed to looking at such as tissue or blood spatter on the ceiling, trash cans for weapons and clothing, bloodstains and fibers on doors and drapes, the toilet seat (hairs and fingerprints), and saliva and dental marks on food in the refrigerator. Also, look for evidence from different vantage points, e.g. floor level and elevated level. It is extremely important to be cautious and take the time necessary for a methodical, systematic search. This approach ensures that critical evidence will not be damaged or overlooked. Also, look for what is not present or missing from the scene. These findings often provide invaluable investigative information, and if that item is later located on the suspect's body, in a vehicle, or at another location, it may provide a critical linkage between a suspect and the crime scene.

Conducting inventories of scenes and objects used during the incident can provide a great deal of information as to what investigators need to be looking for during the search. For example, cases involving firearms that are recovered from the scene or secured from a person at the scene are instances where on-scene inventories are helpful. Examine each and every weapon and determine what is the current bullet capacity and what is the maximum capacity. Photo 5.3 shows the investigation of a homicide weapon found at the scene. When semi-automatic weapons are involved and there are multiple bullet magazines, all magazines possessed by involved individuals (victims, suspects, and witnesses) should be inventoried.

With shootings involving police officers all magazines from every officer who arrived on the scene during any portion of the incident should be inventoried, whether or not the individual officer actually fired a shot during the incident.

While there are numerous exceptions, specific crimes regularly generate

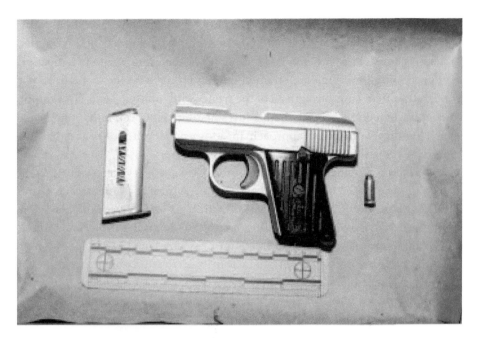

Photo 5.3

A small caliber pistol used in a shooting incident. This photograph documents the state in which the gun was found, one bullet in the chamber and an additional bullet in the magazine.

different kinds of physical evidence. Excellent and productive crime scene searches are based on logic and an analytical approach to the particular scene. While there is an inherent danger of jumping to conclusions and losing objectivity, it is most beneficial to logically deduce the types of evidence expected and potential locations of that evidence based upon the general type of crime committed. 'Logic trees', as discussed in Chapter 7, can be very helpful.

LOCATION OF PHYSICAL EVIDENCE

A crime scene investigator must maintain that fine balance between remaining open-minded and objective, and wondering aimlessly as a result of a lack of direction or focus. Only through training and experience will an appreciation for the necessary balance occur. Generally, there are some guidelines that can provide a focused investigation and still allow for an objective approach to scene analysis.

Primary v. secondary crime scenes

Multiple crime scenes or large, multi-faceted scenes need to be evaluated and triaged. Any scene in which evidence or patterns are subject to destruction or alteration should receive priority. For example, if a portion of a crime scene is located outside, even if the most significant evidence is located within a protected structure, the outdoor scene should be processed first if adverse weather exists or is threatening. Another factor may be the ability or inability to secure a scene or a portion of the scene effectively. Large scenes with no manmade or natural barriers pose problems to adequate security. In addition, a scene located within a high volume of traffic or at a public area should also receive a higher priority than a remote scene with limited access points. Whenever possible, it is better to conduct all of the crime scene investigation and processing by a single well-trained unit and to process the scenes one at a time, rather than rush through all of the scenes with multiple teams. Continuity and consistency are crucial to the investigation. However, situations occur which require a modified approach in addressing multiple scenes that are exposed to adverse weather or other conditions.

Determining whether the scene is a primary or secondary scene can also help determine the order or priority of the scenes. A primary crime scene is the location where the principle elements or activity associated with the particular crime occurred. For example, in a murder investigation this is the location where the victim was actually murdered. In contrast, a secondary scene is a location or locations where secondary or peripheral activity occurred. Common examples of secondary scenes include dumpsites where the body or evidence is deposited after the crime. Photo 5.4 shows a female body which was dumped on the roadside after she was killed by her husband in their bedroom. Primary and secondary scenes can be immediately adjacent to one another or miles apart. Additionally, there may be a trial or evidence located between two or more scene sites. Often, the order of investigation is determined sequentially, not necessarily by importance. It may be that a body is located in a remote area, and even a thorough crime scene search yields only minimal evidence. The primary scene may not be located for months, and in some cases is never found. Therefore, after

Photo 5.4

Secondary crime of 'dumpsite'.

determining that a scene is a secondary scene, one of the greatest investigative priorities is to locate the primary scene as soon as possible. This is necessary to minimize the opportunity for the suspect to clean up or alter the primary scene.

Focal point v. ancillary areas

Logic dictates that when all other factors are equal the first efforts should be on the locations or areas deemed as focal points rather than ancillary areas. Focal points are the areas which, based on available information and the past experience and training of the investigator, are known to have the highest probability of containing relevant physical and pattern evidence. In many cases these focal points include: the point of entry, path traveled by the perpetrator, target area where the crime occurred, and point of exit. Once the focal point area has been completely documented, searched, and all evidence collected and preserved then the ancillary areas can be searched. Finally, the distant curtilage should be examined, in a briefer but nonetheless thorough manner.

Applying this method to processing a burglary scene would be as follows. Search the entire exterior of the structure for any signs indicating points of entrance and exit. Once entry/exit points are identified, search the immediate adjacent area; this area needs to be protected and ultimately searched, as there may be physical evidence and/or pattern evidence, such as footwear impressions, latent fingerprints, and trace evidence. After locating the point of entry follow that into the structure, being mindful of evidence along the pathway from the entrance to target areas. Next, search areas that were obviously disturbed or ransacked. Then examine those locations which there is a reasonable probability that the perpetrator may have accessed. Examples include jewelry boxes, safes, dressers and desks, china cabinets, entertainment centers, gun cabinets, etc. Next search the areas connecting these target areas and the point of exit. The point of exit should also be thoroughly searched, including logical or visible avenues of escape originating from the point of exit. A general search of the curtilage, including neighboring properties, and visible trash canisters may yield evidence related to the crime. Remember to search for items that are not located but that are expected to be present in a particular dwelling. If possible, after the scene has been documented, searched, and evidence collected, have the owner, occupant or relative conduct an inventory of possessions to determine if anything is missing from the scene.

WHAT CONSTITUTES A CRIME SCENE?

Crime scenes come in a wide variety of structures and components. Traditional scenes include indoor crime scenes (house, building, and structures), outdoor crime scenes (yard, park, field, or road), and vehicles (train, airplane, automobile). However, an investigator should consider any area or object that may contain relevant physical and pattern evidence as a crime scene.

The bodies of a victim or suspect are indeed scenes that should be examined in a thorough and timely manner. All types of trace evidence, including hair/fibers, DNA, physiological fluids, latent prints, accelerants, gunshot residue, pollen, soil and debris, etc., are often located on a body associated with a crime. The body condition and position of the body, including color, rigor, lividity, etc., pattern, shape, and location of wounds also provide investigative information.

Orifices may contain foreign objects, fibers, body fluids, and drugs. Body fluids may show the presence of drugs, alcohol, or poisons. These also contain blood group substances and other genetic markers. In addition to the actual body, the articles of clothing and personal possessions often contain evidentiary value. Bodies should receive high priority in searching triages as they are often mobile, or subject to adverse activities such as washing or decomposition. There are many other additional specific types of crime scenes that pose significant issues and problems, such as underwater crime scenes, clandestine drug laboratories, fire and explosion scenes, and excavation sites. These specialized scenes, and techniques to address issues related to these scenes, are addressed in Chapter 9.

Within the past few years a new class of crime scenes have become more prevalent, that is crimes committed within electronic or digital domains, particularly within cyberspace. Criminal justice agencies throughout the world are being confronted with an increased need to investigate crimes perpetrated partially or entirely over the Internet or other electronic media. Resources and procedures are needed to effectively search for, locate, and preserve all types of electronic evidence. This evidence ranges from images of child pornography to encrypted data used to further a variety of criminal activities. Even in investigations that are not primarily electronic in nature, at some point in the investigation computer files or data may be discovered and further analysis required.

CRIME SCENE SEARCH PATTERNS

Crime scene search patterns are varied and outwardly different in style and application. However, they all share a common goal of providing structure and organization to ensure that no physical or pattern evidence is overlooked. There is no single correct method for a specific type of crime scene. Rather, an experienced crime scene investigator will evaluate all available data and peculiarities associated with that specific scene. In addition, available resources may prohibit certain search methods, as some methods require substantial manpower or specialized equipment.

Most of the basic search patterns employ a geometric pattern. The six basic search patterns are the line, grid, spiral, ray, zone, and link method. While these search patterns are in fact fairly easy to implement, they are often the most efficient and productive methods. A common error made by reasonably experienced investigators is to exclude systematic search patterns, as the investigator erroneously believes that his or her experience is a viable substitute. If there is any doubt that some evidence may have been overlooked then a basic search method should be employed. Note that some search methods are best suited for outdoor scenes while others work best for indoor crime scenes.

Figure 5.2
Crime scene search patterns.

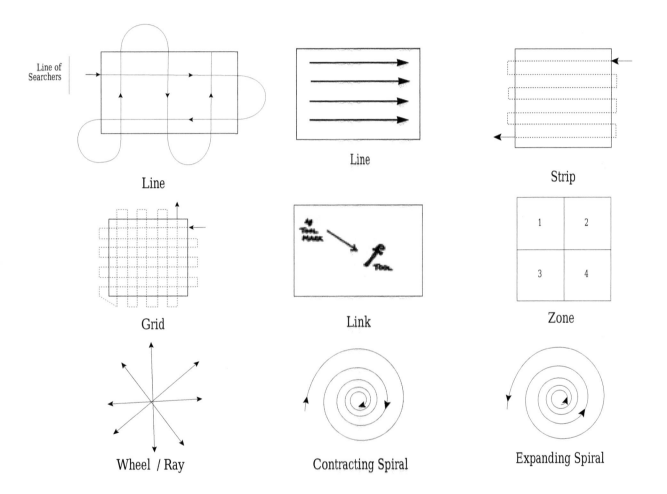

LINK METHOD

The link method is often the most productive and common approach for crime scene searches. This method is based on the four-way linkage theory, seeking to find associations between the scene, victim, suspect, and physical evidence. With this method, the investigators evaluate the scene(s) and then proceed through the area in a systematic and logical fashion to gather physical evidence that can be linked or associated to a particular crime or activity. Although this method is not a geometric pattern, or easily definable, it is nonetheless a systematic approach. The search progression is not random; rather, each step is based upon findings and observations and applying a reasonable probability and simple logic based on training and experience that, regarding that particular crime, evidence will likely be located in a particular location.

For example, a naked body of a female in her early twenties was located at the bottom of an embankment, adjacent to a rural road. A logical assumption, based upon the stated minimal data, is that this scene could be a secondary crime scene. Formulate a search plan to look for footwear and tire impressions along or adjacent to logical pathways between the body and potential avenues of egress. A lack of clothing such as pants, shirt, shoes, or pocketbook suggest that these items had been removed from her. This clothing was left behind at the primary scene, discarded at the secondary scene, or collected by the suspect as a souvenir.

The age, gender, and body condition of the victim might support the hypothesis that the crime may have sexual overtones. Thus the victim's body needs to be carefully examined for evidence associated with sexual assaults, such as seminal fluid, saliva, hair and fiber transfers, as well as the possibility of latent prints on the victim. Failure to identify these evidentiary materials early on in the process may result in the destruction or degradation of the evidence. Developing of latent fingerprints on the skin of a victim must be done as soon as possible, otherwise evaporation, decomposition, or alteration will adversely affect the ability to recover latent prints. One of the more successful methods is to encase the victim in a plastic tent structure and fill the structure with cyanoacrylate fumes (superglue), and subsequently use chemical or physical methods to enhance.

In many cases, linkages are applications of common logic. For example, if a large amount of bloodstain is found at the crime scene, the investigator should look for an injured person; if the victim appears to be stabbed, investigators should search for weapons that may have caused this type of injury.

LINE (STRIP) METHOD

Outdoor crime scenes can be large in scope and difficult to search because of vegetation, topography, water and area to cover. In addition, since there are no identifiable zones it is difficult to search an outdoor scene systematically without some form of a search pattern. One of the easiest patterns to employ, that is still very effective, is the line method. This approach involves the demarcation of the crime scene into a series of lines or strips, as it is sometimes called. First, the area is blocked in the form of a rectangle. Then, members of the search team are arranged at regular intervals, usually arm's length, and then proceed to search along straight lines. The investigator identifies any evidence in his path. This method is also referred to as the strip method. The crime scene coordinator regulates the pace of the search. It is often helpful to mark or tag the evidence for later processing. This method is well suited for searching large areas, such as parks, fields, yards, parking lots, or highways. In addition, it can be conducted by as few as one or two investigators or as many as hundreds. When the search area is extremely large, such as in the case of searching a rural area for a missing person, this method works well.

The members of the search team are not necessarily trained crime scene investigators. Rather, volunteers can be employed if they are given explicit instructions as how to search, what they are looking for, and instructed to stop, don't touch, and immediately notify one of the crime scene investigators if they find anything suspicious or valuable.

Crime scenes that involve multiple gunshots must be searched for all related firearms evidence, shell casings and projectiles. An inventory of the weapons and bullet magazines potentially involved in the incident will identify the maximum amount of cartridges and bullets that may be found at the scene. The information can be supplemented with a preliminary examination of the deceased's wounds. If basic search methods do not recover all of the firearms evidence then an organized line method search should be conducted. In an investigation concerning a police officer-related shooting when the initial scene search was unable to locate one of the expended shell casings, the scene search should include the use of metal detectors. Locating the shell casing is important, as it is information needed to assist in the reconstruction process conducted months later.

For example, in 1999 a police officer on routine patrol observed a suspicious vehicle. Soon after following this vehicle the suspicious vehicle led police officers on a long high-speed chase. Eventually several police vehicles were able to box in the suspicious vehicle. When one of the pursuing officers exited his vehicle and approached the driver of the suspicious vehicle the driver veered toward this officer. Having no place to safely retreat and fearing for his life this officer fired at the driver, fatally wounding him. During the initial scene search one of the expended shell casings from the officer's gun was not located. Months later, during a subsequent reconstruction exercise a line method was employed, and the missing shell casing was located in a grassy area within the original crime scene area (as shown in Photo 5.5). The location of this casing was extremely important in reconstructing the locations of the officer and suspect's vehicle, the direction the officer and vehicle were moving, and the position from which the officer fired the shots at the driver.

Photo 5.5

Investigators conducting a grid search, to look for evidence. During the search a cartridge casing was located.

GRID METHOD

The grid method is a modified double-line search. In this approach, a line pattern is constructed then a second line pattern is established in the same area, running perpendicular to the first line pattern. Searchers follow the first line pattern and search in the same manner as with the line method. Upon completing the first line pattern, the searchers realign on the other line pattern. Thus, the same area is searched twice by a grid pattern format. An additional advantage is that two different searchers search the same area. While this method is more time consuming, it has the advantage of being more thorough and methodical.

ZONE METHOD

Crime scenes that comprise readily definable zones can be effective searched by focusing on the zones in a systematic manner. Indoor crime scenes are examples of such a scene. Depending on the size of the scene, each zone may be subdivided as needed until it is of manageable size.

There are a variety of techniques for conducting a zone pattern search. If the search is to be conducted by a small group of trained crime scene investigators the entire team can work together in a particular zone. For example, if the scene involved a private residence the investigators could enter one room at a time, document, search, and collect all relevant evidence as a unified team. For the primary areas of the scene, this methodology is recommended. However, if there are numerous zones in ancillary areas then the team can be divided and each member conduct a search of a particular zone. If this method is chosen it is good practice to have a particular zone searched twice, by two different investigators. The scope of the search and the type of evidence being sought will help determine the appropriate method to search in a zone format. Zone searching is also advantageous in that the individual zone can be prioritized. Critical zones such as target areas, point of entry, and point of exit can be searched multiple times.

Photo 5.6

Trooper trainees assisting in a homicide investigation by conducting a grid search.

WHEEL / RAY METHOD

With the wheel method, the crime scene is considered to be essentially circular. The investigators start from a critical point and travel outward along many straight lines, or rays, from this point. This search pattern becomes increasingly difficult when searching larger areas and, therefore, is usually used only for special scene situations and with limited applications.

SPIRAL METHOD

Similar to the wheel/ray method, the spiral method considers the crime scene as circular in design. There are two techniques commonly used for spiral methods; one method is generally referred to as an inward spiral, the other is an outward spiral.

With the inward spiral method, investigators start at the outer boundary and circle the crime scene towards the critical point. With the completion of each circuit, the diameter of the circle is progressively decreased until a central point is reached. Meanwhile, the outward method involves starting at the critical point and circling outward. These approaches rely on the ability to trace a regular pattern of fixed diameter. Thus, physical barriers at the scene may pose problems during the search. The spiral method is generally used for special conditions of the crime scene search. However, there is a danger that physical evidence could be destroyed while walking to the central point to initiate the search. A very limited number of situations require the application of these search methods.

PRACTICAL APPLICATION OF CRIME SCENE SEARCHES

No singular crime scene search method will work for all types of scenes. Thus, an experienced scene investigator must select the appropriate method based on a thorough evaluation, considering particular obstacles, available equipment and resources, scope of the search, and evidence sought or anticipated. Often multiple methods or hybrids of several methods are appropriate. The link method can be utilized in conjunction with any of the other geometric patterns. With any crime scene, the most important aspect of the search is that it be conducted in a methodical, logical, and systematic manner. The purpose of a scene search is to recognize and locate the relevant physical evidence.

In addition to the application of the described traditional search patterns, crime scene searching can be augmented by specialized equipment or methods.

Canine teams, trained for evidence recovery, are valuable resources. Known articles of clothing belonging to the victim or suspect may be used to help the canine track that individual. Canines can be trained to detect drugs, accelerants and explosive residues, and decomposing bodies and items containing physiological material. Experience has shown that canines have remarkable olfactory sensitivity. Canines used to detect accelerants have located samples containing accelerants in the parts per million levels, as confirmed through gas chromatography–mass spectrometry analysis.

Arson investigators have used a variety of sniffers and detecting devices with reasonable success. In the very near future, highly specialized remote sensing devices will be used to conduct instrumental analysis. Thus, even trace amounts of evidentiary material may be located at a crime scene, and confirmed before investigators leave the scene. These technologies are being developed in tele-forensic research programs sponsored by the National Institute of Justice, New York, Connecticut, and Massachusetts State Police Forensic Laboratories. These emerging technologies will be discussed in further detail in Chapter 9, Special Scene Techniques.

There are more advanced theories and methodologies that can be used to search a crime scene. Metal detectors and portable x-ray machines are valuable tools. Also, in shooting cases, the scene investigator can employ known data and experience to focus the search pattern. Once a series of expended cartridge casings are located the resulting pattern yields information as to the possible location of the shooter, if shell casing ejection pattern data is known for the particular types of weapons used in the incident. In addition, trajectory determination can help locate bullets or bullet paths. These shooting reconstruction methods will be discussed in greater detail in Chapter 10. Application of other specialized, more advanced methods are addressed in Chapter 9, and include topics such as underwater searches, aerial searches, missing persons, missing vehicles, trails, and combinations of several different search methods.

In general, there are some basic considerations and principles that apply to all crime scenes. In most cases, investigators have only one chance to search the original crime scene. Therefore, the initial search process must be done thoroughly and correctly. When investigators reasonably believe that some pattern or physical evidence may be overlooked or missing it is time to search the scene again, using a structured search method. Do not relinquish the crime scene until all available methods have been used to search the scene. It may be necessary to maintain the security and integrity of the scene until the autopsy or preliminary forensic laboratory examinations are completed. Until it is released, remember to keep the scene guarded by police personnel 24 hours a day until all processing is completed; failure to do this results in the loss of legal integrity of any evidence found after the original search.

Do not allow search methods to interfere with or diminish other critical crime scene functions such as the proper documentation, collection and preservation of evidence. Remember that as established in Locard's Exchange Theory every form of movement through the scene may result in alteration to or destruction of evidence. Thus, search methods involving large numbers of searchers, particularly untrained searchers or officers should be used only after the preliminary documentation and evidence collection and preservation has been completed. Further, do not circumvent established procedures. If evidence is located during a subsequent search, follow your established procedures to document, collect, and preserve that evidence. Chain of custody issues are always paramount and can be addressed by limiting the number of personnel who are authorized to collect evidence at a crime scene.

CHAPTER 6

COLLECTION AND PRESERVATION OF PHYSICAL EVIDENCE

GENERAL CONSIDERATIONS

After the completion of the crime scene documentation and the systematic search of the crime scene for the physical evidence, the collection and preservation of each item of evidence can begin. One person shall be designated as the evidence officer. This singular appointment as evidence officer will insure that all evidence is collected, packaged, marked, sealed, and preserved in a consistent manner. Nothing will be missed, lost or contaminated if one individual has the obligation for collection and preservation of the evidence. There is no set order for the collection of evidence but some general considerations about collection should be mentioned. It is helpful to have a variety of collection, packaging, and marking materials nearby for easy access and convenience. Table 6.1 is an example of contents of an evidence collection kit.

• Various sizes of paper envelopes	• Assorted sizes of plastic ziplock bags
• Assorted sizes of pillboxes	• Metal paint cans of various sizes
• Cardboard boxes	• Sterile swabs and boxes
• Disposable pipettes	• Eye-dropper and bottles
• Strings	• Large butcher paper
• Glassine weighing paper	• Sterile test tubes
• Gun boxes	• Knife boxes
• Labels and markers	• Evidence tape
• Blood collection kits	• Rape kits
• GSR kits	• Post-mortem fingerprint kits

Table 6.1

Basic components of a crime scene evidence collection kit.

If any fragile, easily lost or transient evidence has been identified, it should be collected first. Occasionally some items of evidence or other structures may need to be moved or relocated before the rest of the crime scene can be processed. Carefully move these items while looking for additional evidence. Remember that if any new items of evidence are discovered during the collection process, that item must be documented using the techniques already described. See Photos 6.1a&b.

Photo 6.1a

Crime scene photograph before couch is moved.

Photo 6.1b

Crime scene photograph after couch is moved, revealing bloody knife. (Both photographs are courtesy of Officer Robin Lunsford, Asheville Police Department.)

Most physical evidence will be collected into a primary container or druggist's fold and placed into a secondary container or outer container. Druggist's folds are typically used for small trace evidence but are useful for protecting items of evidence that may 'hold' trace evidence that will need to be collected by the crime scene investigator or laboratory personnel at a later time. Outer containers are frequently envelopes, paper bags, packets, canisters or plastic bags. The outer containers are sealed with evidence tape and marked with documentation information about the item of evidence, identification of the collector, date, time and location collected, agency case number, and a brief description of the physical evidence with its location contained within the secondary container. As shown in Photo 6.2, the evidence tape should completely cover any openings of the container and be marked with the collector's initials, the time of collection, and the date of collection. A variety of packaging materials, sealing tape, and assorted items for marking packaging are commercially available.

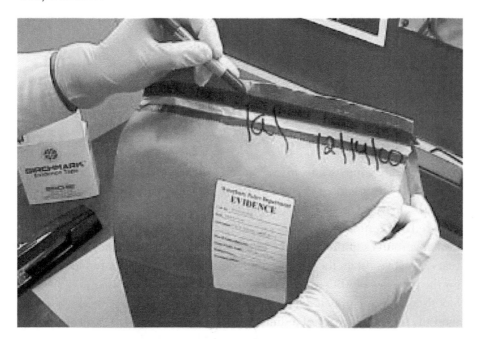

Photo 6.2

Properly sealed and marked evidence bag (courtesy Cindy Lopes, Waterbury Police Department).

Most items of physical evidence are solids and can easily be packaged, stored, and preserved in the above containers. If the physical evidence is volatile or easily lost due to evaporation, airtight containers such as metal paint cans, jars, and specially designed bags are to be used for packaging. Liquid items of physical evidence can be packaged and transported in unbreakable, leakproof containers. Moist, wet, or biological evidence (blood, suspected marihuana plants, etc.) collected by methods to be described, can temporarily be packaged as above and later, in a controlled drying area, be allowed to air-dry and repackaged into non-airtight containers (see Photo 6.3). The original packages must be retained and packaged with the evidence.

Each item of physical evidence must be collected and packaged separately to prevent any cross-contamination between items of evidence. The packages must also be closed and sealed at the time of collection. This procedure will insure that during transportation no intermingling of the physical evidence will occur.

Photo 6.3

Secure drying room for evidence with wet bloodstains (courtesy of Officer Robin Lunsford).

Finally, the crime scene investigator must always keep in mind that all evidence is important to the criminal investigation and should be collected. Forensic analytical techniques are constantly improving, the amount of sample required for testing has also been reduced and the information about the probable sources of the evidence has significantly improved. For example, 15 years ago a bloodstain the size of a dime would have beeen required to be tested for the presence of ABO types and iosenzymes. Analysis ten years ago required a bloodstain the size of half a dime for RFLP DNA typing, five years ago a bloodstain the size of a quarter of a dime for PCR (DQA and PM) DNA typing, and currently, all that is required is a flake of blood which contains nanogram (0.000000001 g) quantities of DNA to virtually identify sources of blood at crime scenes through STR analysis (as depicted in Figure 6.1). Because of these improving forensic techniques and sensitivities, the proper collection and packaging of physical evidence is *extremely* important. Advanced techniques in the laboratory cannot be used if the evidence is lost or contaminated because of improper or poor collection and packaging at the crime scene. Photo 6.2 shows the way bloodstained articles should be dried in a secured location to protect their scientific and legal integrity.

The remainder of this chapter will address the various types of physical evidence that can be encountered at the crime scene. Each type of physical evidence will be discussed in terms of the collection techniques best suited for that evidence and then the proper packaging technique.

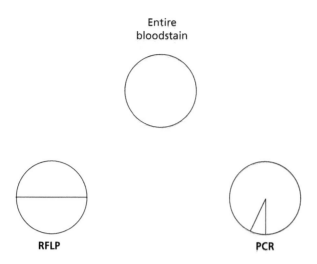

Entire
bloodstain

RFLP   PCR

PCR/STR testing uses 1/10th to 1/100th of the sample
compared to RFLP testing

Figure 6.1

*Relative sample sizes
needed for RFLP v. PCR-
based DNA blood typing.*

FINGERPRINTS

Fingerprints constitute the most important category of physical evidence for positive identification or individualization. In addition, palm prints, bare footprints, lip prints and ear prints are also encountered and should be expected at crime scenes. Fingerprint evidence found at scenes can be in the form of latent, plastic, visible, and wet fingerprints. Each type will require different searching, enhancement or visualization, and collection techniques at the crime scene. Figure 6.2. is a generalized processing procedure for these various types of fingerprint evidence.

Visual examination or searching for fingerprints is accomplished by the use of a variety of lighting methods. Most common is the use of side lighting or oblique lighting. A high-power flashlight works very well. Other forms of lighting sources include portable laser, Xeon arc lamp lasers or forensic light source. Careful handling of physical evidence bearing suspected fingerprints is always expected. Once the fingerprints are found then the next step is photographic documentation of the fingerprint before further processing or enhancement with chemical or physical visualization techniques. Photographing the fingerprints can be accomplished by following the procedure suggested for laboratory examination photographs in Chapter 4. See Photo 6.4. Commercially available instant film and cameras and digital cameras with macro-capabilities work well for this process. The choice techniques for enhancement or visualization are dependent on the type of fingerprint found and the surface upon which the fingerprints deposited. These visualization and enhancement

Figure 6.2

General fingerprint processing procedure.

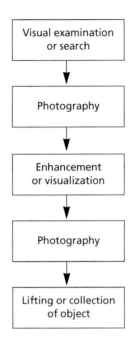

Photo 6.4

Close-up of a dusted latent print, located on a glass (courtesy of Cindy Lopes).

techniques will be discussed below. If the fingerprint is found on an immovable or large object, field processing is warranted and the fingerprints should be collected. If the fingerprint is found on a small, movable object then the object can be packaged for collection. It will be packaged as discussed in Chapter 5.

LATENT PRINTS

Latent (invisible) prints once found at the crime scene are enhanced or visualized by physical, chemical, instrumental, or by combining methods. Physical methods are used for any dry, non-porous surfaces like glass or plastic. These methods include the use of various colored powders and brushes. The physical methods for visualization can be greatly assisted by the use of cyanoacrylate (superglue) fuming before powder application. A variety of superglue fuming devices are available for use both at the crime scene and in a controlled environment like a processing room. Photos 6.5a&b illustrate the application of superglue techniques in crime scene and laboratory.

Photo 6.5a

Investigator using a Cyanoacrylate (superglue) fuming wand to process the exterior surface of a car window.

Photo 6.5b

Superglue fuming tank used for smaller evidence with latent prints (courtesy of Robin Lunsford).

Black powder is the most common powder used for light backgrounds and light color powders for dark backgrounds. Magnapowder, black powder mixed with metal shavings and applied by use of special magnetic wands, is used for shiny surfaces like plastic bags, plastic CD cases, or magazine covers. Once the latent prints have been visualized by the superglue and powder dusting techniques, they should be photographed again. Then the developed latents need to be lifted and placed on backing cards. The latent cards are documented by putting the case number, date and time of lifting, initials of person processing the evidence, and a sketch indicating the location of the lifted latent print on the back of the lift card, as shown in Photo 6.6. The lift card is evidence and should be treated as such. If the item containing the latent fingerprint is movable, then it must be marked as to the location of the lifted latent, packaged and collected as evidence. If the item with the lifted latent is immovable, then a documentation photograph of the surface must be taken.

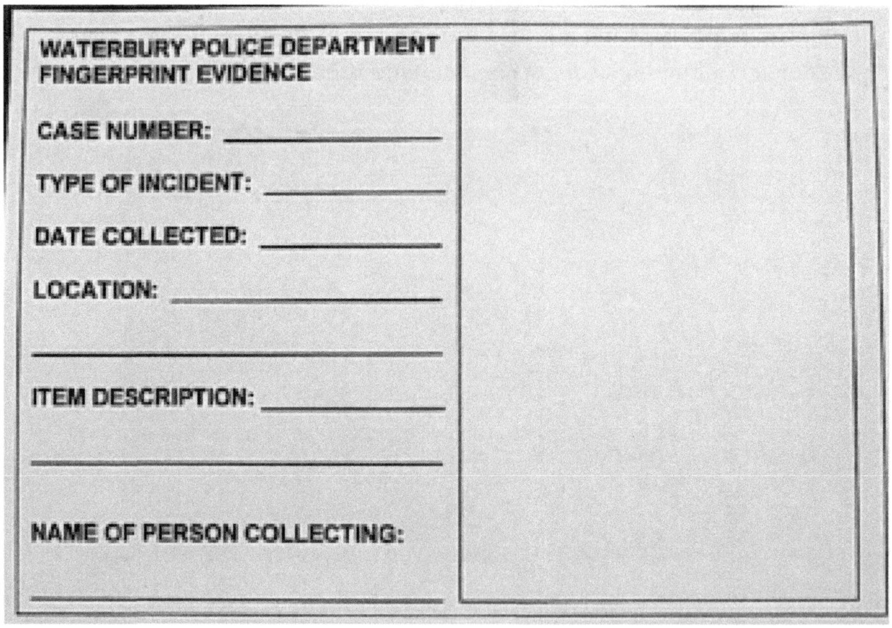

Photo 6.6

Latent lift card. The tape-lifted print is placed on the backside of the card, a sketch of the latent's location is placed to the right side of the card, and case information is placed to the left (courtesy of Cindy Lopes).

```
WATERBURY POLICE DEPARTMENT
FINGERPRINT EVIDENCE

CASE NUMBER: _____

TYPE OF INCIDENT: _____

DATE COLLECTED: _____

LOCATION: _____

_____

ITEM DESCRIPTION: _____

_____

NAME OF PERSON COLLECTING:
```

Chemical processing methods for latent fingerprints can be used on dry and wet surfaces. Various dye staining techniques, like gentian violet, fluorescent dyes or other laser-excitable dyes, followed by lighting or laser excitation, then photography of the developed latent fingerprints work on dry surfaces. Lifting the dye-stained latents is dependent on the type of chemical used and the surface. Wet surfaces with suspected latent fingerprints are processed using small particle reagent spray or physical developer (as shown in Photo 6.16). These types of enhanced latent fingerprints need to be photographed for documentation of the developed fingerprints. A detailed discussion of the procedures and chemical reagents used for developing latent prints can be found in Table 6.2.

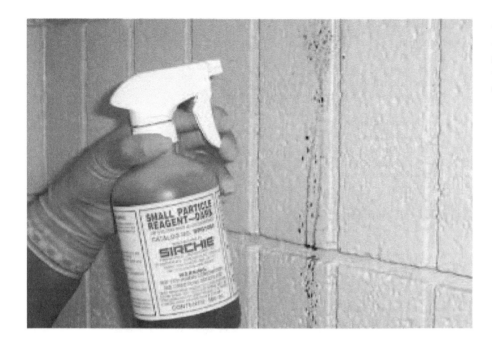

Photo 6.7

Application of small particle reagent for the development of latent fingerprints on a wet surface.

Latent prints on porous surfaces are visualized by the use of chemical methods. Because of the nature of the surface and the fact that the friction ridge secretions are dissolved into the surface, the chemical method chosen for visualization must react with the secretions and not with the surface. Silver nitrate, iodine fuming, ninhydrin and its analogs, and various dye-staining techniques are examples of some chemical methods used for porous surfaces. Once the latent fingerprints have been developed, they will need to be photographed and the object with the fingerprints collected as evidence if possible. Papers and other documents should be individually placed in plastic bags (if dry) or envelopes. If the surface with the developed latents is immovable, then photography becomes the primary source of the latents' documentation.

VISIBLE PRINTS

Visible prints, palm prints or sole prints, generally result when friction ridges are coated with material that is transferred to another surface leaving the outline or impression of the friction ridge. Visible prints do not need to be dusted (occasionally they may need enhancement), the visible prints should be photographed, and the object with the visible print should be packaged and collected. If the object cannot be collected then the photograph will become the evidence.

Frequently the visible print can be enhanced or visualized so that better ridge detail can be obtained. The fingerprint is enhanced using chemical methods that are based on the chemical composition of the transferred material. Bloody

Table 6.2

Chemical reagents used for developing latent prints.

- **Ninhydrin**
  0.8 g ninhydrin
  120 ml acetone
  Spray on item and heat for visualization.
  Note: Shelf life of solution will exceed one year.

- **Zinc chloride solution**
  (for use of ALS/laser after ninhydrin treatment)
  5 g zinc chloride crystals   400 ml 1,1,2-trichlorotrifluoroethane
  2 ml glacial acetic acid   2 ml bleach
  100 ml methanol
  Lightly spray on item. Dry and look for color change to orange. View w/ALS.

- **Iodine spray reagent**
  Solution A: 1 g iodine   Solution B: 5 g naphthoflavone
              1 L cyclohexane   40 ml methylene chloride
  Mix 2 ml of Solution B into 100 ml of Solution A for 5 minutes. Filter.
  Note: Solution A store at rm temp for 30 days and Solution B refrigerate for 30 days.
  When solutions mixed use within 24 hours.

- **Silver nitrate solution**
  5% silver nitrate in distilled water
  Spray on item. Caution: will turn skin black.

- **Small particle reagent**
  30 g molybdenum disulfide
  1 L distilled water
  3 drops PhotoFlo
  Mix together thoroughly. Shelf life of 6–8 weeks. May be sprayed or dipped. Rinse
  object with water and tape lift the latent.

  ### *Post-superglue fluorescent treatments*

- **Rhodamine 6G**
  Stock solution: 100 mg Rhodamine 6G   Working solution: 3 ml stock solution
                  100 ml methanol   15 ml acetone
                                                            10 ml acetonitrile
  Mix in order given.   15 ml methanol
                                                            32 ml 2-propanol
                                                            925 ml petroleum ether

- **7-(*p*-methoxybenzylamino)-4-nitrobenz-2-oxa-1,3-diazole (MBD)**
  Stock solution: 100 mg MBD   Working solution: 10 ml stock solution
                  100 ml acetone   30 ml methanol
                                                            10 ml 2-propanol
  Mix in order given.   950 ml petroleum ether

- **Ardrox**
  2 ml ardrox
  10 ml acetone
  25 ml methanol
  10 ml 2-propanol
  8 ml acetonitrile
  945 ml petroleum ether

fingerprints are the most common type of visible fingerprints found in crime scene investigations. These visible fingerprints can be enhanced or visualized following the flow chart in Figure 6.3 below. Colors are formed by the use of chemical reagents along the friction ridges to allow for better visualization (see Photo 6.9). The reagents are some of the chemicals commonly used for the presumptive or field-testing for blood. These chemicals are applied by the use of atomizers or spray bottles. The reagents have limited shelf lives if kept unrefrigerated, so, for storage purposes, it is better to keep them refrigerated when not being used at the scene. A detailed description of the procedure and reagents can be found in Chapter 9 of this book.

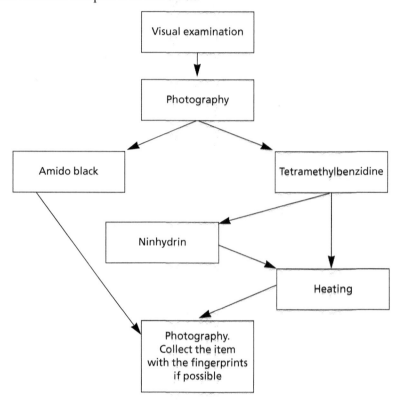

Figure 6.3
Methodology for processing evidence with bloody fingerprints.

PLASTIC/3-DIMENSIONAL PRINTS

These types of prints are produced when the friction ridge on the finger, palm or sole come into contact with a softer surface and makes a three-dimensional impression into the receiving surface. Photographic documentation of impression evidence has already been discussed and those procedures would follow here. The photograph will represent the best evidence in this case and should be treated accordingly. Depending on the surface materials, some casing materials can be used for casting and preserving these impressions. Detailed discussion of other impression evidence will be presented later in this chapter.

ELIMINATION PRINTS

For comparison purposes, the crime scene investigator must obtain known fingerprints (palm prints or footprints) from every person who may have been in the scene. These known fingerprints are referred to as elimination fingerprints. Elimination fingerprints are inked prints onto ten-print fingerprint cards or shortened cards for at-the-scene use. Elimination fingerprints of deceased victims must be taken too. Post-mortem elimination fingerprints and palm prints should be accomplished only after consultation from the medical examiner and only after trace evidence has been collected. The ink will need to be placed on the victim's fingers and the fingers rolled onto the fingerprint card. In some cases this can easily be done, as shown in Photo 6.3. However, if the fingers are difficult to roll then a 'spoon' apparatus is advisable to use.

Photo 6.8

Post-mortem fingerprints are being taken by the use of inking spoon (courtesy of Robin Lunsford).

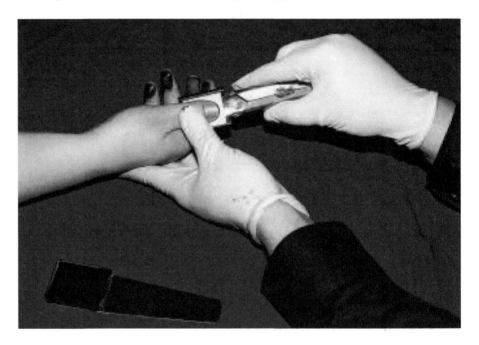

If the deceased has been exposed to water or other fluids (for example, lying in blood) for a length of time so that the deceased fingers' skin is loosely held or the skin is peeling away from the body, then care should be taken to dry and remove the epidermis skin layers so that the friction ridge details are not lost. Once the skin from the fingers is removed it can be placed over a mold or the examiner's own gloved fingers to be inked and rolled on the ten-print card. If any of the ridges are transferred to the card, do not attempt to remove them. Allow the ridges to dry undisturbed and they will generally be easily removed later without destroying the minutiae details.

In extended exposure to heated and dry conditions the deceased can become desiccated or 'mummified'. When this type of result is seen, the fingers of the deceased will lose moisture that makes obtaining of elimination prints difficult. If the drying of the fingers is slight, then the application of skin lotion to the hands will allow for usable inked prints. If the drying of the hands is extensive, then using tissue builder can restore the flesh and skin. The tissue builder is injected into the finger just below and towards the fingertip. The tissue builder material should be added until the tips return to their appropriate size. They can then be inked and rolled (the spoon apparatus is best for this step) with usable elimination prints obtained. Only in extremely rare instances should the deceased fingers be removed from the body. If removal is necessary, then the removal of the fingers or hands should be done only under the supervision of the medical examiner.

FINGERPRINTS ON HUMAN SKIN

The visualization of latent prints on victim's skin most likely involves the presence of a contaminant. The above techniques for visualization of latent prints will not be successful. It is for this reason that the visualization of the latent prints on skin is based on the visibility and reactivity of the contaminant. Searching for the prints on the skin of a victim can be easily accomplished with careful, close examination for ridge detail followed by enhancement if necessary. Visual searching is done with various light sources at oblique angles that reflect or react to the contaminant material. Alternate light sources, lasers, and strong halogen lighting are good for this purpose.

Generally, there are two accepted techniques for the developing or enhancement of latent fingerprints on bodies. These techniques may be used separately or in tandem. The techniques are the transfer lift method and the superglue fuming method. For both methods permission must always be obtained from the medical examiner's office prior to attempting to find latent prints on the bodies of victims. Additionally, any trace evidence should be protected or properly collected prior to using the methods.

Transfer lift method

1   For deceased victims, the skin surface should be 72–80 degrees Fahrenheit and the transfer material should be heated to above 86 degrees Fahrenheit prior to lifting the latent prints (hair dryers work well).

2   Place a nonporous surface transfer material (black plastic, black-developed RC photo paper, mirror, glass, or metal plate) against the area suspected as having the latent print for 15–20 seconds.

3   Remove the surface material and develop with superglue fuming.

Photo 6.9

Bloody fingerprints found on skin of a homicide victim.

4   If necessary, enhance the developed print with dye staining, laser or alternate light source excitation, and powder dusting.

5   Porous paper can be used as the lifting surface with subsequent development using DFO, ninhydrin or PD.

Superglue fuming method

1   Do not refrigerate the body to be processed. If the body has been refrigerated prior to attempting the development technique, then allow the condensation to evaporate.

2   Place the body in an airtight plastic or visqueen tent that allows for heat acceleration of the fuming process.

3   Place a test print inside the tent.

4   Fume the body until the test print is fully developed. Numerous types of superglue formats can be used for this step.

5   Dust using a contrasting powder. Successful results have been obtained using fluorescent powders and magnetic powders.

6   This method is also well suited for small areas on the body if the entire body cannot be fumed.

IMPRESSION EVIDENCE

Impression evidence is one type of physical evidence commonly found at crime scenes. When properly recognized, documented and interpreted, impression evidence can be extremely valuable in the investigation and subsequent reconstruction. It can associate a victim, suspect or witness with a particular location at the scene, and in addition it can provide important investigative leads, such as with footwear impressions that show shoe size, number of persons present at the scene, and give indications of physical conditions and the direction of travel of the person(s) who deposited the impressions.

Two types of impression evidence may be encountered at crime scenes: (1) two-dimensional impressions, sometimes called imprints. This type of impression is normally found at indoor scenes, on objects, and occasionally on non-porous surfaces in outdoor scenes; (2) three-dimensional impressions, sometimes called indentations. This type of impression is usually found at outdoor scenes deposited in softer receiving surfaces. Impression evidence when recognized at crime scenes should be properly documented and collected for further examination and possible comparison. Figure 6.4 shows a general procedure for the recording and collection of impression evidence found at the crime scene and of known standards or origins for comparison to the crime scene impression evidence. Special care must be taken to prevent contamination or destruction of the impression evidence, to maintain its integrity, and to preserve the chain of custody.

IMPRINTS

Two-dimensional residue impressions are referred to as imprints. Their appearance at the crime scene is due to two surfaces coming into contact. The material or residue from one surface is transferred to the second surface. Fingerprints, footwear, and tire tread impressions are the most common types of imprints found at crime scenes. Enhancement and collection techniques for residue imprints are similar to the fingerprint techniques discussed previously and are summarized in the table below. The imprint evidence is searched for using various side-lighting sources (flashlights, alternate light sources, lasers, etc.). Once the imprint is located then it must be photographed as shown in Chapter 4 on Documentation. The collection of the residue imprint is done by lifting techniques dependent on the surface characteristics of the object with the imprint, as shown in Table 6.3.

Porous surfaces

Imprint evidence on porous surfaces cannot be lifted using tape or other adhesive materials. Gel lifters are especially well suited for lifting residue imprints without lifting any of the porous surface's material (see Photo 6.10). Gel lifters consist of three layers: the backing or carrier, the gelatin adhesive, and the protective cover sheet. The backing material is colored or transparent. The choice of backing is dependent on the desired contrasting color of the residue imprint and

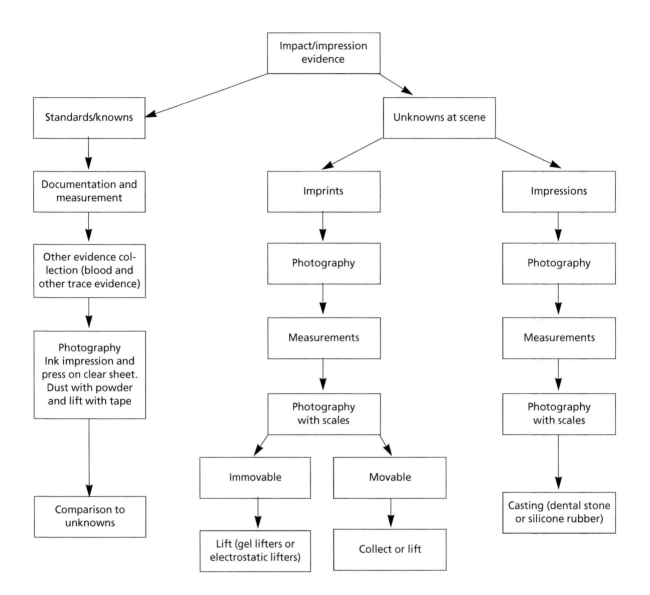

Figure 6.4

General procedures for the collection of imprint/impression evidence.

the gel lifter's backing. The gel lifters are available in a range of sizes and can be cut to any size to fit the imprint. Once the imprint is lifted, it should be photographed without the cover sheet in place. The intact gel lifter should then be placed in an evidence bag or envelope for storage. Because the gelatin layer will melt at temperatures above 104°F, it must be stored at room temperature or below room temperature. The backing material must be marked with the case number, collector's initials, date and time. However, fading of the lifted residue imprints does occur after a period of time (dependent on the type of residue and the storage temperatures, etc.), therefore photographing the imprints after lifting should be done as soon as possible.

Technique	Principle	Applicable surface
Iodine fuming	Reaction w/chemicals (fatty acids or grease) deposited on surface.	Porous surfaces: paper, cloth, walls, etc.
Ninhydrin spray	Reaction w/chemicals (proteins and amino acids) on surface.	Porous surfaces: paper, walls, raw wood, etc.
Blood enhancement reagents	Reaction w/hemoglobin deposited on the surface.	Bloody imprints on any porous surfaces.
Trace metal disposition	Reaction with metals deposited on the surface.	Any imprint containing metal deposits.
Oblique lighting	Light interaction and reflection off residue particles.	Any surface; porous and non-porous.
Ultraviolet, alternate light source	Excitation of visible light and other wavelengths of light.	Any surface; porous and non-porous.
Gel lifters	Tacky surface interaction and adhesion of residue particles.	Any surface; porous and non-porous.
Electrostatic lifting	Static charge on the lifting film attracts dust particles.	Any surface; porous and non-porous.

Table 6.3

Enhancement and lifting techniques for fingerprint and imprint evidence.

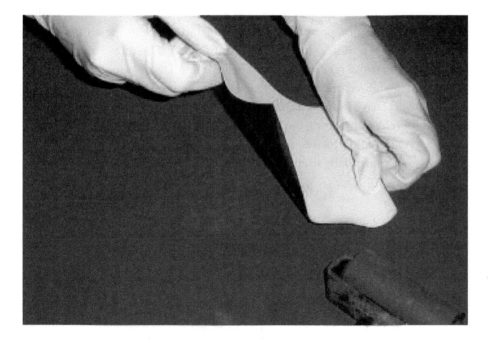

Photo 6.10

Use of a gel-lifter to collect dust residue off an immovable surface.

(a)

(b)

Photo 6.11a–c

Dr Henry Lee using an electrostatic lifter device to capture a dust-based footwear pattern located at a crime scene.

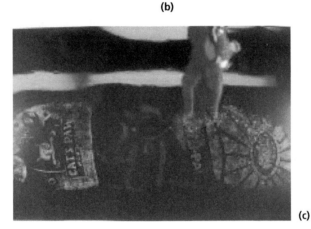

(c)

Electrostatic lifting can also be used as a technique for collection of residue imprints on both non-porous and porous surfaces. Electrostatic lifters are a means for lifting of dust prints (see Photos 6.11a–c). The unit consists of four basic components: a rechargeable power supply, a DC charger, metal ground plate, and metalized lifting film. The battery power is converted to a high voltage static charge on the lifting film that attracts the dust particles of the imprint thereby transferring the imprint to the film. The transferred dust print is then photographed or used for comparison purposes. Electrostatic lifting devices are commercially available from a variety of sources.

Non-porous surfaces

Gel lifters, electrostatic lifting and strongly adhesive lifters are very well suited for the lifting, collection and preservation of residue imprints. Once the imprints are lifted, those lifts should be packaged in plastic bags, envelopes, or other containers. The packaging should be marked and documented as previously described.

INDENTATIONS

Three-dimensional impression evidence is produced like imprint evidence when two surfaces come into contact with one another. Indentations are different from imprint impressions because one of the surfaces is softer than the other surface. The softer surface becomes 'indented' with the shape, length, width and depth of the harder item. In essence the softer surface has an impression with a detailed replication of the pattern of the object.

As previously described, indentation evidence is properly photographed using oblique lighting that is raised slightly so as to cast shadows and illuminate various surfaces of the indentation with an attempt to view details of the indentation. Once the indentation is photographed, it should be cast so as to collect the impression evidence. The casting material is chosen based upon the type of surface containing the indentation. If the indented surface is a hard type of material, like metal or painted hardwood, it may contain microscopic markings, thus silicone rubber material is best suited for the casting. If the indented surface is softer, like dirt or snow, then a material like dental stone is the best casting material. The surfaces of the softer indentations must be prepared before casting is done.

The general procedure for casting with the dental stone is:

1 Remove large pieces of unimbedded debris that may have fallen on the indentation.
2 Prepare the surface of the indentation by gently spraying it with hair spray or snow wax material. Do not spray directly towards the impression; indirect application of the spray works well so as not to disturb the impression but coat it only.
3 Set up barriers to prevent the dental stone mixture from running out of the indentation.
4 Mix the dry dental stone material with water until a pancake batter consistency is achieved. This is approximately two parts batter to one part water. Stir constantly.
5 Carefully pour the mixture so that it flows onto the indentation without disturbing its structure. An interrupted flow over a spatula works well.
6 When approximately half-an-inch of dental stone fills the indentation, add reinforcing material (sticks or screen material) to the cast.
7 Continue pouring the dental stone mixture until the indentation is filled with material.
8 Mark the cast approximately 10 minutes after the cast has been allowed to set.
9 Move and collect the cast of the indentation approximately 30 minutes after the dental stone mixture is hardened. Do not remove any dirt adhering to the cast.
10 Secure the cast in an open box as the primary container and wrap the box with paper as the secondary container. Properly seal and mark the outer container.

Table 6.4 provides the procedures to follow for casting indentations in various surfaces.

Table 6.4

Impression media and casting procedures.

Media	Casting procedures
WET SOIL of a fine, even consistency will produce an impression with a high degree of detail.	1 Remove excess water by sprinkling a small amount of casting material over the impression. 2 Mix and pour as normal. 3 Accelerator may be needed. 4 Drying time 45–60 minutes.
MUD of a fine, even consistency will produce an impression with a high degree of detail.	1 Mix and pour as normal. 2 Drying depends on how wet the mud is: 45–60 minutes.
DRY SOIL of a consistency of talcum powder will retain detail to a varying degree.	1 Spray impression with pump hair spray. 2 Spray paint can to be used to harden and highlight the impression. 3 Mix and pour as normal. 4 Drying time 20–30 minutes.
DRY SOIL with a hard packed consistency will retain detail to a varying degree.	1 Spray impression with pump hair spray. 2 Mix and pour as normal. 3 Drying time 20–30 minutes.
SAND will vary in texture and consistency and will retain detail.	1 Spray impression with pump hair spray. 2 Spray paint can to be used to harden and highlight the impression. 3 Mix and pour as normal. 4 Drying time 20–30 minutes.
When impression is in water: WATER varies in texture and consistency. Detail depends on the amount of water and the amount of pressure applied to the ground. Time consuming process.	1 Build form around the impression, if needed to control water and remove excess water if possible. 2 Sprinkle small amount of casting material over impression until covered. 3 Mix and pour as normal. 4 Accelerator can be added. 5 Drying will vary from 60–120 minutes.
When water is in impression: WATER varies in texture and consistency. Detail depends on the amount of pressure applied to the impression by the water.	1 Remove excess water by pipetting. 2 Sprinkle small amount of casting material over the impression until covered. 3 Mix and pour as usual. 4 Accelerator can be added. 5 Drying time will vary from 60–90 minutes depending on amount of water.
When impression is in snow: SNOW varies in texture, cohesiveness, and impression detail retention with temperature. Excellent detail can be reproduced if care is exercised.	1 Spray the impression area with 'Snow Print Wax'. 2 Mix water and surrounding snow together in order to lower the temperature of the water. 3 Accelerator can be added. 4 Pour as normal. 5 Drying time will vary from 60–90 minutes and may be longer. Depends on outside temperature.

Accelerator = potassium sulfate.

The impression evidence collected from the crime scene will be compared to possible knowns or standards in an attempt to determine the source or origin of the indentation. It is for this reason that any knowns or standards must be collected and submitted, too. The basis for the comparison between knowns and unknowns is to identify any class or individualizing characteristics due to size, pattern, and wear characteristics. It is, therefore, also important to collect the knowns in a timely manner.

HAIR AND FIBER EVIDENCE

HAIR EVIDENCE

Hair evidence found at a crime scene can be used to identify racial origin and somatic origin of the source of the hair. Hairs can also be microscopically examined and compared to possible known sources so that inclusion or exclusion of the hairs' origin can be done. If a root sheath is attached to a hair (such as, anagen or catagen hairs), then PCR-STR DNA typing can be used to identify the contributor of the hair. Mitochondrial DNA typing of hair shaft identification methods have also been used in many court cases.

For these reasons, hair evidence at crime scenes must be carefully searched for, collected, and packaged so that the hairs are not lost. Oblique lighting, alternate light sources, and lasers are useful techniques for observing and finding hairs at the crime scene or on suspects' or victims' bodies and clothing (as shown in Photo 6.12). Once the hairs have been found at the scene, they are collecting by using tweezers or forceps and placed into a druggist's fold as a primary container. The primary container should then be placed into a secondary, outer container. The outer container can be plastic or glassine bags, envelopes, vials, or pillboxes. They should be properly documented, sealed, and marked.

Hairs from same locations may be packaged together. Indiscriminate vacuuming at the crime scene will produce a re-mixing effect of the 'newly deposited' hair evidence and should be avoided in crime scene investigations. Vacuuming of small areas near bodies or primary crime scenes can be useful as a hair collection technique without re-mixing the newly deposited hair. Care should be taken to make sure that a new filter for the vacuum is used. The filter should be packaged separately into a druggist's fold and placed into an appropriately sealed and marked outer container. The use of tape lifts or gel lifters in small, distinctive areas at the crime scene is appropriate, too (see Photo 6.13). If movable objects at the crime scene are suspected to contain hair evidence, they should be wrapped in a primary container and placed in a secondary, outer container (properly sealed and marked) and taken to a controlled environment

Photo 6.12

Oblique or side-lighting is being used to search for hair evidence.

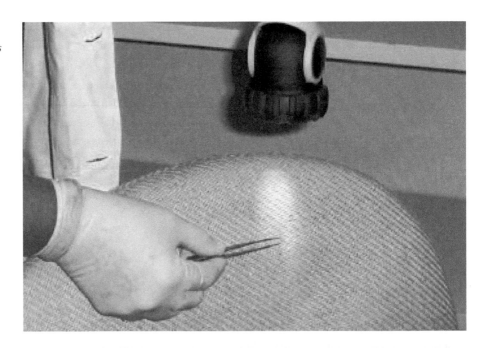

Photo 6.13

Tape lifting for trace evidence (courtesy of Karthika Divakaran, University of New Haven, CT).

or the entire object submitted to the forensic laboratory for searching of the hair evidence. Similarly, if a hair is attached or caught on an item of evidence, as in dried blood or a part of fabric, it should be left on the item and collected in its original condition. It should be packaged within a primary container and placed in an outer container.

The collection of known or standard hairs from victims and/or suspects will be necessary for most criminal investigations. These known hairs should never be cut. A total of 25–50 pulled hairs should be collected from different regions of the area, packaged into a druggist's fold, placed in an outer container, properly sealed, and marked by the collector with their initials, the case number, the date, the time and a brief description. Combings of the head or pubic areas are designed to remove loose hairs on those surfaces and it is not a technique for collecting known standards. Any combings are to be considered as unknown or questioned samples.

FIBER EVIDENCE

Laboratory examination can identify the fiber type and determine the possible origin of the fiber from a fabric source. Fiber evidence is searched, collected, and packaged like hair evidence. The picking, vacuuming, tape lifting and scraping techniques are used for the collection of fibers or threads. Where there is fiber evidence adhering to a movable object found at the crime scene, that object should be wrapped and packaged intact. It is useful for the crime scene investigator to remember that fabrics are easily caught or torn by broken windows, edges of ripped screens, and other damaged or sharp materials.

Other fiber evidence, such as fabrics, thread, cordage, rope, or cloth may also be found at the crime scene. They should be collected as with fiber evidence. They should be photographed, packaged in primary containers and placed in outer containers that are sealed and marked as other evidence previously discussed. Knotted cordage evidence can be found at the crime scene. The knots should never be untied; they should be photographed intact. If removal of the knots and cordage is necessary for transportation, the cordage may be cut at a new location and marked by the person removing the cordage. Removal and cutting at new location must allow the knots to remain intact.

As with hair evidence, known standards of possible sources of the fiber evidence must be collected and packaged for subsequent comparison in the laboratory. If possible, the entire known source should be collected. If not possible, then a representative sample from the source should be obtained. Cuttings from carpets, fabrics, or other materials can be used as the known sample of the possible source. The knowns are packaged into primary containers, placed into outer containers, and preserved as shown previously.

OTHER TRACE EVIDENCE: GLASS, PAINT, AND SOIL

GLASS EVIDENCE

Glass often is found at crime scenes, on vehicles, clothing and bodies. It is persistent and frequently unknowingly transferred from one surface to another surface. Windows are frequently broken in burglaries or robbery cases, headlights in hit-and-run investigations are broken and deposited on victims and suspects, and various glass containers or objects may break and leave tiny fragments on suspects involved in many investigations. Photos 6.14a–c show the securing and documentation of glass evidence prior to collection.

As with other trace evidence, hairs and fibers, any objects that are movable and may contain glass evidence should be wrapped or placed in a primary container to prevent loss of the glass evidence. They should then be placed in an outer container that is sealed and marked properly for preservation purposes. For example, any objects that are contaminated with glass like shoes or clothes should be folded into paper. If the object to contain the glass evidence cannot be moved, then previously described collection methods of picking, tape lifting, scraping, or vacuuming can be done. Large pieces of glass should be placed between pieces of cardboard to prevent further breakage, wrapped in primary container material, and placed into an outer container. Each large piece of glass should be numbered, sealed and marked appropriately. The containers should also be marked that they contain sharp edges and careful handling is necessary.

Special attention should be given to hit-and-run investigations. All glass particles that can be found should be collected and packaged. All pieces of the glass may be necessary for direct edge matching and reconstruction of lenses or glass objects. If glass is found dispersed over a wide distance, particles from similar areas of close proximity can be packaged together. However, different locations must be packaged separately.

Suspected sources which contain glass evidence should be collected also. Any frames holding the glass should be packaged and preserved intact with any broken glass particles. If the possible source of the glass is an exterior window, then be sure to label the source's exterior or interior surfaces. The edges of the fractured glass can be used to reconstruct the side to which force was applied to fracture marks on the glass. Pieces of broken glass may also be used to reconstruct windows by direct-edge matching.

PAINT EVIDENCE

Forensic laboratories examine suspected paint evidence by looking at different layers of paint in chips, and the chemical and elemental composition in each paint layer. The layers of paint found in paint chip evidence are examined for sequence, number and relative layer thickness. It is for this reason that intact paint chips must be collected and preserved. Paint chips are packaged into druggist's folds as primary containers and placed in outer containers like pill vials, pill boxes, or coin envelopes. Paint scrapings are often found in specific

(a)

(b)

(c)

Photo 6.14a–c
Photos depicting the documentation of glass evidence in investigations.

locations at crime scenes or on vehicles. Care should be taken to document locations, specifically heights of paint scrapings on poles, road abutments or on damaged vehicles.

As shown with other trace evidence from crime scenes, representative samples of possible known sources for the paint evidence need to be collected and preserved.

SOIL EVIDENCE

Soil evidence at crime scenes generally fall into three basic types of evidence: soil from impression evidence, clothing with soil adhering to it, and soil evidence that is part of hit-and-run investigations. Soil evidence that is part of an impression at the crime scene should not be collected so as to destroy or disrupt an impression that may be used for subsequent laboratory comparison. Direct sampling of the area can be done after the impression is photographed and cast. A sampling of the soil around the impression should be collected. A tablespoon taken at the four compass points at a distance of 1–2 feet needs to be collected. Tablespoon samples at the compass points at a distance of 25 feet can also be collected. The collected samples should be wrapped into a druggist's fold of paper and placed into non-airtight containers to allow any moisture to evaporate. This technique works well for the soil samples that may contain microorganisms. Clothing containing soil evidence should be wrapped between layers of paper and placed in paper bags for submission to the forensic laboratory. Large pieces of soil debris that are evidence in a hit-and-run investigation may potentially be used in direct edge matching with vehicles. The wheel wells of any vehicles should be sampled for comparison purposes. A sample from the wheel wells should be collected into paper druggist's folds and placed into non-airtight outer containers.

FIREARMS AND TOOLMARKS

Firearms evidence, including weapons, bullets, casings and parts, is often found at the crime scenes involving shooting incidents. This evidence will be subjected to numerous examinations in the laboratory. The firearm should be checked for fingerprints, biological fluids, and other trace evidence. They could be tested for operability by test firing and the test-fired rounds can be microscopically compared to any other projectiles or spent casings found at the crime scene. Spent casings and fired projectiles can be examined for the presence of rifling characteristics that will indicate caliber, type of ammunition used, manufacturer and model of the firearm that discharged the casings and projectiles.

Toolmarks at crime scenes are treated as impression evidence. The marks should be photographed, collected, and, if on a movable surface, packaged and marked. If the toolmark is on an immovable surface, then the toolmark is cast with silicon rubber casting material, and the cast collected as evidence. The laboratory will attempt to compare the toolmark from the scene to a test toolmark made by a submitted suspect tool.

FIREARMS EVIDENCE

Firearms, spent casings, and fired projectiles are frequently found at crime scenes. Firearms are documented by notes, photography, videography, and sketching as discussed in an earlier chapter. Searches for firearms are a commonplace occurrence in criminal investigations. The collection, packaging and preservation of firearms evidence includes some additional documentation before the actual bagging and tagging of the firearm. The additional documentation of firearms is to accurately record the make, model, caliber, and serial number of the evidence. Additional information about location, condition (loaded or unloaded), time of discovery, and identification of other physical evidence present on the firearm should be recorded. If the firearm needs to be moved to determine this information, then it should be carefully handled to avoid disturbing any potential fingerprints or blood spatters that may be deposited on the firearm. The firearm may be picked up or touched on the textured grips without altering or damaging existing fingerprints. Never stick anything in the barrel of the firearm to move it; this may alter or change the rifling in the barrel.

Firearms should never be collected or packaged in a loaded condition. Before the firearm is unloaded, if the firearm is a revolver, then the cylinder needs to be diagrammed (as shown in Photo 6.15 and Figure 6.5. If it is a semi-automatic pistol then the condition of the slide mechanism, the number of live rounds in the magazine, and the presence of any chambered rounds need to be recorded, as shown in Photo 6.16. Spent casings and bullet positions should be noted on the diagram, too. Any unused ammunition must be collected with the weapon, packaged, marked, and described as to its location near or in the firearm.

The firearm should be packaged in a primary container or wrapping and placed in a paper bag, envelope, or cardboard box specific for firearms. Never clean the barrel, chamber, or cylinder of the firearm. Do not take the handguns, rifles or shotguns apart before submission to the forensic laboratory. The live ammunition found in the firearm should be similarly packaged but in a separate container. The forensic laboratory that will be testing the firearm may use the unused ammunition as standards or knowns. Any additional live ammunition or boxes of ammunition found at the crime scene should also be collected and submitted with the firearm.

Photo 6.15
Revolver.

Figure 6.5

Diagramming revolver cylinders.

Cylinder of revolver found at crime scene:

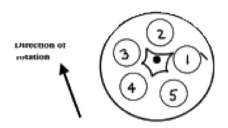

Investigator's Mark	Location in Cylinder	Description	Manufacturer And Type
M1	1	Fired	R-P, JHP
M2	2	Live	Federal, lead RN
M3	3	Live	R-P, JHP
M4	4	Live	R-P, JHP
M5	5	Live	Federal, lead RN

Photo 6.16

Semi-automatic pistol with magazine. and live rounds

Projectiles

Projectiles found at the crime scene should never be marked or scored in any way. They should be wrapped in soft paper and packaged in a secondary container. All projectile evidence must be submitted to the laboratory. Do not attempt to clean the projectiles. If the projectiles are coated in blood or other biological fluids, then they should be allowed to air dry, wrapped in paper, and be placed in an outer pillbox.

Spent casings

Spent casings found at the crime scene should be wrapped with soft paper as primary containers, packaged separately, and placed in outer containers like pillboxes or coin envelopes (as shown in Photo 6.17). The metal spent casings should not be marked. Spent shotgun casings may be marked on the plastic shell material. As with projectiles, all spent casings recovered at the scene must be submitted to the forensic laboratory.

Photo 6.17

Collection of spent cartridge casings at a crime scene.

TOOLMARKS

Toolmarks found at the crime scene are impression evidence. These toolmarks can be static indentations or dynamic indentations called striations. They are discussed above with regards to collection, packaging, and preservation. Frequently, the toolmarks will be compared to tools or other implements that are suspected to have made the scene toolmarks. The comparison and identification of toolmarks is based on the wear or usage damage on the tool. For this reason, careful packaging of suspected tools or implements must occur. Suspect or known tools should be secured in a box to protect the tool's unique markings. Under absolutely no condition should the suspected tool be placed or fitted into the mark found at the scene.

GUNSHOT RESIDUE

Gunshot residue (GSR) found at the crime scene is very fragile and therefore should be collected as soon as possible after firearm discharge. Collection of GSR on live subjects can be done by the use of laboratory supplied kits or commercial kits. Currently, there are the two commonly used techniques for GSR collection: the SEM disc lifting method and AA swabbing methods (as shown in Photo 6.18). Investigators should consult with their local laboratory as to which test the laboratory performs. The collection of the GSR must be done within six hours on live subjects and they should not be allowed to wash their hands or extensively contact their hands with other surfaces in case they loosen the GSR particles. If a body is to be sampled for GSR, the sampling must be done before the body is moved. If no sampling can be done at the scene, then bagging the hands with paper bags should be done.

GSR on clothing can oftentimes be useful in the determination of range of fire. The clothing must be carefully packaged so as not to dislodge any GSR particles. The packaging technique that best accomplishes this is to place clean wrapping paper on each layer of the clothing. Clothing should be placed in a

Photo 6.18

Gunshot residue (GSR) sample collection. Swabbing hands of suspected shooter (courtesy of Karthika Divakavan).

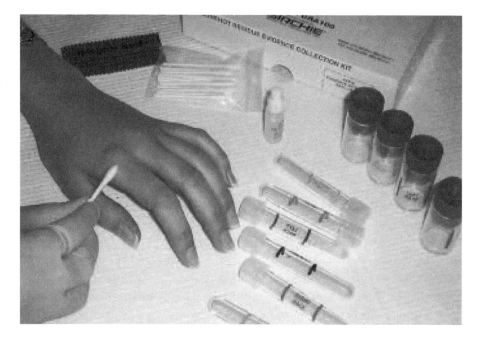

box, and folding avoided as much as possible. For GSR pattern determination of the range of fire, the firearm and matching ammunition must be submitted to the laboratory (as shown in Photo 6.19).

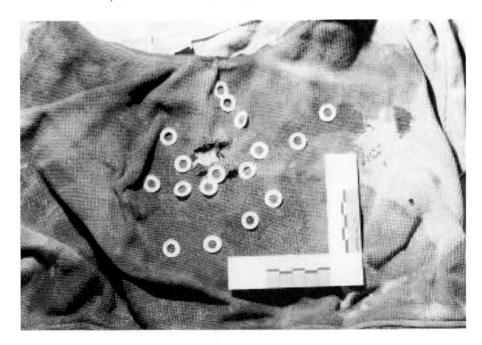

Photo 6.19

Identified GSR particles on victim's dress. The distribution of particles indicates the range of fire compared to test-fired targets.

BIOLOGICAL EVIDENCE: BLOOD, BODY FLUIDS AND TISSUE

BLOOD

General considerations

The collection, packaging, and preservation of blood evidence at the crime scene should never take place until the investigator has taken extra care to make sure that the bloodstain patterns have been extensively documented. Bloodstain evidence and its patterns are extremely useful in crime scene reconstruction. The use of bloodstain patterns for reconstruction will be discussed in Chapter 10. For example, impacted bloodstain patterns on a suspect's bedroom wall may give investigators information as to the sequence of events at a homicide scene, or a blood drip pattern may lead investigators to a victim's body (as shown in Photo 6.20). It is for this reason that the documentation of blood is so important and must be done before any samples are collected.

Recent advances in DNA typing techniques allow for older and smaller bloodstains to be analyzed. The collection of even the smallest of bloodstain samples at the crime scene may significantly add to an investigation. For example small bloodstains belonging to the victim found on a suspect's clothes or shoes can be the only link between the victim and a suspect. New research on DNA in criminal investigations has raised the possibilities of microchip DNA 'on-scene' analysis. With the advent of artificial intelligence systems, like CODIS, a crime scene investigator may be able to identify the donor of a blood-stain by on-scene DNA database search.

The advances in the identification and individualization of bloodstain and the successful court presentation and resolution of an investigation with blood-stain evidence cannot be accomplished *unless the correct procedures are followed for collection, packaging, and preservation of the blood evidence.*

Photo 6.20

Crime scene containing blood stain patterns yield information on sequence of events.

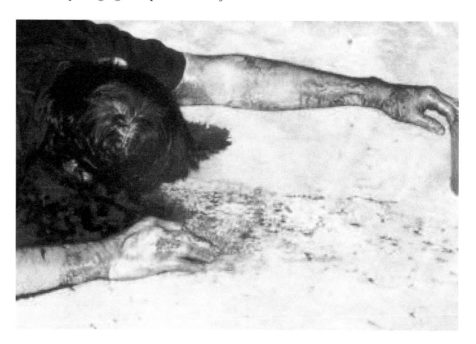

After documentation of the blood evidence at the crime scene, the collection can begin. Generally, the most easily lost blood must be collected first. These are bloodstains that may be located in high volume traffic areas of the scene; bloodstains that are in doorways, hallways or roadsides; or blood that may be present at outdoor crime scenes. Bloodstains that are found on movable objects can be protected by temporarily moving the object to a safer location until the stain or object may be collected.

Whenever biological fluids are encountered at a crime scene, care and pre-cautions should be taken as discussed in Chapter 3. Be sure to wear protective clothing, gloves, masks, and eye protection as the situation warrants. Multiple layers of gloves with frequent changes can be very helpful to prevent biohazards while also preventing cross-contamination of bloodstains at the crime scene.

Blood at crime scenes will be found either as a dried stain or in a liquid state.

Generally, if blood at the crime scene is liquid, then let it air dry! If the object with the blood-stain is movable, then collect the entire object! The packaging of blood and objects with blood will follow the same packaging principles that have been discussed throughout this chapter for all physical evidence. Place blood and bloodstained objects in a primary container (druggist's folds or blood swab box) followed by packaging in an outer or secondary container (envelopes or paper bags), as shown in Photos 6.21 and 6.22. *Blood and bloodstained evidence should never be placed in airtight containers.*

Photo 6.21

Bloody evidence placed into paper wrapper after it dried.

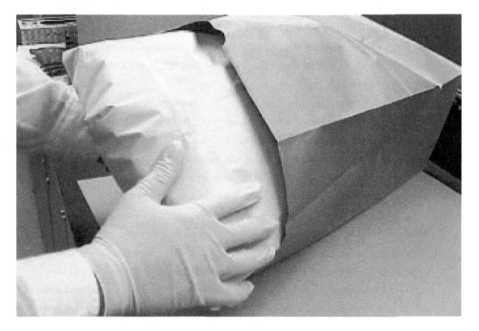

Photo 6.22

Primary container (paper wrapped clothes) placed in a secondary or outer container (paper bag).

The secondary container should be sealed with evidence tape, marked appropriately, and placed in a secure location. Bloodstained evidence frequently will have other trace evidence present. If the blood loosely holds the trace evidence, then it is proper to collect that trace evidence (with techniques previously described). However, if a dried bloodstain holds the trace evidence tightly, do not attempt to collect the trace evidence. Carefully cover or protect the trace evidence while packaging the bloodstain. Bloodstained items should always be packaged separately to prevent cross-contamination. The packaging should be sealed at the scene before transportation.

Do not allow bloodstained evidence to be exposed to excessive heat or humidity (see Photo 6.24a&b). If possible bloodstained evidence should be refrigerated, but the dried bloodstained evidence can be stored safely at room temperature and then submitted to forensic laboratories as soon as possible.

Liquid blood samples

If the wet blood is small, then it should be collected with sterilized cotton swabs and then be allowed to air dry. Alternately, covering the stain with a clean 3x5 index card folded into an inverted V-shape or a clean evidence marker can provide protection of the stain or swab while drying. The stain can be collected by the procedure discussed below for dried bloodstains.

If the liquid bloodstain is large, then it may be collected by the following choices of collection procedures:

1   Absorb the liquid blood sample onto sterile cotton swabs. Allow the swatch to dry. The cotton swab must immediately be inserted into a swab box and sealed with evidence tape. Alternatively, bloodstains can be collected onto swatches that are attached to a 3x5 index card at one end, folding the card into a V shape, and inverting the card with the swatch to allow it to dry. Once the absorbed sample has dried, the card may be marked, and placed in an envelope or paper bag.

2   Using a sterile disposable pippet or syringe, collect a portion of the liquid sample and place it into a purple-topped vacutainer test tube. This container is glass and must be protected against breakage. Mark and label the test tube, then place it in a padded or bubbled plastic bag. Seal and mark the bag. *Do not freeze this evidence*, it must be refrigerated. If the large liquid blood sample has begun to coagulate, then the sample should be collected with both the liquid and the clot (as shown in Photo 6.23).

3   If the large wet bloodstain is located on a movable object, for example clothes or bed sheets, then wait until the bloodstain dries. Then place paper in-between layers of the clothing and collect the item carefully to avoid transfer or alteration of the bloodstain pattern. At the secure location the object should be unwrapped and laid out for continued air-drying (as shown in Photos 6.24a and 6.24b). The original packaging should be maintained and used again for re-packaging if possible. If new wrappings

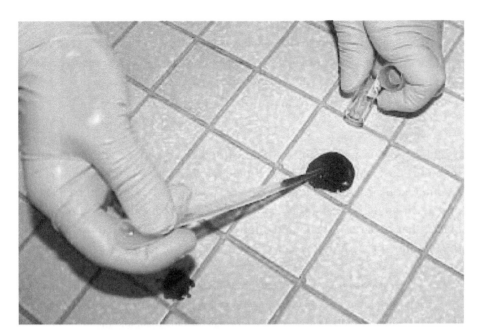

Photo 6.23
Collection of liquid blood at crime scene with disposable pippet.

(a)

Photo 6.24a and b
Depicts bloodstained clothes found outdoors and exposed to adverse elements. These items of evidence should be dry before being packaged.

(b)

and packaging are used then the old materials must be saved as evidence. The blood-stained object should be carefully photographed with scales and without before packaging. Sometimes the object, like bloodstained clothing, must be cut to remove it from the scene, *do not* cut through the bloodstains.

Dried bloodstains

As stated previously, if the object with the dried bloodstain is small and movable, then the entire object should be wrapped in a primary container and placed in an outer, non-airtight container. Whenever possible this is the preferred collection technique however, dried bloodstains are frequently encountered on objects that are large or bulky and cannot be collected intact. In those situations the following procedures for collection should be followed:

1   *Absorbing the bloodstain.* According to the DNA Analysis Board guidelines, dried blood-stains can be absorbed on to sterile cotton swabs or threads. Moisten the swab with saline solution or distilled water. Carefully swab the bloodstain with the swab. Absorb all the stain with a minimum of area consumed. Insert the swab into the swab-drying box. Allow the swab to dry once the stain has been collected. Seal the box and label all the necessary information. A suggested collection kit is shown in Figure 6.6.

2   *Cut out the bloodstain.* If the bloodstain is located on a surface that can easily be removed, then cut an area around the bloodstain including the stain. If the surface material is fragile or easily broken, care should be taken to secure the cutout section to

Photo 6.25

Sterile swab is being used to collect bloodstain from muzzle of firearm used in homicide (courtesy of Cindy Lopes).

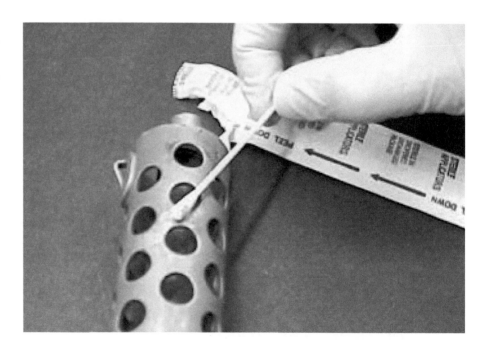

C.D.S. SWAB SAFE®

Collect Dry Store

FORENSIC EVIDENCE COLLECTION KIT

INSTRUCTIONS

1. Open a package of sterile cotton-tipped swabs. Do not touch or handle the cotton at the end of the swabs.

2. Transfer the evidence onto a dry cotton swab or onto a cotton swab lightly moistened with sterile water (use sterile water dispensers provided).

3. Place one or two swabs into perforations #1 and #2 of the foldable drying racks in the CDS SWAB SAFE® box as indicated. Swabs taken from different locations must always be placed into separate boxes.

4. Break swab(s) where indicated. Fold and close the box and seal with three evidence seals. Initial seals. Complete all information as indicated. As an alternative you may design and affix your own adhesive label in order to meet your specific requirements more fully.

5. Place the sealed box in a secure, dry storage area at room temperature. Sealed box(es) can be stored in paper bags (do not use plastic bags).

Orders: Institute of Legal Medicine, University of Bern, Switzerland
Buehlstrasse 20, CH-3012
Tel.: (0041) 31 631 84 12
Fax: (0041) 31 631 84 15
E-mail: dna@ilm.unibe.ch   www.cs.unibe.ch/ilm/
®,© , Pat.pend.

Figure 6.6
Forensic evidence collec-
tion kit for preserving
swabs.
(Courtesy of Dr Manfred
Hockmeister, MD, Insti-
tiute of Legal Medicine,
University of Bern.

prevent breakage of the sample. Wrapping in a druggist's fold made of gauze or sterile swatch material works well (as shown in Photo 6.26).

3 *Scrape the bloodstain.* Use a sterile or clean sharp instrument (razor blade, scapula, or knife blade) to scrape the bloodstain into a druggist's fold of paper. The wrapped sample is then placed in an envelope (as shown in Photo 6.27). This technique can also be used with small gel lifters or fingerprint tape. Static charge will attract the scrapings onto the lifters/tape to efficiently collect the sample. This technique can be difficult to use with very small stains or in windy conditions. Also, it is important to check with the local forensic laboratory to assure the tape used will not inhibit DNA testing.

Photo 6.26

Dried bloodstain collected from an immovable surface (wall). Sample is being cut from wall (courtesy of Holly Dintzner, UNH).

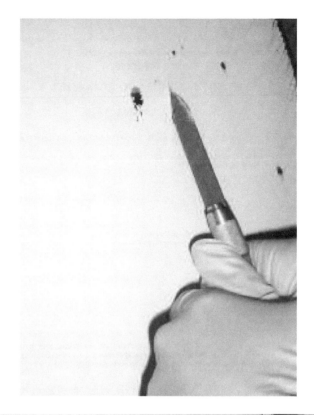

Photo 6.27

Dried bloodstain is scraped from wall using a clean scapula, and scraping blood into druggist fold. Druggist fold is then placed in an envelope (courtesy of Holly Dintzner).

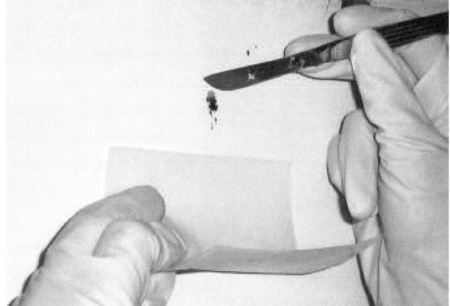

4 *Lifting the bloodstain.* Dried bloodstains can be lifted using selected gel lifters or finger-print tape (use tape that does not interfere with DNA tests). Be sure not to touch the tacky surfaces of the lifters or tape. Place the lifter or tape over the stain and the unstained surface, gently rub, and lift. Cover the tacky surface with the lifter's cover or clear acetate material for the tape. Place in a primary container and outer container like an envelope. Some surfaces may not release the bloodstains, therefore it is a good idea to 'test lift' the surface (as shown in Photo 6.28).

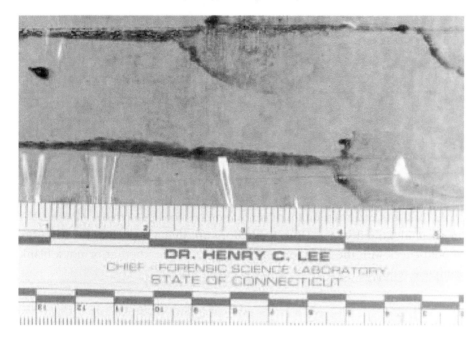

Photo 6.28
Tape-lifting of dried blood-stain sample from an immovable surface.

Known blood samples

Whole blood samples from victims and suspects will be necessary for comparison purposes. The forensic laboratory, in an attempt to individualize unknown bloodstains collected at the crime scene, will do comparison of genetic markers, including DNA. The appropriate known or standard blood sample is whole blood collected from all individuals in the investigation. A nurse or medical personnel collect the whole blood sample into a test tube vacutainer. Generally, blood standards or knowns are collected into purple-top (contains an anti-coagulant EDTA) and red-top (sterile, no additives) vacutainers (as shown in Photo 6.29). The nurse or doctor collecting the blood should mark the tube directly with the name of the source, the date, the time of collection, and the initials of the collector. The tube of blood should then be placed in a padded envelope or box that is sealed, marked and preserved as described previously.

Alternatively, a known blood sample can be collected by a finger-pricking method. Allow the blood drop to absorb onto a standard filter paper sheet.

Photo 6.29

Vacutainers for whole blood standards collection. Top tube (red top) contains no additives and the bottom (purple top) contains EDTA.

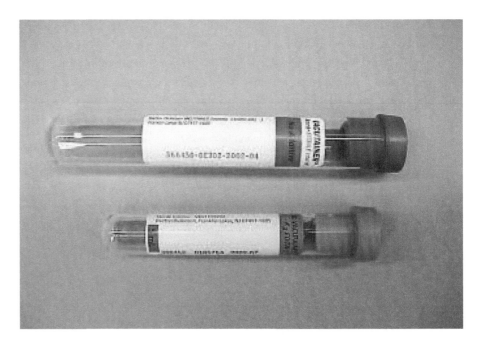

As for blank control samples, it is not required for DNA typing. All the DNA markers identified in the DNA Laboratory are human specific. Investigators should check with the local forensic laboratory to see whether or not a blank sample is required.

SEMINAL STAINS

Seminal stains in crime scene investigations are usually found in the form of rape crisis center or hospital specimens taken from victims of sexual assault or in the form of dried stains on objects at the scene. The dried stains at the crime scene are collected, packaged, and preserved in a similar way to bloodstains as discussed above.

In sexual assault investigations the crime scene investigation will also include the collection of evidence from the victim at the hospital. The victim of a sexual assault should be taken to the hospital for examination as soon as possible. A doctor assisted by a nurse will usually conduct the examination and collect evidence. Forensic training for nurses is available nationwide and should be encouraged for hospital staff. Commercially available or forensic laboratory prepared sexual assault collection kits are used for the collection of the hospital specimens. These kits will include swabs, microscope slides, and various containers for the collection of a variety of evidence from the victim (Photo 6.30).

At the crime scene dried seminal stains may be present on movable and immovable surfaces. Using an ultraviolet light or forensic light sources will

Photo 6.30

Sexual assault evidence collection kit (courtesy of Robin Lunsford, Asheville PD).

facilitate the searching for these stains. Once the possible stains have been found and documented, collection can occur. As with dried bloodstains, a variety of collection methods may be used, but because of the nature of seminal stains (Photo 6.31), minimize handling of suspected stains. The collected evidence should be placed in a primary container – swab box or druggist's fold – followed by an outer, secondary container that is not airtight. The container is

Photo 6.31

Overall view of a sexual assault/homicide victim. Several bite marks were noticed on her right shoulder. Blood stains and seminal evidence were also found on her body and at the scene.

sealed with evidence tape, marked appropriately, and preserved by refrigeration if possible. As with bloodstains, seminal stains may be stored at room temperature for a limited period of time until submitted to the laboratory as soon as possible.

SALIVA, URINE, PERSPIRATION STAINS

The above biological fluid stains are collected, packaged, and preserved in a similar way to the methods and techniques described for blood and seminal stains. Liquid saliva samples should be collected with the sterile cotton swab method. Saliva stains or bite marks can be collected with a moistened swab. Swab the area with a single swab and concentrate it in a limited area. The saliva standard is collected by having the donor place their saliva sample on a filter paper circle in a designated area collects the dried saliva sample. The saliva standard is then placed in a primary container inside an outer envelope that is appropriately marked. The saliva standard is best stored frozen or refrigerated but can be stored at room temperature for a limited period of time before submission to the forensic laboratory.

ACCELERANTS AND FLAMMABLE FLUIDS

The collection, packaging, and preservation of suspected accelerants or flammable liquids at a fire scene should be done as soon as possible. However, the safety and security of the scene should be considered before any attempts of collection are done. Flammable fluids can be present at the fire scene in various forms. They may be absorbed into numerous materials or exist as liquids. The collection method is dependant on the form of accelerant found – absorbed or liquid. Regardless of the form, accelerants are volatile and will evaporate if not properly packaged into airtight containers. See Photo 6.33.

LIQUID SAMPLES

Liquid samples of suspected accelerants found as pools mixed with water or in other containers at the scene (gasoline cans, plastic jugs, etc.) should be placed in an airtight container. Unused, unpainted metal paint cans are best suited for this collection. Glass jars can be used as a last resort if paint cans are not available, but should be transferred as soon as possible. Absorbing the liquids to clean cloth material or even sanitary napkins can be done. The absorbed samples should then be placed in airtight containers – paint cans or KAPAK bags – as soon as possible. The airtight container should have a piece of evidence tape placed over the opening and marked as previously described. Due

(a)

(c)

(b)

Photo 6.32a–c
Dr Lee and fire scene investigators working on an arson scene.
(Courtesy of Sgt Joe Sudol, CT State Police – Office of Fire Marshall.)

Photo 6.33
Proper documentation label on airtight can used for arson evidence collection.

to the nature of arson investigations, the labels placed on possible accelerant evidence must have details about the location where the evidence was found.

ABSORBED ACCELERANT SAMPLES

Burned and unburned carpeting, padding, furniture, bedding, flooring, wood, and walls at fire scenes are examples of materials that may have absorbed accelerants that have been used to start a fire. The forensic laboratory will be able to separate the fire debris and water from the accelerant used. As with suspected liquid accelerants the absorbed accelerant must be packaged into an airtight container. However, the size and location of the absorbing materials may preclude its intact collection. If the object with the absorbed accelerant can be packaged into the paint cans or KAPAK bag in its original condition, then it should be collected intact. If the item is too large or difficult to remove from the scene, then a representative sample containing the accelerant should be collected and placed in the airtight paint can as described above. The fire debris and accelerant should approximately fill only two-thirds of the can's volume. *Do not fill the paint can.*

EXPLOSIVE MATERIAL

Bomb scenes are characterized by mass destruction and unsafe conditions. This destruction and unsafe nature makes searching at bomb scenes very difficult, as discussed in previous chapters. It also makes the collection, packaging and preservation of the physical evidence a difficult task. Generally, physical evidence at bomb scenes consists of explosives, fallout, timers, fuses, and bomb parts. Some of those items can be fragmented. The small size of evidence means that it is often overlooked or missed while searching and collecting. Most guidelines for the collection of evidence at the bomb scene suggest collecting everything. The forensic laboratory is normally given the responsibility for sifting through the scene debris for the explosive residue, ignition devices or other explosion-related materials that will be identified.

QUESTIONED DOCUMENTS

Questioned documents are documents whose origin or authenticity is unknown or is uncertain. Any written material found at the crime scene that falls into this category of physical evidence must be collected (see Photo 6.35). The document in question should never be directly marked, folded or defaced in any manner. Handling of the document should be kept to a minimum. Gloves and forceps should be used for all handling of the document, as illustrated in Photo 6.34. The document should be packaged into a clear plastic bag or envelopes with clear windows on one side.

Photo 6.34

Collection and packaging of item of evidence for questioned document examination (courtesy of Holly Dintzner, UNH).

EXEMPLARS

Various exemplars or standards for comparison purposes are often collected in this type of investigation. There are two types of exemplars for questioned document examinations: requested writings and non-requested writings.

Requested writings are standards that are obtained when the conditions for writing are exactly the same as in the questioned document. For example, the same type of ink, pen, paper and content of a letter are used. The conditions should minimize stress. The requested writing should be repeated at least 10 to 12 times. The writer should never be shown the document in question.

Non-requested writings are exemplars that are obtained from the normal writing activities of the suspected writer. Examples of non-requested writings include cancelled checks, journals, letters, etc. Any written document from the normal course of living is considered a non-requested exemplar. Photo 6.35 consists of three pages of ransom notes found on the staircase in the house. The writing on this note consists of discarded printing. Similar examplars should be collected for comparison.

Exemplars from mechanical writings are those documents that may be type-written, printed or produced by copy machines. Matrix-dot printers also are included in this group of writings. The machine suspected to have been used to make the questioned document should be collected. However if it is not available, then numerous samples from each machine are necessary for laboratory comparison and should be collected. If typewritten or computer printer documents are to be examined, then the ribbon on the typewriter or printer

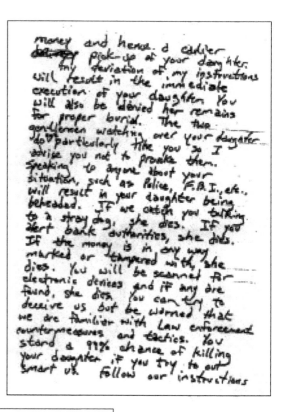

Photo 6.35

Copy of ransom note in
Jon Bennet Ramsey
homicide investigation.

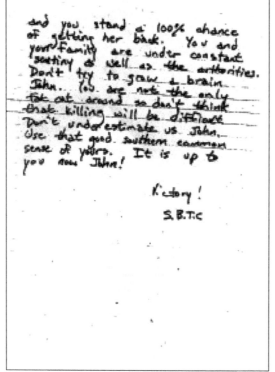

must also be collected.

DRUG EVIDENCE

General crime scene processing procedures should be followed with the collection, packaging, and preservation of drug evidence. At the present time, often criminal investigations will involve some aspect of suspected drug evidence. The suspected drug evidence may be directly involved or indirectly related to the investigation. For example, a homicide investigation may indirectly involve the investigation of illicit drug activity of victims and/or suspects. As such, suspected drug evidence will be found and therefore must be properly collected, packaged, and preserved. The suspected drug evidence will fall into two basic categories: illegal controlled substances or medicinal preparations. Both types of drug evidence must be collected, packaged and preserved as physical evidence.

CONTROLLED SUBSTANCES

All suspected controlled substances should be collected intact, packaged in sealed containers, and preserved for laboratory analysis. If the controlled substance is biological in nature, then it should be packaged in non-airtight containers. For example, marihuana, illicit mushrooms, and opium poppy plants should be packaged in paper bags or wrapped in paper. Never package the live plants in airtight containers! All tablets and capsules should be carefully

Photo 6.36
Drugs and paraphernalia found during a crime scene search.

described in the notes, counted or weighed prior to collection or packaging. The forensic laboratory will sample and test a representative sample from the submitted drug evidence.

Frequently, paraphernalia and other items will be present at a crime scene, as shown in Photo 6.36. These items may have residue coatings and trace quantities of drugs on their surfaces. For this reason, every attempt should be made to preserve these residues on the items from the crime scene. Many times it will be necessary to collect the residue from the items before it is collected and packaged. The scraping or rinsing of these items must be packaged separately from the item itself. If the department procedures prohibit the crime scene investigator to isolate the residue prior to laboratory submission, then the investigator must follow the department procedure. The forensic laboratory must be made aware that residue quantities are remaining on the item. Do not attempt to process the items for fingerprints or other trace evidence if the residual drug substance is present.

MEDICINAL PREPARATIONS

In investigations where prescription vials are found, the labels on the vials provide useful information that can be used in the investigation. The vial labels will often identify the user of the pharmaceutical, the identity of the preparation, the quantity prescribed, when the preparation was filled, and the vial can be easily processed for fingerprints. The contents of the vial can always be compared to the label, too. The vial and its contents should be collected, packaged and preserved in an intact condition using procedures discussed previously in this chapter.

BITEMARK EVIDENCE

When bitemark evidence is discovered at a crime scene, it will need to be preserved as soon as possible. Photographic preservation with scales and without scales is best suited for this type of evidence, as shown in Photo 6.37. The crime scene investigator should consult with a forensic odontologist as soon as possible. Trace quantities of saliva may be present on the bitemark and should be collected and preserved using the swab techniques discussed above.

ENTOMOLOGICAL EVIDENCE

Forensic entomology is based upon the study of the insects that colonize a decaying corpse and the development of their offspring. This process can begin almost immediately after death, as shown in Photo 6.38. The collection and

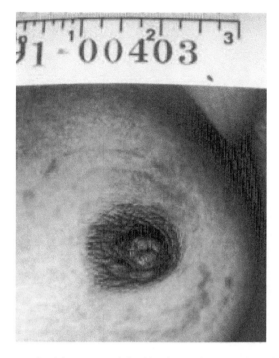

Photo 6.37

Close-up photograph of bitemark impressions located on the breast of a homicide victim. (Courtesy of Dr C. Karazulas.)

analysis of this type of evidence as with all other crime scene evidence depends upon the proper procedures being followed in the correct order.

The proper procedures to follow when collecting entomological evidence follow two steps: obtaining the crime scene information and collection of the insect evidence present. Crime scene information includes a description of the locality, the corpse, and the insect fauna. In order to generate an accurate estimate of how long a body has been exposed to the fauna of an area it is crucial that exacting and detailed information be gathered at the crime scene. The information (as shown below) about the locality should be a recording of the general habitat, the terrain, the vegetation, the type of soil present, and any recent weather patterns.

DESCRIPTION OF LOCALITY

- *General habitat:* any structures or manmade intrusions, swamps, water, fields, or woods.
- *Terrain:* flat land, hillside (direction facing), altitude, plateau, and exact location on topological maps.
- *Vegetation:* all plants growing near the corpse, trees, shrubs, grass and the height of each.
- *Soil type:* sandy, rocky, clay, mud.
- *Recent weather:* include up to five days prior to the earliest date the body could have been exposed, daily highs and lows, amount and type of precipitation, and be aware that the location of the body might be a 'microclimate' that will affect the type and rate of insect infestation.

Photo 6.38a–b

Entomology specimens located on a decaying body. These specimens can be studied to help determine the time of death interval.

The description of the corpse should include identification of the sex, age, weight, and height of the body, type and extent of clothing present, the position of the body, the possible cause of death, and an estimation of the degree of decomposition of the body. Insect fauna description includes the type, number of each type, and the location of each type on, near, or under the body (as shown in Figure 6.7).

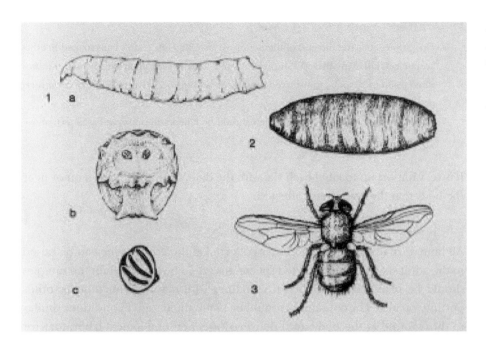

Figure 6.7
Diagram of entomology
specimens found on
decaying bodies.
(Courtesy of Dr Wayne
Lord, FBI.)

COLLECTION OF INSECT EVIDENCE

The techniques for the collection of the insect evidence are dependent on the presence or absence of the corpse and the type of insect present – flying or crawling (see Figure 6.7). When possible, insect collection should be done prior to body removal.

Body present

Flying insects should be collected as soon after the discovery of the body as possible. Any standard insect hand net can be used. Alternatively small sheets of a commercially available sticky paper may be used to passively capture insects heading to or away from the body.

For crawling insects, the immature stages of all different types of insects on, in, or under the body should be collected with a gloved hand. The use of forceps may generate marks or indentations in the insect body that will make future identification difficult. Eggs and a mixed sample of larvae (several hundred) should be collected.

Body removed

The final stages of many fly and beetle larvae will migrate from the body and into the ground immediately under and around it. In order to collect these insects, samples of leaf litter (several handfuls), and soil (several four cubic inch samples), should be collected from the area under the body.

Preservation of any killed specimens

- *Flying insects:* placing the end of the net into a jar with a few cotton balls soaked in ethyl acetate can kill flying insects caught with a net. This will kill them within a few minutes whereupon they can be transferred to vials containing 75% ethanol. Some of the insects may be pinned and stored dry.
- *Immature insects:* all larval stage insects should be killed and preserved as shown above with the adult insects (75% ethanol).

It is very important to label each vial with the date, time and location on or near the body that the insect was collected.

Raising immature specimens to adult stage

All immature insects and egg masses collected at the crime scene can be raised to the adult stage. If the collected specimens are to be reared, then the samples should be placed in a cardboard container with damp vermiculite or other potting soil mix. The containers should be maintained under conditions similar to those found at the body until delivered to an entomological laboratory for further rearing.

CHAPTER 7

LOGIC TREES

GENERAL CONCEPT

A logical and systematic approach to any crime scene is essential to the successful outcome of that investigation. Approaches will vary in particulars depending
upon the nature of the crime, but will share many common features or underlying principles. General classes of crimes can be logically diagramed in a 'logic
tree'. Referring to a relevant logic tree before, during, or immediately after
investigating a specific crime may help prevent some of the many critical
mistakes that have plagued all too many criminal investigations. However, it
should be noted that logic trees are designed to be the foundation for a particular investigation and should not be viewed as all-encompassing or comprehensive detail action plans. An open objective approach must always be maintained.

COMMON FEATURES

RECOGNITION

Recognition of an item or pattern as potential evidence or significance is the
first critical step. Failure to recognize crucial evidence will be detrimental to the
investigation by failing to establish the vital links between the suspect, victim,
crime scene, and physical evidence (four-way linkage theory). Successful recognition is dependent on the ability to not only know what to look for, but where
to look for relevant evidence. The next phase of recognition is the ability to sort
through numerous items and objects and determine those with potential or
actual relevance from those without value. Mastery of this skill is only acquired
through substantial training and experience.

IDENTIFICATION

Identification of various forms of evidence is the next logical approach. Essentially, identification is a classification scheme. We all use forms of classification
in everyday life. Identification involves sorting items based on similar general
characteristics. The more characteristics two or more items have in common
the more complex or discriminatory the identification. Within forensic science,

items are identified by comparing selected class characteristics of an unknown object with similar characteristics of a known standard. For example, a strand of fibrous material may be classified as a hair after microscopic examinations reveal the presence of scale and medulla patterns. If the selected class characteristics are essentially the same between the known and unknown samples, then the unknown object can be classified with the known. Moreover, these two samples could have originated from the same source and further analysis is advisable. If, however, there are significant differences in some of the selected class characteristics, then the unknown sample can be absolutely excluded as coming from the same source, and is not a member of that classification.

INDIVIDUALIZATION

Following identification, forensic scientists will continue with their analysis to determine if a particular sample is unique, even among other members of the same class. This process is referred to as individualization. While not all evidence has sufficient measurable characteristics to obtain individualization, laboratory examinations will be conducted toward that ultimate goal. If subsequent examinations identify any characteristic that is not common between the known and questioned sample then the samples are excluded from having the possibility of originating from a common source. Often, examinations will conclude with a conclusion that the compared objects are similar in all measurable natures, but cannot be conclusively linked to a common origin. Statistical analysis of the significance of the common features may be helpful. Matches in disciplines such as DNA typing will generally be subject to statistical analysis. Statistical interpretations are only as reliable as the database upon which the conclusions were deduced.

RECONSTRUCTION

Reconstruction is the final phase in the process, and is entirely dependent on proper recognition, identification, and individualization of relevant evidence. Reconstruction utilizes investigative information, crime scene information, and laboratory analysis of physical and pattern evidence. The amount of information that a reconstruction may provide is limited by the above factors. The more relevant, accurate the data the greater the chance that a reconstruction exercise will be of value to the investigation. The reconstruction process has been defined as one which involves the use of both inductive and deductive logic, and can be a complex task, linking many types of physical evidence, pattern information, analytical results, investigative information, and other documentary and testimonial evidence into a complete entity. For additional information relating to reconstruction see Chapter 10.

LOGIC TREE APPLICATIONS

Logic trees can be best explained by application to a case scenario. Below are illustrations of logic trees for many of the most commonly encountered types of crime scenes and investigations. In the scenarios presented, consideration of the elements articulated in the logic tree(s) can prevent unnecessary mistakes or oversights, and increase the probability that all relevant evidence has been recognized, identified, and individualized if possible, and subsequent examination results made available for a reconstruction.

THE DEATH SCENE (SEE LOGIC TREE 1)

The naked body of a young female was found in a wooded area adjacent to an apartment complex. Examining the scene from a scene profile perspective may assist in the investigation, and give understanding as to what may have occurred. Is this a primary scene or rather is it a secondary dumpsite? By the body positioning, damage of clothing or lack thereof, external injury pattern, and other general characteristics, it may be possible to distinguish an active from a passive scene, or a crime perpetrated in an organized versus disorganized fashion. Was the overall scene relatively natural in appearance, or was it staged? These questions may be useful in identifying classes of potential suspects.

The actual body is a crime scene unto itself. Identification of the body is a critical first step. Rapid identification is beneficial as the ability to successfully solve a case diminishes over time, and the starting point is often with the victim. If personal belongings, clothing, or markings will not provide identification, other means must be employed. Basic anthropological features will provide class characteristics, and occasionally individualizing characteristics. Dental identification is reliable, but is contingent upon obtaining known dental records. If decomposition is not advanced fingerprint identification is a good option. However, once again there is a need for a known source of prints for comparison. In this case, family members made a positive identification of the young woman's body.

Unfortunately, she was naked; thus there was no evidence associated with her clothing at the scene. Clothing can be examined for any defects or damage, as well as for trace evidence. Her naked body was carefully examined for pattern evidence such as shoeprints, fingerprints, bite marks, or injury patterns revealing information as to possible weapons. Examination of the body was conducted with the assistance of a forensic light source. Further, her body was examined for latent fingerprints by building a tent structure around her body and filling the tent with superglue fumes. If her body had been in advanced stages of decomposition and there was maggot and insect activity, entomologi-

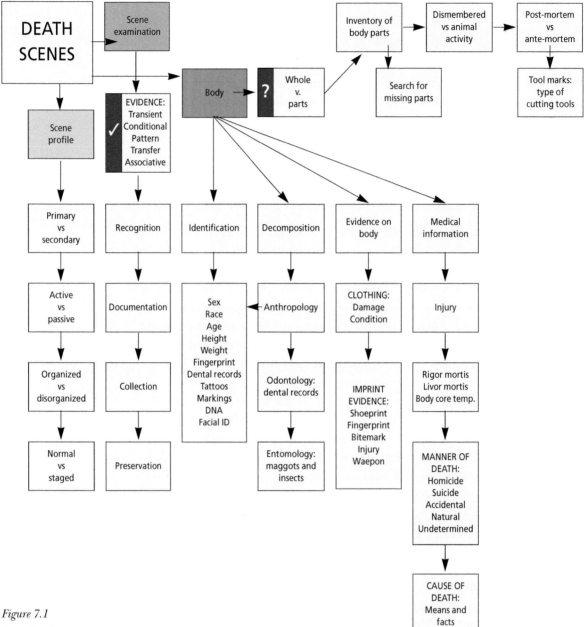

Figure 7.1
Logic Tree 1.

cal samples could be collected and preserved. Entomology samples can be used to help determine the time of death, whether this was a secondary site, and the presence of narcotics or toxic substances in the host (her body).

The medical examiner or coroner should develop relevant information during the initial at site examination as well as during the autopsy. The nature and degree of each injury should be documented, as well as the types of instruments or weapons that may have caused the injuries. The presence of rigor mortis or livor mortis may assist in determining the approximate time of death as well as post-mortem movement of the body. Monitoring changes in the body core temperature are of value for time of death estimations. It is imperative that the environmental temperature and factors be recorded. Ultimately, the medical examination will determine the manner and cause of death.

A critical inquiry is to determine if the body is whole or if some parts have been dismembered or are missing. With skeletal or buried remains a comprehensive bone-by-bone inventory is required. A forensic anthropologist is a tremendous resource for this task. If parts are separated or missing, was it a result of dismemberment or post-mortem animal activity? Were any of the injuries or cuts inflected post mortem versus prior to death? If the body was dismembered carefully preserve the cut ends for further examination as they may provide both class and individual information as to the weapon or tool that caused the cuts, injuries. Scene efforts must continue until all parts are recovered, or it is determined that some of the parts were removed from the site.

Examination of the overall scene included searching areas immediately adjacent to her body, pathways leading to or from her body, surrounding areas (how large an area will depend upon the type of scene, e.g. active versus passive, or on whether any evidence or body parts are unaccounted for). If relevant evidence is located at a remote or separate location, consideration should be given to searching intervening areas or any vehicle or mechanism potentially used to transport the object from the primary scene. As suspects or suspect vehicles are identified, search areas will expand. In this case, preliminary examinations indicated that the deceased female was a homicide victim and likely had been subject to some form of sexual assault. Thus, one would want to reference the sexual assault logic tree as well. Evidence that may be encountered could include transient (odors – cigar smoke), conditional (body exposed to rain), pattern (blood spatter, clothing damage), transfer (semen, hairs and fibers), or associative (tool belt from apartment complex, landlord near body). Regardless of the type of evidence, all evidence must be properly documented, collected, and preserved. Also, be sure to collect all necessary known control samples, such as soil samples from adjacent to the body.

RAPE/SEXUAL ASSAULT (SEE LOGIC TREE 2)

Sexual assault victims can be either living or deceased when police learn of the crime. Investigations with living victims have the distinct advantage of information obtained during an interview with the victim. An effective interview will not

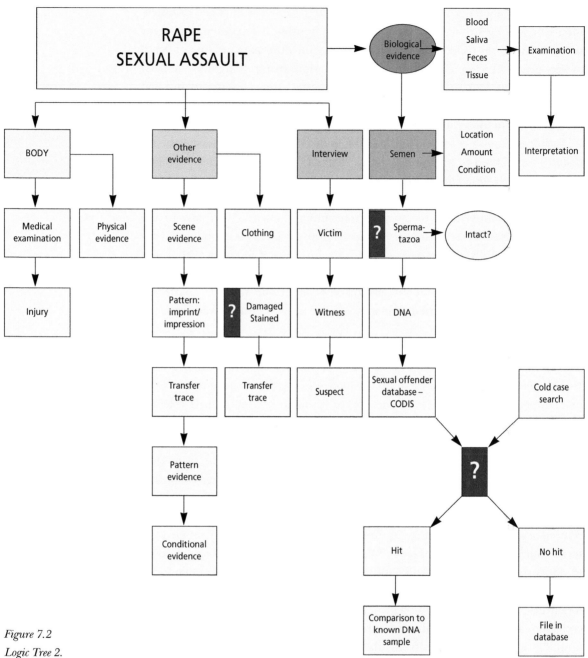

Figure 7.2
Logic Tree 2.

only provide investigative leads, but also can help in the collection of all relevant samples and evidence. However, with alarming regularity rape victims are unable to provide valuable testimony, as they were rendered unconscious by inadvertently drinking a drink spiked with one of the many 'date rape' drugs, such as GHB.

A woman spent the evening at a local restaurant and bar. She recalls having brief conversations with a few individuals, some whom she had not previously met. She vaguely remembers planning to leave, as she had to get up to go to work in the morning. The next thing she remembers is awakening on the ground in an alley, several blocks from the restaurant. Her clothes are disheveled and her nylons are torn and pulled down. She is quite sore and proceeds to find a telephone and call 911. There were no witnesses to this incident.

The victims should be transported to a medical facility as soon as possible. In addition to providing her with medical treatment and evaluation, a timely examination is essential for the collection and preservation of a great deal of evidence associated with sexual assaults. Moreover, most of the date rape drugs metabolize rapidly and are not easily detected in either blood or urine samples. If date rape drugs are suspected an additional blood and urine sample should be obtained and submitted as soon as possible to a qualified laboratory for analysis.

Samples were taken by swabbing the victim's vaginal, anal, oral, and nasal openings. If semen was deposited in any of these openings it will be of great value to the investigation. Identification of intact spermatozoa by a forensic scientist means a recent ejaculation. Also, it is possible to obtain the DNA profile of the offender. If the suspect's DNA is typed the suspect can be identified either by direct comparison with a known blood sample or through a sexual offender (CODIS) database. If the suspect is identified by a CODIS hit then the DNA results are confirmed with a known blood sample obtained by court order or search warrant.

Other body fluids such as saliva, blood, urine, and feces can be encountered in sexual assault cases such as this one. Examination of these body fluids may provide individual genetic information that would include or exclude a potential suspect. Other forms of trace evidence should not be overlooked. Hairs and fibers are common forms of trace evidence in these cases. Trace evidence can provide links between the suspect, victim, and crime scene. In addition to trace evidence, various forms of pattern evidence may be encountered. Fingerprints, shoeprints, bloodstain transfer patterns, vaginal drainage, seminal ejaculation, or bite marks may be present.

The victim's clothing should be carefully examined not only for trace and biological evidence, but also for any tears or signs of damage. Clothing forcibly removed may be torn, stretched, or have buttons or fasteners missing. These findings may indicate a forceful encounter rather than a consensual passive act.

The area where the sexual assault occurred should be treated as a primary crime scene and subjected to a thorough search, documentation, and general processing. As with this scenario, the victim may not recall the exact location.

Thus, several potential sites may have to be searched for evidence that would suggest a sexual assault occurred at that location. Ultra-violet lights and forensic light sources can aid in locating seminal stains and other types of trace or transfer evidence.

SHOOTING SCENES (SEE LOGIC TREE 3)

Shooting scenes can be associated with a variety of cases, most commonly aggravated assaults, homicides, and robberies. Investigation of shooting cases may include gunshot residue and pattern analysis, bullet trajectory reconstruction, microscopic examination and comparison of bullets and cartridge cases; firearms evidence database searches, and weapon registry and record inquiries.

Police responded to a report of a robbery at a service station located on a main road. First responding officers noted that the front glass door had been smashed, apparently with a metal garbage can that was located next to the door. Once inside, officers located the night clerk who was suffering from a gunshot wound to the arm. The clerk stated that after closing time a masked gunman smashed the glass, entered the station and pointed a handgun at him. During a verbal argument, the gunman fired several shots, took cash from the register, and fled in a full-size dark-colored sedan. Medical personnel and x-rays determined that a bullet-like object had entered and remained in the clerk's upper arm.

In addition to shooting-related evidence, shooting scenes should be searched for other types of trace and pattern evidence. Investigators located tire marks in the sand edge of the parking lot, where the clerk indicated the gunman had parked his vehicle. These tire marks were photographed and sketched. In addition a plaster cast was taken to further preserve the tire marks. A subsequent examination of the photographs and cast by laboratory personnel revealed that the tire marks were consistent with a Goodyear brand tire. The metal trash can, glass doorway, and cash register were processed for latent prints with powder dusting techniques. Two latent prints were developed, photographed, and secured onto lifting tape. These prints can be entered into an automated fingerprint identification system.

A search of the scene located two bullet holes, one in the wall directly behind the cash register, and the other in a shelf between the register and adjacent wall. Placing a colored trajectory probe into the bullet hole and extending the trajectory line from the end of the probe with colored line determined trajectories of each of bullet. These trajectories were documented with photographs and measurements, including determinations of the angles of incidence. The wall and wood containing the bullets were cut free and submitted to the laboratory. At the laboratory the bullets were carefully extracted from the material in a

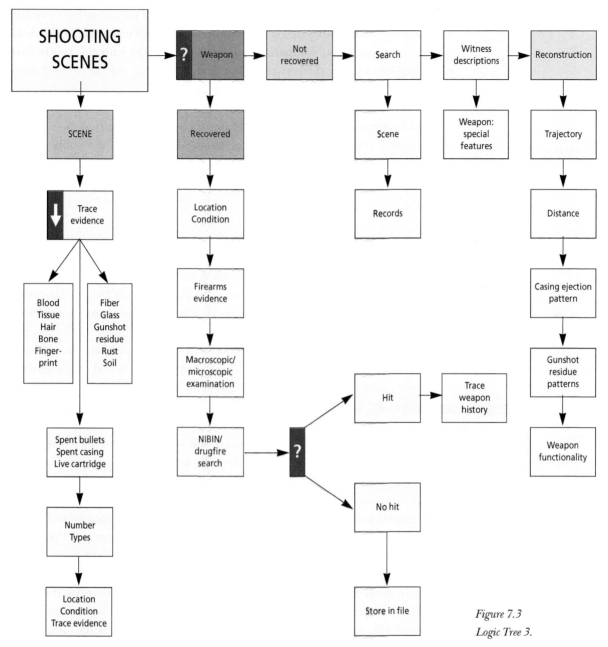

Figure 7.3
Logic Tree 3.

manner that would not harm the striations or any trace evidence located on the bullets. Despite a thorough search, no cartridge casings were located at the scene.

During the crime scene search a video monitoring system was discovered. The videotape was reviewed and the actual robbery and gunman were depicted on the tape. The clothing and characteristics of the gunman, as viewed in the tape, were helpful in identifying the gunmen during a neighborhood canvass by investigators. A search and seizure warrant was obtained for the suspect's home, and a revolver with obliterated serial numbers was found inside the home. Subsequent test firing and comparison of the known bullet with the two bullets recovered from inside the service station concluded that they were fired from the same weapon, the suspect's .357 magnum. Further laboratory analysis was able to raise the obliterated serial numbers. A weapons registry inquiry traced the gun back to an individual in a neighboring town who reported the revolver stolen over a year ago. Ultimately, the suspect confessed to the robbery and shooting as well as to the theft of the revolver during a burglary.

BOMBING, EXPLOSION, FIRE SCENES (SEE LOGIC TREE 4)

Fire and explosive scenes can be challenging scenes in which to locate physical evidence due to the destructive nature of fires and explosions. However, if a comprehensive, analytical approach is taken with these scenes valuable information can be obtained from the scene. This logic tree will help investigators address the critical components necessary for a successful arson/explosive scene investigation.

Los Angeles fire department responded to a late night fire alarm at a large manufacturing plant, during the month of January. Flames had fully engulfed the entire north end of the factory. Dense black smoke was bellowing from the active fire. In accordance with standard protocols, fire investigators also responded to the scene. Soon after their arrival at the scene, and after basic scene photographs recording the spread of fire and smoke had been taken, fire investigators observed a set of footprints in the snow leading to the north end of the building as well as away from the building. These footprints came from the general direction of a large housing development adjacent to the factory. After photographing the footprints, several of the footprints were treated with snow seal wax and subsequently cast with dental stone. Observations at the scene indicated that the footprints were consistent with large size, 12–14, work boots.

Once the fire was suppressed, investigators located glass debris on the outside of the north end of the building, near the end of the footprint trails. An additional Molotov cocktail (capped glass bottle filled with flammable substance, with a partially burned cotton strip tied around the bottle) was found lying against the brick faced, badly charred building exterior. Subsequent internal searches located additional glass fragments on the floor, adjacent to a window opening in the same general area at the north end of the building.

A major component of fire/explosive scene investigation is to determine the cause and origin of the fire/explosion. Causes include natural, accidental, and planted (arson) mechanisms. Generally, planted determinations are made after eliminating natural and accidental causes, as well as finding some form of

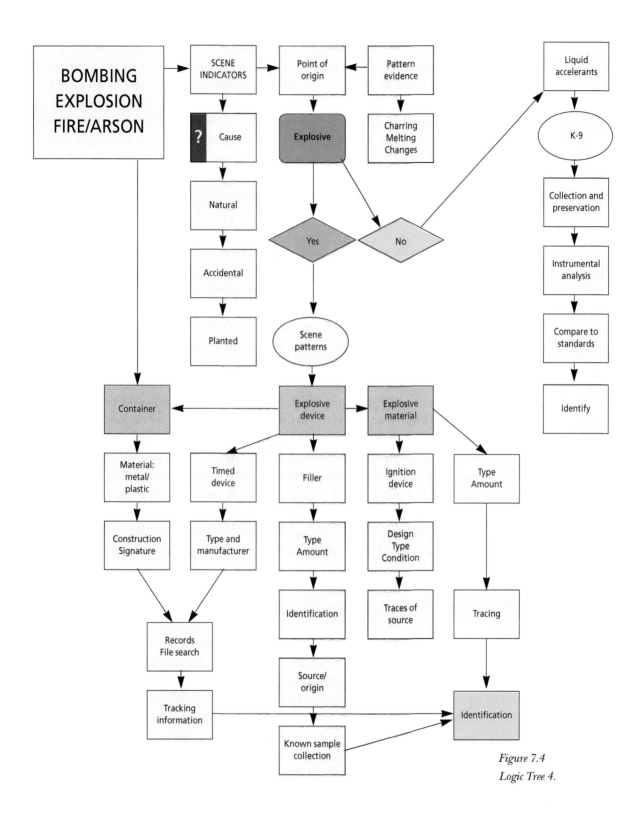

Figure 7.4
Logic Tree 4.

physical evidence or investigative information to support a theory of arson.

Identification of the point of origin is preliminarily determined by studying burn patterns. In this case the most significantly fire-damaged portion of the building was in the area where the glass fragments and Molotov cocktail had been located. A trained canine was brought through the fire scene to identify accelerant residues. The canine alerted (a term indicating that the canine's olfactory senses detected accelerant residues) to areas adjacent to the glass fragments inside the building as well as those glass fragments adjacent to the exterior of the building. The glass fragments as well as samples of the charred debris collected from the alert sites were placed in sealed clean metal paint cans.

These items were submitted to the laboratory for analysis. The debris was analyzed by gas chromatography–mass spectroscopy and revealed a mixture of low to medium and medium-high petroleum distillates, consistent with a mixture of gasoline and lamp oil.

Analysis of any explosive device, such as a Molotov cocktail, includes three basic areas: examination of the container, explosive device, and explosive material. The container, a glass bottle was processed for fingerprints and trace evidence. The collected broken glass fragments were reassembled and were then processed for latent prints. Superglue fuming, followed by fluorescent powder dusting, was the method for latent print development. Two latent prints were developed. These latent prints were entered into an AFIS (Automated Fingerprint Identification System) and a match occurred. These prints identified a tenant of the adjacent housing complex who had an extensive criminal history, including a prior conviction for reckless burning. The explosive device consisted of a cotton wick, which provided no additional investigative leads. Further analysis of the accelerant mixture showed similar instrumental properties to samples of lamp oil seized during a subsequent search of the suspect's apartment.

DRUGS AND POISONING (SEE LOGIC TREE 5)

Deaths and serious illnesses associated with drug usage or poisoning can be overlooked or poorly investigated unless investigators consider all relevant factors, and the type of valuable investigative information that can be obtained if the investigation is conducted logically.

Morristown police officers as well as local emergency medical technicians responded to a medical assist call at a private residence. The victim's husband reported that upon waking he found his wife unconscious on the bathroom floor, where she was still located. There was vomitus in the bathtub and on the bathroom floor. Several hours later, after being stabilized at the hospital, the

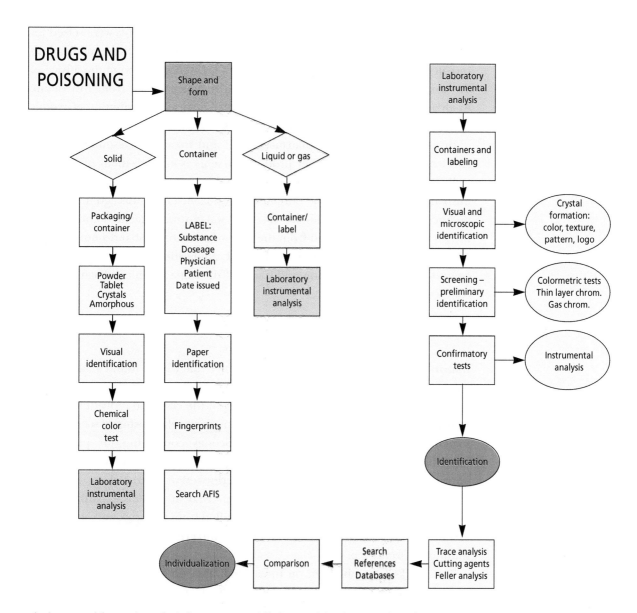

Figure 7.5
Logic Tree 5.

victim was able to give a brief statement. All she could relay was that she was not feeling well and she had been feeling sick on and off for the past several months. Toxicological analysis of her blood at the hospital revealed a blood alcohol content of 0.03%. Standard acetic and basic drug screens were all negative.

Back at the house, investigators continued their search with the husband's consent and located four vials of medicine in the bathroom cabinet. One vial was prescription blood pressure medication, prescribed to the victim's husband. Another prescription container was for the victim, and was an anti-depressant medication. There was also an over-the-counter allergy medication as well as a bottle of cough syrup. These vials and their contents were seized for laboratory analysis. Comprehensive toxicological testing of these medications revealed trace amounts of arsenic in the cough syrup. Following the advice of the toxicologist, investigators obtained head hair samples from the victim. Analysis of these hair samples revealed the presence and distribution of arsenic that was consistent with long-term, low dosage arsenic poisoning.

Investigators researched pharmaceutical and toxicology resource material and learned that among other products, arsenic is an ingredient in commercially available rat poisons. Investigators obtained a credit history for the husband and learned that he purchased rat poison 11 months ago through an on-line garden supply wholesaler. A search warrant was executed and some of the rat poison was recovered from the basement of the husband's home. Additional instrumental analysis demonstrated similarities between other minor components of the rat poison and traces of the same chemicals located in the cough syrup.

IMPRINTS (SEE LOGIC TREE 6)

Imprint evidence is a valuable type of evidence that can be found at almost any type of crime scene. Recognition and proper documentation of imprint evidence is essential. A good understanding of the class and individual characteristics associated with imprint evidence, and their relationship to scene reconstruction cannot be over-emphasized. Scenes containing, or potentially containing, imprint evidence must be logically analyzed or it is likely that imprint as well as other evidence will be overlooked or destroyed.

One Monday morning bank officials arrived at the local bank only to discover that the ATM machine had been pulled from the brick wall of the bank at some time during the weekend. Detectives and crime scene investigators were summoned to the scene.

Tire marks were observed on the asphalt adjacent to the hole in the bank where the ATM had been located. These skid marks were consistent with a vehicle spinning its tires, indicating that a vehicle was used to pull the ATM machine from the bank wall. These tire tracks were photographed and measured. Measurements were taken of the wheelbase between the marks as well as the width of each mark. As the marks curved, marks associated with each of the four tires were observed. One of the tires was different to the other three.

The interior bank floor in the area of the missing ATM unit had examined a light film of dust. Investigators examined this area of the floor with an oblique lighting technique. Footwear patterns were observed in the dust. A forensic light source was used to further examine these two-dimensional footprint impressions. Three distinctively different footwear patterns were observed. An

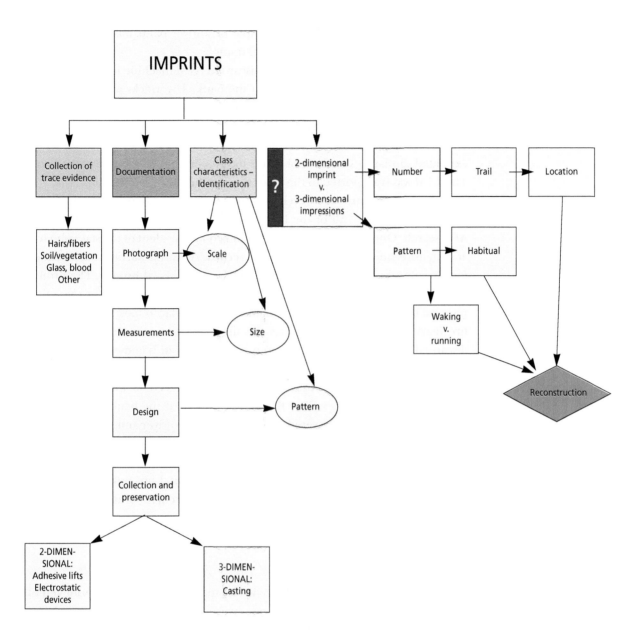

electrostatic lifter device was used to capture the footwear imprints. Detectives learned that several of the bank employees had walked through this area before notifying police. Known inked impressions were taken of their footwear. It was readily apparent that one of the dust impressions had class characteristics consistent with a bank employee's footwear.

Examination of the remaining steel frame that held the ATM unit in place revealed sliding pry marks, and several round indentations consistent in shape with the head of a large hammer. These marks were photographed and silicon

Figure 7.6
Logic Tree 6.

casts of the marks were taken. A sample of known paint was taken from an adjacent, undamaged area of the metal frame.

Ten days later a hiker located the discarded ATM machine in a wooded area located approximately five miles from the bank. Tire tracks were observed in the dirt roadway. These tire marks exhibited similar class characteristics to the tire marks observed at the bank. Sliding pry marks and numerous round indentations were observed on the face and edges of the ATM machine. These marks exhibited similarities to the tool marks located on the ATM frame at the bank. The ATM was transported to the laboratory for further examination.

Latent fingerprints were developed using superglue fuming and fluorescent fingerprint powders. All of the lifted latent fingerprints were submitted to an AFIS search. One of the latent prints was linked to a resident of the state who had an extensive burglary/larceny criminal record. A search warrant was obtained for the suspect's home and registered vehicle, a 1997 Ford Bronco. The Bronco had three standard tires and one different style tire. Examination of these tires revealed both class and individual characteristics similar to those observed at the tire marks at the bank, as well as the tire impressions in the dirt near the discarded ATM machine. Also, a large screwdriver and hammer were found in the rear of the Bronco. Subsequent laboratory examination of the tools concluded that they were consistent with having produced the tool marks located on the ATM machine as well as the piece of frame at the bank. Further, trace amounts of paint were recovered from both the screwdriver and hammer. Instrumental analysis of these paint transfers demonstrated similar chemical and microscopic characteristics to the sample of known paint taken from the bank frame.

In this scenario, imprint evidence was instrumental not only in developing investigative leads, but also provided the necessary corroborating evidence to obtain an arrest and conviction.

ENHANCEMENT METHODS (SEE LOGIC TREE 7)

Pattern evidence is valuable evidence whose importance is often overlooked or underrated. In addition, even when investigators painstakingly search for pattern evidence they can leave an active violent crime scene with minimal usable pattern evidence. Even very bloody scenes can be a challenge to find quality pattern evidence that will yield individualizing characteristics. However, a logically constructed search process and the use of enhancement reagents can dramatically increase the quantity and quality of pattern evidence recovered from a crime scene.

A 72-year-old female was found face down on her kitchen floor, Thanksgiving morning, by her nephew. She had expired as a result of numerous (27) stab wounds to her chest.

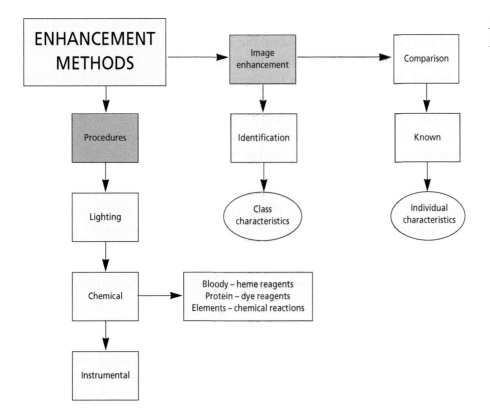

Figure 7.7
Logic Tree 7.

Investigators immediately became suspicious of the lack of blood present on the kitchen floor. With some many stab wounds there should have been considerable pooling. This led investigators to suspect that a majority of the blood had been cleaned up. Thus, a decision was made to apply bloody print enhancement reagents to the floor in an effort to locate any trace amounts of residual blood. A tetramethylbenzidine (TMB) spray reagent was applied. Seven imprint patterns were developed. Two discernible patterns were identified. One footwear pattern had a parallel line construction. The other pattern was consistent with a sneaker pattern. These enhanced footwear patterns were photographed with and without scales. These patterns were entered into a footwear pattern database back at the lab. The sneaker pattern was identified as being consistent with a Puma brand size 12 sneaker. The other pattern was found to be consistent with a size 10 work boot, similar to several different boot manufacturers.

Detectives decided to conduct a search of all trash canisters in the area. In a trash dumpster located behind a 24-hour convenience store, two miles from the crime scene, a pair of size 12 Puma sneakers were located. A few blood-like droplets were observed on the top of the sneakers, and reddish brown transfer smears were observed on the sole of the sneakers. Subsequent laboratory examination also revealed a Negroid body hair. STR DNA analysis was conducted on the blood located on the Puma sneakers. The extracted blood yielded genetic profiles consistent with the victim's known blood.

During the robbery murder the perpetrators stole the victim's wallet and credit cards, some jewelry, and a VCR machine. During an interview with detectives the victim's daughter mentioned that the stolen VCR had been malfunctioning for the previous week. Detectives also decided to keep the victim's credit cards active and trace any activity on the account. Two days later, at an electronics store in a neighboring state, a telephone order was made for a new VCR using the victim's credit card. Detectives arranged to make a controlled delivery of the VCR. After delivering the VCR detectives obtained a search warrant and searched the suspect's apartment. Several of the victim's credit cards were recovered. Also, a pair of size 10 work boots were located and seized. Subsequent laboratory examination revealed trace amounts of blood on these work boots that yielded a STR DNA profile consistent with the victim's genetic profile.

As demonstrated in this case, enhancement reagents can help investigators locate that critical missing evidence. Besides bloody print enhancement reagents, enhancement reagents are available for proteins, other components of latent print residues, as well as gunshot residue (as shown in Figure 7.7).

CHAPTER 8

FIELD TESTS AND ENHANCEMENT REAGENTS

INTRODUCTION

Field test and enhancement reagents often provide valuable assistance in crime scene processing and laboratory examinations. These field test and enhancement reagents are designed for the following applications:

1　Assisting in the recognition and identification of physical evidence.
2　Enhancement of pattern evidence found at a crime scene or on items of evidence, clothing, or a body.
3　Assisting in interpretation and reconstruction of events.
4　Identification of samples to be collected for further laboratory examination.
5　Screening evidence and materials at a crime scene so valuable resources are not wasted on unwarranted laboratory analysis.
6　Providing investigators with preliminary results in a timely manner, such as the fact that blood-like material was present, or that a certain substance is possibly a controlled substance.
7　Providing a general indication of the existence of a chemical, physical or biological substance.
8　Providing investigative leads.

Generally, these field tests are capable of detecting biological materials or chemical substances. To be effective and useful in field applications these tests and reagents should be relatively easy to use in non-laboratory environments, require little specialized equipment, be as sensitive and specific as possible, and utilize only small amounts of sample during testing. Results obtained from a field test should also be easy to interpret in a short period of time. Many of these tests are equally valuable for forensic scientists as preliminary or screening tests during the examination of physical evidence within the laboratory environment.

As valuable as these tests and reagents may be to investigators and forensic scientists, there are certain precautions that must be heeded. Field tests are designed for screening purposes and should not be utilized in lieu of laboratory analysis and confirmation testing. As a general rule, if the amount of available

Photo 8.1a–e (opposite)

Photographs from the State v. Richard Crafts 'wood chipper' murder trial.
(a) Crime scene supervisor standing next to the wood chipper rented by the suspect and believed to have been used to shred portions of his wife's body.
(b) Close-up view of fibers, hairs, wood, and tissue debris located along the river bank where the suspect was seen operating the wood chipper during night hours.
(c) Dr Henry Lee, Medical Examiner, and detectives conduct an experiment with wood chipper, to determine the distribution of flesh and bone material (a slaughtered pig was placed in the wood chipper) and obtain known fragments for microscopic analysis of the tool marks on bone, associated with the chipper.
(d) One of the largest pieces of tissue located along the river bank. This specimen was the upper portion of a human finger.
(e) Close-up view of a fingernail with nail polish. A sample of this polish was instrumentally analyzed and compared to a sample of nail polish recovered from the victim's home.

sample for testing is so minute that there may not be sufficient material for a full array of testing, then, if at all possible, avoid field tests so as to preserve the sample for laboratory analysis.

Training a crime scene investigator to use the majority of these reagents is not difficult or complex. Following a simple sequential procedure with prepared reagents is all that is required with most tests. The interpretation of testing results is often straightforward and simple, such as observing a color shift or formation or fluorescence. However, some results require interpretation by more experienced or trained personnel. Unfortunately, the novice or relatively inexperienced personnel using these tests may not even be aware that they are observing a false positive or problematic result and thus can reach an erroneous conclusion. One way to minimize this problem is to require formalized training in the use of these reagents and testing procedures before allowing their application to actual case or crime scene applications. This training should include considerable practical exercises and interpretation of results. Ideally, only trained personnel are allowed to use field tests and enhancement reagents. Despite the simplicity of the basic procedure, it is helpful to have an understanding of the underlying chemical reaction or mechanism.

However, this form of presumptive testing should not be taken too lightly as results of field tests may provide important investigative leads. For example, in an investigation into the disappearance of a wife, investigators received information that the suspect was operating a large wood chipper along a river bank during the general time frame when his wife was reported missing. In addition, extensive cleaning of bed sheets and removal of carpet and furniture had also taken place after his wife's disappearance. Luminol and tetra-methyl benzidine reagents were sprayed onto washed bed sheets, towels, bathtub, and floors. A large number of samples yielded positive results. Subsequently, the actual wood chipper rented by the suspect was seized as evidence and systematically disassembled. No visible signs of blood, tissue or suspicious trace material were found. Fragments of hair and fiber evidence were recovered. Presumptive tests for the presence of blood were conducted in the blade and bearing assemblies, yielding positive results for blood. Although there was insufficient sample available to conduct any confirmatory testing due to extensive cleaning these results provided detectives with valuable investigative leads. Photos 8.1a–e depict investigators and laboratory scientists working together as a team searching for physical evidence.

In addition, tissue and blood crusts were located on pieces of a disassembled chain saw recovered from a river bottom. Also, numerous items were located on the riverbank. Fifty-six bone chips, a tooth, a portion of a finger and attached nail, and 2660 hairs were among the recovered items. These findings were instrumental in the conviction of her husband for murder.

(a)

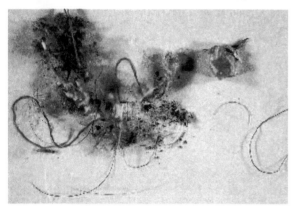

(b)

(c)

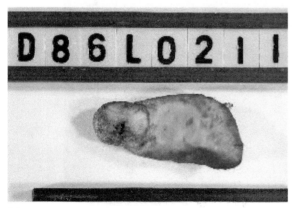

(d)

(e)

Enhancement reagents are used to visualize and to increase the contrast of transfer patterns such as fingerprints, footprints, shoe imprints, and other physical patterns. In some instances, enhancement reagents can be used for dual purposes: presumptive tests for biological substances, and the development of physical patterns.

For example, in the late spring, the nude body of a female was found face down on the kitchen floor in her apartment. Her former boyfriend discovered the body and reported his findings to the police. He informed investigators that he only touched her arm to check for vital signs and did not disturb the scene. The victim's throat was cut with a sharp instrument. Blood enhancement

(a)

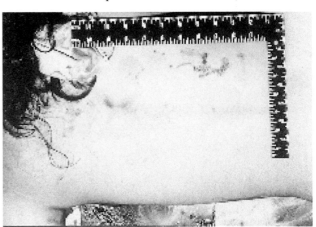

(b)

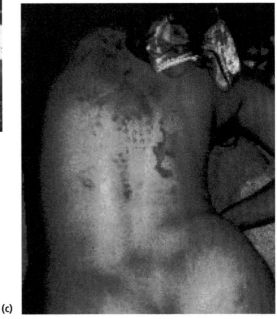

(c)

reagents were sprayed onto her back, and three partial shoe imprints were developed. These imprints contained circular dot sole patterns; designs which resembled the 'Puma' brand of sneakers. Investigators found when checking the boyfriend's shoes that they had a similar type sole pattern. In addition, trace amounts of blood were found in the groves of the sole. This information indicated that the boyfriend had given a false statement. It is more likely that he stepped on the victim's back and cut her throat. Subsequently, this evidence induced the boyfriend to confess to the murder.

FIELD TEST REAGENTS

Numerous field test reagents have been reported. In general, the most commonly used field tests can be classified into the following categories.

I   Tests for the presence of blood
1   Phenolphthalin (Kastle-Meyer)
2   Leucomalachite green (LMG)
3   Ortho-tolidine
4   Luminol
5   Tetra-methylbenzidine (TMB)
6   Fluorescin

II Tests for the presence of body fluids
1   Semen – acid phosphatase tests
2   Saliva – amylase tests
3   Urine – creatinine, urea tests
4   Fecal material – urobilinogen
5   Gastric contents – gastric acid

III Test for gun shot residue (GSR) and explosives

IV Tests for controlled substances and drugs

TESTS FOR THE PRESENCE OF BLOOD

Presumptive blood tests are designed to detect minute traces of heme or heme-like derivatives. Heme, a principle component of hemoglobin, is a ferrous-bearing molecule located within a red blood cell. This hemoglobin molecule is responsible for carrying oxygen through the body. The ferrous element is generally in a reduced state. The presumptive blood tests discussed hereafter are designed to detect the presence of the reduced ferrous molecule through

Photo 8.2 (opposite)

(a) Dr Lee examines the floor where the female victim was found for pattern and trace evidence.

(b) Close-up view of the victim's back, depicting an area where a faint pattern was detected.

(c) View of the victim's back after the treatment with a Bloody Print Enhancement Reagent (TMB). Note the developed footwear imprint.

an oxidation-reduction reaction that will convert a colorless reagent to a colored by-product. With Luminol, a positive test is indicated by fluorescence rather than a visual color formation. The oxidation-reduction reaction, catalyzed by heme, may be written generally as:

$$AH_2 + H_2O_2 \xrightarrow{\text{Heme}} A + 2H_2O$$

This reaction can also be expressed as:

$$\text{oxidizable chemicals} + \text{hydrogen peroxide} \xrightarrow{\text{Heme (peroxidase)}} \text{Oxidized}$$
$$\text{(colorless)} \qquad \text{compound and water} \qquad \text{(colored)}$$

A positive reaction, as indicated by the formation of a colored product, merely indicates the possibility of the presence of blood. There are many substances that will also catalyze this same reaction such as plant peroxidase or strong chemical oxidants. Therefore, none of these presumptive tests should be considered as conclusive as to the presence or absence of blood. Both false positives and false negatives are possible. In addition, a positive test result will yield no information as to the species of the blood sample or any individualizing genetic markers. However, in most cases if the testing reagents have been tested on known standards of blood prior to testing the suspected stains, the lack of a reaction on the unknown stain can be deemed as meaning that blood is absent.

False positives occur when a 'positive' reaction occurs within the presence of blood. These results can occur for a variety of reasons. Heme's role in the test reaction is to catalyze the reaction, thus catalyzing the oxidation-reduction reaction to occur rapidly – generally within a few seconds after the testing reagents have been applied to the suspect sample.

Since the basis for these tests is the formation of a colored complex as the result of an oxidation-reduction reaction, the presence of a strong oxidizing agent may rapidly complete the oxidation reaction without the presence of heme, thus mimicking a positive tests result. Many household cleaning agents contain strong oxidizing agents. In addition, the presence of plant peroxidases will yield false positives. Many common fruits and vegetables contain sufficient peroxidases to yield false positives, e.g. apples, horse radish, broccoli, etc. Many of the false positive reactions can be identified during the presumptive testing procedure if the examiner closely follows the prescribed procedure, carefully observes any changes and the exact point in the reaction of these changes, and has conducted extensive laboratory testing on known standards, so as to have a good basis for understanding how the reaction should proceed in the presence of blood.

False negatives are less common but even more problematic in that an actual blood sample may be overlooked or left at the scene. These results occur when there is some interference with the oxidation-reduction reaction. A common culprit is the presence of a strong reducing agent, resulting in the prevention of significant delay of the oxidation reaction, giving a colored formation. The most effective remedy is to collect additional samples for subsequent laboratory testing anytime a negative test result occurs and it was not anticipated or the examiner believes there is any possibility that blood samples are actually present.

Because of the possibility of false positives and false negatives with presumptive reagents, confirmatory testing is necessary. Confirmatory tests are conducted at the laboratory and generally consist of either a microcrystalline tests or immunological tests. With microcrystalline tests, such as Takayama or Teichman, chemical reagents only react with heme components of the blood and produce distinctly characteristic crystals. The immunological test uses anti-human hemoglobin serum to react with human hemoglobin and forms a white precipitin line. This test also confirms that the blood is of human origin.

General procedure for blood tests

Despite the variety of testing reagents available, a general procedure could be used for all types of presumptive tests for blood.

1 Swab a small amount of the suspect stain on a clean cotton swab moistened with saline.
2 Swab a non-stained area from an adjacent area of the suspect stain, on the same surface as a control swab.
3 Add two drops of the testing reagent, e.g. Kastle-Mayer reagent, onto each of the swabs.
4 Wait 30 seconds. If a color transformation occurs at this point in the reaction it is indicative of a false positive associated with the presence of a strong oxidizing agent or peroxidase activity.
5 Add two drops of hydrogen peroxide (3%) to each swab.
6 Depending upon the particular testing reagent a predictable colored complex will form within a brief period of time; ranging from almost immediately to within 15 seconds.

Note: The colored formation must be observed within the prescribed time frame as these same result can be observed in time, even absent the presence of heme or other catalyzing agents. Photo 8.3 shows a positive reaction with Kastle-Mayer reagent.

The lack of color formation is generally indicative of the absence of blood in the suspect sample. However, it is possible that chemical interferences resulted in a false negative.

Quality control testing is necessary and should be conducted with known blood samples on every new batch of test reagents, and periodically so as to verify that the reagents are working as expected. Many of these reagents deteriorate over time. Some of the reagents will change color, demonstrating the deteriorated state, and should be discarded. For example, o-tolidine when fresh is a light straw-colored solution; when deteriorated, o-tolidine will turn dark brown.

Photo 8.3

Photo demonstrates the pink color formation which is indicative of a positive Kastle-Meyer test for the presence of blood. A sample of the reddish-brown stain was swabbed from the knife blade.

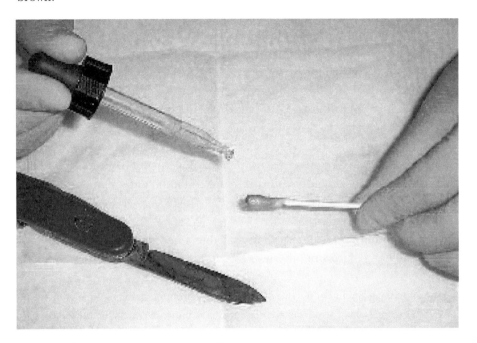

Commonly used presumptive testing reagents

Since the peroxidase-like activity of the blood was first discovered in 1857, many chemicals were discovered which could be used as an oxidizable substance for the catalytic color tests. Among these chemicals, in the past, Benzedine and O-tolidine were frequently used. These two chemicals are colorless in their reduced form, and they will turn to dark blue in their oxidized form, in the presence of a catalyst such as heme. Due to their high sensitivity and highly visible color transformation, benzidene and O-tolidine have been widely used. However, benzidine was found to be an extremely hazardous and carcinogenic substance. Breathing its vapors or touching the chemical may lead to cancer. In 1974, the Occupational Safety and Health Administration (OSHA) banned its use and manufacture in the United States. O-tolidine has been reported to induce neoplasm. It has been considered as a potential carcinogen. OSHA has limited the exposure of O-tolidine to 5 ppm per eight hours and the vapor concentrations are limited to 22 mg/ml.

Different chemicals have different sensitivities, different reactions to alkaline or acidic conditions, and different color transformations. The following are some commonly used chemical presumptive tests for blood:

1 *Phenolphthalin (Kastle-Meyer)*

Sensitivity: 1:100,000

Year introduced: 1901

Positive reaction: A positive reaction is a pink to red color on the swab within 15 seconds.

Reagent preparation:

Stock solution:

Phenolphthalein	2 g
Potassium hydroxide	20 g
Distilled water	100 mL

Reflux the stock mixture with 20 grams of powderized zinc for two hours until the solution becomes colorless.

The stock solution should be stored in a dark bottle and refrigerated with some zinc added to keep it colorless.

Working solution:

Phenolphthalein stock	20 mL
Ethanol	80 mL

2 *Leucomalachite green (LMG)*

Sensitivity: 1:20,000

Year introduced: 1904

Positive reaction: A positive reaction is a greenish-blue color that will appear almost immediately on the area of the swab containing blood.

Reagent preparation:

Leucomalachite green	0.1 g
Sodium perborate	3.2 g
Glacial acetic acid	66 mL
Distilled water	33 mL

3 *Ortho-tolidine*

Sensitivity: 1:100,000

Year introduced: 1912

Positive reaction: A positive reaction is indicated by an intense blue color.

Reagent preparation:

O-tolidine	1.6 g
Ethanol	40 mL
Glacial acetic acid	30 mL
Distilled water	33 mL

4 *Luminol*

Sensitivity: 1:5,000,000

Year introduced: 1937

Positive reaction: This reagent is sprayed onto the area to be checked for the presence of suspected bloodstains, but it must be viewed in total darkness. In a positive reaction, bloodstains will luminesce within five seconds. The luminol test works best to discover an area where an attempt has been made to clean up blood, thus the sample is fairly dilute.

Reagent preparation:

Solution I:

3-Aminophthalhydrazide (luminol)	0.1 g
Distilled water	50 mL
Ethanol	20 mL

Solution II:

Sodium carbonate	0.5 g
Sodium perborate	0.7 g
Distilled water	30 mL

Immediately before use mix solutions I and II.

5 *Tetramethylbenzideine (TMB)*

Sensitivity: 1:1,000,000

Year introduced: 1974

Positive reaction: If blood is present the swab should turn a greenish-blue color. This reagent can be mixed in a collodion suspension and used as a bloody print enhancement reagent, sprayed onto both horizontal and vertical surfaces.

Reagent preparation:

Acetate buffer:

Sodium acetate	5 g
Glacial acetic acid	43 mL
Distilled water	50 mL

Tetramethylbenzidine (TMB)

3,3',5,5' tetramethylbenzidine	0.4 g
Acetate buffer	20 mL

Dissolve 0.2 grams of TMB into 10 mL of acetate buffer. The mixture is thoroughly mixed for five minutes. The solution is then filtered to remove any undissolved particles. TMB solution should be stored in a brown reagent bottle and could be kept in the refrigerator for six months.

For information on using as a collodion mixture see the bloody print enhancement reagent caption below.

6 *Fluorescin*

Sensitivity: 1:500,000

Year introduced: 1979

Positive reaction: intense green fluorescence

Reagent preparation: Fluorescin can be prepared from fluorescein in the same way that phenolphthalin is prepared from phenolphthalein.

Effects of presumptive tests on subsequent serological/DNA testing

While presumptive tests are an extremely valuable screening or searching tool for blood evidence they do not supplant the need for subsequent more comprehensive confirmatory or DNA testing.

Unfortunately, any testing which requires the application of a chemical or foreign substance to the suspected sample area may interfere with subsequent testing procedures. These presumptive reagents may have adverse effects on species determinations, ABH antigen, isoenzyme typing, or RFLP DNA typing. In general, many of the testing reagents had some detrimental or destructive effects on subsequent testing; therefore, if possible, avoid direct application of these potentially harmful chemicals to dried bloodstain evidence. Yet, if these problems are recognized and accounted for it is possible to use presumptive reagents and still acquire some additional serological or DNA testing results.

It is often necessary to evaluate all potential sources of information that can be obtained from a source of evidence and conduct a carefully designed sequential scheme, addressing the most evidentiary concerns. For example, with bloody fingerprint or footwear imprint evidence, pattern evaluation and comparison is often equally or more valuable than blood testing results. Thus, it is advantageous to use blood enhancement reagents to help identify and enhance the quality of the pattern. However, it may also be valuable to conduct additional serological and DNA testing on the blood sample comprising the pattern area. This is of particular significance in cases involving multiple suspects and/or victims, or scenes where mixtures of blood are suspected.

This problem can most easily be resolved by collecting a small portion of the stain prior to the application of presumptive or enhancement reagents. Care must be exercised to select a portion of the stain for collection that will not adversely affect the pattern interpretation. In addition, with recent advances in STR DNA typing, under normal conditions, most presumptive testing reagents will not have a detrimental effect on subsequent STR DNA typing.

TESTS FOR THE PRESENCE OF BODY FLUIDS

It is not uncommon to encounter other body fluids at a variety of crime scenes such as burglary, sexual assault, assault, and murder scenes. Semen, saliva, urine, vaginal secretions, perspiration, gastric contents, fecal material, and nasal mucus are examples of body fluids that may be located at crime scenes or on evidence associated with a criminal investigation. Recognition and identification of this body fluid is essential, and presumptive testing reagents can be of great benefit both in the field and in the laboratory for screening purposes. If presumptive testing indicates the presence of one or more body fluid the remaining sample should be collected and preserved for additional laboratory testing. The laboratory can conduct testing that will detect ABO blood group substances, isoenzymes, and DNA typing. Particularly with recent advances in DNA typing these individualizing characteristics of the body fluid can exclude an individual as a potential donor of the body fluid, and positively identify an individual as the donor with a significant degree of discrimination.

1   *Semen*

Semen is a heterogeneous mixture that contains both fluid and cellular components. Many of the fluid components are amenable for detection with presumptive testing reagents. Examples of these seminal components include acid phosphatase, spermine, and choline. While these components are found in relatively high concentrations in semen, tests that detect them should not be considered as a positive means of identification. Seminal stains can also be located and preliminarily identified by their characteristic whitish crusty appearance and fluorescence under ultra-violet light and forensic light sources.

Photo 8.4

Sexual assault victim's underpants being examined with ultraviolet lights for semen stains. Fluorescent semen stains can be seen in the crotch area.

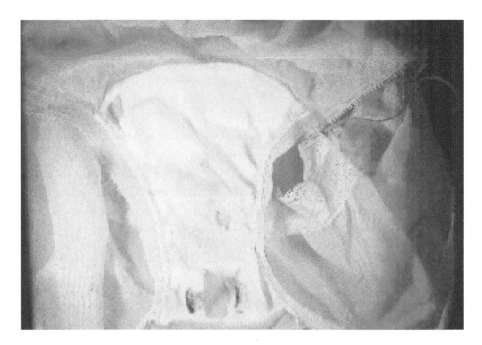

Acid phosphatase

Substrate solution:

Calcium-2-naphyl-phosphate	200 mg
or Na-alphananphthyl-phosphate	187 mg
Sodium acetate	2 g
Glacial acetic acid	1 mL
Distilled water	to 100 mL

Color reagent:

Fast blue B salt	2 g
Distilled water	100 mL

Filter the color reagent solution after dissolving the Fast blue B salt in the distilled water.

These reagents should be prepared fresh, shortly before use. Their shelf life is limited.

Procedure:

(a) Swab a sample of the suspected stain with a cotton swab moistened with saline. Alternatively, cut or scrape a small portion of the stain into a clean well in a disposable spot plate.

(b) Add (1) drop of the substrate solution.

(c) Wait (10) seconds.

(d) Add (1) drop of the color reagent.

(e) The development of a bright purple-pink color within 10–15 seconds indicates the presence of acid phosphatase activity.

2 *Saliva*

Saliva can be encountered on many different circumstances. Saliva may be recovered from partially eaten food items, cigarettes, on and around bite marks, and from swabs taken from a sexual assault victim, clothing, face masks, pillows and various other materials. Saliva contains a starch-digesting enzyme, amylase. The identification of high concentrations of amylase usually indicates the presence of saliva.

However, while amylase is present in relatively high concentrations in saliva it is also present in other body fluids. Thus, as with other presumptive test reagents, these reagents are not conclusive as to the presence of saliva in a sample. Sometimes the suspected area will fluoresce under examination with ultra violet or forensic light sources.

3 *Urine*

The detection of urine is based on its characteristic color and odor, as well as the presence or characteristic chemical components, such as creatinine or urea.

Creatinine–Jaffe test

Picric acid solution:

  2–3 g picric acid saturated in 100 mL of dH$_2$O

NaOH – 10% solution:

Procedure:

(a) Swab a sample of the stain with a cotton swab moistened with distilled water.

(b) Add (1) drop of picric acid solution to the sample.

(c) Add (1) drop of 10% NaOH solution.

A positive result is indicated by a dark reddish-orange color. A negative result will be indicated by the bright yellow color of the picric acid. It is important to compare results against the negative and positive controls.

4 *Fecal material*

Fecal material usually has a characteristic color and odor. Chemical tests for the presence of urobilinogen are also used to help identify the presence of fecal material. Current fecal material detection tests are not easily adaptable for field use.

5 *Gastric contents*

Gastric contents can be identified by the presence of pepsin, a digestive enzyme. Also, specific contents of the gastric material such as the type and amount of food or drink may be determined visually, microscopically, or chemically. Further, the degree of digestion of certain food items may be relevant in helping determine the time of death or ingestion before being vomited. Current gastric content detection tests are not easily adaptable for field use.

TESTS FOR GUNSHOT RESIDUE (GSR)

When a firearm is discharged, it creates gases, soot, and burned or partially burned gunpowder. These materials are generally referred to as GSR (gun shot residue). GSR originates from detonation of the primer, gunpowder, lubricants, or components of the projectile. These materials are propelled forward with the projectile toward the target as well as backwards onto the shooter's hands and clothing. GSR may be detected if samples are collected from the hands or clothing of the shooter, before washing or loss by other means. Detection of GSR may aid in identification of the shooter or an individual who handled a recently discharged firearm. In addition, the screening of suspect surfaces at crime scenes for GSR can help locate those areas where additional samples should be collected for laboratory analysis and confirmation of GSR. Photos 8.5 and 8.6 show laboratory test SEM results and chemical test on gunshot residues.

The components of GSR can be categorized in the following classes.

1. Primer residues:
   (a) Initiating explosive, consisting of lead styphnate, lead azide, diazodinitrophenol.
   (b) Oxidizing agent, consisting of barium nitrate, calcium peroxide, magnesium peroxide and magnesium dioxide.
   (c) Fuel, consisting of antimony sulfide, calcium silicide, aluminum, titanium, zirconium, and lead thiocyanate.
   (d) Sensitizing agent, consisting of tetracene, powdered glass, titanium, and calcium silicide.

2. Gunpowder:
   (a) Smokeless (common modern variety): nitrocellulose – single base, nitrocellulose and nitroglycerin – double base.
   (b) Black powder (muzzle loader type weapons): 75% potassium nitrate, 15% sulfur, 10% charcoal.

3. Lubricants:
   Materials used to ease the bullet into or out of the casing, antifriction agents to speed the projectile down the barrel, gun oil and cleaning residues, and additives used in shaping and compounding the propellant.

4. Components of the projectile:
   Metallic materials such as lead, copper, zinc, antimony, arsenic, bismuth, and chromium can be detected. These metals originate from metal transferred from the barrel, projectile, or cartridge casing.

GSR tests

Detection of GSR has two primary objectives: to determine whether an individual fired or handled a recently discharged firearm or whether a surface was in close proximity to a weapon during discharge. Interior surfaces of automobiles can be tested to determine if a gun was fired from inside the vehicle. The second primary use of GSR detection is to analyze the pattern of GSR for the purpose of determining the muzzle-to-target distance. Distance determination can play a vital role in helping to distinguish between a self-inflicted gunshot wound and a distance shot attributed to a murder. Any test designed to detect GSR must be used in a manner that minimizes the potential for damaging the GSR pattern. Like other presumptive or screening tests the color tests suitable for detection of GSR at crime scenes must be confirmed by more precise laboratory testing, such as atomic absorption spectroscopy, induced coupled plasma spectroscopy, or scanning electron microscopy with elemental analysis.

Photo 8.5

Scanning electron microscope image of gunshot residue particle located on right hand of suspect.

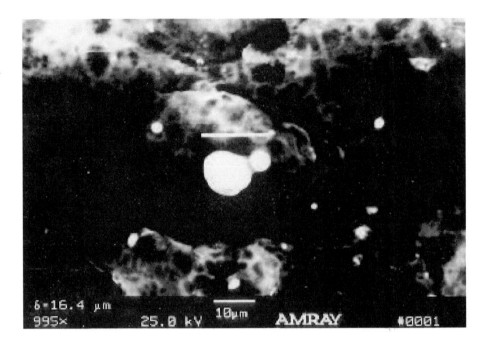

Photo 8.6

Supervising Criminalist Robert O'Brien performing the Modified Griess Test to visualize a gunshot residue pattern on a homicide victim's shirt.

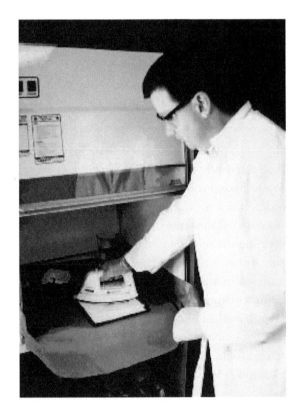

GSR test reagents

These reagents react with nitrate and nitrite compounds in GSR, yielding a colored pattern. Reagents can be used with swabs to merely indicate the presence of GSR on a surface or can sprayed onto a target surface to visualize the GSR particle distribution pattern. A developed GSR pattern can aid in distance determinations. Commonly occurring substances such as cigarette smoke, urine, and fertilizer may sometimes also react with these reagents.

Diphenylamine (DPA)

Procedure:

1 Swab the area to be tested with a cotton swab moistened with distilled water.
2 Add a drop of the DPA in sulfuric acid solution.
3 The immediate development of a dark blue color indicates the presence of nitrates/nitrites.

Modified Griess test

1 Process desensitized photographic paper with a mixture of 50% alpha-naphthol solution and 50% sulfanilic acid solution – allow paper to dry.
2 Place the evidence item, questioned side down, on the gelatin-coated side of the treated photographic paper.
3 Place a piece of cheesecloth soaked in 15% glacial acetic acid solution on the questioned item and press with a hot iron.
4 Any orange indications on the photographic paper are the result of chromophoric (color-producing) reaction specific for the presence of nitrite residues (as shown in Photo 8.7a)

Reverse modified Griess test

For thick or otherwise non-porous materials through which acetic acid solution 'steam' will not penetrate.

1 Tape a piece of filter paper on the back of a piece of desensitized and treated photographic paper.
2 Place the photographic paper emulsion side down on the questioned surface.
3 Wipe the emulsion-coated side of the photographic paper with a piece of cheesecloth saturated with 15% glacial acetic acid solution.
4 Immediately place the photographic paper emulsion side down on the questioned surface.
5 Apply a hot iron to the back of the photographic paper.
6 Separate the photographic paper and questioned item.
7 Any orange indications on the photographic paper are the result of chromophoric (color-producing) reaction specific for the presence of nitrite residues.

Photo 8.7a

Close-up view of a gunshot residue pattern developed with the modified Griess test.

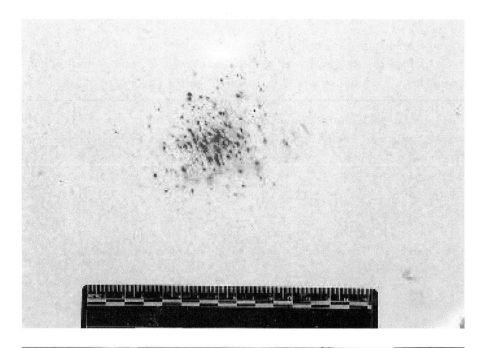

Photo 8.7b

Close-up view of a gunshot residue pattern developed with the sodium rhodizonate test.

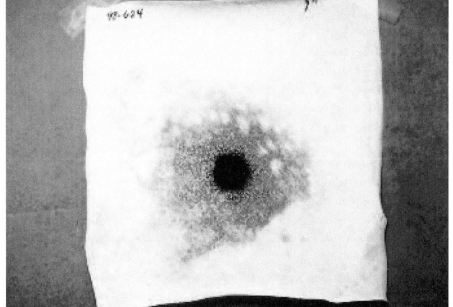

Sodium rhodizonate test

This reagent is a specific chromophoric test for lead in GSR.

1 Spray the questioned surface with a saturated solution of sodium rhodizonate in distilled water.

2 Spray the same area with the tartaric acid, sodium bitartrate buffer solution.

3 Spray the same area with a 5% hydrochloric acid solution.

4 The previous pink color will fade out and the blue violet area constitutes a positive reaction for lead. Prompt note taking is essential because a positive result may fade (as shown in Photo 8.7b).

Note: A modification, the Bashinsky transfer technique, can be used for lead residues located on dark colored items.

TESTS FOR EXPLOSIVE RESIDUES

Explosive residues may be encountered in numerous forms at scene. Explosive residues may be located at storage or production sites as well as in vehicles or containers used to transport explosive material. Also, these residues may be on the hands and clothing of a suspect. At post-blast scenes these residues may consist of both unchanged explosive material and products of the explosion.

Explosives are chemical substances, which are unstable in their natural form. When heated, shocked or struck, they are capable of rapid decomposition, producing an explosion by the liberation of large quantities of heat and gas. Explosives are classified into three primary categories.

1 Low explosives: Stable under ordinary conditions, violent explosions will occur if these explosives are confined and detonated. Examples are black and smokeless gunpowders and fireworks.

2 Primary high explosives: This type of explosive is sensitive to heat and shock and used to initiate detonation of secondary high explosives. Examples include blasting caps, det cord, and nitroglycerine.

3 Secondary high explosives: These explosive materials are insensitive to heat, shock, or friction, and are used as a booster charge. Common examples are TNT, RDX, dynamite, ammonium nitrate, and monomethylamine nitrate.

Presumptive test for explosive materials

Portable hydrocarbon or ion sniffers are available for detecting explosive residues on objects or persons. Many jurisdictions have developed canine programs, and have reported significant success with the use of dogs to detect minute amounts of explosive materials. In addition, there are various reagents that will give characteristic color reactions when the suspect sample is tested.

As with many other presumptive tests, both false negatives and positives are possible. Therefore, laboratory confirmatory testing is essential. Some commonly employed color tests and their reactants are provided in Table 8.1.

Table 8.1

Color test reagents and reactions for explosives.

Explosive component	Color reaction			
	Griess	Diphenylamine	J-acid	Alcoholic KOH
Chlorate	No color	Blue	Orange-brown	No color
Nitrate	Pink to red	Blue	Orange-brown	No color
Nitrate	Red to yellow	Blue	Orange-brown	No color
Nitrocellulose	Pink	Blue-black	Orange-brown	No color
Nitroglycerine	Pink to red	Blue-black	Orange-brown	No color
PETN	Pink to red	Blue	Orange-brown to red	No color
RDX	Pink to red	Blue	Orange-brown	No color
Tetryl	Pink to red	Blue	Yellow to orange	Red
TNT	No color	No color	No color	Red violet

Table 8.2

Common color tests for drugs.

Reagent	General application	Expected result
Marquis	Alkaloids	Morphine – purple Heroin – purple PCP – colorless to light pink Amphetamine – orange to brown LSD – orange to brown to purple Mescaline – orange Psilocybin – orange
Mandelin	Amphetamines	Morphine – blue-gray Heroin – blue-gray Amphetamine – green LSD – orange to green to gray Psilocybin – green
Nitric acid	Morphine v. heroin	Morphine – orange to red on standing Heroin – yellow to green on standing
Ehrlich	Hallucinogens	LSD – purple
Duquenois	Marijuana and THC	Marijuana – gray-blue Hashish – gray-blue THC – gray-blue
Cobalt thiocyanate	Cocaine and derivatives	Cocaine – blue precipitate Procaine – blue precipitate Methadone – blue precipitate
Dille-Koppanyi	Barbiturates	Barbiturates – red-violet

TESTS FOR CONTROLLED SUBSTANCES AND DRUGS

Police officers, narcotics agents, and forensic scientists need to identify controlled substances and drugs of many types and in many forms. Current laboratory techniques, such as gas chromatography–mass spectroscopy, are very sensitive and discriminating. However, there is often a need for a quick screening test or field test to analyze a material suspected of being a drug or controlled substance. In many situations, this field test helps provide the necessary probable cause to substantiate an arrest for sale and/or possession of a controlled substance.

Color tests are often used as screening tests in drug analysis. Certain drugs will react with selected chemical reagents to give characteristic color changes or precipitates. Kits are commercially available which contain these reagents in convenient single-test vials. Some commonly used drug-screening reagents and their characteristic reactions are shown in Table 8.2.

PATTERN ENHANCEMENT REAGENTS

Several reagents have been developed for enhancement of imprint evidence at crime scenes. Following are examples of some of these reagents.

I   Bloody print enhancement reagents.
II Protein enhancement reagents.
   1   Ninhydrin
   2   Amido black
   3   Coomassie blue
   4   Crystal violet
III Fatty acid, elements and compounds, enhancement reagents
   1   Iodine fuming
   2   Small particle reagent
   3   Superglue (cyanoacrylate) fuming

BLOODY PRINT ENHANCEMENT REAGENTS

At times it may not be possible or practical to remove the stained evidence and utilize a staining procedure that requires soaking the object in a tray of solution. In addition, some of those soaking methods are not that practical for either field or crime scene applications. Further, some stains may be located on vertical surfaces. In those instances if staining reagents are sprayed onto the vertical surface there is a potential that the staining solution may drip, thus damaging or altering the underlying pattern. Photos 8.8a–d show the results of

(a)

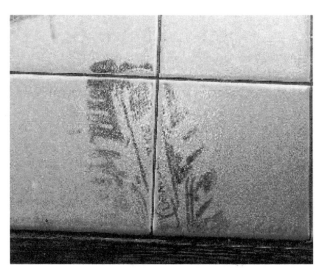

(c)

(b)

(d)

enhancement of bloody foot patterns. A collodion-based reagent has been designed for application to a variety of surfaces encountered at crime scenes, including vertical surfaces.

Solution:
Acetate buffer:

Sodium acetate	10 g
Distilled water	100 mL
Glacial acetic acid	86 mL

(Refrigerate for up to six months)

O-tolidine	0.12 g
Sodium perborate	0.20 g

Collodion:

Ethanol	6 mL
Collodion	15 mL
Ethyl Ether	60 mL

Combine ethanol and collodion before adding ether to prevent precipitation.

Caution: ether is highly flammable. Ether can be substituted with other carrying solvents.

Mixing instructions:

1 Place O-tolidine and sodium perborate in a test tube with 4 mL of acetate buffer and shake vigorously for one minute.
2 Measure 60 mL of the O-tolidine solution to the collodion mixture and mix.

Procedure:

1 Photograph the area containing any bloody print prior to treatment.
2 Spray surface lightly 2–3 times (*Do not over-spray*).
3 Photograph any developed prints.
4 Some of the prints, which are developed, can be lifted with regular fingerprint tape.

PROTEIN ENHANCEMENT REAGENTS

There are a variety of protein-based materials present at a crime scene. Proteins are components in many body tissues and fluids, including but not limited to skin, tissue, blood, and milk. In addition, other animal matter and food

Photo 8.8a–d (opposite)

A couple brutally beaten to death in their home: there was such a large volume of blood downstairs, adjacent to their bodies that it was difficult to obtain quality bloody footwear impressions. However, when treated with a BPER, the second-floor bathroom yielded excellent quality footwear and footprint imprints.

(a) Overall view of the bathroom floor before application of the BPER.

(b) Overall view of the same floor after an application of BPER. Both footwear and footprint patterns were observed.

(c) Close-up view of a developed footwear pattern; note you can read the brand name, 'Newbalance.'

(d) Close-up view of a footprint pattern. No friction ridge details were developed, as the suspect wore a sock. Note the protrusion on the right side of the base of the foot. This was consistent with a birth defect and used as means to positively identify that print as belonging to the suspect.

products may also contain proteins. Amino acids are basic building blocks for proteins. A suspect or victim may deposit large or trace quantities of these substances at a crime scene, even during relatively minor contact. Common sources of protein located at a crime scene are associated with contact transfer or a direct deposit of body fluids, such as sweat, tears, blood, urine, semen, or saliva. Ninhydrin usually can be used as a presumptive test reagent for the presence of protein.

Latent finger, palm, footprints, lip, and ear prints can be located by the use of amino acid detecting reagents such as ninhydrin, Amido Black, Coomassie Blue, crystal violet, and bloody print enhancement reagents. Each of these reagents has slightly different sensitivities, limitations, and methods of application; however, they all are proven to be very effective at locating and/or enhancing pattern evidence containing proteins or amino acids. The following are some commonly used chemical protein reagents that enhance protein evidence.

1 *Ninhydrin*

Ninhydrin detects trace amounts of amino acids associated with body secretions. The amino acids are transferred with the sweat from pores of a finger, palm, or sole. These amino acids are easily absorbed into absorbent and partially absorbent surfaces such as paper, unfinished wood, cardboard, leather, etc. The absorbed amino acids are rather stable. Under special conditions, ninhydrin methods have successfully enhanced fingerprints decades old.

Solution:

2,2 Dihydroxy –1,3- indanedione monohydrate	25 g
Acetone	4 L

Mix the ninhydrin crystals with acetone, stirring well. Store in dark bottle for use.

Procedure:

(a) Fill spray bottle with working solution.

(b) Spray the surface evenly from a distance of six inches.

(c) Allow the solvent to evaporate. Repeat the spraying process as necessary.

(d) To speed development after spraying, the surface could be heated with a steam iron for a short period. Do not overheat the surface. Alternatively, the sample could be left at room temperature until the latent print fully develops.

2 *Amido Black*

Amido Black is an effective method to enhance blood contaminated latent prints. Amido Black is a protein dye, which will react to the protein in blood and will turn it a blue-black color.

Photo 8.9

Amido Black enhanced bloody footprints at homicide scene (courtesy of Cindy Bales, Sarasota Sheriff's Office).

Solution (water-based formula):

Citric acid stock solution:

| Citric acid | 38 g |
| Distilled water | 2 L |

Combine and stir until citric acid is thoroughly dissolved.

Developing solution:

Citric acid stock solution	2 L
Naphthalene 12 B (Amido Black)	2 g
Kodak Photo Flo 600 solution	

Place beaker containing citric acid stock solution on stirrer and slowly add the naphthalene 12 B, stir for 30 minutes. Add the Photo Flo solution.

Solution (organic-based formula):

Step 1 – Working solution:

Naphthalene 12 B	2 g
Glacial acetic acid	100 mL
Methanol	900 mL

Combine and stir until well mixed.

Step 2 – Rinse:

Glacial acetic acid	100 mL
Methanol	900 mL

Step 3 – Rinse:

Glacial acetic acid	50 mL
Distilled water	950 mL

Procedure:

Step 1 – Fix blood on surface of the evidence:

Immerse evidence in tray of methanol for one hour. (If the blood print is on a painted surface or other substrate, which can be damaged by the methanol, use the water-based formula.) Spot-test an uncontaminated piece of the evidence or similar surface if uncertain.)

Step 2 – Using the working solution:

Soak evidence in working solution for two to three minutes or until latent prints become blue-black in color.

Step 3 – first rinse:

(a) Immerse evidence in tray and gently rock the tray.

(b) When excess dye has been removed from the background of the print take the evidence out of the rinse.

Step 4 – second rinse:

(a) Immerse evidence in tray and gently rock for 30 seconds.

(b) Allow evidence to dry at room temperature.

3 Coomassie Blue

Coomassie Brilliant Blue (R250) is a general protein stain that works well with bloodstains. Coomassie is a more sensitive, general protein stain, than crystal violet stains. Also, Coomassie has a distinct advantage over crystal violet in that Coomassie stain utilizes a destaining solution to clear the background.

Solution:

Coomassie staining solution:

Coomassie Brilliant Blue R250	0.44 g
Glacial acetic acid	40 mL
Methanol	200 mL
Distilled water	200 mL

Coomassie destaining solution:

Glacial acetic acid	40 mL
Methanol	200 mL
Distilled water	200 mL

Alternatively, another newly developed stain that does not use methanol and therefore prevents running of some inks is Crowle's Double Stain.

Crowle's staining solution:

Crocein scarlet 7B	2.5 g
Coomassie Brilliant Blue R250	150 mg
Glacial acetic acid	50 mL
Trichloracetic acid	30 g

Dilute to 1 L with de-ionized water

Crowle's destaining solution:

Glacial acetic acid	3 mL
Deionized water	1 L

Procedure:

(a) Bloodstained articles are placed in staining solution for up to 30 minutes, depending on the surface and age of print.

(b) Agitate.

(c) Immerse article in destaining solution, and agitate for one minute.

If more detail is desired the staining process can be repeated.

4. *Crystal (gentian) violet*

Crystal violet works exceptionally well on adhesive surfaces such as tapes. Once latent or partially patent prints are visualized with crystal violet they can be photographed and used for comparison and analysis.

Solution – Formula A:

Stock solution:

Gentian violet	1.5 g
Ethyl alcohol	100 mL

Working solution:

Stock solution	2 mL
Water	100 mL

Solution – Formula B:

Stock solution:

Crystal violet	5 g
Ethyl alcohol	50 mL
Phenol	10 g

Working solution:

Stock solution	1 mL
Water	100 mL

Procedure:

(a) Carefully remove adhesive tape from surface. Freezing tape in liquid nitrogen can help separate layers of tape adhered together.

(b) Immerse the tape into the working solution and ensure that the surface is completely covered.

(c)   Soak the tape in solution for several minutes, gentle agitating the solution.

(d)   Remove the sample from the dye solution.

(e)   Rinse the surface with cold tap water.

FATTY ACID, ELEMENTS AND COMPOUNDS, ENHANCEMENT REAGENTS

Reagents designed to detect the presence of fatty acids in the imprint residues can detect imprints and patterns. Iodine fuming procedures and Small Particle Reagent–molybdenum solution are used with good success both at the crime scene and in a laboratory setting.

1. *Iodine fuming*

    Iodine fuming works well on a variety of absorbent smooth surfaces such as paper and human skin. The vapors sublimed from warmed iodine crystals dissolve in the skin oils in a latent print, yielding a yellow brown print. These developed prints must be photographically recorded immediately, as they will quickly fade. However, the prints can be developed numerous times by re-fuming. While it is possible to fix the developed prints with a starch or chemical solution it is often better to document the prints photographically and submit the print surface, if possible, to the laboratory for further development.

    Iodine fuming is an excellent screening process in that it is non-destructive and does not interfere with other development procedures such as ninhydrin or superglue fuming methods.

    Methods:

    Iodine fuming wand/gun:

    (a) Iodine fuming wand can be constructed or purchased as already made disposable units.

    (b) Warm the fuming gun with hands and slowly blow air through the connecting tube.

    (c) Iodine vapor generated is first applied generally over the whole surface until an outline of any latent print becomes visible.

    (d) Once a latent print is located, treat further with iodine vapors until maximum intensity is obtained.

    (e) Photograph the developed prints.

    (f) Fix with starch solution or 7,8-benzoflavone if desired.

    Fuming chamber:

    (a) Place 1 gram of iodine in a sealed chamber. For field applications a zip lock baggie is a suitable chamber.

    (b) Leave at room temperature or warm crystals to 50°C.

(c) Prints will develop within minutes to an hour.

(d) Photograph developed prints; fix with starch or chemicals if desired.

2 *Molybdenum solution 'Small Particle Reagent'*

Small Particle Reagent is designed to detect fatty acids and lipids on nonporous surfaces, including damp surfaces. Small Particle Reagent has been successfully used to develop latent prints on the exterior surfaces of automobiles that were exposed to rain after deposition of the latent prints, and to develop prints located on weapons and other objects recovered from bodies of water. Small Particle Reagent procedures can be employed while the suspect surface is still wet.

Solution:

Molybdenum disulfide	30 g
Distilled water	1 L
Photo Flo '2000'	3 drops

Procedure:

(a) Fill a tray with the working solution. Alternatively, a reagent may be applied to large surface areas with a spray bottle.

(b) Completely immerse the object in the solution.

(c) Gently agitate the tray.

(d) Latent prints should develop within approximately two minutes.

(e) Remove the object and allow the excess solution to drain off.

(f) Rinse the object in clean water until all small particles have been removed.

(g) Air dry at room temperature

3 *Superglue (cyanoacrylate) fuming*

Superglue is comprised of an acrylate resin, cyanoacrylate. While most glues require heat or evaporation to set properly, liquid superglue forms a solid polymer upon contact with microscopic amounts of moisture. Virtually any moisture on the surface is sufficient to trigger the instantaneous polymerization. The fuming reaction of superglue with latent prints is based on this same principle. The vapors of superglue react with the residues of water, lipids, fatty acids, amino acids and proteins, and deposits along the ridges forming an irreversible cyanoacrylate polymer complex.

The resulting fumed print is a visible white, durable print. Subsequently, these fumed prints can be further enhanced by dusting with magnetic or ordinary fingerprint powders, or visualized with forensic light sources or laser.

Superglue works well on a variety of surfaces, such as plastic bags, glass, metals, leather, and even human skin. There are various methods for exposure of the suspected surface or item to the superglue fumes. A fuming chamber can be used on smaller objects. Large objects or an entire body can be fumed by constructing an airtight tent or chamber around the object, and then filling that area with superglue fumes (as shown in Photo 8.10). Interiors of houses or vehicles can be processed by fuming with the doors and windows closed. Superglue can be applied by chemical packages, fuming wands, or by heat or chemical reaction accelerators.

There are a few general precautions or guidelines for superglue fuming methods. Good ventilation is required, and caution should be exercised to avoid contact of the liquid superglue with the examiner's skin. Do not over-fume the latent prints, as excess development will cause the ridge details to become unclear.

LEGAL AND SCIENTIFIC CONSIDERATIONS

Jurisdictions vary; however, there are some fairly universal legal implications and issues related to the ultimate admissibility of results obtained from field tests in court proceedings. One of the principal legal issues is a concern that the prejudicial factor of presumptive tests may outweigh any probative value associated with the tests results. For example, given the possibility of false positives associated with presumptive tests some jurisdictions preclude testimony about the results of a presumptive test unless an acceptable confirmatory test is performed and confirms the presence of the substance.

Photo 8.10

A portable tent was constructed around the naked body of a sexual assault/homicide victim for the purpose of forming a superglue fuming chamber.

Once enclosed the tent is filled with superglue (cyanoacrylate) to develop latent prints on her skin.

Connecticut courts, in *State v. Moody*, held that testimony regarding a small stain on one of the soles of the defendant's shoes which gave a positive result for the presumptive test for blood was inadmissible. In this case the stain in question was too small to conduct any confirmatory or additional testing. The court ruled that the result of the presumptive test for blood had no probative value whatsoever. The test result did nothing toward establishing the likelihood of the presence of human blood on the sole of the defendant's shoes. Therefore, the court held that the test result was entirely irrelevant, and results of that presumptive test should not be admitted into evidence.

Other legal issues involve the ability to obtain samples for testing. These issues have constitutional overtones, particularly protections afforded individuals against unreasonable searches, as guaranteed by the Fourth Amendment of the United States Constitution and comparable State Constitutional provisions. These issues often arise when attempting to collect samples for field tests from an actual person, or in cases involving the street testing of suspected controlled substances.

For example, suppose that during an unruly demonstration involving 25 individuals protesting the production and sale of fur coats, balloons full of blood were hurled at employees of the fur manufacturers. Police officers were able to detain five protestors who were in the general vicinity of where the blood-filled balloons had originated. A crime scene processing team was available to conduct presumptive blood tests from swabbing taken from the suspect's hands. The physical act of swabbing of an individual's hands can be construed as a detention and subsequent search of that individual, subject to Fourth Amendment protection. American legal doctrine requires either a court-authorized search warrant, consent from that individual, or some articulable exigent circumstance to effectuate that search lawfully. Given the specific facts of this scenario many American courts may entertain an exception to the search warrant requirement based on the exigent circumstances. This ruling would be supported by the need to identify the perpetrator in a timely manner, to prevent the possible destruction or loss of evidence, namely trace amounts of blood on the guilty party's hands.

While this scenario and conclusion are not intended to establish the law that governs these situations it should be taken as a precautionary note to investigators that in certain circumstances field tests have been deemed as searches that must be afforded some form of constitutional protection.

Ideally, sometime in the near future a universal multiple application reagent will be developed to address all uses for presumptive tests of biological samples. To be effective and practical for field as well as laboratory applications this hypothetical reagent should have the following attributes. First and foremost the reagent must be easy to administer in a crime scene setting. Further, the interpretation should be objective and readily visible. Reagents such as luminol are excellent heme detection reagents, but their utility is hindered by the need to visualize a positive reaction in a dark environment. This reagent should have an extended shelf life at room temperature. Crime scene investigators do not want the burden and complications of preparing these testing reagents in the field or immediately prior to their use. Often, the request for crime scene processing comes at non-business hours, and there are circumstances such as adverse weather conditions requiring timely response. Likely the universal reagent will be a complex mixture, requiring research and validation to ensure that the various chemical components will not interfere with one another. In addition, this reagent should be designed with the health and safety of the crime scene investigators as a priority. Several of the initial presumptive blood testing reagents were later to be determined as highly carcinogenic, e.g. benzidine. Moreover, some of the current reagents require a highly volatile organic solvent that can be hazardous to use in crime scene environments. A prime example is the use of ether in the tetra-methylbenzidine formula used in a bloody print enhancement reagent. However, it would be most beneficial if this reagent had the same qualities as ether-based bloody print enhancement reagents in that they could be applied to vertical surfaces without damaging the developing patterns. The solvent base of the reagent needs to evaporate quickly, thus minimizing the potential of creating a drip or run through the enhanced pattern. Finally, as indicated by the stated goal of this research challenge, this universal agent should be able to detect the commonly encountered biological materials found at crime scenes and on physical evidence seized in conjunction with an investigation. Thus, the reagent will be able to detect blood, proteins, seminal fluid, and other bodily fluids such as saliva or urine.

Field tests and enhancement reagents provide valuable and timely assistance to crime scene technicians and laboratory analysts. However, it is important to know the limitations and potential complications associated with a particular test. Further, over-interpretation of a presumptive test result may mislead the investigator and crime scene technician, and in some cases be an inadmissible conclusion. Finally, while most of these tests are fairly straightforward and easy to use they must not be employed until the user has received adequate training, and the actual procedure and reagents have been validated and tested on known controls.

CHAPTER 9

SPECIAL SCENE TECHNIQUES

INTRODUCTION

Essentially, no two-crime scenes are alike. Each scene presents its own unique challenges and characteristics. While most crime scenes can be adequately addressed if a comprehensive crime scene management system is implemented there are certain types of scenes that present a number of special difficulties or dangers not found at more common crime scenes. Outdoor crime scenes can be large and challenging to search, as well as exposed to detrimental elements and conditions. Evidence is often disposed of or hidden in the ground or in water, requiring special equipment and techniques to locate and recover the evidence. Many times a body represents a segment of the main scene, while at other times the evidence and information associated with the body is best identified and preserved by treating the body as a crime scene unto itself. Fire and explosive scenes pose additional hazards and complications. Also, clandestine drug laboratories are types of scenes that must be approached in a manner that minimizes inherent hazards, while preserving essential evidence. Finally, with greater frequency crime scenes contain electronic and digital evidence mandating specific collection and preservation requirements. Because of the complex nature of these types of crime scenes, the preplanning and investigative team organization are extremely important to the eventual outcome of the investigation. Since these specialized scenes can be identified at the outset and generally do not suddenly appear or necessitate emergency responses, they can be successfully processed by a well-designed and implemented crime scene processing approach. Evidence lost due to a lack of planning or a hasty crime scene investigation is impossible to recover at a later time.

OUTDOOR CRIME SCENES

Outdoor crime scenes present several issues not associated with indoor scenes. These issues include security concerns, large and diverse areas to be searched, and adverse conditions.

SECURITY OF THE SCENE

Outdoor scenes can be difficult to physically secure and are accessible at many points by many people. To further complicate matters, often the scope of the scene is unknown at first, and on many occasions ultimately determined to be adjacent to or beyond the originally identified and secured areas. This problem is best addressed by initially securing an area larger than what is believed to be the crime scene. Moreover, throughout the process it is important to be aware of the possibility that the evidence is beyond the designated area, and be flexible, willing to adjust the boundaries as necessary. Many times the crime scene area is redefined subsequent to a detailed organized search such as a line or grid search.

As described in earlier chapters the crime scene should be secured with multiple perimeters of varied levels of security. The innermost area is the area known to or believed to contain relevant evidence, and access to it should be strictly monitored and regulated. Once a perimeter has been established an outdoor crime scene is investigated much like an indoor scene, but with a number of complicating factors involved which will be delineated below. If the outdoor crime scene cannot be readily located or identified then an organized, well-planned search must be performed.

SEARCHING AN OUTDOOR AREA

It is important to remember that the search of an outdoor crime scene is usually not an emergency situation and as much time as is needed should be allocated to carefully consider every aspect of the search. However, if circumstances such as inclement weather or the need to rapidly find a child or injured victim exist, then following a pre-planned protocol, emphasizing the following factors, can mitigate many problems.

Even if the exact parameters of a search area are not known, a rough estimate of the potential size and duration of the search is essential to determine the human and support resources necessary for the search. If a large area is to be searched consider employing volunteers. While it is not essential, it is helpful to have adult volunteers with some form of relevant training or experience. Consider local fire departments, emergency response personnel, civil patrols, National Guard or military personnel, or civic groups.

However, if this type of personnel is utilized it is imperative that the search party is instructed as a group as to the scope of the search, purpose of the search, a brief synopsis of the current investigation, and protocols as how they should respond if they find relevant evidence or have questions. A trained individual with crime scene and investigative experience should separate these volunteers into manageable groups and a leader. Also, a structure must be implemented so that all information is channeled through a single command center, and groups are updated and debriefed on a regular basis.

Support equipment may include trained canines, helicopters and fixed-wing aircraft, all-terrain vehicles, portable communications, and scuba diving equipment. Photos 9.1a–c are examples of special searching techniques. Canine units can be used to locate missing individuals, dead and decaying remains, as well as objects touched by sought individuals. Canines should be used early in the search process, as the presence of large search parties will interfere with the ability of the canines to track and locate individuals and evidence. Air searches can be a great asset, particularly if the search area is large and covers remote areas. Either fixed-wing aircraft or helicopters are effective. However, helicopters are advantageous in that they may move slower and closer to the ground. Further, helicopters can be equipped with forward-looking infrared (FLIR) devices. FLIR units detect thermal patterns and can help identify a living or decaying body due to the heat being emitted. These units also work at night as the infrared images can be seen even in total darkness. If vast areas of rugged terrain are involved all terrain vehicles will be needed to move supplies and equipment to ground search parties, and assist in the removal of any identified evidence.

Regardless of the search process good communications are essential. Different search groups must be able to communicate with the command center and relay vital information in a timely manner. With large search parties the available law enforcement communications system and equipment may be insufficient to handle the search. Most likely there will not be enough portable radios. Therefore, other communication devices must be obtained and used to further communications. The advent of cellular telephones, and the ability to acquire numerous phones, may provide the additional communication links between field units and the command post. However, many remote areas lack sufficient cellular coverage. If bodies of water are part of the search area these may require underwater searches by trained personnel.

Inclement weather or adverse conditions add a set of issues that often need immediate attention and response. If possible, searches should be delayed until weather conditions improve. However, if a crime scene is located, rapid measures must be taken to minimize loss or destruction of evidence (as shown in Photo 9.2). Imprint and blood patterns, and many forms of trace evidence will be damaged by wet weather. At a minimum, areas containing this type of evidence need to be protected by protective coverings such as large tarpaulins. Often it is advisable to document, preserve, and collect if possible these items of evidence without delay.

Evidence located in outdoor scenes in winter conditions presents challenges,

Photo 9.1a

Training canines to detect accelerants at fire scenes.

Photo 9.1b

Sheriff Department divers prepare to conduct an underwater search and evidence recovery.

Photo 9.1c

Investigators using a helicopter to aid in the search for a missing person, who was believed to have been murdered and dumped in a remote area.

Photo 9.2

Portable heaters and a tarp are used to melt snow and ice to aid in the collection of skeletal remains and evidence located in a wooded area.

as it is often impractical to wait for weather patterns to change. The physical evidence may be frozen in the ground and difficult to locate and remove. One solution is to utilize portable heating units and thaw the specific area where the evidence is located. Building a temporary structure/tarp roof and walls around the area to be warmed enhances this process.

Other adverse conditions include crime scenes located on highways or in heavily populated areas where there is a potential for a large gathering or hostile crowd. Crime scenes on highways range from secondary scenes, dump sites, to primary scenes, shooting scenes. Police officer-involved shooting scenes are one of the most scrutinized and high profile scenes that crime scene investigators will face. Unfortunately, many police-involved shootings transpire on busy roadways, making it difficult to safely secure the scene and minimize potential loss of evidence. Broken glass debris, ejected cartridge cases, empty pistol magazines, and imprint patterns are all types of valuable evidence commonly associated with police shootings. These types of evidence can easily be destroyed or moved from their original location, thus greatly diminishing the possibility of conducting a thorough crime scene reconstruction.

In order to prevent this problem the highway should if possible be shut down and traffic diverted from the area as soon as possible (as shown in Photo 9.3). Some highways are almost impossible to close as the volume of traffic is too great and there are insufficient alternative routes.

Particularly in urban areas it is not uncommon for large gatherings to occur as the result of a crime and the establishment of a crime scene area. Usually,

Photo 9.3

Crime scene located on a busy highway. Use of police cars and yellow tape to divert vehicular and pedestrian traffic away from the crime scene.

these individuals are supportive of law enforcement's role in dealing with the tragedy and working toward a successful resolution of the case. However, occasionally the crowd has a hostile temperament and it may become difficult to maintain the integrity of the scene. In these cases the scene should be quickly but effectively documented and, wherever possible, the evidence gathered and transported to a more secure location for further analysis. For example, the deceased could be placed in a clean shroud and transported to the medical examiner's office for close-up photographs, preliminary examination, and removal of trace evidence. During the documentation process, additional police manpower should be deployed to the scene to maintain the security and safety of investigators.

PROCESSING OUTDOOR CRIME SCENES

Once a crime scene has been located, the investigation should be handled like any other scene. A perimeter should be established around the immediate site and security enforced. Before any aspect of the scene is disturbed it should be fully documented. The actual clearing and investigating of an outdoor site requires the incorporation of several specific techniques and tools.

All maps of the scene and access should originate from a base, or datum, point. This datum point should be any relatively permanent feature so that map coordinates can be re-established if future investigation is necessary. All evidence taken from the site should include the distance and compass direction from the base point.

Alternatively, specific locations can be identified and recorded by a global positioning system (GPS). GPS devices can be purchased as portable hand-held devices, and are relatively inexpensive. Depending upon the sensitivity of a unit they can locate and record a specific location to accuracy within a few feet. Also, many GPS units can integrate with personal computer software programs, designed to map a series of GPS coordinates identified by the user. Ideally, the GPS would be used to locate fixed points and the perimeter of the scene, while traditional measurements could be used to determine precise distances from the GPS points. To assist in orienting photographs and video images at a later time the base points or GPS coordinates should be visualized and labeled with fluorescent paint or other forms of visible markers. Then, as a photograph or video image is recorded the photographer should try to include one of the marked reference points in the photo or video to aid in orientation.

Necessary equipment specific to outdoor scenes

The list below describes the minimal equipment needed to investigate an outdoor scene and a short description of the purpose of each.

1 Pruning shears, axes, and saws – to clear vegetation from the core search area. If large areas need to be cleared, rent or purchase gas-powered brush cutters.
2 Marking devices or placards – to mark located evidence or areas in which a metal detector yielded a positive signal, requiring excavation.
3 String and police line tape – to mark the perimeter of the search area, any large areas of specific interest and entrance and egress paths to avoid inadvertent destruction of evidence.
4 Shovels, hand trowels, and rakes – for removal of dirt in excavation and digging.
5 Paint brushes – for the careful removal of soil that is in contact with buried evidence.
6 Large buckets – to remove soil and other debris from the crime scene to other areas for further processing.
7 Sifting screens – to screen soil and other debris for small objects that may have been overlooked at the excavation site.
8 Evidence bags and boxes – to store any evidence recovered until it can be analyzed further.
9 Portable generators – to provide power for equipment, lighting, and heating equipment.
10 Tarps and tent apparatus – for temporary structures to protect scene and evidence from the elements.
11 Mapping equipment: GPS devices, tape measure, ruler, compass (a transit is ideal), and protractor – for the generation of a three-dimensional map of the crime scene if needed.
12 Metal detector – to detect any small metallic objects buried in soil or other debris.
13 Access to ground-penetrating radar – to help identify buried bodies or evidence.
14 Communication devices – cell-phones, two-way radios.

BODIES AND PHYSICAL EVIDENCE LOCATED ON THE SURFACE

Fortunately, most bodies and evidence are located on the ground surface as it is quicker and easier to dispose of evidence in this manner. There are general guidelines that should be followed when dealing with bodies and evidence on the ground. Care to follow established protocols will enhance evidence recovery and preservation.

As with a crime scene a perimeter must be established. Since the exact size of the crime scene is not known it is important that the initial perimeter established be generous in size. Two perimeters should be laid out: the core, an area immediately around the body, and the extended perimeter, an area that includes any adjacent areas that may contain other evidence. Once these are established, entrance and egress points should be determined and followed by all crime scene personnel. Avoid obvious pathways, as they were most likely the routes taken by the perpetrator and may contain evidence such as footprints or blood trails.

Documentation of the scene must be thorough and done progressively. As layers of brush or debris are removed the search process must stop and additional documentation must occur – photographs, videotaping, and sketches if relevant. Care must be exercised with photographs and videos so that their orientation may be determined. As previously described this can be accomplished by marking reference points within the scene.

All vegetation and natural debris should be cleared from the core area in a slow systematic process. Photo 9.4 shows an example of a cleared area at an outdoor scene. All vegetation should be cut down to within $1/2$ to $3/4$ of an inch to the ground, bagged and removed to the command post to be searched for evidence. In addition, maintain samplings of the vegetation. The samplings may be needed as control samples when examining a suspect's footwear, clothing, or vehicle. With recent advances in DNA typing, particularly Amplified Fragment Length Polymorphism (AMFLP) techniques, vegetative material can be individualized similar to human DNA and used to compare different samples of vegetation and determine a common origin. Currently this technology is not routinely available for casework, as further validation is needed as well as acquiring relevant DNA databases for statistical relevance.

An effective way to ensure that the area is totally searched is to grid the area. Forming a square or rectangle around the core area and forming a grid with string can establish a grid. In addition to searching advantages this grid can assist in measurements as it provides baselines from which to obtain coordinate measurements of specific objects. The sides of the grid may be oriented east/west and north/south if possible. One corner of the grid should contain the base point.

Photo 9.4

Densely wooded area where a state trooper was engaged in a gun battle with a suspect. Investigators cut and cleared all vegetation in the area so a thorough search could be conducted.

The entire area must be scanned with a metal detector. All positive readings should be flagged with a wooden stake and subsequently excavated with a trowel and screen. The exact depth of the object should be recorded. Once a metallic object is located and removed the area should be re-examined with the metal detector to ensure that all of the metallic debris has been located. Most metal detectors have varying degrees of sensitivity. Adjustments should be made to optimize the metal detector. Calibration of the unit is important. For example, if the metal detector were being used to locate missing cartridge cases it would be helpful to calibrate the detector on a known shell casing.

As evidence is located, and after it has been documented in place, it should be carefully removed and packaged. Be sure to note the precise location and depth of the recovered evidence as that information may have bearing on the investigation. If substantial plant growth has enveloped the object it indicates that the object has been present at the location for at least the required growth period. This would be a good example of a time where the involved vegetation should be seized and the assistance of a botanist obtained.

After removal of a body or larger piece of evidence the underlying area should be excavated to a depth of approximately six inches. This dirt should be screened and visually examined to ensure that no evidence has been overlooked.

Once the core area has been fully searched, documented, and evidence seized the adjacent areas should be searched. The extent of the outer search area will vary, and depends upon the type of case, evidence missing or sought,

Photo 9.5a

A metal detector is used to locate any metallic objects at a scene. A hand trowel is used to unearth objects slightly below the surface.

Photo 9.5b

Dr Lee and crime scene investigators locate a cartridge case after the area had been cleared of brush and searched with a metal detector.

(Courtesy of CT State Police – Major Crime Squad.)

trails leading to or from core area, and general terrain considerations. Some form of systematic search method should be employed to increase efficiency and the probability of finding evidence. The precise location of any evidence found in the outer area can be recorded in reference to a base point or a separate reference or GPS coordinate.

SUB-SURFACE EVIDENCE AND BURIED BODIES

Evidence located underground poses two challenges; locating the evidence, and removal of that evidence. A variety of techniques can be employed to help identify potential burial sites. None of the methods are 100% effective and many require specialized equipment and/or trained personnel. Once a potential burial site is identified efforts are focused on recovering the buried body or objects without damaging or losing any of the evidence. These two challenges must be conquered by careful planning and a systematic process, understood by all participants. The need for consultation or assistance from other experts may be beneficial.

Burial-site indicators

The primary indicator of a buried body will be the gravesite. Any of a large number of factors will impinge upon what a burial site will look like and, therefore, what indicators should be looked for in a search. Gravesites have the advantage of conditions associated with the decomposition process. These conditions may result in the emission of odors detectable by trained canines, or result in bodies partially unburied by indigenous animals. If possible, it is important to try to determine how long the body has been buried and at what time of the year it was buried. There are a number of burial-site indicators worthy of consideration.

Buried bodies or objects may be camouflaged or hidden. Brush or debris piles may be placed over the burial site thus making it difficult to detect. Removing all surface debris may be necessary, and may require the use of heavy equipment such as a bulldozer. However, if heavy equipment is used caution must be exercised not to damage the buried objects. Only small layers of dirt should be scraped away, a layer at a time. Digging with heavy equipment is not recommended.

Vegetation or plant growth can be analyzed. Uprooted or visibly disturbed vegetation may be an indicator of a fairly recent disturbance or burial. Over time vegetation will grow over the burial site (as shown in Photo 9.6). However, it may take years for vegetation over the burial site to return to normal. A botanist may provide valuable information as to average growth cycles for particular types of plants in a specific climate.

The decomposition and settling of the soil used to refill the grave will leave a depression in the ground over the actual hole. This depression may be visible. A secondary compression may be visible in the larger compression from the rapid decomposition and settling of the abdominal cavity. Cracks may also be present around the edge of the hole from shrinkage of the disturbed soil. The size of the depression area may also indicate the approximate size of the hole that was dug, or the approximate size of the buried object. These depression areas will need to be marked for further examination, either excavation or analysis with ground-penetrating radar.

Any potential burial site can be analyzed by ground-penetrating radar. Ground-penetrating radar units are portable, but are somewhat cumbersome and require a fair amount of surface preparation and clearing. A ground-penetrating radar unit can be slowly moved across a grid and will detect variations in soil compositions below. All undisturbed soil is found in layers; these layers are lost when the soil is disturbed. The radar unit will show the change in soil composition and layer structures and also show anomalies at given depths. This will provide the necessary information to conduct an excavation or exhumation process.

Analysis of soil conditions and consideration of the topography can assist in identifying areas where it is difficult if not impossible to bury a body or larger object. For example, at or near the water line the water level in the soil will prevent a body from being buried deeply. Also, packed clay or shale layers are difficult to dig through and therefore not as likely burial sites.

Once the burial or gravesite is identified a systematic process must be implemented for the successful recovery of remains and evidence. As stated earlier, the recovery of human remains does not constitute an emergency situation and as much time as is needed should be utilized to plan and acquire the resources, both human and equipment, needed for the investigation. A forensic archeologist or anthropologist can be of great assistance during the excavation process.

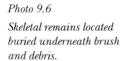

Photo 9.6

Skeletal remains located buried underneath brush and debris.

Most of the tools used in the excavation are similar to those used in more traditional archaeological digs or are from standard archaeological tool kits. Most are designed for the removal of small amounts of dirt at a time so that the preservation of delicate evidence will be eased.

As with all crime scenes, gravesites should be intruded upon as little as possible until the entire region has been documented. A gravesite differs from an outdoor crime scene in that the datum point serves in three dimensions; the third dimension is important in the determination of the exact location of any evidence, including depth.

A core area for investigation should be established and marked by four perimeter walls, which will aid measurements. The excavation should not begin until the surface has been cleared. An airlift, hydraulic dredge, or water jet can be used to remove large quantities of overburden from the site to be excavated. Material should be removed only from one small grid or region at a time in controlled layers. All materials removed should be screened through a $^1/_4$ inch mesh to trap any small items excavated.

After the initial gross excavation, the excavation process must be conducted with small hand tools that are capable of skimming off thin layers of dirt, rather than shovels which remove larger amounts of dirt from a thicker region. The dig will proceed in two to four-inch layers that cover the entire grave one level at a time. Before the removal of a layer, including the first, a metal detector should be passed over and any readings marked with small wooden stakes. As the layer of soil is removed a small pedestal of soil should be left around the marker flag, the soil in the pedestal should be removed and screened separately. The thickness of the layer removed is dependent upon the sensitivity of the metal detector. As a layer is removed a one-inch buffer of soil should be left between along the grave walls. After a layer is removed this soil can be removed with more care to protect any tool marks or severed roots that mark the exact location of the grave wall. Soil from each layer should be passed through a screen to recover any small items of evidence. If desired, the soil from each layer can be removed from the grave in small grid regions and each of these regions screened separately.

When exhuming bodies or remains, normally the first part of a body to be uncovered is either the skull or the pelvis. As soon as any part of the body is uncovered, all evidence further discovered should be left in place and treated as being in direct contact with the body. The actual clearing of the body should be performed with the smallest wooden tools and brushes available. Debris should be removed from each portion of the body separately.

Once cleared, the body should be photographed, sketched, and the position of all evidence mapped. After full documentation of the cleared scene, the body and associated evidence can be removed using normal crime scene procedures for the handling of evidence. If enough flesh remains on the body so that it is intact, it can be removed by sliding a plywood board under it or by sliding the body onto a body bag.

UNDERWATER CRIME SCENE

During outdoor searches it is possible to locate a body of water within the area to be searched. The water source may be a shallow swamp, river with strong

Photo 9.7a

Underwater crime scene: a rusted metal drum containing a skull and assorted bones was located on the ocean bottom in a harbor.

Photo 9.7b

Close-up view of some of the remains and the barrel top after they were recovered by divers. The evidence is maintained in the water for transportation to the laboratory to minimize further oxidation and deterioration.

currents, deep quarry or lake, covered by a layer of ice, and composed of either fresh or salt water. Each of these water bodies has its own unique characteristics and will require slightly different search and recovery operations. Trained personnel in consultation with crime scene investigators should conduct the actual underwater search process. Ideally, some of the dive team members will have training or an understanding of the crime scene process and need to document and properly collect all relevant evidence. Minimally, crime scene personnel should be available to assist with the preservation and packaging of recovered evidence. Photos 9.7a and b show the underwater searching operation and the recovery of evidence.

In addition to the personnel dive and safety equipment, specialized equipment is helpful. Waterproof cameras and video cameras, as well as accessory lighting, are necessary to document evidence and the overall underwater scene. However, the water clarity may be so poor that photographic documentation is not possible. If underwater photography is not possible documentation will be limited to sketching and good notes. Global positioning systems can aid sketching and recording the location of evidence. Once the evidence is located containers must be available to preserve the evidence during transportation from the site to the laboratory for examination.

If the area to be searched is relatively shallow, and searches can walk through the water with boots or waders, then waterproof metal detectors can be employed. Other types of advanced electronic equipment can aid in underwater searches. A proton magnometer detects variations in the Earth's magnetic field caused by ferrous metals. A side-scan sonar unit can be used to detect any objects that protrude above the bottom of the body of water. Sub-bottom profiler instruments generate high-resolution images of the bottom and some objects buried just beneath the bottom surface.

Accurately locating the underwater scene or evidence is often the largest challenge. If the location is not known investigators must utilize witness statements, currents or water flow rates, wind direction and speed, water depth and clarity, and available information or maps detailing the bottom topography. Not only will this information aid in the search, but it is also beneficial for planning the safest possible dive mission. If the surface can be searched by boat then sonar devices, grappling hooks, or specially trained canines can aid in the search process, particularly in the search for bodies. Experts agree that dogs can detect people underwater at depths as great as 150 feet. If suspect areas or items are located during the search these areas must be marked for further diving and exploration by either placing buoys or identifying the location with a GPS unit. As with land-based searches, it is important to identify perimeters and establish a search pattern or grid, thus ensuring that the entire area is searched. Searches for submerged bodies have further complications. As decomposition progresses the body will fill with gas and float; any current or tide may remove it from the original site and deposit it elsewhere. For this reason it is important to attempt to determine if the location of the body is the primary crime scene.

Once the search area has been narrowed, evidence or a body can be located by one of the above-described methods, or if the body of water is relatively small then the divers will be sent in to conduct an underwater search. Divers can utilize search methods such as the spiral or grid methods. The underwater area to be searched needs to be marked with anchors and lines, or other forms of visible markers. When visibility is reduced two divers can cover an area with a snag line search. With one diver on each end of the rope, the rope is towed over the search area in an effort to snag any protruding objects. Working off a line is also beneficial for diver safety.

Once evidence or a body is located the scene and evidence should be documented before recovery is attempted. All small items recovered can be placed individually into plastic bags or containers and brought to the surface by the diver. However, for a heavy or large item a lift bag or power winch will be required.

The recovery of a submerged body requires careful recovery techniques to ensure that all of the evidence is recovered (as shown in Photo 9.8). Special attention should be drawn to the position of the body and clothing, as these factors will change during the removal process. Once the body is carefully brought to the surface the body can be transported to the medical examiner's facility for further study. In addition to recovering the body, a sample of water should be obtained and the water temperature determined, both at the surface and the bottom if applicable.

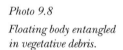

Photo 9.8
Floating body entangled in vegetative debris.

Recovery of evidence or objects also requires special handling and procedures. Most objects tend to deteriorate much more rapidly in water than on land, especially if they have been recovered from salt water. Moreover, once items are removed from the water oxidation or other deterioration processes will often occur rapidly. Evidence is usually recovered in one of three general conditions, which determine how the item is handled after being removed from the crime scene.

Evidence with little or no visible deterioration may be dried off and forwarded for analysis. Certain objects, such as ferrous metals, e.g. firearms, will oxidize rapidly once removed from the water. Therefore, it is recommended that the ferrous object be packaged in a container of the water from which it was removed, and transported to the laboratory as soon as possible. Items displaying moderate to substantial deterioration may need to be preserved by a variety of techniques, e.g. electrolysis, by a professional in the field of preservation. If items are so severely deteriorated that salvage is unlikely, then the item should be thoroughly documented in place. The item can be encased in plastic to preserve the physical state until it is determined whether any preservation is possible.

Raising large objects from a soft muddy bottom is difficult as there is a suction effect. The amount of suction depends upon the size and shape of the object as well as the condition of the bottom. Caution must be exercised to avoid injury to divers or damage to the object, as it suddenly breaks free from the bottom suction. To minimize these dangers when lifting large objects, divers should utilize buoyant lift bags. When slowly inflated these lift bags will help raise a large object to the surface in a controlled manner.

FIRE AND EXPLOSIVE SCENES

FIRE SCENES

The greatest single factor in the successful resolution of an arson case is the quality of the physical evidence recovered from the scene. The most valuable evidence will be collected at or near the point(s) where the fire started; therefore the majority of the effort at a fire scene goes into locating the point(s) of origin of the fire.

Despite the importance of a thorough fire scene investigation, a number of major complications are associated with fire investigations. In a recent research report issued by the Technical Working Group on Fire/Arson Scene Investigation these major complications were identified.

1   A fire can be a complex event whose origin and cause are not obvious. Qualified fire scene investigators are essential; however, their training and preparation is time consuming and costly, requiring dedication to the profession over many years.

2   The destructive power of the fire itself compromises evidence from the outset. In addition, further destruction may occur by the normal and necessary duties of fire personnel carrying out rescue, suppression, overhaul, and salvage tasks.

3   Representatives from numerous law enforcement, fire, public health, and utility agencies are necessarily at the scene for different critical functions. With so many people at the scene there is an increased risk that evidence will be lost, destroyed, or its integrity brought into question.

4   Responsibility for the investigation of fires is bifurcated. While the fire service has the primary responsibility of establishing the fire's cause, if the conclusion was that the fire was purposely set, a crime has been committed and law enforcement officials investigate the criminal aspect.

   Ideally, the investigation will proceed with a unified team consisting of representatives with expertise in fire services and other members with law enforcement investigative experience.

5   A lack of commitment to conduct fire investigations exists on the part of some law enforcement and fire agencies. This lack of commitment is often attributed to a lack of resources or competing responsibilities.

Documentation of fire scenes

The optimal situation is for the investigator to arrive at the scene while the fire is ongoing. This will allow for documentation of the characteristics of the fire and smoke, and the crowd watching the fire. After the fire, photographs should be taken of all aspects of the scene, especially of any destruction caused by the fire department.

Traditional documentation methods such as photography, videotaping, sketches, and notes are required. Photography and videotaping can be difficult in that special techniques must be used to ensure proper exposure, as the black fire scene absorbs a majority of available light. Documentation of undisturbed or normal conditions is extremely important. For example, all electrical circuits should be inspected and documented to demonstrate whether they did or could not have contributed the cause of fire. Documentation should continue throughout the process.

Investigating the fire scene

The first priority is the safety of the investigative team. Many fire scenes are structurally unstable. Moreover, fire scenes contain many caustic or otherwise hazardous materials that require special handling and personal protective equipment. Scene investigators should not enter the scene until all suppression activities have subsided and the atmosphere quality and structural integrity are determined. However, nothing at the scene should be moved before the initial examination of a fire scene unless absolutely necessary for safety reasons.

The main motivation in the search of a fire scene is to discover the point of origin. The search should start in areas away from the point of origin, those with little or no damage. The team should work towards the point of origin, to areas with the greatest amount of damage. Through observation of the level of destruction and degree of charring the path of burning can be followed back to the origin. The following factors should be evaluated:

1   Exterior damage – examination of the charring and smoke pattern on the exterior of the structure will indicate the direction the fire moved, if the fire started externally and what windows and doors were open.

2   Doors and windows – greater damage to one side of a door or window than the other will indicate the direction of the fire and if the door or window was open during the fire.

3   Char pattern – when fire envelopes a wooden beam it will round the edges away from the fire and create an alligator pattern on the charred surface. The intensity of a fire at a particular point will be reflected in the charring pattern. Photo 9.9 is an example of a burn pattern on wood beams.

Photo 9.9

Burn patterns on 2 × 4 wooden studs, showing the direction of fire.

Collection and preservation of evidence

There is a variety of evidence that may be located at a fire scene, some unique to fire scenes, others common at many other crime scenes. Arson fires are commonly started with the aid of an accelerant. Accelerants include gasoline, other flammable liquids, flammable solids, and flammable gases. Generally, there is some form of ignition device, such as matches, cigarettes, candles, timing devices, or explosives. More common types of evidence that may be located at fire scenes include imprint and impression evidence, such as fingerprints, footprints, tire tracks, and tool marks. In addition, various forms of biological evidence may exist, such as bone, blood, tissue, and teeth.

Any debris at or near the point of origin should be examined carefully to determine if any evidence of the cause of the fire remains. Odors, particularly petroleum-based products, may remain from an accelerant. Pieces of a timing device or plant designed to ignite a combustible material at a time after the initiating action may remain in the debris.

Trailers may have been used to spread fire from one point to another. If more than one point of origin is located the areas between the separate origins should be carefully examined for potential trailers. There are a variety of containers that an arsonist may have used to transport accelerant to the scene including bottles, cans, or boxes. The arsonist may leave behind any tools used to enter the structure or start the fire hoping that the fire will destroy the evidence. A mass of paper or books near the point of origin may have been placed there to destroy incriminating evidence and may still contain salvageable evidence. All samples of debris and soil or other evidence should be taken from the crime scene and analyzed for petroleum or other possible accelerant products.

Care must be taken to properly collect and preserve arson samples. To minimize changes in the condition of arson-related samples certain procedures should be followed. Use clean tools for collecting items of evidence from different locations within the scene. Place evidence in clean, airtight, and secure containers. Clean metal paint cans of various sizes are excellent containers for fire debris. As many of these samples contain volatile materials the samples should be transported to a forensic laboratory in a timely manner.

EXPLOSIVE SCENES

Generally, post-blast explosive scenes are handled with the same basic procedures, tools, and objectives as arson scenes. Therefore, basic scene security, documentation, and need for recognition, collection, and preservation of the evidence remain vital objectives. However, there are different dynamics associated with certain explosive materials, and modifications in the process must be possible. Also, with post-blast scenes there is always the concern that some unexploded material is still present, thus posing a significant danger to crime scene personnel.

Once the security and integrity of the scene is ensured the preliminary scene evaluation should focus on several key objectives. In many cases, post-blast scenes are massive catastrophic events, which will require substantial equipment, personnel, and resources to complete the task. Photo 9.10 shows the site of the Oklahoma bombing. Safety concerns are paramount. Investigators must be alert for structural damage, secondary explosive devices, unconsumed explosive materials, failed utilities, and a wide variety of hazardous materials. If these factors are encountered crime scene personnel should immediately vacate the scene until qualified personnel render the particular hazards safe. Evidence preservation will continue to be a challenge and concern as many people and machinery move throughout the scene to complete the process. Anytime there is a large cadre of people and equipment a very structured, centrally managed control system is essential.

Investigators must locate the seat, or location where the explosive devices were positioned at the time of detonation. The seat will be a major source of potential evidence. Additional evidence and debris may be located at a considerable distance from the seat, depending upon the type of explosive material. There are two general categories of explosives, high explosives and low explosives. A low explosive is made by confining a low explosive in a container and igniting the material, the confined gases increasing the internal pressure until the container bursts. The rate of detonation for low explosives is below 3280 feet per second. Common examples of low explosives include black powder, single or double base smokeless gunpowder, or flares. Conversely, high explosives detonate instantly, and in that they must, in general, be initiated by the shock of an additional primary high explosive, such as a blasting cap. Rates of detonation can far exceed 3280 feet per second. Common examples include dynamite, military C4, and ANFO – ammonium nitrate and fuel oil mixture.

As a result of these significant differences, primarily with rates of detonation, the blast forces, and resulting residue and fragment distributions differ. Low explosives exhibit pushing or heaving power. As a result the fragments are larger, with 90-degree angles, and a majority of residues consumed in the process. High explosives have shattering power. This results in smaller fragment pieces with knife-like edges, pitting on the surface, and some unconsumed fragments.

Collection of evidence at post-blast sites should include the following types of evidence.

1 Suspected bomb components and fragments – do not forget to make arrangements to recover and preserve fragments removed from victims.
2 Material associated with the construction and transportation of explosives and devices should be collected, including batteries, tape, booklets, vehicles, and containers.
3 Carefully examine the bomb seat and take numerous debris samplings and swabbing from the seat.
4 Residues can also be swabbed off of surfaces facing the seat.

Photo 9.10

An overall view of the Murrah Federal Building in Okalahoma after a terrorist attack, by placing a large quantity of explosives in a vehicle parked in front of the building.

5   Remember to take adequate control samples to eliminate indigenous materials as the source of the explosion.

6   As with fire scenes other traditional types of evidence such as fingerprints, footprints, tire tracks, trace evidence, and blood should not be overlooked.

Explosive devices located at crime scenes

Crime scene personnel should always evaluate suspicious packages and objects at crime scenes with the possibility that the scene may be booby-trapped or contain explosive devices designed to injure unwelcome intruders at the scene. Even the mere suspicion of explosive devices warrants immediate action. All personnel should be removed from the scene and the perimeter re-established so that all personnel are at a safe distance until the scene has been systematically searched and all hazardous devices located and rendered safe by bomb technicians. Booby-traps have been located at clandestine drug laboratory sites, organized crime facilities, and other crime scenes.

Booby-traps come in various forms. Light switches have been wired to containers of flammable liquids, and detonate when an individual inadvertently throws the light switch. Appliances such as refrigerator doors can be wired with explosives. Monofilament trip lines attached to pipe bombs or homemade shotguns are other possibilities. There have even been cases where videotape cassettes have been altered to detonate an internal explosive when the tape is placed in a video player.

There are some universal precautions that may minimize the potential of falling victim to booby-traps. Stay alert, and visually check everything before you touch or disturb the item. Check furniture and appliances before using them. Do not use light switches or electrical appliances in the suspect area. Do not smoke. Do not consume food or drink in the area as chemical contamination may occur through the air or contact.

Photo 9.11a

Examples of 'booby traps' or anti-personnel devices found within the home of an individual who had shot several police officers.

Photo 9.11b

Pipe bombs located around the perimeter of this same individual's home.

In a rural part of Connecticut, police officers responded to a minor neighborhood complaint. The individual being questioned by police drew his weapon without provocation and began firing at police officers. During the ensuing gun battles three troopers were critically injured by gunfire. A cursory examination of the curtilage, vehicles, and outbuilding revealed numerous weapons, and explosive ingredients. A systematic search by bomb technicians uncovered over 20 booby-traps designed to injure or kill individuals moving throughout his residence, as shown in Photos 9.11a and b. Failure to act on the early warning signs and implementation of a bomb search and removal plan would most likely have resulted in additional casualties to law enforcement personnel.

CLANDESTINE DRUG LABORATORIES

The operations of an illicit laboratory are so varied in nature that a full discussion of the topic is not possible. Clandestine laboratories can produce a variety of illicit or controlled substances. Different types of labs or processes may be located at a single location. Yet, of all the clandestine laboratories seized in the United States during the past 10 years over 80% have been associated with the production of methamphetamine. Some processes are designed to extract an illicit substance from raw (plant) material, such as morphine from opium. Other labs synthesize the illicit substance using combinations of raw materials and/or chemicals. Other procedures are designed to convert an undesirable form of a drug into a more desirable form, the illicit or controlled form of the drug.

Despite law enforcement efforts current trends show no signs of stopping despite an increase in the number of clandestine laboratories located and seized every year. Lab seizures are increasing in almost every state in the United States. While regulations and monitoring has improved, chemical ingredients necessary for synthesis are still readily available. Further, the use of some of these illicit compounds, such as methamphetamine, is on the rise.

Clandestine laboratories are unregulated and often very unsafe laboratories. Many of the chemicals used in synthesis are inherently hazardous, and even more so when used and disposed of improperly. Chemicals are rarely labeled, seldom in original containers, and may be mixed with other chemicals. Apparatus may be improperly constructed or used. Further, the site may have been intentionally abandoned in a hazardous condition or booby-trapped. The following general precautions should be taken when seizing a clandestine drug laboratory, under the supervision of trained chemists or clandestine laboratory personnel. Once these precautions are implemented, the clandestine laboratory site should be treated as any other crime scene when identifying, collecting and preserving other types of physical evidence. Evidence such as fingerprints, documents, money, records, computers and supplies could be extremely important for further investigation.

1   Never enter a laboratory operation without having a qualified chemist as technical advisor present. Call the forensic lab or toxicology lab for technical assistance. In addition to laboratory personnel, the team should have personnel trained and equipped to handle potentially explosive material.

2   Never smoke, eat or drink within or near the clandestine laboratory.

3   Do not dispose of, or destroy anything by pouring into water or by pouring water into it.

4   Do not shut off any heaters, stirring motors or other mechanical or electrical apparatus.

5   Secure the clandestine laboratory and vicinity. Give no unauthorized or unnecessary personnel access to the premises.

6   Maintain security until a qualified chemist reaches the scene to dismantle and shut down laboratory operations.

During the search of a clandestine laboratory or site suspected of one housing such a laboratory careful attention should be given to chemicals and chemical containers. These chemical containers may provide leads and corroborating evidence as to the types of illegal drugs or illicit compounds manufactured at this laboratory. Tables 9.1 and 9.2 list reagents for specific drug

Chemical reagent	Drug synthesis
Phenylacetone	Amphetamine
	Methamphetamine
Formamide	Amphetamine
Methylformamide	Methamphetamine
Cyclohexanone	Phencyclidine – PCP
Piperidine	Phencyclidine – PCP
Piperonal	Heliotropine – MDA
Nitroethane	MDA
Isosafrole	MDA
Indole	Dimethyltryptamine – DMT
Diethylamine	DMT
Olivetol	Tetrahydrocannabinol
Citral	THC
Verbenol	THC
Ergotamine	LSD
Lysergic acid	LSD
Benzoyl chloride	Cocaine
Succinaldehyde	Cocaine
Diphenylacetonitrile	Methadone
Phenylacetonitrile	Methylphenidate
2,5-Dimethoxy-4-methylbenzaldehyde	STP
3,4,5-Trimethoxybenzoic actd	Mescaline

Table 9.1

Reagents associated with the synthesis of specific drugs.

Table 9.2

Hazards associated with certain chemicals commonly found at clandestine laboratories.

Chemical	Caution
Acetic acid	Caustic
Acetone	Flammable and toxic
Benzene	Flammable and toxic
Boron trifluoride	May inflame on contact with water
Chloroform	Toxic
Ethanol (ethyl alcohol)	Flammable
Ethyl ether	Highly flammable
Lithium aluminum hydride	Inflames and may explode on contact with water
Magnesium metal	Flammable
Methanol or methyl alcohol	Flammable and toxic
Sodium or potassium hydroxide	Caustic

synthesis and general synthesis. Purchase of many of these chemicals in large quantities is often monitored by law enforcement and regulatory agencies.

Documentation is essential. Sketch, photograph, and video all equipment and apparatus in place. Document all chemicals and containers and the amounts of materials in each of these containers. This information may be valuable in determining the potential approximate yield of the particular laboratory. Samples of all chemicals should be seized and maintained for further analysis. Large quantities of chemicals may be disposed in a safe and environmentally sound manner by licensed contractors. Remember to swab empty apparatus as residues may remain and can provide information as to previous compounds synthesized at this laboratory.

SCENES CONTAINING BIOLOGICAL/CHEMICAL AGENTS

Incidents involving weapons of mass destruction, nuclear, chemical, or biological in nature, require a high degree of cooperation and coordination between many agencies at many levels of government, as well as the private sector. This team should have representatives from local, state, and federal law enforcement, fire department officials, specially trained bomb disposal technicians, personnel trained in handling and transporting hazardous materials, scientists capable of performing presumptive or screening tests in the field to determine the nature of the hazardous material, scientists to perform laboratory analysis, physicians or public health officials, and members of the military. Each of these groups can offer their own unique perspective, and can provide invaluable resources to a response team. While it may be administratively necessary to elect a lead agency, none of these groups should be minimized in their function.

Training programs should be implemented at all levels. First responders to incidents or threats of weapons of mass destruction will need basic training as how to quickly and effectively minimize the hazards and exposure to citizens as well as investigators. These personnel will need to know the basic action plan so that these necessary notifications can be made without delay. Most often the first responder role will be performed by uniformed police officers. Highly technical training is necessary for the bomb and hazardous device technicians who will be tasked with handling the materials, as well as any personnel assigned to perform analysis on the suspect material. Military personnel can provide the required mass of personnel should the need arise. Protocols should be clearly established so that the interjection of military personnel is done in a timely and cohesive manner. All involved personnel, including medical staff, will need training in the proper use of protective clothing and equipment, and the various forms of protective equipment to defend against different nuclear, chemical, or biological threats.

GENERAL PROCEDURES

Standard operating procedures for dealing with weapons of mass destruction will vary among jurisdictions, mainly due to differences in available resources, and the types of communities served by those jurisdictions. However, there are basic steps that should be uniform. If weapons of mass destruction are encountered, suspected, or a potential based on other circumstances it is imperative to implement the relevant procedures as quickly as possible. While protection and preservation of human life are of greatest importance, a properly implemented plan will allow for the proper recognition, documentation, collection, preservation, and analysis of evidence.

First responders must be prepared to begin containment and evacuation procedures. Whenever possible, without needlessly endangering themselves, they should render aid and remove injured parties from the immediate area. They should be aware of contamination issues, protecting themselves, and trying to avoid unnecessary spreading of the agents. A brief situation analysis will assist in determining what additional personnel or agencies are needed.

Since approximately 70% of all weapons of mass destruction are deployed by means of explosive devices, bomb disposal technicians should always be summoned to the scene. As additional members of the response team arrive a more detailed analysis and response plan can be generated. Only after the situation is stabilized and contained should search and recovery efforts be attempted. Once a suspect material is located, if possible, presumptive testing should be done immediately to determine if the threat is real, and what additional measures should be taken to decontaminate the area and treat affected individuals. Once the material is collected it must be packaged in a manner to avoid the possibility of spillage or contamination. Packing requirements will vary due to different types of hazardous compounds. This material should be brought to a laboratory that is equipped to conduct analysis on hazardous materials.

Only after the hazardous material is removed and the area is decontaminated or deemed safe should crime scene personnel enter the scene to perform their normal crime scene documentation and processing functions. Finally, as with any major incident, an after-action report and meeting among the team members would be an invaluable learning experience.

Table 9.3

Chemical and biological agents associated with weapons of mass destruction.

Anthrax
Botulism
Brucellosis
Q fever
Ricin
Sarin
Smallpox
Soman
Staphylococcal Enterotoxin B
Tularemia
Venezuelan Equine Encephalitis
Viral Hemorrhagic Fever
VX

SCENES WITH ELECTRONIC AND COMPUTER EVIDENCE

INTRODUCTION

Computers and electronic telecommunication devices are not new for much of the developed world; however, these items and our reliance on these items have increased at an exponential rate in a very short period of time. Our daily dependence on these technologies both for business and pleasure is demonstrated by the fact that the worldwide Internet population is approximately 350 million strong and growing. As a result, computers and other various electronic devices are becoming associated with criminal activities or investigations. These objects may be a fruit of the crime, evidence of the crime, means of a crime, target of a crime, tool for a criminal act, or a repository for information related to criminal activity. Moreover, not only are computers and electronic evidence associated with computer-based or Internet crimes, such as child pornography or e-commerce fraud, but also with many if not all types of criminal activity, including, larceny robbery, threatening, kidnapping, homicide, narcotics trafficking, fraud, etc.

Thus, the criminal justice system is being forced to change procedures, priorities, training objectives, and initiatives to address the high-tech reality that has been embraced by the criminal domains. Many jurisdictions are significantly behind the learning curve and need to rapidly invest significant resources for equipment, training, and related resources to combat computer, Internet, and other forms of high-tech crime. Crime scene investigations should expect to encounter some form of computer or electronic evidence at an increasing majority of crime scenes. Hence, they need to develop protocols and provide training so that their personnel can accomplish this mission without damaging or losing this form of evidence. Until a crime scene has the appropriate internal expertise they must be willing to secure the assistance of someone with sufficient expertise to avoid loss of valuable evidence. In addition, it is preferable to have plenty of time to plan a computer/data search.

Of course, sometimes there is not enough time to coordinate the execution of a search warrant with expert assistance, in which case the following suggestions will help to maintain the integrity of the evidence.

RECOMMENDED PROCEDURES FOR COMPUTER SYSTEM SEARCH AND SEIZURE

1   Through investigation, surveillance and/or intelligence sources, identify the type of computer (IBM-compatible, Apple, DOS-based) and whether it is a stand-alone system or attached to a network. Also ascertain, if possible, where the computer is located and whether it is in a protected place that will necessitate a warrant (like a home) or in a place in which a warrant might not be necessary (such as a private employer's place of business).

2   If seizure is pursuant to a search warrant, review the warrant to determine the scope of the search.

3   Secure the scene and remove any individuals from the proximity of the computer or power sources. If legally permissible, detain potential defendants away from the computer and interview them regarding password protection devices, encryption programs or any special program that the computer system or individual files may require. (Consider whether Miranda warnings and waiver may be appropriate.)

4   Check for remote infrared or voice-activated devices in possession of anyone at the scene.

5   Check the roof and area outside. (In a recent search warrant execution, there was a satellite uplink on the roof.)

6   Do not allow any unauthorized or untrained personnel to touch the computer or its peripherals. (The FBI considers any touching of the computer to be a forensic examination.)

7   Photograph:
    (a) The room in which the computer is located
    (b) Any images on the screen

      (c) The computer, peripheral devices, cabling, etc.

      (d) DIP switch settings

      (e) Area surrounding the computer, media, papers, manuals, access codes, passwords, etc.

8 If the computer is on, pull the power plug from the wall. If the computer is on and it appears as if a self-destruct program is running, immediately pull the power cord from the wall. (DO NOT TOUCH POWER SWITCH ON COMPUTER.) *If there is an uninterruptible power supply (UPS), pull the power cord from the back of the computer.*

9 Scan the area for any large magnets that may be used to damage electronic media.

10 Insert a prepared seizure diskette or wiped non-system disk into each drive bay and seal with evidence tape.

11 If the computer is connected to a modem line, disconnect the cable at the wall. Test for dial tone with a telephone handset and make a written note if the telephone line is operational at the time of the search.

12 Remove cover and photograph internal components and jumper settings. Disconnect power to any hard drive.

13 Seize and record:

      (a) Computer and peripherals

      (b) Software and hardware manuals

      (c) Notes, or notebooks that appear associated with the computer or peripherals

      (d) All media (e.g. floppy disks, CD-ROMs, Zip disks)

14 Tag and label all cables and note connections to peripheral devices. Tape and label any empty ports or slots not in use. Take photographs that clearly display the wiring configurations before disassembling the computer system.

15 Carefully label, log, package and prepare all seized evidence using Evidence Inventory Sheets especially drafted for computer seizures. Remember to maintain a tight chain of custody.

16 Ensure that all components and media are kept away from two-way radios while being transported to or stored in the Evidence Room.

You may want to dust the keyboard or certain switches for fingerprints. Fingerprint evidence would be helpful if you need to establish whether the suspect used the computer and/or if she had exclusive control.

EVIDENCE HANDLING CONSIDERATIONS

Treat the evidence just as you would treat narcotics or a murder weapon or any other kind of evidence. Just as you would not pick up a gun suspected of being the murder weapon in a homicide and pull the trigger a few times to see if it works, do not turn on the computer or touch anything when you seize a computer or data *unless you know what you are doing!*

Do not examine original evidence such as files on the subject's disks. You wouldn't snort white powder if you found it in a vial during a search, would you? Preserve the original evidence in its original state. Make a true copy of the original evidence. If possible, have the subject sign a stipulation that the copy is an exact duplicate of the original.

Make an extra copy to use as your 'working copy.' Then you can open up the files on the 'working copy' and look to see what is inside. (Don't forget to run a virus scan before opening any files.) Figure 9.1 shows a case view of a program designed to assist forensic data examiners in computer crime investigations.

WHEN TO OBTAIN A SECOND WARRANT

One can include only as much information in an affidavit and application for a search warrant as one possesses at the time. As is frequently the case with any other search warrant execution, police may encounter situations in which it will be appropriate to obtain a second search warrant. This may be the case when a computer turns up unexpectedly during a search and is not addressed in the first warrant. However, if you particularly described the computer system and data in a search warrant application and included language requesting analysis of the computer system and/or data, you should not need to obtain a second search warrant to perform a forensic examination. Be aware that rules may vary from jurisdiction to jurisdiction.

If, for example, an officer executed a search warrant that authorized the seizure of videotape, she would not need a second search warrant that authorized viewing it with the assistance of a VCR. Everyone assumes that you may seize the tape's container, because without it the tape would be destroyed or useless. In the same sense, you must, of necessity, seize the container of electronically stored data when you seize the data because the data depends on the container (the physical diskette) for its continued existence.

Electronic data is similar to orange juice. You cannot carry orange juice unless it is in a container. You have to put orange juice in a glass or plastic container in order to transport it, or you'll not only make a mess, but you will lose your orange juice as well. Data stored in electronic format must be held in a container – just like orange juice. If you have the authority to seize the data, you have to take custody of it in the diskette or the hard drive on which it is held. If you have a warrant that authorizes seizure of a videotape, you would not make a copy of the tape at the search scene.

If you have a warrant authorizing seizure of orange juice, you would seize the orange juice and the containers. You would not pour the orange juice into a different glass. You wouldn't take a picture or video of the orange juice and call the picture or video your evidence. You would seize the orange juice in its original container.

It is axiomatic that if you possess the authority to seize the data, that implies that you also can utilize the means necessary to view/feel/hear the data. When you have a search warrant that authorizes seizure of an audiotape, you may listen to it using a tape player. You do not apply for a second search warrant to listen to the tape. It follows that you should not need to apply for a second warrant to view data contained on electronic media if you have a warrant that authorizes you to seize and analyze the 'data.' If you have any doubts, and in any case involving a question of law, you should consult the appropriate state's attorney.

A search warrant may particularize the items to be searched and seized, but not include computer hardware, software and files. It may become apparent, during the course of a search, that a computer, computer system or data is an instrumentality of criminal activity, contraband or evidence. If you wish to seize the computer system and/or the data stored within or on diskette or other storage facility, and your search warrant did not address the possibility of electronic evidence, you should secure the scene and obtain a second search warrant to allow both seizure and off-site laboratory analysis of the computer, peripherals and information contained therein.

Generally, if you seize a computer, diskettes or other electronically stored data /and you do not possess a warrant or consent that explicitly allows you to search the computer and/or its contents, you should obtain a warrant that allows you to do so. Consult with your local District or State's Attorney to determine the current law in your jurisdiction regarding these matters. Until this issue is squarely addressed as to electronic evidence, a warrant is advisable. Whenever there is any question, the investigator should consult the appropriate state's attorney.

THE INTERNET CRIME SCENE

Just as with any other crime scene, when crimes are committed via the Internet, the perpetrator leaves evidence behind. But, the electronic evidence is delicate and, if not handled properly, subject to alteration or destruction. It requires investigators and evidence technicians who are skilled in gathering and preserving electronic evidence in its many forms to ensure the integrity of the evidence so that it may be used successfully in court.

The Internet comprises a number of areas with different functionalities, each of which could be the scene of a crime. Internet evidence contains electronic communications, which are subject to the strictures of the Electronic Communications Privacy Act of 1986 (ECPA) (18 USC § 2701 et seq.). The ECPA restricts the type of communications government agents may obtain and what legal process agents must use. In addition to the ECPA, there are a number of federal laws, such as the Federal Privacy Protection Act (affecting how evidence may be obtained from 'publishers,' 42 USC § 2000aa), the federal wiretap law (affecting the interception of real-time electronic communication, Title III, 18 USC §§ 2510–22) and the Cable Communications Policy Act (affecting access to cable subscriber information, which probably includes cable access to the Internet, 47 USC § 551) that regulate how the government may obtain Internet and electronic evidence. Similarly, there are a host of state laws that further restrict access to Internet and electronic evidence that investigators should be familiar with before executing an Internet search and seizure of evidence. For example, the State of Connecticut has laws governing the interception of wire communications (CGS § 54–41 et seq.) and search of a news organization (CGS § 54–33i). A complete discussion of the ECPA and all of the laws that govern access to Internet communications is beyond the scope of this text, but it bears repeating that investigators should be familiar with the laws that govern search and seizure of electronic evidence in their jurisdiction.

The four most often-used features or areas of the Internet are email, news-groups, chat and websites. Each of these areas will be described and best practices for evidence preservation and collection discussed in the following section.

Email

Email is an electronic form of communication that can contain letter-type cor-respondence as well as graphic images or attached data such as spreadsheets, computer software or graphic images. Email is similar to conventional mail in that it is addressed from one individual to another and is usually intended to be private. Because email traverses through a number of computer servers, it is more like a postcard because its contents are not 'sealed,' but open to view by any of its handlers.

Email usually contains a message header that gives information about the individual who originated a particular message or graphic and the return address in order to respond to them. Individuals who have an Internet email address usually have a subscription to, membership in or affiliation with an organization or commercial service that provides access to the Internet. A provider of Internet access is referred to as an Internet service provider or 'ISP.'

The ISP operation is similar to a post office. Email sent to an ISP account owner is held in storage electronically on the ISP server. Whenever a message is sent or received by a user, a copy of the correspondence is maintained on the ISP server for a period of time, dependent upon the amount of storage space available on the server and the policies of the ISP regarding storage.

Email sent, accessed, processed and maintained by a computer system may be important to a criminal investigation in two distinct and important respects:

(1) the objects themselves may be instrumentalities, fruits, or evidence of crime, and/or (2) the objects may have been used to collect and store information about crimes (in the form of data).

Information available from Internet service providers (ISPs) is as follows:

1 *Subscriber information.* In order to establish an Internet access account, one usually must provide a name and address for billing purposes. The word 'usually' is important here, because service providers are not required to maintain any information on subscribers. Some Internet service providers (ISPs) set up an account 'for life' for a one-time fee. Other ISPs do not require a credit card number and do not verify address information. This is true with some web-based email account providers.

2 *Account and billing information.* Account information includes how the subscriber is billed, such as to a credit card account and the account number, when the account was established and by whom. Billing information includes charges for which the subscriber was billed. You may obtain detailed billing information from some ISPs if you specifically request it in your warrant. Detailed billing will give you a history of when an account was accessed, under what screen name (if applicable) and for what amount of time. The following language may be helpful when requesting subscriber and billing information.

3 *Buddy lists and favorites.* Some ISPs allow users to maintain a 'buddy list' or 'favorites.' A buddy list or address book contains email addresses of other Internet users to whom the subject often sends messages. A 'favorites' list contains addresses of frequently visited sites to facilitate moving from one website to another quickly without typing the whole address.

4 *Email and files attached to email.* There are three forms of email maintained on an ISP's server – new mail, sent mail and read mail. The three forms differ substantially in the amount of time the ISP retains them. New mail is mail that has been sent to the subscriber but has not yet been read. New mail resides on the ISP server until the subscriber accesses (or 'logs on to') the Internet account. New mail is kept the longest – usually about a month. Sent mail is mail sent by the subscriber. Sent mail may be maintained on an ISP server for as long as a month. Read mail is mail that the subscriber received, opened and read. Read mail has the shortest retention. America Online keeps read mail for only two days, but many ISPs keep read mail longer.

It is important to note that the subject's hard drive should contain the same information that you will obtain from the ISP (with the exception of new mail). Even if the subject deletes the information, it is often possible to reconstruct files and data.

It is possible to ask the ISP to preserve an account in anticipation of a search warrant. Many ISPs 'freeze' the account when they preserve it, denying access by the subscriber. If you are investigating ongoing criminal activity and do not want to alert the subject that s/he is the target of an investigation, freezing the Internet account may not be the best approach. You may need a court order requiring the ISP not to divulge the existence of the investigation in order to avoid alerting the subscriber of your inquiries.

Chain of custody

Prior to executing a search warrant for out-of-state data, it is essential to determine how the chain of custody will work and to document it for later reference. Always ensure that the ISP and, if possible, the other state law enforcement agency involved possesses a true copy of the data. If the data must be transported to you by any means that requires it to be out of the possession of a law enforcement officer, an acceptable means is to send it registered/certified mail, return receipt requested.

For example, America Online (AOL) and the Loudoun County Virginia Sheriffs' Office (the law enforcement agency that possesses jurisdiction over the area where the AOL server is located) have worked out the following procedure. The Loudoun County Sheriff obtains a search warrant based on the search warrant application provided by an officer in the state in which the subscriber's computer is located. The Sheriff executes the warrant by serving it on AOL. AOL makes a copy of the requested data and stores it on a diskette, which it hands over to the Loudoun Sheriff. The Sheriff takes the diskette back to her office and makes a copy of the AOL diskette. The Sheriff then arranges to mail (certified, return receipt) the AOL diskette to the officer who requested it. Should a question arise about the authenticity of the data, the prosecution may subpoena an AOL representative who can testify that the data is a 'true copy.'

Secondary email

It is possible to obtain limited World Wide Web access in order to send and receive email with only a computer, modem and dial line (Juno, for example). It is also possible to obtain an anonymous email account through the Internet if one has an Internet account. In addition to anonymity, an added benefit to a secondary, web-based email account is that one is not limited to accessing the email from one telephone line or computer. If the provider is a secondary email provider (such as MSN Hotmail), all the information you may have is the Internet protocol address through which the Internet was accessed, the date and time of access. With that information, you may get a search warrant or other appropriate legal process (refer to the Electronic Communications Privacy Act) to determine the sender of the email.

Mail lists

Mail lists are private message centers where only subscribers are able to read or send messages. Because mail lists are private and reach multiple individuals, they are often abused. Threats, child pornography and fraud are frequently committed through mail lists.

Newsgroups

Newsgroups allow any number of Internet users to communicate about their common interest. Newsgroups are named, and usually are named after the interest that will be discussed. For example, alt.sex.pedophilia, alt.sex.teen are fictitious examples of the names of newsgroups through which participants may discuss their sexual predilections, share graphic images and other information. The names of the newsgroups change, but they usually suggest the content in the name for the group. When a user posts a newsgroup message, readers around the world are able to read and respond to it. As with email, a user of a newsgroup can attach computer files, including but not limited to graphic images. Newsgroups allow a reader of the message to download the attached computer file or image. Some newsgroups are monitored, but most are not.

In monitored newsgroups, the monitor reviews messages and edits the content prior to posting. In theory, at least, a monitored newsgroup on the topic of cooking should only contain entries about cooking.

Newsgroups are similar to electronic bulletin boards (BBS) and chat rooms. In fact, newsgroups are very similar to the physical bulletin boards located in public places like grocery stores where people may post and view written paper messages. A key difference is that newsgroups proliferate throughout the Internet. One can find tens of thousands of newsgroup topics and interact with millions of people. A user of a newsgroup can read postings of interest, or can participate in posting discussions.

Chat rooms and instant messaging

A chat room can be the scene of a crime. A chat room is a vehicle available through the Internet through which any number of people can 'chat'. Like newsgroups, chat rooms, or 'channels', have topics of conversation. Some chat rooms are moderated, in which case someone, usually from the online service sponsoring the channel, moderates the chat. The moderator censors the content and has the ability to exclude inappropriate content and individuals. Most chat rooms are not moderated, however, and even though a topic may be the title of the room, the content of the conversation may not have any connection to the topic.

Individuals may opt, through their browser software, to log chat conversations, but the online service provider or server that 'hosts' the channel usually does not maintain any record or the actual conversations. The most information that an online service provider might keep that would be helpful to law enforcement in a criminal investigation would be when an individual signed on to the channel and how long they remained there.

Instant messaging is like a chatroom in that it is a real-time communication between individuals signed on to the Internet. The distinguishing feature of instant messaging is that the initial communication is made from one individual computer signed on to the Internet through an Internet service provider or online service through to another individual computer.

Once the connection is made from one computer to another, the ISP or online service drops out of the picture and does not record or log any information about the instant message activity. That makes it extremely difficult to obtain evidence when instant messaging is the scene of criminal activity. Like chatroom conversations, instant messages can be logged by setting browser software to log the messages. If the messages are not logged, forensic data analysis can sometimes determine some evidence of instant messages inadvertently stored by the personal computer.

Any criminal activity that can be conducted or furthered by telephone can be conducted or furthered in a chatroom or by instant message. Real-time communications on the Internet are usually through typed message. However, chat may include sound and video.

Websites

The World Wide Web (hereinafter 'www') is a service available on the Internet. The www increases the capability of the Internet to share information by using hypertext to create a mouse-based, point-and-click interface. The www utilizes 'web pages', which are actually documents. The software languages used to create web pages allows computers with different operating systems (Apple, Microsoft, Sun) to read the same files without first converting the files to the format of the different computers. A collection of web pages is known as a 'website'.

The www provides access to billions of pages of information. 'Surfing', that is, moving from one website to another on the www, is done utilizing a web browser bundled within the computer system or is provided by the Internet service provider as part of their proprietary package. Websites are often crime scenes. Individuals have been known to 'hack' into websites in order to gain access to other databases stored on the server. Customer information such as credit card numbers can be used to make fraudulent purchases. Websites may also be 'attacked' by hackers, such as in denial of service attacks, in which hackers bombard computer servers with so many pieces of information that the website either slows its response time or brings it down completely so that legitimate users cannot have access. Websites have also been used to distribute child pornography and illicit narcotics, to name only a few misuses.

Figure 9.1

Case view of Encase program, used for forensic data analysis in computer crime investigations.

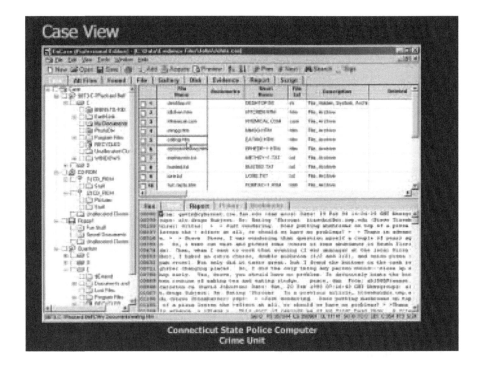

CHAPTER 10

CRIME SCENE RECONSTRUCTION

INTRODUCTION

Crime scene reconstruction is the process of determining or eliminating the events and actions that occurred at the crime scene through analysis of the crime scene pattern, the location and position of the physical evidence, and the laboratory examination of the physical evidence. Reconstruction not only involves scientific scene analysis, interpretation of the scene pattern evidence and laboratory examination of physical evidence, but also involves systematic study of related information and the logical formulation of a theory.

IMPORTANCE OF CRIME SCENE RECONSTRUCTION

It is often useful to determine the actual course of a crime by limiting the possibilities that resulted in the crime scene or the physical evidence as encountered. The possible need to reconstruct the crime is one major reason for maintaining the integrity of a crime scene. It should be understood that reconstruction is different from 're-enactment', 're-creation' or 'criminal profiling'. Re-enactment in general refers to having the victim, suspect, witness or other individual re-enact the event that produced the crime scene or the physical evidence based on their knowledge of the crime. Re-creation is to replace the necessary items or actions back at a crime scene through original scene documentation. Criminal profiling is a process based upon the psychological and statistical analysis of the crime scene, which is used to determine the general characteristics of the most likely suspect for the crime. Each of these types of analysis may be helpful for certain aspects of a criminal investigation. However, these types of analysis are rarely useful in the solution of a crime. Reconstruction is based on the ability to make observations at the scene, the scientific ability to examine physical evidence, and the use of logical approaches to theory formulations.

NATURE OF RECONSTRUCTION

Reconstruction is based partly on scientific experimentation and partly on past experiences. However, its steps and stages, as found in forensic science, closely follow basic scientific principles, theory formation, and logical methodology. It involves consideration and incorporation of all investigative information with physical evidence analysis and interpretation molded into a reasonable explanation of the crime and its related events. Logic, careful observation, and considerable experience, both in crime scene investigation and forensic examination of physical evidence, are necessary for proper interpretation, analysis and, ultimately, crime scene reconstruction.

BASIC PRINCIPLES FOR PHYSICAL EVIDENCE AND RECONSTRUCTION

The foundation of crime scene reconstruction is established by following the basic principles used in the forensic examination of physical evidence. The Locard theory of transfer is the fundamental basis of any forensic analysis. Although the lack of transfer has limited value in forensic laboratory examinations, it still has significant importance in crime scene reconstruction. Figure 10.1 shows the stages commonly involved in the examination of physical evidence at the crime scene and the laboratory.

RECOGNITION

Any type of forensic analysis usually starts from recognition of the potential evidence and separation of this from those items that have no evidential value. As discussed in the previous chapters, once the evidence is located, every effort and precaution should be used to preserve, to document and to collect this evidence. Laboratory analysis and comparisons of physical evidence are used to identify objects, substances, and materials, and to trace its origin. Once an item is identified it is then compared with known reference materials or standards. Depending upon the outcome of the comparison between the questioned sample and the known samples, one can then attempt to individualize the evidence and determine its origin. Once the crime scene appearance has been studied and the examination of physical evidence carried out, the crime or case can then be reconstructed.

Any type of reconstruction generally starts from recognition. Unless the potential evidence can be recognized, no further reconstruction can be carried out. Although the examination of a *macroscopical scene* or a *microscopical scene* is different, however, the general approach remains the same. Once potential

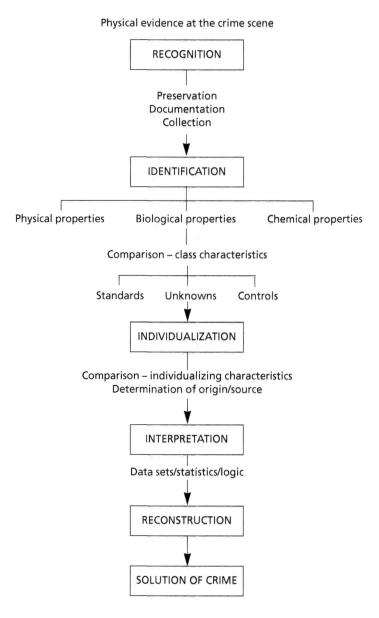

Figure 10.1
Stages of physical evidence examination.

physical evidence has been recognized the investigator should always make every possible effort to properly document, collect, and preserve the evidence. If a question arises, the investigator should always contact an expert in the field before any alteration of the evidence is done. This is important because most conditional evidence and pattern evidence can be easily altered or destroyed. It is very important to emphasize that *once such evidence has been altered, the ability to conduct a reconstruction, will be limited.*

IDENTIFICATION

Identification is a comparison process, which utilizes the class characteristics of a standard object or known substance to compare with the evidential item collected from the crime scene – by comparing the physical properties, morphological properties, chemical properties and biological properties. Table 10.1 is an example of some of the physical and morphological properties to be compared for identification purposes.

Table 10.1

Identification by physical and morphological properties.

Physical properties	Morphological properties
Size: Large, medium, small	State: Liquid, gas, solid
Shape: Round, square, amorphous	Source: Vegetation, insect, animal, human
Color: Red, blue, white . . .	Origin: Nature, man-made
Weight: Heavy, medium, light	
Length: Long, medium, short	
Width: Wide, medium, narrow	

Even the identification of persons also starts with the same logical process of physical type of identification that uses properties such as the height, weight, size, race, and hair and eye color, etc. to include or eliminate someone. Then more specific measurement can be carried out to individualize a person. The types of physical measurements are referred to as anthropometry, a system developed by Alphonse Bertillon in the early 1900s. However, if one identifies a friend or relative, one generally uses a combination of class characteristics and the special features (individualizing characteristics) of the person and then compares them to a mental picture of the person. This process of comparison is the same process used to identify a hair, weapon, or clothing.

When an item of physical evidence is identified but cannot be truly individualized, it will always have similar class characteristics; for this reason, statements about how similar these characteristics are can sometimes be made. The degree of similarity of particular evidence or characteristics depends on many factors, and varies from being fairly easily calculated, as in the case of blood groups, to being limited to only broad estimates of similarity. Tables 10.2 is a list of the specific areas used in reconstruction through identification of serological evidence class characteristics.

1	Species determination
2	Sex determination
3	Race determination
4	Age determination
5	Source determination
6	Genetic marker typing
7	Population distributions
8	Pattern interpretation

Table 10.2
Serological evidence laboratory results for reconstruction.

INDIVIDUALIZATION

Individualization is unique to forensic science; it refers to the demonstration that a particular sample is unique, even among members of the same class. It may also refer to the demonstration that a questioned piece of evidence from a crime scene and a similar known sample of evidence have a common origin. Thus, in addition to class characteristics, objects and materials possess individual characteristics that can be used to distinguish members of the same class. The nature of these individual characteristics varies from one type of evidence to another, but forensic scientists try to take advantage of them in efforts to individualize a piece of physical evidence. Some types of evidence can be truly individualized, but with some other types an approach to the goal of individualization is possible. These types of individualizations are referred to as partial, and in some cases they are nothing more than refined identifications, such as genetic marker determination from a bloodstain, DNA typing of semen evidence, or trace elemental analysis of paint chips. The term identification is sometimes used to mean personal identification (the individualization of persons). Fingerprints, for example, can be used to 'identify' an individual. The terminology is unfortunate, since this is really an individualization. Likewise, dental evidence and dental records may be used by a forensic odontologist in making personal individualizations in situations where dead bodies cannot be readily identified otherwise (such as in mass disaster or in cases of fire and explosions).

The identification and individualization analyses of physical evidence and the conclusions drawn from them are important ingredients in a final reconstruction.

RECONSTRUCTION

Reconstruction is based on the results of crime scene examination, laboratory analysis, and other independent sources of information to reconstruct case events. Reconstruction often involves the use of inductive and deductive logic, statistical data, information from the crime scene, pattern analysis, and laboratory analysis results on a variety of physical evidence. Reconstruction can be a very complex task, linking many types of physical evidence, stain pattern information, analytical results, investigative information, and other documentary and testimonial evidence into a complete entity.

The developing fields of artificial intelligence (CODIS and AFIS, for example) and expert systems have opened up a new dimension in reconstruction. These systems allow forensic scientist modeling and representation of laboratory analysis results, reasoning and enacting of a crime scene, logic, comparing and profiling of a suspect, and making logic decisions concerning the case. Advances in hardware and software have added systematic problem solving to the forensic scientist's repertoire. Computer technology allows communication between the user and the expert system – in a sense each is helping the other to solve a specific forensic problem. Reconstructions are often desirable in criminal cases in which eyewitness evidence is absent or unreliable. They are important in many other types of cases, too, such as automobile and airplane accidents, fire and arson investigation, and major disasters.

STAGES IN RECONSTRUCTION

Reconstruction is considered a *scientific fact-gathering process* (see Figure 10.2). Reconstruction generally involves a group of actions that will set the stage for crime reconstruction. The following are the five separate stages commonly used in the process of reconstruction:

1 *Data collection:* all information or documentation information obtained at the crime scene, from the victim, or witnesses. Data including condition of the evidence, obvious patterns and impressions, condition of the victim, etc., are reviewed, organized, and studied.

2 *Conjecture:* before any detailed analysis of the evidence is obtained, a possible explanation or conjecture of the events involved in a criminal act may be done, but it must not become the only explanation being considered at this stage. It is only a possibility. There may be several more possible explanations, too.

3 *Hypothesis formulation:* further accumulation of data is based on the examination of the physical evidence and the continuing investigation. Scene examination and inspection of the physical evidence must be done. Scene and evidence examination includes

interpretation of bloodstain and impression patterns, gunshot patterns, fingerprint evidence, and analysis of trace evidence. This process leads to the formulation of an educated guess as to the probable course of events, a hypothesis.

4 *Testing:* once a hypothesis is formulated, further testing must be done to confirm or disprove the overall interpretation or specific aspects of the hypothesis. This stage includes comparisons of samples collected at the scene with known standards and alibi samples, chemical, microscopical and other analyses and testing. Controlled testing or experimentation of possible physical activity must be done to collaborate the reconstruction hypothesis.

5 *Theory formation:* additional information may be acquired during the investigation about the condition of the victim or suspect, the activities of the individuals involved, accuracy of witness accounts, and other information about the circumstances surrounding the events. All the verifiable investigative information, physical evidence analysis and interpretation, and experimental results must be considered in testing and attempting to verify the hypothesis. When it has been thoroughly tested and verified by analysis, it can be considered a plausible theory. Figure 10.2, is a model for theory building during crime scene reconstruction.

TYPES OF RECONSTRUCTION

There are many types of reconstruction depending on the nature of the crime, the questions needing to be answered, the types of events that have taken place, and a reconstruction that is based on the degree of involvement of the reconstructionist. As shown in the outline below, there are five common ways to classify the types of reconstruction services that may occur.

CLASSIFICATIONS OF RECONSTRUCTION TYPES

A Specific type of incident reconstruction:
  1 Accident reconstruction:
    (a) Traffic accident reconstruction: automobiles, trucks, motorcycles, etc.
    (b) Other transportation accident reconstruction: trains, airplanes, boat accidents, etc.
    (c) Industrial or construction accident reconstruction: 'on the job' or employee accidents, building collapses, machinery, etc.
  2 Specific crime reconstruction:
    (a) Homicide reconstruction
    (b) Arson scene reconstruction
    (c) Rape case reconstruction
    (d) White-collar crime reconstruction
    (e) Other specific crime scene reconstruction

Figure 10.2
Fact-gathering process.

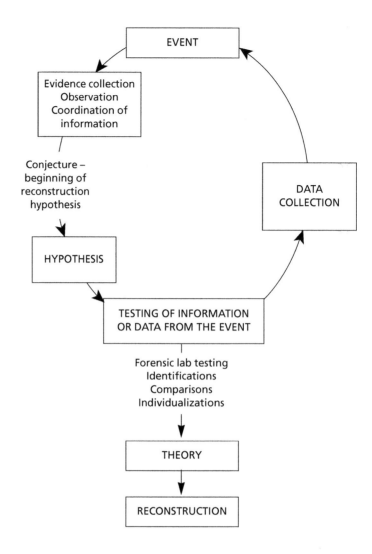

B   Specific events reconstruction

    1   Sequence determination

    2   Directional determination

    3   Position determination

    4   Relational determination

    5   Conditional determination

    6   Identity determination

C.   Degree of involvement reconstruction

    1   Total case reconstruction

    2   Partial case reconstruction

    3   Limited event reconstruction

    4   Specific pattern reconstruction

D Specific type of physical evidence reconstruction:

   1   Pattern evidence

   2   Shooting investigation evidence

   3   Serological evidence

E Special areas or determinations in reconstruction:

   1   Criminal profiling – including MO, motive, and psychological determinations, or organized or disorganized crime scene determination.

   2   Scene profiling – Primary scene or secondary scene determination, etc.

For the purposes of this text, the reconstruction of an event, the criminal act, will be discussed using the classification based on the specific type of physical evidence created by the event and found at the crime scene. This reconstruction process will follow the 'information gathering process' as shown above that leads to the reconstruction theory. The theory incorporates all the previously discussed processing of the crime scene with its physical evidence and the investigator's knowledge of the value and use of forensic testing methods. The physical evidence resulting from the crime and found at the crime scene to be discussed with regards to reconstruction will be pattern evidence, shooting investigation evidence, and serological evidence.

PATTERN EVIDENCE IN RECONSTRUCTION

Pattern evidence is one type of physical evidence encountered at a majority of crime scenes. Often, forensic scientists do not take this type of evidence seriously enough, and think of it as 'not being very scientific'. Pattern evidence at crime scenes is, however, extremely valuable in the reconstruction of crimes and the activity that has taken place at the crime scene (see Photo 10.1a–c). It can be used to prove or disprove a suspect's alibi or a witness's version of what took place at the crime scene, to associate or dissociate the involvement of persons or objects in particular events, or to provide the investigators with new leads or information for further investigation.

Pattern evidence is generally created by the contact of two surfaces (persons, vehicles, or objects) that results in the formation of impressions, imprints or markings. These impressions may be from static or stationary contact or dynamic or moving contact and may be two-dimensional or three-dimensional. In some cases, the contact may be a transfer of material from one surface to another resulting in pattern evidence in the form of a stain or deposit. Pattern evidence also results from the fracture, breaking or cutting of an object. The following is a list of pattern evidence commonly found at different crime scenes:

1 Bloodstain patterns

2 Glass fracture patterns

3 Fire burn patterns

4 Furniture position patterns

5 Track-trail patterns

6 Tire or skid mark patterns

7 Clothing article damage or position patterns

8 Modus operandi and crime scene profile patterns

9 Projectile trajectory and powder residue patterns

10 Injury or wound patterns

Photo 10.1a–c

A Connecticut State Police Lieutenant was struck and killed by a tractor trailer unit as he was assisting a disabled motorist on the shoulder of an interstate highway.

(a) Overall view of the right side of a truck matching the description of the evading suspect truck. Note the swipe mark in the dirt below the trailer number, 160.

(b) View of the Lieutenant's shirt, depicting the Connecticut State Police shoulder patch.

(c) Close-up view of the mark on the trailer after the image was enhanced and photographed. The State Police shoulder patch is clearly visible.

(a)

(b)

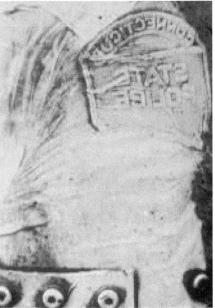

(c)

Pattern evidence found at crime scenes should be carefully documented, processed, enhanced, or collected using all the techniques discussed earlier chapters of this text. The techniques used for pattern evidence reconstruction are the same as those examinations of other types of physical evidence: Recognition → Identification → Individualization → Interpretation → Reconstruction. Figure 10.3 is a flow chart showing these basic stages of reconstruction of pattern evidence.

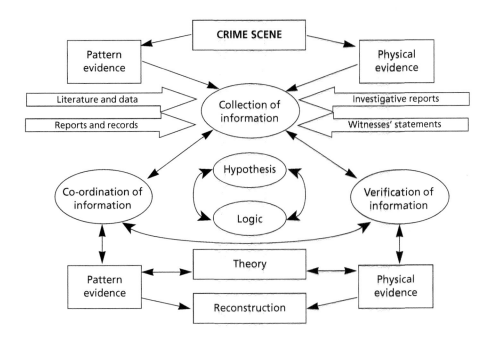

Figure 10.3

Flow chart depicting the basic stages in crime scene reconstruction.

BLOODSTAIN PATTERN ANALYSIS FOR RECONSTRUCTION

Reconstruction from bloodstain patterns has long been a neglected area, but it has received more attention recently from the law enforcement and legal communities. Bloodstain pattern analysis has been defined in several ways. Bloodstain pattern analysis seeks to define the facts surrounding an investigation by the use of the physical nature of bloodstains. It is the evaluation of the static aftermath of bloodshed in an attempt to determine the actions that created the bloodstains found at the crime scene. Oftentimes, the bloodstain patterns provide a window to the past. The totality of these definitions is that the size, shape, and distribution patterns of the bloodstains found at a crime scene where bloodshed has occurred can be used to reconstruct the bloodshed event(s).

The bloodstain pattern analysis is in some cases more useful and significant than the serological or DNA information obtained from the blood. The bloodstain patterns reveal not 'who' but 'what' with regard to the circumstances of bloodshed.

The 'what' of bloodshed is the result of careful examination and study of the blood-stains' appearance at the crime scene. The following are some examples of how reconstruction can be made by the study of the bloodstain evidence:

- Direction of travel of the blood droplets.
- Distance of blood source to target surface.
- Angle of impact of blood droplet.
- Type of blood droplets.
- Determination of blood trails, their direction, and the relative speed of motion.
- Nature of the force used to create the bloodshed.
- Nature of the object used to cause bloodshed, the number of blows involved, and relative location of persons/objects near bloodshed.
- Sequencing of multiple events associated with the bloodshed.
- Interpretation of contact or transfer patterns.
- Estimation of elapsed time and volume of bloodshed.

Basic bloodstain patterns

Bloodstain patterns found at crime scenes will fall into three broad categories: dropping bloodstain patterns, impacted bloodstain spatters, and special blood-stain configuration patterns. Each category of pattern will be briefly discussed so as to provide basic information of bloodstain patterns for reconstruction. Additional reading, careful study, control experiments, and practice must be undertaken for proper bloodstain pattern analysis.

Photo 10.2

The diameter of the blood-stain increases as the distance falling is increased until the distance reached is 48 inches or greater. At this distance the diameter remains constant.

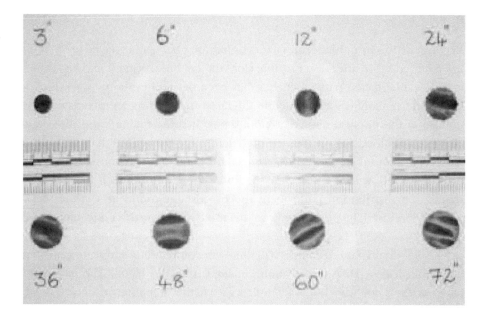

Dropping blood patterns

The patterns produced by dropping blood found at the crime scene are based on the biochemical and physical properties of liquid blood. The surface tension of the liquid blood causes the blood drops produced from a blood source to be spherically shaped. The blood drops have a viscosity four times that of water. An average volume of a drop of blood is approximately 0.05–0.06 ml (roughly 20 drops in one milliliter) under normal conditions. The blood drop when released from the blood source will oscillate slightly during free fall. It possesses an adhesive quality that provides for a small amount of blood to adhere to most surfaces.

(a)

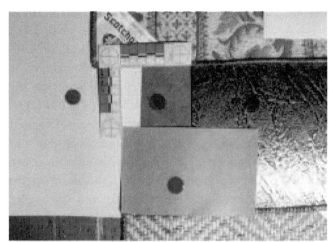

Photo 10.3a–c

Effect of target surface on shape of blood droplet.

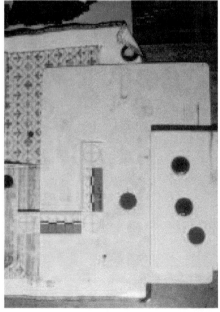

(b)   **(c)**

Additionally, a drop of free-fall blood has terminal velocity ranging from 20–25 ft/sec. Many factors will influence the size and shape of the bloodstain once it reaches a target surface. A free–falling drop of blood when impacting a surface will generally produce circular shaped patterns. If the distance a drop of blood falls is increased it produces a circular pattern showing an increase in the stain's diameter until the terminal velocity of drop is reached (see Photo 10.2). At this height and above, the diameter of the resulting circular stain will remain constant. It is for this reason that an interpretation of a drop of blood's *distance fallen* can be done by examination of a bloodstain's diameter.

The target *surface texture* for dropping blood can also affect the size and shape of the bloodstain pattern. Hard, non-porous surfaces will produce circular stain patterns that have smooth edges, whereas softer, porous surfaces will produce spatter stains that are scalloped or have rough edges. Photos 10.3a–c demonstrate the relationship of the surface texture vs. the diameter of stains.

The shape of the resulting bloodstain is changed when the angle at which a blood drop impacts a surface is changed. As the angle of impact is made smaller or more acute, the bloodstain pattern will become more elongated, elliptical, or oval in shape (as shown in Photo 10.4a–c). The impact direction of a drop of blood can also be determined. The 'tail' of the bloodstain generally points to the direction of travel of the blood drop. In turn the blood origin of a drop can be determined. This direction of travel along with the angle of impact is referred to as the *directionality* of a bloodstain pattern.

The *angle of impact* can be determined from measurements of the length and the width of bloodstain. The trigonometric relationship between the ratio of the long axis (length) v. the short axis (width) of a bloodstain can be measured. Its angle of impact can be calculated with a simple trigonometric formula:

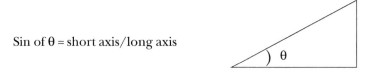

Sin of θ = short axis/long axis

Figure 10.4
Diagram of impact angle.

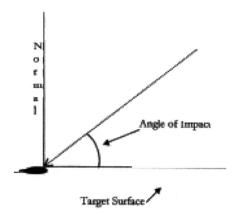

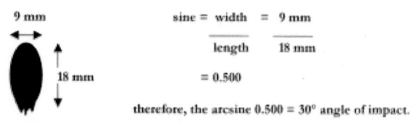

Sine of Impact Angle = Width of Bloodstain / Length of Bloodstain

9 mm

18 mm

$$sine = \frac{width}{length} = \frac{9 \text{ mm}}{18 \text{ mm}}$$

$$= 0.500$$

therefore, the arcsine 0.500 = 30° angle of impact.

Figure 10.5
Trigonometric calculation of impact angle.

Figure 10.5 shows an example of calculation of impact angle of a blooddrop.

Photo 10.4a–c
Effect of impact angle on shape of blood droplet.

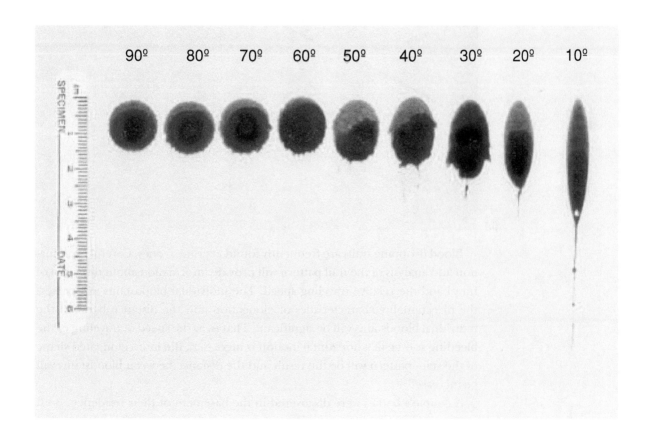

Photo 10.5a–b

Husband and wife were beaten to death in their basement. Examination of the depicted blood trails, and DNA testing of samples of these blood trails assisted in the reconstruction and determining which blood trail, associated with which victim, and the sequence of events at the crime scene.

(a)

(b)

Blood dropping trails are frequently found at crime scenes. Careful examination and analysis of the trail pattern will provide information about direction of travel and the relative traveling speed. The individual bloodstains will possess the directionality characteristics of elongation and the distance between the individual bloodstains will be significant. That is, as the speed of traveling of the bleeding source in a horizontal motion is increased, the more elongated shape of the stain pattern will be the result and the distance between bloodstains will be increased.

A couple's bodies were discovered in the basement of their residence. Both of them were beaten to death. Photos 10.5 a and b show two views of the crime scene. Blood dripping pattern, contact smear pattern, medium velocity impact spatters and large pooling stains were observed on the floor. Through study of the bloodstain pattern, the sequence of events was able to be reconstructed. Their adopted son breaks into the house and kills his father first by hitting him with a sledgehammer. He then drags his father's body to a distant corner and covers him with a bedsheet. He then waits in ambush for his mother to enter the basement. He kills her with a hammer and carries her outside the basement. The mother's blood drips on top of the bloody drag-mark from his father. Subsequent serological analysis identified the mother's and father's blood types and was helpful in the reconstruction of events.

Impacted bloodstain spatters pattern

Bloodstains that have been produced with more energy (force) than gravity is referred to as impacted blood. The force added to the drop of blood causes the drop to break into smaller-sized spatters of blood. These smaller drops of blood are broken into smaller sizes of spatters relative to the amount of force or energy involved. This force (energy) generally comes from two sources: internal or external. Internal force results from the body's internal blood circulation system. Blood travels at a constant speed in arteries, veins, and capillary vessels. As a consequence, the resulting bloodstain patterns will be different. The external force (energy) results from the force that created the bleeding or the force exerted on the blood source. Photo 10.6 shows medium velocity impact spatter found at a homicide scene. The drop's directionality property remains unchanged, however. It is for this reason that blood that has been impacted can be analyzed or examined and a determination of the origin of impact force or the origin of blood source can be determined.

Photo 10.6
Overall view of impact spatter.

The *point of origin* of impact or bloodshed is determined by a two-step process:

1 Determination point of convergence (2-D); and
2 Determination of point of origin (3-D).

The *point of convergence* is the process of determining the two-dimensional point of origin of impacted blood spatter. As shown in Figure 10.6, a line or axis is obtained through the center of a representative sample of each impact blood spatter. Once the axis from all the selected blood spatters have been obtained then a line (direction of impact) can be established by projecting back to its origin. When all the lines converge in a small area, this area is the two-dimensional convergence of the impacted blood or bloodshed source. The second step in the point of origin of impacted blood or bloodshed source requires that each of the stains in the convergence be measured and their angle of impact determined. Once the angle of impact has been calculated then the axis line will need to be set by the use of a protractor. Stringing of lines or graphic tape can be used for this process.

Figure 10.6a

Two-dimensional point of convergence of impact spatter.

Figure 10.6b

Impact spatter's three-dimensional point of origin determination.

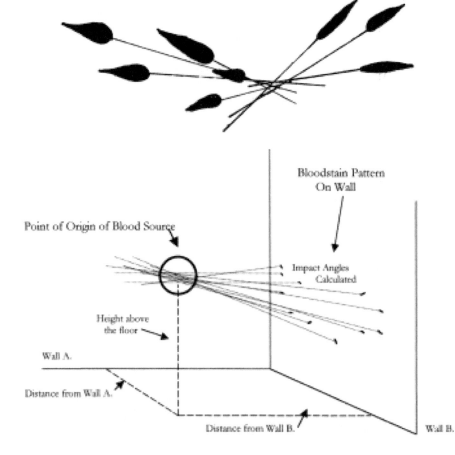

Figure 10.6a shows the step I of 2-D point of convergence determination and Figure 10.6b demonstrates the step II 3-D point of origin determination. The 2-D point of convergence and corresponding impact angles are used to determine location of impact. An experienced bloodstain analyst can assist in the determination of which individual spatters to use for this reconstruction step. It is good practice to use more individual spatters than fewer spatters. The point of origin of bloodshed or point of impact determinations will allow the reconstruction of the nature of the force used, the sequence of events, and the relative position of persons or objects near the impacted source.

Impacted bloodstain patterns are frequently grouped or classified by the relative amount of force used to create the bloodstain pattern. These classifications can also assist in the interpretation as to the type of weapon used to cause bloodshed. *Low velocity impact spatter* produces bloodstain patterns where the majority of drops of blood are not broken into smaller droplets. The majority of spatter produced is large with diameters of 4 mm or more. *Medium velocity impact spatter* is produced when the majority of larger drops of blood are broken into smaller spatter with diameters of 2–4 mm. The force associated with this type of impact spatter is greater than 25 ft/sec. Impact spatter that measures 2 mm or less is generally the result of *high velocity impact spatter.* The force necessary to produce spatter of this size is in excess of 100 ft/sec and is associated with higher energy sources, such as explosions, gunshot wounds, and high-speed collisions. Photo 10.7 shows the high velocity impact spatter found on the wall behind the victim's head, who dies as a result of gunshot wounds. The overall appearance of this high velocity blood spatter is a mist-like distribution pattern. Aspirated blood from a bloody mouth or nose can sometimes be confused with high velocity impact spatter. Upon close examination the bloodstain pattern analyst should be able to distinguish these two types of patterns.

Photo 10.7
High velocity impact spatter.

Special bloodstain patterns

Numerous other types of bloodstain patterns are found at crime scenes that can be used for reconstruction purposes. These patterns involve analysis of individual stains, overall patterns of stains, and a combination of individual stains within overall patterns of stains.

Dispersion effects of forward spatter and back spatter are found with both medium and high velocity impact bloodstain patterns. Photos 10.8a and b show

Photo 10.8a

Shooting experiment apparatus designed to demonstrate forward as well as backward spatter associated with high velocity impacts.

Photo 10.8b

Close-up view of forward and backward high velocity impact spatter on surfaces located 6 inches from the source of blood.

the experimentation of such blood spatter patterns. If the dispersion patterns are absent, then the investigator must be able to reconstruct the crime scene so as to explain their absence. In bloodstain pattern analysis, the absence of bloodstain patterns is equally as important as the presence of bloodstain patterns. Oftentimes the absence of spatter is in the form of an outline of the intermediate target or object that received the blood spatter. Therefore, this intermediate target can be identified.

A quantity of blood impacting a surface with a certain amount of force is known as *projected blood*. This type of special bloodstain pattern is commonly associated with major injuries with open wounds with a large amount of blood projected on vertical surfaces, such as arterial gushes. Photo 10.9 shows one example of arterial gushing pattern. This pattern has sharp, spineous edges and frequently shows movement or motion. The larger quantity of blood is deposited on vertical surfaces and then flows downward as it is acted upon by gravity and produces a *flow pattern* of the blood. Larger quantities of blood deposited on a horizontal surface then flowing downward because of the topography of the surface also produce a flow pattern of blood, as shown in Photos 10.10a and b.

Photo 10.9

Arterial gushes. Shooting victim's two arterial gushes on wall and vacuum cleaner as an intermediate target.

Blood dripping into a pool of blood can produce a special feature bloodstain pattern. The appearance of this type of bloodstain pattern is different from the projected bloodstain pattern. The edges of these types of blood spots are not as spineous and sometimes referred to a rebound spatter patterns. The *repetitive dripping pattern* shows no motion that is commonly found with the projected bloodstain pattern, as depicted in Photo 10.11.

Photo 10.10a–b
Examples of blood flow
patterns.

(a)

(b)

When an object or body part is used to inflict injury or contact a sufficient amount of liquid blood, blood will transfer to the object or body part. The arc motion of the bloody object will produce a *cast-off bloodstain pattern*. The linear nature of the pattern and the repeating shape changes of the resulting individual blood drops deposited on a target surface distinguish this pattern, as shown in Photo 10.12. The blood drop shape changes due to the changes in the impact

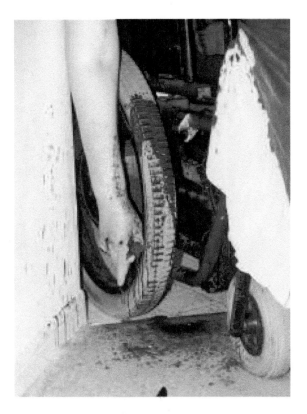

Photo 10.11

Pattern associated with repetitive blood dripping into pool of blood.

angle. The cast-off pattern also allows for a determination of the number of blows inflicted on the blood source. Any bloody object that is given a flinging motion including moving hands, arms, and legs can produce cast-off patterns at a crime scene, as shown in Photo 10.12. Ceilings, walls, furniture, and the clothes of the person inflicting the trauma are usual targets for depositing of cast-off bloodstain patterns.

Once bloodshed has occurred, it is common to find pools of blood. The *pooling of blood* provides information about the amount of blood deposited and the type of injury the person received. The pools of blood can be transferred to other surfaces by contact. *Contact-transfer bloodstain patterns* are the result of blood adhering on an object or body through direct contact and then transferred onto a new location, as shown in Photo 10.13. This new location can be at distances both large and small. The contact-transfer pattern is in the shape of the object due to a stationary or static transfer, and then the object's shape can be determined. For example, a bloody knife blade that is placed on a bed sheet will leave a contact-transfer pattern in the shape of the knife blade.

If the contact-transfer patterns are due to folding of the receiving surface, then two similar bloody imprints may result from the same object, or one image from the other bloody image, hence a 'butterfly' or mirror image of the original stain is created.

Photo 10.12

Examples of cast-off bloodstain patterns.

Photo 10.13

Examples of contact transfer patterns formed when footwear is in direct contact with a bloody surface.

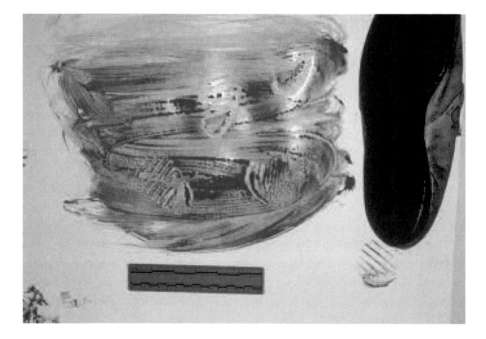

The contact-transfer pattern can show the presence of an interrupted or discontinuous pattern. This type of interruption of the pattern is generally produced due to motion of a repetitive nature or folding of the receiving surface materials. The direction and the sequence of the motion can be determined from examination of these types of bloodstain patterns.

Contact-transfer patterns can often be created though dynamic motions. This type of transfer pattern is commonly referred to as a blood smear or blood smudge. When an unstained object moves through a blood surface the resulting pattern is called a *wipe pattern*. The smear pattern can exhibit 'skeletonization' and show directionality of motion of the original unstained object. A swipe pattern is also produced when a bloody object contacts an unstained surface. Motion and direction can also be identified with these patterns, as shown in Photo 10.14.

Photo 10.14
Bloody swipe patterns located on a wall directly above a homicide victim.

Documentation of bloodstain patterns

Bloodstain patterns found at a crime scene or on items of physical evidence that are to be used for reconstruction *are evidence*. Therefore, they should be subjected to the same documentation protocols as discussed in earlier chapters. However, by their nature there are some documentation techniques that are especially useful for bloodstain patterns. As with general crime scene documentation purposes, any documentation is useful for any subsequent examinations, reconstructions, or as a tool to prepare for trial.

Photography of bloodstain patterns

Photography of bloodstain patterns follows the same basic process as with general crime scene photography – general, overall views followed by specific, close-up views. Because measurement and exact sizing of bloodstain patterns is important, the bloodstain pattern photographs must have scales placed in the photograph. The scales are important even in the overall views so as to give perspective and dimension to the documentation. Labels, arrows, and other markers as previously described are especially important in bloodstain pattern photography. Photos 10.15a–c show the photographic documentation of bloodstains.

Because photographs may have to be printed to actual size, scales should be placed at right angles along the edges of the pattern. For larger areas or overall views a process of 'road-mapping' by the placing of tape measures along entire walls or surfaces is useful, as shown in Photos 10.16 and 10.17.

Photo 10.15a–c

Photographing bloodstain patterns.

(a) Overall.

(b) Stains identified.

(c) Close-up of bloodstain.

(a)

(b)

(c)

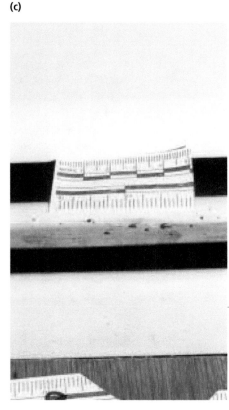

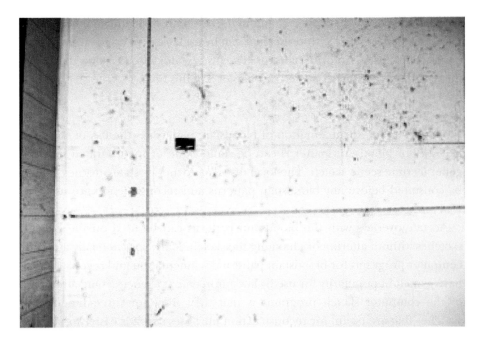

Photo 10.16

Example of road mapping technique for the photographic documentation of blood spatter patterns.

Close-up or laboratory examination quality photographs of bloodstain imprint patterns or individual spatters (as depicted in Photo 10.17) follow the lighting and tripod placements previously discussed. Flashes should be diffused or bounced to prevent burn-out of the bloodstain images.

Frequently, borderline quality bloodstain imprint patterns must be enhanced prior to documentation or reconstruction can be attempted. The

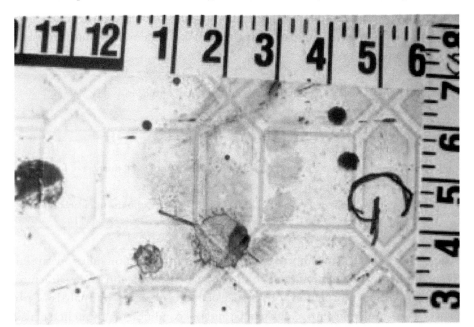

Photo 10.17

Close-up view of bloodstain patterns with ruler, markings, and proper illumination.

field enhancement reagents, like luminol, tetramethylbenzidine, amido black, leucomalachite green, or fluorescence, can be used to spray on to large areas to enhance bloodstain imprint patterns. The investigator should follow the procedures and precautions discussed in Chapter 8 of this book.

Sketching of bloodstain patterns

The final step of documentation of bloodstain patterns is the use of sketches. Sketches of bloodstain patterns can be stand-alone or incorporated into the general crime scene sketch. The local district attorney or state attorney should be consulted before any bloodstain patterns and reconstruction are used for trial purposes.

Acetate overlays with the bloodstain patterns can be used on the general sketches without altering or changing the sketch. Many commercially available computer programs for bloodstain pattern documentation and reconstruction have gained in popularity for use by law enforcement agencies. One advantage of the computer sketch programs is that they allow for three-dimensional sketches that are useful for reconstruction purposes and it is easier to plot the bloodstain evidence in scale.

GLASS FRACTURE PATTERNS

Broken glass at crime scenes can sometimes aid in reconstruction, providing information about the events which took place, and assisting in proving or disproving an alibi or witness's story. Glass fracture patterns are most often associated with burglary, criminal mischief, shooting incidents, and fire scenes. The most common types of information that can be obtained by studying glass fracture patterns are:

- Direction of impact force applied (from inside out or outside in).
- Approximate force of impact.
- Approximate angle of impact of force.
- Determination of the type of glass fracture.
- Determination of the sequence of firing, direction of firing, and the type of firearm for the projectile holes present.
- Estimation of the fire temperatures, direction of fire travel, and the intensity of heat from the melted glass.

The use of glass fracture patterns in crime scene reconstruction relies on careful recognition, documentation, and study of radial and concentric glass fracture markings. Other information for reconstruction is obtained by analysis of rib marks, spatial relationships, crack marks, and the condition of any melted glass.

To conduct even a basic reconstruction based on glass fracture evidence, investigators should be familiar with the different categories of glass and generally how each type of glass fractures. Glass is an amorphous, super-cooled liquid, composed primarily of silicon dioxide (sand). There are three general classes of glass: plate, tempered, and safety. Each type of class has certain characteristics, and will fracture differently.

Plate glass is a common variety of glass used to make windows and mirrors. When plate glass is exposed to a force significant enough to rupture the surface tension and break the glass, characteristic pie-shaped glass shards are formed. If broken glass remains in the frame the observed fracture pattern will consist of a center point, where the force contacted the windowpane, with radiating (radial) fracture lines going out from the center point. In addition, there will be fracture lines running perpendicular to the radial lines, concentric fracture lines. Photo 10.18 shows the radial and concentric glass fractures. By carefully examining a broken edge of a piece of glass along a radial line, you can determine the direction of force. This analysis is helpful in determining from which side of the glass the window was broken. Investigators can use this information to confirm a false burglary report by showing that the window was broken from the inside out rather than outside in as reported by the homeowner.

Safety glass is found in automobile windshields. Basically, safety glass is two separate panes of plate glass adhered together with a clear laminated layer. While this glass fractures in a similar way to plate glass it remains intact after breaking due to the laminate layer. Safety glass was designed to reduce injuries

Photo 10.18

Glass fracture pattern depicting radial and concentric fracture lines.

Figure 10.7

Rib and hackle marks on side of broken glass.

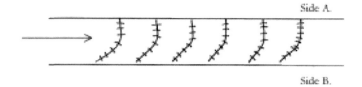

Side A.

Side B.

The large curved lines are the rib marks. The smaller lines perpendicular to these rib marks are the hackle marks. In the above illustration the glass fracture opened on Side A, moved toward Side B, and then progressed from the left to the right (arrow).

Photo 10.20a–d (opposite)

(a) Depicts all of the diced glass fragments recovered from the scene of a shooting in which the fatal bullet penetrated the driver's door window.

(b) The fragments are sorted in preparation of a reconstruction process designed to locate and reconstruct the area of the window where the bullet penetrated.

(c) The bullet hole was reconstructed and an intervening section of glass between the hole and a window edge was also reassembled so that the precise location of the bullet hole could be determined.

(d) Close-up view of the reassembled bullet hole.

to passengers should they be propelled into the windshield as the result of a traffic accident. Caution must be exercised when interpreting safety glass fracture patterns in that there are two separate panes of glass, which will have independent radial and concentric fractures.

Since safety glass remains intact it can provide valuable information in shooting incidents. The direction of each gunshot can be determined by locating the crater, which is located on the side of glass facing the impacting force. Also, if more than one bullet penetrates the windshield it is possible to sequence the shots if the bullet holes are close enough together that their separate radial fracture lines converge. The subsequent bullet hole can be determined because radial lines from that bullet hole terminate where they meet the existing radial line from the prior fracture. Figure 10.7 explains the formation of fracture marks and the direction. Photo 10.19 shows the radial fracture and the concentric fracture on the windshield of a vehicle.

Tempered glass is a single pane glass that is durable and difficult to fracture

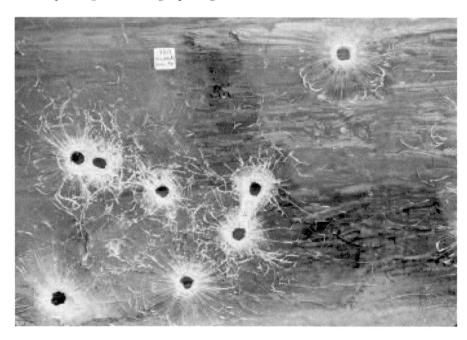

Photo 10.19

Multiple bullet holes in automotive windshield.

due to its significant surface tension. When enough force is applied to break this surface tension the entire pane of glass fractures into thousands of small pieces, commonly referred to as dicing. Tempered glass is used in side windows of automobiles. In most cases a vast majority of the diced glass falls from the window frame, into the car and on the ground. Many investigators fail to realize the potential value of this evidence, and therefore fail to collect all of the glass fragments. While it is a daunting task to reassemble the thousands of diced glass fragments this precise exercise can yield valuable information. Photos 10.20a–d show reconstruction of a bullet hole location from diced window fragments. It is possible to reassemble the diced window and determine the location at which the projectile struck the window, the direction of the projectile flight, an

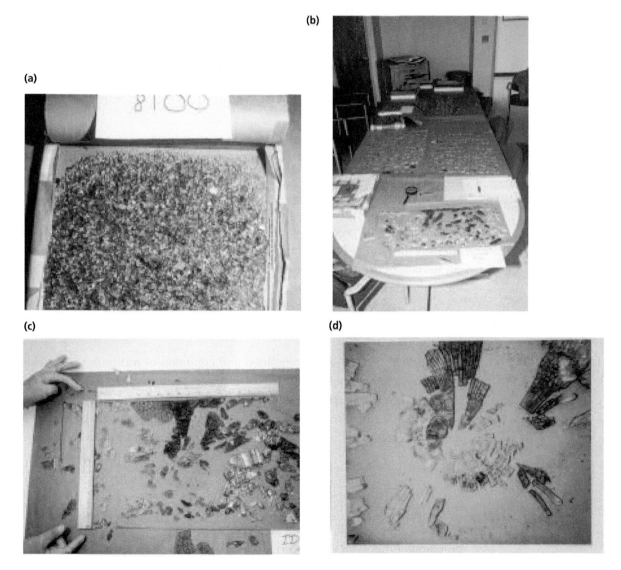

approximate angle of incident, and in some cases whether more than one projectile struck that window. This type of reconstruction is very helpful in shooting reconstruction cases where one or more side windows have been broken by bullets.

FIRE BURN PATTERNS

Fire burn patterns often provide information on the various factors which led to or caused a fire. Detailed study of the burn patterns generally helps in determining the point of fire origin, the direction of fire travel, and the degree of damage of a fire, which may contain clues for arson investigations. The following is a partial list of common patterns found at fire scenes:

- Inverted cone or 'V' pattern
- Multiple points of origin burn patterns
- Low burn pattern configurations
- Depth of charring patterns or alligator patterns
- Trailer patterns
- Smoke stain patterns
- Melted material patterns
- Concrete spalling patterns

Every fire forms a pattern that is determined chiefly by the configuration of the environment, the availability of combustible material, and the type and intensity of the fire. From a study of the fire patterns, and a determination of any deviations from normal or expected patterns, an experienced fire investigator can reconstruct a fire scene.

FURNITURE POSITION PATTERNS

At an indoor crime scene, the position and condition of furniture often yields information about the events that caused the pattern, their sequence, and possible actions of perpetrators and victims. Displaced or broken furniture can indicate that a struggle took place. Patterns of disarray in ordinary or expected furniture placement or condition may further reveal actions taken by suspects or witnesses.

TRACK-TRAIL PATTERNS

Occasionally, track-trail patterns are encountered at crime scenes. Proper interpretation of them can yield information about how many persons were present at a scene, whether they were moving about, the nature of the movement (walking, running) and the direction of travel, and whether heavy objects were being carried or dragged. Some of these types of patterns can give class characteristic information or data about the individual responsible for producing the patterns, such as shoe size, stride length, sex, weight, or any abnormalities in movement or gait.

(a) **(b)**

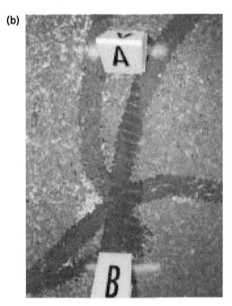

Photo 10.21a–d

Tire marks on the pavement and snow covered shoulder from a vehicle that went off the road at high speeds.

(a) Overall view of the tire skid and yaw marks on the pavement.

(b) Close-up view of a portion of the yaw marks.

(c) Additional skid marks before the vehicle left the paved portion.

(d) Tire marks in the snowy shoulder after the vehicle left the road.

(c)

(d)

TIRE AND SKID MARK PATTERNS

Tire or skid mark patterns are often seen at outdoor crime scenes, and can provide important reconstruction information for the crime scene investigator. The value of skid mark patterns in traffic accident reconstructions is well known and documented. However, the use of these patterns in crime scene investigation and reconstruction is often neglected. These markings can yield information about the number and types of vehicles involved, the possible speed of travel, direction of travel, whether or not brakes were applied, and whether turns were made. Photos 10.21a–d show some of the skid marks and yaw marks found at an accident scene.

CLOTHING OR ARTICLE PATTERNS

This type of pattern evidence can be subtle or, at times, very obvious! Detailed observation, measurement, documentation, and correct interpretation of these patterns can be valuable and essential in crime scene reconstruction. Some examples of the types of information that can be obtained from these patterns are whether a suspect ransacked a scene, proof or disproof of an alibi, direction and route taken by a suspect, physical contact between persons, persons and vehicles, or between vehicles, disturbances of expected patterns at the crime scene, and possible information about the sequence of events. Photo 10.22 shows a bloody fabric pattern left behind at the scene.

Photo 10.22

Bloody fabric impressions on a wall.

MODUS OPERANDI AND SCENE PROFILE PATTERNS

These patterns are more subtle, and require careful observation, as well as extensive knowledge of criminals and details of their previous crimes. Modus operandi (MO) patterns can link apparently unrelated crimes together at the investigative stage. These patterns include information such as methods used to gain entry to a premises, types of weapons preferred, types of force used, types of language used, the sequence of actions followed by the suspect, types of property taken, and the types of any materials left behind at the scene.

Scene profiles often reveal information with regards to identification of primary v. secondary scenes; active scenes v. passive scenes; organized scenes v. disorganized scenes. A detailed discussion of the different types of crime scenes can be found in Chapter 1 of this text.

SHOOTING SCENES – INVESTIGATION AND RECONSTRUCTION

Reconstruction of shooting scenes is often necessary to determine several factors critical to the investigation. Determining the manner of death – homicide, suicide, or accidental – may be difficult without a reconstruction. In addition to providing investigative information and assisting in accurate conclusions, shooting scene reconstructions can be used to help a grieving family cope with the harsh reality that a loved one took their own life. A reconstruction can also provide information as to the relative location(s) of the shooter(s) and victim throughout the incident. Moreover, a reconstruction can help determine the muzzle-to-target distance, which can be a pivotal factor in distinguishing between a homicide and suicide. Also, trajectory reconstructions can be performed to provide valuable information that can in many cases prove or disprove suspect, victim, or witness accounts of shooting scenarios. While reconstruction in the investigation of shooting cases should be a routine procedure for crime scene investigators, it has historically not been utilized to its maximum ability.

The components of a successful shooting investigation include investigative information, crime scene processing, autopsy and medical records, laboratory examination of physical and pattern evidence, and related reconstruction experiments. As with most investigations the ability to conduct a meaningful reconstruction in shooting cases is highly dependent upon the quality of crime scene documentation, searching, and the collection and preservation of all relevant evidence. In shooting cases evidence such as gunshot residue is prone to destruction or loss if efforts are not made to expeditiously locate and preserve such evidence. Also, in all too many cases not all of the relevant evidence is located before the crime scene is released or lost.

PRELIMINARY STEPS FOR SHOOTING INCIDENT INVESTIGATIONS

Investigative information, including statements from all involved parties, is valuable not only to the overall investigation, but also to crime scene personnel. While crime scene investigators must remain open-minded and objective, investigative information can assist them in their duties. For example, if witness statements or the scenario indicate that the ability to see movements was hindered by poor lighting it would be critical for crime scene personnel to take available light photographs. It would be beneficial to know the scope of the incident and how many potential parties were involved with or witnesses to the incident. Documentation should be taken to corroborate or refute stated observations or perceptions.

Gunshot residue analysis can be of great value in helping determine who may have been involved in the shooting and approximate muzzle-to-target distances. However, gunshot residue can be easily lost if not properly collected and protected. In most cases it is advisable to swab the hands of the victim and any potential shooter for the presence of gunshot residue as soon as possible. Gunshot residue can be collected by swabbing with 5% nitric acid solution and/or collected on SEM collection disks. Collection should be done as soon as possible as gunshot residue will dissipate over a relatively short period of time. A gunshot victim's clothing should be preserved as a gunshot residue distribution pattern can assist in distance determinations. The clothing must be carefully removed, not folded, and allowed to dry.

Clothing from both victim and potential shooters should be seized as it may contain gunshot residue, blood spatter, glass fragments, other forms of trace or transfer evidence, or tears, damage or soil patterns that may be useful for reconstruction purposes. The presence of trace evidence or damage to the clothing may be used to corroborate a statement regarding movement or events during and after the shooting incident.

In cases where multiple shots were fired by one or more shooters it is imperative to account for and locate all associated firearms evidence. This can be best accomplished by conducting a thorough inventory of the total number of bullets each firearm could store and how many are 'missing', number of recovered shell casings, number of bullet holes (entry v. exit if possible), any bullet strikes or deflections, number and type of wound, and to a lesser extent witnesses' accounts of the number of shots fired. Once this accounting has been completed investigators should attempt to reconcile the data and ensure that they have accounted for all possible shots, and recovered all firearms evidence. The shooting scene should not be released until all evidence is accounted for. At times it is necessary to x-ray the victim or conduct an autopsy to get a clear understanding as to how many bullets or fragments struck the victim, and how many are located within the victim.

ROLE OF MARKINGS ON PROJECTILES

Projectiles found at crime scenes can be examined by forensic laboratories and provide valuable information that can be used in the reconstruction process. Firearms examination by the forensic laboratory can provide information about the type of firearms used in the investigation, such as the caliber of the firearm, type of ammunition used, and rifling characteristics that may provide a list of possible manufacturers and models. Microscopic examination of the projectile may also provide information about the types of surfaces contacted by the projectile after firing.

Weapon-specific markings on projectiles

Markings found on fired projectiles are either class characteristics, individualizing characteristics, or markings received after leaving the muzzle. Class characteristics are markings that are common to a type of firearm, its manufacturer or the particular model of the firearm. Common class characteristics are the number of lands and grooves, their direction of twist, the degree of pitch, and the widths of the lands and grooves.

Individualizing characteristics found on fired projectiles are markings that are usually the result of use or wear from the firing of the firearm or were created during the manufacturing process. These markings include striations received by the projectile as it passes down the barrel of the firearm, skid marks, shavings, and uneven wear markings.

Post-muzzle markings and trace evidence

Additional markings that can be used for reconstruction of trajectory are the markings placed on a projectile after it leaves a muzzle. These markings used for reconstruction can be attributed to silencers, intermediate target impacts, and the final impact surface or terminal trajectory marking. Silencers may place additional striations on the projectiles specific to the silencer. Every time the fired projectile impacts with an intermediate target it will maintain the Locard Exchange Principle and receive trace material from the intermediate target. This trace evidence can be identified and individualized to a target on the crime scene. If the projectile passes through the intermediate target, then a pathway of direction will be made and useful for reconstruction. Some additional useful types of trace evidence from intermediate targets for reconstruction are gunshot residues on hands and clothing and patterns of cylinder and muzzle flash. The size and shape of the terminal trajectory surface marking can be useful for reconstruction, as discussed below. The markings on the projectile from the terminal surface will confirm terminal trajectory and as such, are useful in reconstruction. Photos 10.23a and b show the red fiber found on the bullet which provided a crucial link between the bullet and the victim.

Photo 10.23a

Close-up photograph of the end of a bullet, suspected of having passed through a shooting victim. Note the red fiberous material.

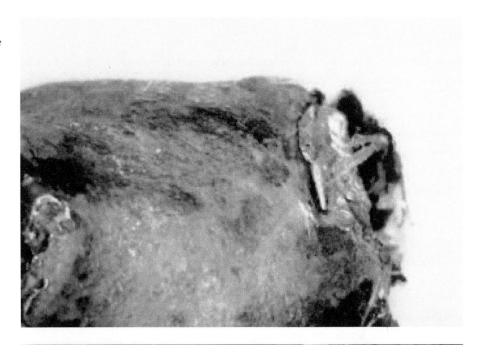

Photo 10.23b

Photomicrograph of the red material removed from the bullet. This material was examined and found to be consistent with fibers from the victim's coat.

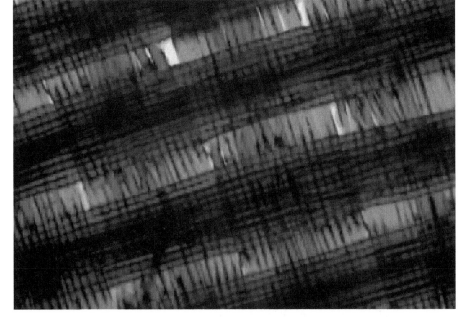

MUZZLE-TO-TARGET DISTANCE DETERMINATIONS

Muzzle-to-target distance determinations have been successfully used by firearm examiners for over 75 years. Over the years modern refinements of instrumentation and detection levels have improved the destructive and non-destructive methodologies used. Generally, distance determinations involve a comparison of gunshot residue distribution found on the item collected at the crime scene to laboratory-prepared gunshot residue patterns acquired at various distances. Each step in the preparation, detection, and comparison of the gunshot residue should be carefully documented. Some of the basic steps in the process are:

- Proper at-scene documentation and handling of evidence.
- Visual examination of the target surface – macroscopically and stereo-microscopically.
- Infrared photography (as shown in Photos 10.24a and b).
- Enhancement and mapping of distribution of GSR particles by chemical reaction for nitrites or lead. See Gunshot Residue Enhancement in Chapter 9.
- Identification and measurement of shotgun pellet patterns if a shotgun was used.
- Control tests – particle loss/redistribution control, environmental or condition controls, test target material selection, angle effects, etc.
- Preparation of test targets – proper ammunition use.
- Objective comparison and evaluation of targets.
- Determination of range of firing.

Care must be employed in the interpretation of gunshot residue patterns or the lack thereof. There are several relevant factors that may affect the anticipated pattern. The composition of the target surface will impact the ability of that surface to hold and retain the gunshot residue. Also, if the target surface is

Photo 10.24a–b

(a) Black-and-white photograph of bullet hole in dark-colored polyester pants.

(b) Infra-red photograph of the same area; note the gunshot residue pattern around the bullet hole in the center of the photograph.

(a)

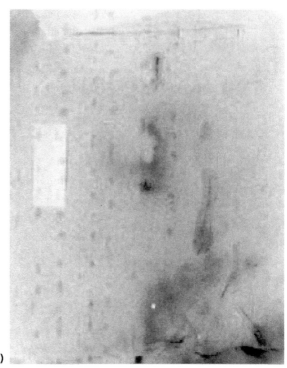

(b)

blood-soaked or wet from rain or environmental factors the ability to recover gunshot residue or locate a GSR pattern will likely be diminished. An acute angle of incident may also reduce the amount of GSR deposited on the target surface. A trajectory reconstruction can help determine the angle of incident.

GEOMETRIC PROJECTION METHODS FOR TRAJECTORY DETERMINATIONS

The crime scene investigator can use two geometric methods for trajectory determinations. One method of trajectory reconstruction is based on physical methods (probes, rods and strings) and the other method is based on optical projection methods (visual sightings and the use of low-power lasers). Whichever method is chosen careful documentation of the entire reconstruction process should be accomplished.

Physical projection methods

1 *Entry hole geometry:* The shape of projectile entry and exit holes in target surfaces can be measured and an estimated angle of entry can be calculated. Most projectile holes are elliptical shaped and by the use of trigonometry (cosine of the ratio of the width to the length of the hole) the angle of impact can be determined.

2 *Probes and rods:* Probes are useful for establishing projectile trajectories if the projectile holes are close together and there is no access to the blind side of one of the projectile holes. Be careful to avoid altering or damaging projectile holes when inserting the probe. Wooden rods, solid metal rods, or hollow metal tubes are useful for this reconstruction method. Use a rod in width close to the approximate diameter of the hole; however, do not use a rod so thick that you have to force the rod into the hole.

3 *Strings:* Longer distances between projectile holes can be aligned using probes with attached strings. Care should be taken not to allow the strings to sag or be deflected by the sides of the holes; this would produce significant error.

Optical projection methods

1 *Optical sighting:* One of the simplest means of assessing the alignment of projectile holes in reconstruction is to align them visually by looking through them. The alignment achieved is only preliminary and lacks precise direction. Photographing the trajectory reconstruction alignment through one projectile hole to the other hole should be attempted.

2 *Low power lasers:* The laser is useful for aligning projectile holes over simple optical sighting because it is capable of defining a straight line over a longer distance. Care should be used with long distances because projectile trajectories are influenced by gravity, which can curve the projectile path. This is especially true with lower velocity projectiles.

3 *Alignment of laser path with projectile holes in walls:* When trajectories end within walls,

Photo 10.25a

A bullet hole was found in the interior surface of a garage. A string was extended from the inside of this same wall also depicting the flight path of the bullet.

Photo 10.25b

Optical sighting method. Hole in wooden wall found near bullet.

observational access to the termination point must be attained without disturbing the projectile entry hole. Cutting into the wall close to the projectile hole will allow access. Another technique for gaining access to a blind projectile hole is to use a probe with the laser. The probe (hollow probes work very well) is inserted in the projectile hole (carefully avoiding damaging the hole) and the laser is aligned with the probe to effectively 'extend' the probe.

4 *Documentation of laser beam:* Documentation (video and photographic) should be con-

Photo 10.26a

View through cut-out showing the general direction of the bullet trajectory.

Photo 10.26b

Close-up of a bullet hole located in a wooden wall. A woodenprobe was used to demonstrate the trajectory.

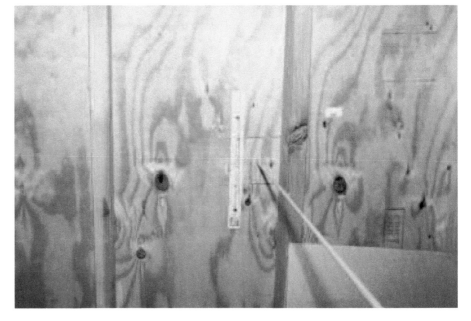

tinuous, but at least done when the laser beam is aligned with two or more projectile holes. Visualization of the laser beam path is enhanced by the addition of smoke or dust. It is difficult to use visualizing smoke outdoors or in any area with air circulation.

5 *Positioning stages:* Commercially manufactured positioning platforms for lasers are available to facilitate the positioning of the laser. The laser head is mounted on a multi-axis stage with appropriate scales for calculations and documentation purposes.

Photo 10.27
Use of laser light to locate
bullet trajectory. A smoke
agent was used to help
visualize the laser beam.
The tarp was held in place
to reduce air flow.

6   *Angle information from the aligned laser beam:* Protractors and tape measures can be used to
    establish the orientation and document the location of the projectile holes in relation to
    fixed points at the crime scene. Plumb bobs, inclinometers, and levels are useful for
    further insuring correct measurements of angles. After a projectile trajectory has been
    obtained and documented, a second determination of trajectory should be done.

7   *Placement of intermediate targets in the laser beam:* Using a laser beam allows for easy inter-
    posing of objects or people in the laser so as to check reconstruction scenarios. In the
    case of soft intermediate targets (mattresses, pillows, cushions, etc.), a hollow probe is
    very useful. Be careful to prevent possible errors by preventing deflections.

8   *Dual-opposed co-axial lasers:* As shown above for soft objects a hollow probe is useful for
    reconstruction alignment of projectile holes. Using a substitute object of the same
    shape, size, weight, etc. can duplicate scenarios without damaging actual evidence. If
    projectile holes exist in objects like bodies, two lasers must be used to establish trajec-
    tory alignments. The first laser's alignment is established and the second laser is
    mounted in the beam of the first laser. This placement of the second laser allows for
    moveable placement of subject 'bodies' in the laser beams.

9   *Auxiliary alignment targets and lighting issues:* It is difficult to utilize lasers for trajectory
    reconstruction at outdoor scenes. Night-time experimentation of reconstruction
    scenarios can work well for these types of scenes. Temporary or auxiliary targets, white
    index cards or reflective strips can be used to facilitate experimentation in the
    daylight. Placement of the cards or strips at various locations in the laser beam can
    allow for successful reconstruction of outdoor scenes in the daytime.

Precautions and sources of error

Post-impact trajectories of projectiles can present errors in reconstruction. Predictions are difficult if the projectile has grazed, ricocheted, or hit a target with a large angle of impact.

For all trajectory reconstructions with intermediate targets, the possibility of *deflection* must be taken into account. In other words, when a projectile passes through an object, there will be some degree of deflection. The degree is established by the nature of the object, its shape, and the way in which the projectile interacted with it. See Table 10.3 for possible sources of error due to deflection factors.

Table 10.3

Factors influencing deflection of projectiles.

Intermediate target properties
- Hardness.
- Surface features.
- Degree of internal heterogeneity.
- Directionality of internal heterogeneity.
- Thickness, compliance, and elasticity.

Projectile properties
- Hardness.
- Shape.
- Mass and mass density.
- Cross-sectional area and density.
- Velocity and flight stability.

Angle of flight path relative to target
- Entry surface.
- Exit surface.

Although two points can be used to establish a projectile trajectory, this is insufficient if deflections have possibly taken place. It is for this reason that the least amount of points is three or more for relatively accurate trajectory reconstructions. In addition, an assessment of the likelihood and possible degree of deflection is necessary for a reconstruction that is scientific in nature. Well-designed controlled experimentation may be indicated. The experimentation should include a range of deflection scenarios and test firings of the weapon to determine its variability.

SHELL CASING EJECTION PATTERNS

Shell casings located at a crime scene can provide valuable information. These casings can be used for subsequent comparisons to suspect guns, to determine if they fired that particular cartridge. If no weapon is found, the cartridge case can be entered into a firearms database, such as Drugfire, IBIS, or NIBIN and compared to a database of cartridge cases. The location of the shell casings may be useful in determining the approximate location of the shooter in reference to the ejected shell casing. Photos 10.28a and b show the casing ejection pattern experiments. While a majority of semi-automatic or automatic firearms eject to the right, experimentation must be conducted with the actual weapon used, or

(a)

Photo 10.28a–b

Shell casing ejection pattern experiment. The different distribution patterns depicted in the photographs are due to a change in the shooter's hand position.

(b)

a similar make and model, to determine the ejection pattern of that particular gun. When test firing a weapon to determine the ejection pattern for that gun, several factors must be considered as they may influence the ejection pattern. These factors include: type of ammunition, shooter's hand-hold and body position, whether the shooter was stationary or in motion during the ejection, the ground surface that the ejected casings land on, environmental factors such as rain and wind. In addition to considering these factors, caution must be exercised in reaching conclusions regarding shell casing ejection patterns in that the observed location of one or more of the casings may not be the true ejection location – the casing may have been kicked or moved by vehicular traffic after being ejected.

OTHER CONSIDERATIONS

Glass fracture distribution patterns

When bullets strike or penetrate glass the subsequent fracture lines can reveal information as to the location of the projectile hole, direction and approximate angle of incidence, and number of sequence of projectiles fired through the glass. Refer to the glass fracture pattern section earlier in this chapter. In addition to the information obtained by examination of the fracture patterns, the distribution of glass debris can be helpful in shooting reconstructions. The starting and ending points, as well as the length of the glass debris field, may provide information as to where the window(s) were initially broken, and the movement of the vehicle after the window(s) were broken.

Blood spatter patterns

Blood spatter analysis is also an important component of shooting incident reconstructions. High velocity impact spatter is associated with high-energy injuries, such as inflicted by gunshots. Refer to the previous section on blood spatter pattern analysis for additional details. Locating a high velocity impact spatter pattern can help determine the relative location of the victim, and corroborate that a shooting occurred in the particular location. When a bullet strikes a blood source both forward and back spatter occurs. This fact can be useful in reconstructions. The presence of high velocity spatter on the back of a suicide victim's hand helps establish the manner of death as suicide, as shown in Photos 10.29a and b.

Accident reconstruction – vehicle dynamics

When a vehicle is involved in a shooting incident the vehicle dynamics and motion must be accounted for during the reconstruction process. It may be beneficial to utilize an accident reconstruction expert to examine skid marks

Photo 10.29a

Bloodstained hand of suicide victim. Note the fine droplets among the bloody residual on the back of the hand.

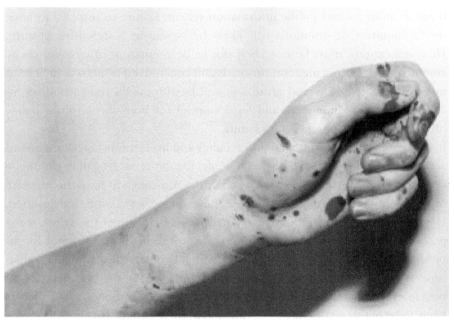

Photo 10.29b

High velocity impact spatter on the palm of a homicide victim's hand. The victim's hand was in close proximity to his head when he was shot.

and vehicle damage to approximate the speed and direction of travel before, during, and after the shooting incident. While accident reconstruction alone will rarely answer all of the relevant issues, it is one of the many available methods or examinations that may be used to conduct a comprehensive shooting scene reconstruction.

SPECIAL ISSUES ASSOCIATED WITH POLICE OFFICER-INVOLVED SHOOTINGS

While the basic issues and needs for proper crime scene documentation and processing are the same whether or not the shooting incident involves a police officer, there are special issues associated with police shootings. If police-involved shootings are not investigated and handled correctly and thoroughly the involved police agency, individual officer(s), and entire criminal justice system will likely face severe criticism, loss of public trust and confidence, and exposure to large civil liability. Police chiefs, District Attorneys, and government leaders need to prepare for the high level of scrutiny the incident and their subsequent actions will undergo. Also, they must formulate their plans in a manner to guarantee as much independent objectivity into the investigation as possible. Further, they must recognize difficulties that often complicate police-involved shootings such as lack of witnesses.

Police shootings will certainly attract significant media attention and public interest. Often public impressions are established in the early hours of the investigation, and with minimal or no input from the police department. It is imperative to expeditiously and accurately report relevant information to the media through an organized public information system. Failure to respond to basic media inquiries or questions will likely be viewed as a defensive posture. However, caution must be exercised not to be premature in conclusions or comments. As the investigation proceeds and concludes it is often beneficial to meet with civic leaders and groups as well as with media representatives, in addition to family members and legal counsel for both the involved police officers and the shooting victim's family.

Perceptions are a reality that police chiefs and leaders must be aware of and account for in their actions. Where possible, the entire investigation should be conducted by an external agency. The District Attorney will have the ultimate responsibility of determining whether the shooting was lawful and justified. However, police or laboratory personnel will likely conduct the crime scene processing and investigation. If there are insufficient local resources for an outside agency to provide the crime scene and investigative functions then supervisors need to ensure that all personnel involved in the investigation are not closely associated with any of the involved officers. Further, since this case is likely to be highly scrutinized, and litigated in some forum – likely civil court – every available resource and expert should be utilized. If the forensic laboratory or crime scene unit has expertise in shooting reconstruction or related disciplines it would be advantageous to involve them as soon as possible, most likely at the initial crime scene.

There are some common characteristics in police shootings that can create investigative challenges. In many cases, there is a lack of witnesses, at least available witnesses within the early portion of the investigation. The individual wounded during the encounter may be dead or incapacitated to the point where they are unavailable to interview.

The officers involved in the shooting are more frequently exercising their constitutionally protected rights and availing themselves for questioning at a later date in the presence of legal counsel. As a result it is possible that the crime scene processing unit will need to perform their functions with little or no background information.

REQUIREMENTS FOR RECONSTRUCTIONS AFTER CRIME SCENE RELEASED

All crime scene photographs, autopsy reports and photographs, videotapes of scene, measurements, notes, crime scene reports, and laboratory reports of physical evidence testing that are available must be thoroughly studied. Whenever possible, visiting the crime scene at the time of the incident and direct observation of the scene and patterns is most desirable. Complete and accurate documentation of a scene is also important. Direct examination of the physical evidence to observe any type of damage, stains and conditions will provide the best opportunity for later reconstruction analysis. It should be noted that complete reconstructions are often not possible. However, partial reconstructions – reconstructing certain facts or aspects of the events without necessarily being able to reconstruct all of them – can be extremely valuable for the case investigation. Information developed through reconstruction can often lead to the successful solution of a case. Investigators and laboratory personnel (as well as medical examiner personnel in death cases) must cooperate and work together to document every important aspect of a scene, carry out analysis of the physical evidence, and conduct a thorough and unbiased investigation of a case and share all the necessary information for reconstruction. A team approach concept should always apply to crime scene investigation and reconstruction.

WRITING A RECONSTRUCTION REPORT

GENERAL RECOMMENDATIONS

1 Two examiners should review and sign the report.
2 State what materials were reviewed and used as a basis for the report.
3 Be accurate and in complete agreement with notes taken during the review and reconstruction process.
4 Use labeled photographs to aid in articulating your observations and comments.
5 Do not interject or rely on unsubstantiated information.

6 Clearly state any relevant facts or circumstances not known to you.

7 If your interpretations are limited due to a lack of data state this.

8 Do not over-commit or too narrowly limit your opinions and observations:
   (a) Use words like: consistent with, similar to, most probable, inconsistent with available data or facts, inconclusive, cannot be determined with the available information, etc.
   (b) Keep an open, objective mind.

9 Restrict stating opinions until the summary or conclusion; keep facts, observations, and data separate.

10 Be prepared to objectively evaluate a hypothetical with the stated facts, arriving at a different conclusion or opinion.

11 Be general; many of the underlying details should be reserved for oral testimony – remember, anything written will be carefully reviewed by other experts.

12 *Stay objective and true to the facts.*

Any reconstruction can only be as good as the information provided. Information may come from the crime scene, physical evidence, records, statements, witness accounts, and known data. The process of information gathering and its use in reconstruction show the scientific nature of crime scene reconstruction and will allow for its successful use by investigators.

APPENDIX I:
CRIME SCENE INVESTIGATION
EQUIPMENT INVENTORY

SUPPLIES FOR SCENE SECURITY

- Barrier tape
- Rope and cord
- Saw horses
- Signs and poles
- Color spray paints
- Road flyers
- Security and safety lighting devices
- Police or marked vehicles
- Emergency response equipment
- Tents and traps

EQUIPMENT FOR CRIME SCENE DOCUMENTATION
PHOTOGRAPHY

- Polaroid
- Numbered markers
- 35 mm SLR with accessories
- 1:1 or close-up cameras, larger format
- Black and white films
- Color films
- Scales and rulers
- Remote or auxiliary flash units with synch. cords
- Tripods
- Video cameras and equipment including extra batteries and tape
- Filters

SKETCHING EQUIPMENT

- Assorted papers, pens, clipboards
- Tape measures, various lengths
- Rollers
- Protractors, angle measuring devices
- Grid overlays – volume determination, droplet count

- Hand-held GPIs (Ground Positioning Instruments)
- Drafting templates
- One and three-inch stick-on scales

EQUIPMENT AND MATERIALS FOR PROCESSING CRIME SCENES

EVIDENCE PACKAGING MATERIAL

- Paper bags and envelopes (various sizes)
- Butcher paper
- Boxes
- Zip lock bags (various sizes)
- Metal paint cans
- Pillboxes (various sizes)
- Sharps containers
- Swabs and swab boxes
- Blood tubes: with and without EDTA
- GSR collection kits
- Sexual assault evidence collection kits – victim
- Sexual assault evidence collection kits – suspect
- Tape and gel lifters
- Evidence tags/labels
- Strings
- Labels and markers
- Glassine weighing paper for druggist's folds
- Evidence tags and labels

REAGENTS

- Presumptive blood tests
- Presumptive protein tests
- Bloody print enhancement reagents
- Latent print processing chemicals
- Entomology sample preservatives
- Chlorox/cleansing reagents
- Saline/distilled water
- Drug field tests reagents

COLLECTION EQUIPMENT

- Tweezers
- Disposable scalpels
- Disposable pipettes
- Paper for pharmacy folds

- Nets for flying insects
- Assorted hand tools: saws, drills, knives, screwdrivers, chisels, etc.
- Assorted yard tools: rakes, shovels, trowels, buckets
- Screens and sieves
- Casting material: plaster and silicon
- Vacuums

LIGHTING EQUIPMENT

- Auxiliary lights
- Generators
- Flash lights
- Forensic light units
- Ultra-violet lights

LATENT FINGERPRINT KIT

- Assorted color fingerprint powders
- Fingerprint brushes
- Magna brush and magna powder
- Lifting tape
- Lift cards
- Gel lifters
- Fingerprint cards
- Backing latent lift cards
- Inked pad
- Assorted development/enhancement reagents
- Flashlight
- Magnifier

IMPRINT AND IMPRESSION COLLECTION KIT

- Electrostatic dust lifter
- Dental stone
- Mixing bowls and spatulas
- Retaining borders
- Reinforcing material
- Release agent
- Silicone rubber
- Snow wax
- Cardboard box
- Large tape lifters

TELECOMMUNICATIONS

- Cellular telephones
- Hard wire telephones, wires and jacks
- Fax machines
- Laptop computer with modem
- Portable printer/copier
- Video conferencing – digital image transmission
- Audio tape recorder.

HAND TOOLS

- Scissors, knives, scalpel, and blades
- Forceps, assorted hand tools
- Power tools as needed, saws, screwdrivers, hand saws, etc.
- Portable generators
- Dissecting tools
- Spatulas
- Toothpicks
- Mirrors with extension rods
- Metal scribes
- Portable vacuum with filters or evidence trap
- Ladder, step stool
- Folding card table and chairs
- Metal detector, spade, and shovel

CRIME VAN

- Sufficient to carry equipment and evidence
- Refrigeration
- Hard line and generator power sources
- Four-wheel drive, off road capabilities

PERSONNEL PROTECTION

- Surgical and latex gloves, heavy rubber gloves
- Disposable gowns and booties
- Dust filter masks
- Gas masks, hepa-filters
- Self-contained breathing apparatus
- Boots
- Eyewash
- Cleaning solutions
- Tissues and paper towels
- Jump suits and lab coats
- Insect repellent

APPENDIX II:
GAME PLAN FOR PROCESSING

Managing the crime scene properly has a direct relationship to successful crime scene processing. A 'game plan' should be followed and used where applicable at each scene processed. Sometimes even the most conscientious investigator can forget simple tasks/information which should be completed or recorded. An investigative guide and assignment record should be maintained for each scene processed and should contain the following information/checklist:

POLICE INFORMATION

Major Crime Squad case number:
Town:
Date:
Scene location:
Time: Assigned/arrived
Scene cleared: Date/time
Major Crime Squad case officer:
Assisted agency case/evidence officer:
Jurisdiction assisted/address/telephone:
Assisted jurisdiction case number:

DISCOVERED BY/FIRST RESPONDER

Discovered by: Name/DOB/address/telephone
Interviewed by:
First police responder:
Interviewed by:

VICTIM INFORMATION IF AT SCENE:

Name/DOB/address/telephone
Rigor and post mortem lividity consistent with position of body when found.
Blood flow.

Blood spatter.
Identity of victim confirmed: By whom:
Dental records available: (dentist)
Fingerprints/palmprints available:

VICTIM INFORMATION IF NOT AT SCENE

Name/DOB/address/telephone:
Hospital/address/telephone:
How transported:
Investigator assigned to hospital:
Prognosis:
Victim's clothing obtained by:
Other evidence obtained: Sexual assault kit, GSR kit, etc.

SCENE ASSIGNMENTS

Polaroids: Investigator
Video: Investigator
Color prints 35 mm: Investigator
Color slides 35 mm: Investigator
Crime scene sketch: Investigator
Latent prints: Investigator
Latent print photographs: Investigator
Aerial photographs: Investigator

PHYSICAL EVIDENCE SEARCH

Blood: From victim/scene/suspect
Semen: From victim/scene/suspect
Saliva: From victim/scene/suspect
Hairs: From victim/scene/suspect
Fibers: From victim/scene/suspect
Clothing: From victim/scene/suspect
Control devices: Rope/tape/handcurfs/other
Footprints/shoeprints:
Fingerprints/palmprints:
Tire tracks:
Bite marks:
Tool marks:
Other impressions:
Live ammunition:

Cartridge cases:
Fired bullets:
Shot gun shell wadding:
Glass:
Soil:
Questioned documents:
Charred documents:
Sink drains:
Septic systems:
Garbage compact:
Rubbish containers:
Newspapers: Dates
Mail: Dates
Drugs: Prescription/illegal
Poison:
Fly larvae:
Area search:
Answering machine tapes:

WEAPONS

Weapon: At scene/missing
Revolver/auto pistol/rifle/shotgun/machine gun/other firearm
Knife/ice pick/razor/scissors/machete/ax/hammer/tire iron/jack
handle/club/bat/stick/bottle/rock/screwdriver/other
Hands/fist/feet/shoes/boots/rope/cord/wire/pantyhose/scarf/belt/chain/
other ligature

STRUCTURES

Weather conditions:
Temperature: Interior/exterior
Lighting fixtures: On/off/not working
Heating system: Type/on/off
Air conditioning: Type/on/off
Household appliances: On/off/not working
Doors/windows/hatchways: Locked/unlocked/open/closed/forced entry
Last food preparation/refrigerator contents:
Clocks:
Pets: feces
Laundry:
Telephone/electric service lines: Cut or disconnected

MOTOR VEHICLE

Engine: running
Ignition: On/off/jumped
Doors: Locked/unlocked
Windows: Up/down
Accessories: On/off
Fuel reading:
Battery charged:
Odometer reading:
Vehicle damage:
Trunk:
Vehicle stolen:
Radio station:
Mirrors:
Ash trays:
Contents of vehicle:
Light switch:

MEDICAL EXAMINER

Name: Was Medical Examiner at scene/date/time
Date and time notified:
Notified by:
Victim pronounced dead by: Time/by whom:
Removal time:
Medical Examiner case number:
Removal of deceased authorized by:
Undertaker: Name/address/telephone/date/time
Deceased removed to: Address
Autopsy scheduled: Date/time/Investigator assigned

STATES ATTORNEY

Name/date and time notified: By whom:
Inspector notified: Date/time/by whom:

FORENSIC LABORATORY

Technician requested: Time/date/by whom:
Forensic laboratory case number:

NEXT OF KIN NOTIFIED

Name/address/telephone:
Relationship:
Date/time/by whom/how (telephone)
Family member needed at autopsy for positive identification

WARRANTS

Search and seizure:
Judge:
Affiants:
Consent to search:
Officer assigned return of warrant:

COMMAND POST

Established: Time/date/address/telephone

BODY SURVEY

On _____, 200____ from approx. _____ to _____ , the following body survey was completed in connection with a _____ investigation in _____, Connecticut.

Victim identification
    Age, DOB

General scene observations:

Physical description:
    Sex, height, weight, build, hair, eyes, scars, tattoos, jewelry, other

Clothing description:

Glasses/contacts:

Dentures:

Description of injuries:

Blood patterns:
    Flow, direction, spatters, transfers

Body temperature:

Color of lips:

Color of fingertips:

Pupils:

Petechial:

Lividity:

Rigor mortis:

Other observations:

HOUSE SURVEY

On _____, 200____ from approx. _____ to _____ hours, the
residence/establishment of _____,
located at_____ , Connecticut, was processed
and surveyed in connection with a _____ investigation
which occurred in _____, Connecticut.
The following survey was completed by _____ during the
execution of a _____ upon this residence/establishment.

WINDOWS:

DOORS:

AIR CONDITIONER:

LIGHTS:

MAIL:

NEWSPAPERS:

TELEVISION:

RADIO:

THERMOSTATS:

INSIDE TEMPERATURE:

OUTSIDE TEMPERATURE:

LAST FOOD PREPARATION:

CLOCKS:

DISHES/UTENSILS:

LAUNDRY:

OTHER OCCUPANTS:

VEHICLES:

APPENDIX III:
RESOURCES AND SUPPLIES

Abbey Camera, Inc.
8040 Georgia Avenue
Silver Spring, MD 20910
(301) 587-3600, (888) 587-0712
www.abbeycamera.com

Academic Press
525 B Street, Suite 1900
San Diego, CA 92101-4495
(800) 321-5068
www.academicpress.com

AFIP Office of the Armed Forces
Medical Examiner Offices
6825-16th Street Northwest
Building 54, Room G018
Washington, DC 20306-6000
(202) 782-2468

AccessData Corporation
2500 North University Avenue,
Suite 200
Provo, UT 84604
(800) 489-5199
www.accessdata.com

Activation Laboratories Ltd
1336 Sandhill Drive
Ancaster, ON L9G 4V5, Canada
(888) 228-5227
www.actlabs.com/forensics

Advanced Chemistry Development, Inc.
133 Richmond Street West, Suite 605
Toronto, ON M5H 2L3, Canada
(800) 304-3988
www.acdlabs.com

Advanced Imaging Magazine
445 Broad Hollow Road, Suite 21
Melville, NY 11747
(631) 845-2700
www.advancedimagingmag.com

Agilent Technologies
2850 Centerville Road
Wilmington, DE 19808
(302) 633-8000
www.agilent-tech.com

AirClean® Systems
PO Box 17614
Raleigh, NC 27619
(919) 876-6142
www.aircleansystems.com

American Academy of Forensic Science
PO Box 669
Colorado Springs, CO 80901
(719) 636-1100
www.aafs.org

American Board of Criminalistics
Massachusetts State Police Labs
59 Horse Pond Road
Sudbury, MA 01776
(508) 358-3101

ARTEL Inc.
25 Bradley Drive
Westbrook, ME 04092
(207) 854-0860
www.artel-usa.com

ASCLD-LAB
139 J Technology Drive
Garner, NC 27529
(919) 773-2600
www.ascld-lab.org

Astec Microflow Systems
2180 Andrea Lane, Suite 5
Fort Myers, FL 33912
(800) 382-8537
www.ductless.com

Avid Technology, Inc.
Ocean Systems
700 13th Street, NW, Suite 950
Washington, DC 20005
(800) 497-2843
www.avid/government

Beckman Coulter, Inc.
4300 North Harbor Boulevard
Fullerton, CA 92834
(800) 742-2345

Bill Deaton Systems/JSD-LLC
200 Paw Paw Avenue
Benton Harbor, MI 49022
(616) 927-2781
www.jsd-llc.com

Biochemical Diagnostics, Inc.
180 Heartland Boulevard
Edgewood, NY 11717
(516) 595-9200
www.biochemicaldiagnostics.com

Biophotonics International
2 South Street, Berkshire Common
Pittsfield, MA 01201
(413) 499-0514
www.Photonics.com

BioSynthesis
612 East Main Street
Lewisville, TX 75057
(800) 227-0627
www.biosyn.com

BioTechniques Books – Eaton Publishing
154 East Central Street
Natick, MA 01760
(508) 655-8282
www.BioTechniques.com

The Bode Technology Group, Inc.
7364 Steel Mill Drive
Springfield, VA 22150
(703) 644-1200
www.bodetech.com

Bristlecone Corporation
1474 North Point Village Center, #314
Reston, VA 20194
(703) 318-1343

Bruker AXS Inc.
5465 East Cheryl Parkway

Madison, WI 53711
(800) 234-XRAY
www.bruker-axs.com

Bulbtronics Inc.
45 Banfi Plaza
Farmingdale, NY 11735
(800) 624-2852
www.bulbtronics.com

California Criminalistics Institute (CCI)
Room A – 104 DLE/CCI
4949 Broadway
Sacramento, CA 95820
www.ns.net/cci

Canon USA
2110 Washington Boulevard, Suite 150
Arlington, VA 22204
(703) 807-3862

Carlson Software
1340 Soldiers Field Road, #2A
Boston, MA 22204
(877) 221-6199
www.carlsonsw.com

Cellmark Diagnostics
20271 Goldenrod Lane
Germantown, MD 20876
(301) 515-6150
www.cellmark-labs.com

Centennial Products, Inc.
6900 Phillips Highway
Jacksonville, FL 32216
(904) 332-0404

CETAC Technologies
5600 South 42nd Street
Omaha, NE 68107
(402) 733-2829
www.cetac.com

ChoicePoint
8330 Boone Boulevard
Vienna, VA 22182
(703) 734-6200
www.choicepoint.net

Chromex, Inc.
2705-B Pan American Freeway, Northeast
Albuquerque, NM 87107
(505) 344-6270
www.chromex.com

CMI, Inc.
316 East Ninth Street
Owensboro, KY 42303
(270) 685-6454
www.alcoholtest.com

College of American Pathologists
325 Waukegan Road
Northfield, IL 60093
(800) 323-4040

Cogent Systems Inc.
209 Fair Oaks Avenue
South Pasadena, CA. 91030
(626) 799-8090
www.cogentsystems.com

Computer Cop Corp./
NetWolf Technologies
80 Orville Drive
Bohemia, NY 11716
(800) 311-3114

CRC Press, LLC
2000 Corporate Boulevard, Northwest
Boca Raton, FL 33431
(800) 272-7737
www.crcpress.com

Cross Match Technologies, Inc.
777 South Flagler Drive
East Tower, Suite 1200
West Palm Beach, FL 33401
(561) 802-3442
www.crossmatch.com

Data Unlimited International, Inc.
362A Christopher Avenue
Gaithersburg, MD 20879
(240) 631-7933
www.duii.com

DBT Online, Inc.
4530 Blue Lake Drive
Boca Raton, FL 33431
(800) 279-7710
www.dbtonline.com

Department of Energy
Forrestal Building
1000 Independence Avenue, Southwest
Washington, DC 20585

Defense Group Inc.
2034 Eisenhower Avenue, Suite 115

Alexandria, VA 22314
(877) 233-5789
www.defensegroupinc.com

Diagnostix, LTD
400 Matheson Boulevard East
Suites 14 and 15
Mississauga, Ontario
Canada L4Z 1N8
(800) 282-4075
www.diagnostix.com

Digital Biometrics, Inc.
5600 Rowland Road
Minnetonka, MN 55343
(952) 932-0888
www.digitalbiometrics.com

Digital Descriptor Systems, Inc.
2010-F Cabot Boulevard West
Langhorn, PA 19047
(800) 799-0963
www.ddsi-cpc.com

Draeger Safety, Inc. – Breathalyzer
Division
185 Suttle Street, Suite 105
Durango, CO 81301
(800) 385-8666
www.draeger-breathalyzer.com

EAI Corporation
1308 Continental Drive, Suite J
Abingdon, MD 21009
(410) 676-1449
www.eaicorp.com

Eastman Kodak-Scientific
Imaging Systems
4 Science Park
New Haven, CT 06511
(877) SIS-HELP
www.kodak.com/go/scientific

EDAX Inc.
91 McKee Drive
Mahwah, NJ 07430
(201) 529-6277
www.edax.com

Edmund Scientific Co.
101 East Gloucester Pike
Barrington, NJ 08007
(609) 573-6250
www.edsci.com

Elephant Engineering
PO Box 968
Dahlgren, VA 22448
(540) 663-2137
www.latentmaster.com

Environmental Criminology
Research Inc. (ECRI)
Suite 212, 1807 Maritime Mews
Vancouver, BC V6H 3S4, Canada
(604) 718-2060
www.ecricanada.com

Evans, Conger, Broussard & McCrea Inc.
(The Expert's Expert)
One Bala Plaza, Suite 640
Bala Cynwd, PA 19004
(610) 668-7100
www.ecbm.com

EVI-PAQ
PO Box 18276
Tucson, AZ 85731-8276
(800) 377-0450
www.evipaq.com

Expert Pages.com
150 Shoreline Highway
Building E
Mill Valley, CA 94941
(800) 487-5342
www.ExpertPages.com

Fairfax Identity Laboratories
3025 Hamaker Court, Suite 203
Fairfax, VA 22031
(800) 848-4362
www.fairfaxidlab.com

Fisher Hamilton, Inc.
1316 18th Street
Two Rivers, WI 54241
(920) 793-1121

Fisher Scientific Worldwide
Pittsburgh, PA
(800) 772-6733
www.fishersci.com

Forensic Research Training Center
PO Box 826
Meriden, CT 06451

The Forensic Science & Crime Scene
Technology Expo, Frenzy Expo, LLC

731 Main Street
Monroe, CT 06468
(203) 445-1224
www.frenzyexpo.com

Forensic Solutions, Inc.
3 Schoolhouse Lane
Waterford, NY 12188
(518) 233-7272
www.forensicsolutionsinc.com

Forensic Technology Inc.
1901 Research Boulevard, Suite 250
Rockville, MD 20850
(301) 838-9141
www.fti-ibis.com

Foster and Freeman
25 Swan Lane
Evesham Worcestershire
UK WR11 4PE
(013) 864-1061
www.fosterfreeman.co.uk

Fuji Photo Film USA
555 Taxter Road
Elmsford, NY 10523
(800) 755-3854
www.FUJIFILM.com

Gamma Metrics
5788 Pacific Center Boulevard
San Diego, CA 92121
(858) 450-9811
www.gammametrics.com

GW Medical Publishing
2601 Metro Boulevard, Suite 101
St. Louis, MO 63043
(314) 298-0330
www.gwmedical.com

Government Scientific Source, Inc.
8460 Tyco Road
Vienna, VA 22182
(800) 248-8030
www.govsci.com

Graphco Technologies Inc.
41 University Drive, Suite 205
Newtown, PA 18940
(215) 497-9321
www.graphcotech.com

Guidance Software
572 E. Green Street, #300
Pasadena, CA 91101
(626) 229-9191
www.guidancesoftware.com

Hamilton Company
4970 Energy Way
Reno, NV 89502
(775) 858-3000
www.hamiltoncompany.com

H & M Scientific
5340 North Dixie
Elizabethtown, KY
(877) 561-1511
www.hmscientific.com

HEMCO Corporation
111 Powell Road
Independence, MO 64056
(800) 779-4362
www.HEMCOcorp.com

High Tech Crime Network
759 Bloomfield Avenue
PMB 155
West Caldwell, NJ 07006
(973) 726-9328
www.htcn.org

Hitachi Genetic Systems
1201 Harbor Bay Parkway, Suite 150
Alameda, CA 94502
(510) 337-2041
www.hitachi-soft.com/gs

Humana Press Inc.
999 Riverview Drive
Totowa, NJ 07512-1165
(973) 256-1699
www.humanapress.com

i2 Inc.
6551 Loisdale Court, Suite 600
Springfield, VA 22150
(888) 546-5242
www.i2group.com

IAAI-International Assn of Arson
Investigators
12770 Boenker Road
St. Louis, MO 63044
(314) 739-4224
iaaihq@aol.com

Identicator, Inc.
7055 Gentle Shade Road, #204
Columbia, MD 21046
(877) 344-4810
www.identicatorinc.com

Identigene, Inc.
7400 Fannin, Suite 1250
Houston, TX 77054
(713) 798-9510
www.identigene.com

Identix Inc.
510 N. Pastoria Avenue
Sunnyvale, CA 94086
(888) 500-7018
www.identix.com

IMAGIS
1300-1075 West Georgia Street
Vancouver, BC N6E 3C9 Canada
(604) 684-4691
www.imagis-cascade.com

Immunalysis Corporation
560 East Arrow Highway
San Dimas, CA 91773
(909) 394-2203
www.immunalysis.com

Image Content Technologies LLC
185 Main Street, Ste 211
New Britain, CT 06051
(860) 229-4122

Integritek Systems Inc.
111 Bermuda
Tampa, FL 33606
(813) 258-6882

International Assoc. for Identification
IAI
2535 Pilot Knob Rd, Suite 117
Mendota Heights, MN 55120-1120
(651) 681-8443
www.theiai.org

International Diagnostic Systems
Corporation
2620 South Cleveland Avenue, Suite 100
St Joseph, MI 49085
(616) 428-8400
www.ids-kits.com

IPIX (Interactive Pictures Corporation)
1009 Commerce Park Drive
Oak Ridge, TN 37830
(423) 482-3000
www.ipix.com

Isotec Inc.
3858 Benner Road
Miamisburg, OH 45342
(937) 859-1808
www.isotec.com

J & M Analytische Mess – und
Regeltechnik GmbH
Robert-Bosch-Strasse 83
D-73431 Analen Germany
+49 7361 9281-0
www.j-m.de

J & W Scientific
91 Blue Ravine Road
Folsom, CA 95630
(800) 223-3424
www.jandw.com

JEOL USA, Inc.
11 Dearborn Road
Peabody, MA 01960
(978) 535-5900
www.jeol.com

JEWETT Inc.
750 Grant Street
Buffalo, NY 14213
(716) 881-0030
www.JEWETTINC.com

JusticeTrax, Inc.
2501 W. Behrend Drive, Suite 27
Phoenix, AZ 85027
(800) 288-LIMS
www.justicetrax.com

Kapak Corporation
5305 Parkdale Drive
Minneapolis, MN 55416
(800) KAPAK57
www.kapak.com

KARA Company
5255 Dansher Road
Countryside, IL 60529
(800) 369-KARA
www.karaco.com

Kinderprint Company Inc.
PO Box 16
Martinez, CA 94553
(800) 227-6020
www.kinderprint.com

LabCorp
1912 Alexander Drive
Research Triangle Park, NC 27709
(800) 533-0567
www.labcorp.com

Lab Safety Supply
(800) 356-0783
www.labsafety.com

LabVantage Solutions
245 Highway 22 West
Bridgewater, NJ 08807
(908) 707-4100
www.lims.com

Law Enforcement Technology Magazine
1233 Janesville Avenue
Fort Atkinson, WI 53538
(800) 547-7377
www.letonline.com

Leica Microsystems
111 Deer Lake Road
Deerfield, IL 60015
(800) 248-0123
www.leica-microsystems.com

Leisegang Medical, Inc.
6401 Congress Avenue
Boca Raton, FL 33487
(561) 994-0202
www.leisegang.com

Lifecodes Corporation
550 West Avenue
Stamford, CT 06902
(800) 543-3263

Life Technologies, Inc.
9800 Medical Center Drive
Rockville, MD 20850
(301) 610-8696
www.lifetech.com

Lightning Powder Co. Inc.
1230 Hoyt Street, SE
Salem, OR 97302
(800) 852-0300

Lipomed Inc.
One Broadway
Cambridge, MA 02142
(617) 577-7222
www.lipomed.com

Lippincott, Williams and Wilkins
Publishers
187 Ridgecrest Drive
Napa, CA 94558
(707) 265-8055

Lunar Lite Inc.
955 Connecticut Avenue, #6003
Bridgeport, CT 06607
(203) 336-3482
www.lunarlite.com

Lynn Peavey Company
PO Box 14100
Lenexa, KS 66285-4100
(800) 255-6499
www.peaveycorp.com

Mack Information Systems, Inc.
1 North Avenue
Wyncote, PA 19095
www.mackinfo.com

The Mattman Company
1220 Industrial Avenue
Escondido, CA 92029
(800) 245-2865
www.gomattman.com

Melles Griot
2051 Palomar Airport Road, 200
Carlsbad, CA 92009
(760) 438-2131
www.mellesgriot.com

Microflex Corp.
127 Woodland Avenue
Reno, NV 89523
(800) 876-6866
www.microflex.com

Mideo Systems, Inc.
15234 Transistor Lane
Huntington Beach, CA 92649
(800) 258-1066
www.mideosystems.com

Misonic Inc.
1938 New Highway

Farmingdale, NY 11735
(800) 645-9846
www.misonix.com

MYRIAD Genetic Laboratories
320 Wakara Way
Salt Lake City, UT 84108
(801) 584-3572
www.myriad.com

National Center for Forensic Science
PO Box 162367
Orlando, FL 32816
(407) 823-6469
www.ncfs.ucf.edu

National Forensic Center
17 Temple Terrace
Lawrenceville, NJ 08648
(609) 883-0550

National Forensic Science Technology
Center, Inc.
Allstate Center
3200 34th Street South
St Petersburg, FL 33711
(727) 549-6067
www.nfstc.org

National Law Enforcement and
Corrections Technology Center
2277 Research Boulevard, MS-8J
Rockville, MD 20850
(800) 248-2742
www.nlectc.org

National Patent Analytical Systems Inc.
2260 North Main Street
Mansfield, OH 44903
(419) 526-6727
www.npas.com

NEN Life Science Products
549 Albany Street
Boston, MA 02118
(800) 551-2121

Neo Gen Screening
110 Roessler Road
Pittsburgh, PA 15220
(412) 341-8658
www.neogenscreeening.com

Neogen Corporation
628 Winchester Road

Lexington, KY 40505
(606) 254-1221
www.neogen.com

Nicolet Instrument Corporation
355 River Oaks Parkway
San Jose, CA 95134
(408) 433-4808
www.nicolet.com

Nikon Inc.
1300 Walt Whitman Road
Melville, NY 11747
(516) 547-4200
www.nikonusa.com

NIST Office of Law Enforcement
Standards
100 Bureau Drive
Gaithersburg, MD 20899
(301) 975-2757
www.nist.gov

NuAire, Inc.
2100 Fernbrook Lane
Plymouth, MN 55447
(800) 328-3352
www.nuaire.com

ODV, Inc
PO Box 180
South Paris, ME 04281
(800) 422-3784
www.odvinc.com

Olympus America Inc., Scientific
Equipment Division
Two Corporate Center Drive
Melville, NY 11747
(800) 446-5967
www.olympus.com

One Mile Up, Inc.
7011 Evergreen Court
Annandale, VA 22003
(800) 258-5280
www.onemileup.com

Optronics
175 Cremona Drive
Goleta, CA 93117
(800) 796-8909
www.optronics.com

Oxford Instruments Inc.
130A Baker Avenue Ext.
Concord, MA 01742
(978) 369-9933
www.oxford-instruments.com

Pacific Concepts Inc.
PO Box 84463
Seattle, WA 98124
(800) 827-2247
www.bagexperts.com

Payton Scientific Inc.
244 Delaware Avenue
Buffalo, NY 14202
(716) 855-1314

PE Biosystems
850 Lincoln Center Drive
Foster City, CA 94404
(650) 638-5715
www.pecorporation.com

Photodyne Technologies, Inc.
19441 Business Center Drive
Suite 134
Northridge, CA 91324
(818) 701-8877
www.photodyne.com

Polaroid Corporation
2750 Prosperity Avenue, Suite 501
Fairfax, VA 22031
(703) 641-8547

Porter Lee Corporation
906 South Roselle Road, Suite C
Schaumburg, IL 60193
(847) 985-2060
www.PorterLee.com

Promega Corporation
2800 Woods Hollow Road
Madison, WI 53711
(608) 277-2497
www.promega.com

Qiagen, Inc.
28159 Avenue Stanford
Valencia, CA 91355
(800) 426-8157
www.qiagen.com

QORPAK DIV. ALL-PAK
1195 Washington Pike

Bridgeville, PA 15017
(412) 257-3100
www.gorpak.com

Quincy Technologies
5650 Brookstone Drive
Acworth, GA 30101
(770) 590-0966
www.quincytech.com

Radian International
PO Box 201088
Austin, TX 78720-1088
(512) 238-9974
www.radian.com/standards

Rainin Instrument Co., Inc.
5400 Hollis Street
Emeryville, CA 94608
(510) 654-9142
www.rainin.com

Rees Scientific Corporation
1007 Whitehead Road Ext.
Trenton, NJ 08638
(609) 530-1055
www.ReesScientific.com

ReliaGene Technologies, Inc.
5525 Mounes Street, Suite 101
New Orleans, LA 70123
(504) 734-9700/(800) 256-4106
www.reliagene.com

Renishaw, Inc.
623 Cooper Court
Schaumburg, IL 60173
(847) 843-3666
www.renishaw.com

Restek Corporation
110 Benner Circle
Bellefonte, PA 16823
(814) 353-1300
www.restekcorp.com

RJ Lee Instruments, Ltd
515 Pleasant Valley Road
Trafford, PA 15085
(724) 744-0100
www.rjleeinst.com

Roche Diagnostics Corporation
9115 Hague Road
Indianapolis, IN 46256

(317) 845-7071
www.Roche.com

Sanyo Gallenkamp
900 North Arlington Heights Road
Suite 310
Itasca, IL 60143
(800) 848-8442

Schleicher and Schuell, Inc.
10 Optical Avenue
Keene, NH 03431
(603) 352-3810

S.E.E. Inc.
801 Mahler Road, Suite G
Burlingame, CA 9410
(650) 259-3910
www.see-incorp.com

Sempair Corporation
PO Box 659
Chestertown, MD 21620
(888) 778-7829
www.semper.co.uk

SensIR Technologies, LLC
15 Great Pasture Road
Danbury, CT 06810
(203) 207-9700
www.sensir.com

Shandon Inc.
171 Industry Drive
Pittsburgh, PA 15275
(412) 788-1133
www.shandon.com

Shimadzu Scientific Instruments, Inc.
7102 Riverwood Drive
Columbia, MD 21046
(410) 381-1227
www.shimadzu.com

The Sirchie Group
100 Hunter Place
Youngville, NC 27596
(800) 356-7311
www.sirchie.com

Skeltrak, Inc.
63 Sarasota Center Boulevard
Sarasota, FL 34240
(941) 342-8707
www.skeltrak.com

Spectrum Laboratory Products
14422 South San Pedro Street
Gardena, CA 90248
(800) 777-8786
www.spectrumchemical.com

Spex Forensics Division
3880 Park Avenue
Edison, NJ 98820
(732) 494-8660
www.crimescope.com

STC Technologies, Inc.
1745 Eaton Avenue
Bethlehem, PA 18018
(610) 882-1820
www.stctech.com

Tetra Scene of Crime Ltd
Hygro Farm, Kennel Lane
Great Burstead
Billericay, Essex CM11 2SU, England
+44(0)1277 626100
www.tetrasceneofcrimeuk.com

T & L Products, Inc.
7856 Reinbold Road
Reese, MI 48757
(517) 868-1550
www.tlproducts.com

Transgenomic Inc.
2032 Concourse Drive
San Jose, CA 95131
(408) 432-3230
www.transgenomic.com

Tri-Tech Inc.
4019 Executive Park Blvd, SE
South Port, NC 28461
(910) 457-6600
www.tritechusa.com

United Chemical Technologies, Inc.
2731 Bartram Rd.
Bristol, PA 19007
(215) 781-9255
www.unitedchem.com

University of Bern
Institute of Legal Medicine
Buhlstrasse 20
CH-3012, Switzerland
(0041) 31 631 84 12
www.cx.unibe.ch/irm/

Varian, Inc.
3120 Hansen Way
Palo Alto, CA 94304
(650) 424-5499

VertiQ Software, LLC
16275 Monterey Road, Suite L
Morgan Hill, CA 95037
(408) 782-7470

VWR Scientific Products
(800) 932-5000
www.vwrsp.com

W.B. Saunders/Mosby
4307 Inlet Road
Stockton, CA 95219
(209) 951-9434

Whatman FITZCO
5600 Pioneer Creek Drive
Maple Plain, MN 55359
(612) 479-2880
www.fitzcoinc.com

Zymark Corporation
68 Elm Street
Hopkinton, MA 01748
(508) 435-9500
www.zymark.com

APPENDIX IV:
BIBLIOGRAPHY

BOOKS

ATF Arson investigation guide (1997, May). Washington, DC: The Department of the Treasury.

Bevel, T. and Gardner, R. (1997). *Bloodstain pattern analysis with an introduction to crime scene reconstruction.* Boca Raton, FL: CRC Press.

Bodziak, W. (1990). *Footwear impression evidence.* New York: Elsevier Science Publishing Co., Inc.

Casey, E. (2000). *Digital evidence and computer crime: Forensic science, computers and the internet.* New York: Academic Press.

Computer Analysis and Response Team (1997, 21 February). *Conducting searches in a computer environment.* Washington, DC: Federal Bureau of Investigation, US Department of Justice.

DeForest, P., Gaensslen, R. and Lee, H. (1983). *Forensic science: An introduction to criminalistics.* New York: McGraw-Hill, Inc.

DiMaio, V. (1985). *Gunshot wounds: Practical aspects of firearms, ballistics, and forensic techniques.* New York: Elsevier Science Publishing Co., Inc.

Dix, J. (1999). *Handbook for death scene investigators.* Boca Raton, FL: CRC Press.

Eckert, W. and James, S. (1989). *Interpretation of bloodstain evidence at crime scenes,* 1st edn. New York: Elsevier Science Publishing Co., Inc.

Fisher, B. (1992). *Techniques of crime scene investigation,* 5th edn. New York: Elsevier Science Publishing Co., Inc.

Gaensslen, R. (1983, August). *Sourcebook in forensic serology, immunology, and biochemistry.* Washington, DC: National Institute of Justice and US Department of Justice.

Hawthorne, M. (1999). *First unit responder: A guide to physical evidence collection for patrol officers.* Boca Raton, FL: CRC Press.

Lee, H. and Gaensslen, R. (1991). *Advances in fingerprint technology.* New York: Elsevier Science Publishing Co., Inc.

Lee, H., *et al.* (1991). *Physical evidence in criminal investigations.* Westbrook, CT: Narcotic Enforcement Officers Association.

Lee, H., Gaensslen, R., Ladd, C., Bourke, M., Gibbs, D., Maxwell, V., Mills, R.,

Novitch, B., O'Brien, R., Pagliaro, E., Penders, P., Tramantozzi, D. and Zercie, K. (1994). *Crime scene investigation.* Taoyuan, Taiwan ROC: Central Police University Press.

Lee, H. (assistant editors Pagliaro, E., Maxwell, V. and Zercie, K.) (1994). *Physical evidence.* Enfield, CT: Magnani & McCormick, Inc.

Lee, H. and Harris, H. (2000). *Physical evidence in forensic science.* Tucson, AZ: Lawyers & Judges Publishing Co., Inc.

McDonald, J. (1992). *The police photographer's guide.* Arlington Heights, IL: PhotoText Books.

McDonald, P. (1989). *Tire imprint evidence.* New York: Elsevier Science Publishing Co., Inc.

National Medicolegal Review Panel (1997, December). *National guidelines for death investigation.* Washington, DC: National Institute of Justice and US Department of Justice.

Ogle, R. (1995). *Crime scene investigation and physical evidence manual.* Vallejo, CA: Robert Ogle, Jr.

Redsicker, D. (1994). *The practical methodology of forensic photography.* Boca Raton, FL: CRC Press.

Technical Working Group for Bombing Scene Investigation (2000, June). *A guide for explosion and bombing scene investigation.* Washington, DC: National Institute of Justice and US Department of Justice (NCJ #181869).

Technical Working Group on Crime Scene Investigation (2000, January). *Crime scene investigation: A guide for law enforcement.* Washington, DC: National Institute of Justice and US Department of Justice (NCJ #178280).

Technical Working Group on Fire/Arson Scene Investigation (2000, June). *Fire and arson scene evidence: a guide for public safety personnel.* Washington, DC: National Institute of Justice and US Department of Justice (NCJ#181584).

LEGAL

Mincey v. Arizona, 437 US 385 (1978).
State v. Moody, 573 A.2d 716, 214 Conn. 616 (Conn. 1990).

ASSORTED ARTICLES, JOURNALS, AND PAPERS

Basic laboratory protocols for the presumptive identification of bacillus anthracis. [Online]. Centers for Disease Control and Prevention, Department of Health and Human Services. Available:

http://www.bt.cdc.gov/documents/biological/B.anthracisv8BasicProtocol. doc (2000, 4 May).

Douglas, J., Ressler, R., Burgess, A., and Hartman, C. (1986). Criminal profiling from crime scene analysis. *Behavioral Sciences & the Law*, **4**(4), 401–421.

Drug Enforcement Administration (No date). *Clandestine laboratory awareness.* US Department of Justice, Office of Training, Quantico, VA. (Pamphlet).

Forensic diving. (1998, April). *FBI Law Enforcement Bulletin.*

Franz, D. (No date). *Defense against toxin weapons.* United States Army (pamphlet).

Hamm, E. (1983, June 23). *Enhancement and development of blood prints.* Presented at summer workshop, Georgia State Division, International Association for Identification, Savannah, GA.

Lee, H. (No date). *Blood and bloodstains.* (Paper).

Lee, H. (No date). *Bloodstain pattern interpretation.* (Paper).

Lee, H. (No date). *Survey of methods used in forensic science.* (Paper).

Lee, H., Hazen, R. and Nutt, J. (No date). *TMB as an enhancement reagent for bloody prints.* University of New Haven.

Lee, H. and Attard, A. (1979) The comparison of fluorescamine O-phthaladehyde and ninhydrin in latent prints detection. *J. Police Science and Administration*, **7**(30).

Lee, H. and Gaensslen, R. E. and DeForest, P. (1979) An evaluation of fluorescein as a presumptive test reagent for blood. *Eastern Analytical Symposium Abstracts*, **138**(69).

Lee, H. (1984) TMB as an enhancement reagent for bloody prints. *Identification News*, March.

Lee, H. and DeForest, P. R. (1984) Forensic hair examination. *Forensic Sciences*, Vol. 2, Chapter 37A.

Lee, H. and Gaensslen, R. E. (1984) Analytical techniques used in homicide investigation. *Eastern Analytical Symposium Abstract.*

Lee, H. and Gaensslen, R. E. (1984) Cyanoacrylate. *Identification News*, **34**(6), June.

Lee, H. and Gaensslen, R. (1984). *Cyanoacrylate fuming: Theory and procedures.* University of New Haven.

Lee, H. *et al.* (1985) Methods for the recovery of accelerant residues from arson debris. *Forensic Science*, 2nd ed.

Lee, H. and Gaensslen, R. E. (1987) Electrostatic lifting procedure for two-dimensional dustprints. *Identification News*, January.

Lee, H. *et al.* (1989) The effect of presumptive test, latent fingerprint and some other reagents and materials on subsequent serological identification, genetic markers and DNA testing in bloodstains. *J. of Forensic Identification*, **39**(6), 331–350.

Lee, H. and Gaensslen, R. (1989, August). The effect of presumptive test, latent fingerprint and some other reagents and materials on subsequent serological identification, genetic marker and DNA testing in bloodstains. *Journal of Forensic Identification*, **39**(6), 339–342.

Lee, H. *et al.* (1991) DNA analysis in human bone tissue: RFLP typing. *J. Forensic Science Society*, **31**(2), 209–212.

Lee, H. *et al.* (1991) DNA analysis in human bone and other specimens of forensic interest: PCR typing and testing. *J. Forensic Science Society*, **31**(2), 213–216.

Lee, H. *et al.* (1991) Guidelines for the collection and preservation of DNA evidence. *J. Forensic Identification*, **41**(5), 344–356, September.

Lee, H. (1994). *Benzidine or o-tolidine? Identification News.*

Lee, H., Ladd, C., Bourke, M., Pagliaro, E., Trinady, F. (1994) DNA typing in forensic science. *The American Journal of Forensic Medicine and Pathology*, **15**(4), 269–282.

Lee, H., Bigbee, P., Kearney, J., Lindsey, J. and Doyle, J. (1997, January). *Guidelines for the collection and preservation of DNA evidence.* Presented to Technical Working Group on DNA Analysis.

McCracken, K. (1999). To-scale crime scene models: A great visual aid for the jury. *Journal of Forensic Identification*, **49**(2), 130–133.

Noblett, M., Pollitt, M. and Presley, L. (2000, October). Recovering and examining computer forensic evidence. *Forensic Science Communications*, **2**(4).

Norkus, P. and Noppinger, K. (No date). *New reagent for the enhancement of blood prints.* Florida Department of Law Enforcement, Pensacola Regional Lab.

Ressler, R., Burgess, A., Douglas, J., Hartman, C. and D'Agostino (1986, September). Sexual killers and their victims. *Journal of Interpersonal Violence*, **1**(3), 288–308.

Staff (No date). Responding to terrorism victims – Oklahoma City and beyond. *Executive summary.* [Online]. US Department of Justice. Available: http://www.ojp.usdoj.gov/ovc/fores/respterrorism/executive.html (2000, 28 November).

Staff (1985, August). Crime scene and profile characteristics of organized and disorganized murderers. *FBI Law Enforcement Bulletin.*

Staff (1995, November). Multiagency response to clandestine drug laboratories. *Bureau of Justice Assistance Fact Sheet*, US Department of Justice.

PARTIAL RECONSTRUCTION (FOCUS POINT: BLOOD STAIN PATTERN ANALYSIS)

If a crime scene is properly documented, relevant evidence is obtained through a logical, systematic search, related laboratory investigations, and if medical reports are available, then a full reconstruction is possible. A partial reconstruction will provide investigators with logical interpretations that may assist in determining or eliminating certain events and actions that occurred at the crime scene. An experienced investigator could conduct a partial reconstruction based on scene photographs, examination of physical evidence, and review of relevant reports. The following scenario involves a homicide investigation in Hilo, Hawaii, that was solved through a reconstruction of bloodstain patterns – much to the credit of Deputy Attorney General Kurt Spohn's direct involvement and Hilo police Lt. Paul Fasseira, officer Martin Ellazam and other investigators, who skillfully acquired the necessary information and scene documentation.

On November 27, 1992 Sergeant Kenneth Mathison of the Hawaii Police Department and his wife, Yvonne, were driving north on the Volcano Highway. According to Sergeant Mathison, Yvonne was driving their tan van during that rainy night. Sergeant Mathison admitted that, while his wife was driving, they were involved in a verbal argument over family affairs. During this argument she suddenly jumped from the moving van. Sergeant Mathison gave several versions regarding the events during the investigation. First responding officers arrived at the scene and observed Sgt. Mathison holding his critically injured wife in the rear cargo area of the van. Sergeant Mathison told witnesses, as well as the first responding officer, that – after his wife jumped from the moving van – he drove the van in the area looking for her, and found her lying on the road edge, apparently having been struck by an unknown vehicle. Later, Sgt. Mathison stated that, while driving slowly looking for his wife that dark rainy night, he felt a bump, got out of the van and realized that he had run her over with the van.

Yvonne Mathison was transported to a local hospital were she was pronounced dead as a result of her injuries. She suffered from a severe skull fracture and had a corresponding laceration on the left side of her head. The autopsy revealed that the skull fracture was consistent with a perpendicular blow, rather than an injury associated with having been run over by a passing vehicle. She also had a broken forearm. There was a tire mark impression on her left chest corresponding to a tire mark from the van that would be expected if she had been run over by the van.

INVESTIGATIVE INFORMATION

Initially, the matter was investigated as a fatal traffic accident. In addition to a preliminary investigation and report by patrol personnel other investigative and technical personnel were assigned to assist in the investigation. Officer Martin Ellazan, an accident scene reconstructionist, was assigned to the case. In addition, Detective Paul Ferreira and other investigators were assigned to assist in the background portion of the investigation. After completing their respective preliminary investigations, both the detective and accident scene specialist became suspicious that foul play may have been involved with Yvonne's death. The investigative information was forwarded to Deputy Attorney General Kurt Spohn for review and recommendation. He also concluded that there was more to this death than a fatal motor vehicle accident. Unfortunately, Yvonne's body had been expeditiously cremated, and so further medical examinations could not be conducted.

On May 7, 1993, at Kurt Spohn's request, Dr. Henry Lee traveled to Hilo to examine the Mathison's van. Dr. Lee conducted a detailed examination of the interior and exterior of the van and noted blood stain patterns and other evidence that were inconsistent with Sgt. Mathison's story. Some of the key findings by Dr Lee were as follows:

1. Multiple bloody hair swipe patterns on the driver's side sun visor shows that these patterns are the result of contact and transfer from the victim's head.
2. Blood crust and hair were observed on a hexagonal nut located above driver' side door. The pattern of this hexagonal nut corresponds to the injury pattern on her right face.
3. Hundreds of medium velocity impact blood spatters were found on the face of the instrument panel, suggesting multiple impacts.
4. Bloody imprints of a fist and fingers were located on the sliding cargo indicating that the victim was against the cargo wall and subsequently slid down the wall.
5. A mixture of soil, blood was located in the cargo area. Through further examination it was determined that the blood was deposited before the soil.
6. A rope fragment, bundle of hairs, and vegetative material were collected from the step-up into the driver's door area. These hairs had crushed cut ends.

LABORATORY REPORTS

Physical evidence was sent to the Federal Bureau of Investigation Forensic Laboratory for analysis. The victim's hair and blood were identified in samples taken from within the rear cargo area of the van, as well as from the driver's seat area. With blood pattern analysis, and the result of physical evidence examination a reconstruction of this case, the sequence of events and location of victim when attacked was able to be determined.

FINAL RECONSTRUCTION

As a result of the comprehensive crime scene documentation, thorough post-mortem examination, examination of forensic evidence, as well as the investigative information developed it was possible to conduct a meaningful full reconstruction in this case. Despite the fact that Yvonne's body was cremated and unavailable for further examination, the Mathison's van *was* available for further analysis and examination. It should be noted that there was a legal challenge to integrity of the evidence obtained during subsequent examination, by claiming that there was not an unassailable chain of custody regarding the van. These concerns and challenges were overcome by a comparison of the detailed photographs which were taken during the initial investigation with the same state of the van as when examined by Dr. Lee six months after the homicide.

The actual final reconstruction report, which was prepared and the basis for reconstruction testimony during the criminal trial. Sergeant Mathison was convicted of Kidnapping and Murder as a result of the investigation and reconstruction into the tragic death of Yvonne Mathison.

The following is a copy of the summary portion of the detailed reconstruction report.

SUMMARY

1. The incident occurred on November 27, 1992 at an evening hour on the southbound side of Route 11, near Mt. View, HI. The exact location and the exact time of the incident could not be established at this time.

2. The vehicle involved in the incident is a beige colored 1984 Ford van, Model Econ E150 with Hawaii registration # HRJ 038. This van is equipped with a manual hand gear shift type of system. A foot control clutch pedal was noticed on the floor board of the driver side.

3. Chemical testing for the presence of blood was positive with some areas of the under carriage of the passenger side. Hair/fiber-like trace materials were also noted. According to the information provided by Det. P. Ferreira, tissue, blood, and hairlike materials have been collected from these areas. If those materials originated from the victim it would be clear that the passenger side under carriage had contact with the victim at one point in time.

4. A tire-like impression was observed on the left chest area of the victim. This fact suggests that a tire had contacted her left chest area at one point in time. No tire marks were noticed on her face and the rest of the body, which indicates that there has been no direct contact between a tire and the rest of her body.

5. Based on the autopsy report, there is clearly a lack of typical automobile injury patterns observed on the lower extremities of the victim's body. This fact suggests that the victim was not hit by the vehicle while in an upright position.

6. Based on the report issued by Dr. Alvin Omori, the injuries found on the victim's head could not be explained by a traffic accident.

7. Medium velocity blood spatter was found on the plastic cover of the instrument panel. The pattern, amount, and distribution suggests that the blood spatter was deposited in a left to right and downward direction with an energetic source. These patterns could have been produced by arterial or venous gushing from the victim's wounds. This type of blood pattern could not be explained by a vehicle running over the victim.

8. Medium velocity blood spatters found in the driver compartment indicate that these blood spatters were produced by several separate impact sources. Photographs #65 and #66 depict two views of the reconstruction of those blood spatters.

9. Contact transfer smears with hair swipe patterns were found on the sun visor and on the roof area near the dome light. This indicates that at one point in time a blood source was in contact with this area causing a transfer.

    The hair swipe pattern could have been produced by hair soaked with blood. The pattern indicates movement from left to right which is also inconsistent with an incident in which the victim was run over by the vehicle.

Photo 65

10. Bloodstains and blood spatter were observed on the driver's side window, door, and door frame. The pattern, distribution, and condition of those stains are indicative of multiple depositions at different points in time.

11. The heavy, crusty stain found near the nut above the window frame indicates that there has been heavy contact between a blood source and this particular area. Hair and tissue-like material were observed in this area which could suggest that the victim's head had impacted this particular location at one point in time. These patterns also are inconsistent with a simple traffic accident.

12. A large amount of medium velocity blood spatter was found on the roof of the cargo bay and on the interior wall of the passenger side near the spare wheel. The patterns, amount, and distribution suggest that at one point in time a medium velocity force was applied to a blood source thus causing some of the deposits.

13. The enhanced imprints found on the interior wall of the passenger side of the cargo bay indicate that an individual's hand covered with blood has contacted the wall surface with two separate motions in a downward direction.

14. After a study of the blood patterns both on the inside and outside of the van, the location of hair, tissue, and heavy crusty blood stains found, a review of the medical examiner's report, crime scene investigative reports, and a study of the original crime scene photographs, the following conclusions were derived:

a. The blood stains found on the under carriage of the passenger side are consistent with contact transfer smears from a blood source. These could have resulted from an incident in which the victim was run over.

b. The blood spatter patterns inside the van are inconsistent with a traffic accident. These patterns are consistent with that which would result when multiple impact forces are exerted on a blood source.

Henry C. Lee, Ph.D.   Stanley S. Lee, D.M.D.
Director   Sr. Scientist

FORENSIC RESEARCH TRAINING CENTER
MERIDEN, CONNECTICUT

Reconstruction Report

SUBMITTING AGENCY: DATE OF SUBMISSION:
    Hilo Police Department   March 11, 1993
    County of Hawaii
    349 Kapiolani Street
    Hilo, Hawaii 96720   DATE OF REPORT:
                                                  June 20, 1993

REPORT TO:
    Chief Victor V. Vierra   Det. Paul Ferreira
    Chief of Police   Detective Division
    Hilo Police Department   Hilo Police Department

CASE NO: D-99428   LAB CASE NO: HL930311HA

A. Examination of Photographs and Records
On March 11, 1993 a set of investigative reports, an autopsy report, and a set of crime scene photographs were submitted by Detective Paul Ferreira of the Hilo Police Department with a request for a reconstruction of a traffic fatality which occurred on November 27, 1992.

A total of one hundred seventy-five (175) photographs were submitted for evaluation. This set of photographs could be divided into four major groups:

Group A consists of fourteen (14) pictures which were taken on the night of the incident by Detective S. Guillermo of Hilo Police Department. The majority of these photographs depict a variety of views of the beige colored van at the crime scene.

In addition, there are six (6) photographs showing the bloodstains found at various locations inside of the van. Since most of those photographs are distance views of the van, no further interpretation on the blood spatter patterns could be made at this time.

Group B consists of eleven (11) photographs which were taken on December 21, 1992 by Officer M. Ellazar. This group of photographs depicts the interior views of the vehicle. Blood-like stains can be seen in the cargo area, middle console, roof area near the dome light, plastic cover of the speedometer, steering wheel, and the driver side door and window. Some of those blood-like stains are consistent with contact transfer smears, others are similar to medium velocity impact type of spatters.

Group C consists of thirty-two (32) photographs which were taken on February 25, 1992 by Detective P. Ferreira. Three (3) of the photographs in this group show the exterior views of the van. The remainder are various views of the interior conditions of the van. Blood-like stains can be seen in various areas inside of the van. These patterns can be summarized into the following subgroups:

1. Blood-like stains found on the drywall panel and the spare tire in the cargo area consist of low velocity passive blood drops, contact transfer type of blood smears, and medium velocity blood spatter.
2. Blood-like stains found on the roof near the dome light, sun visor, steering wheel, and the side of the driver seat are consistent with contact transfer patterns. Some of those are similar to a hair sweep type of pattern.
3. Blood-like stains found on the driver door, window, and door frame areas are mainly contact dripping patterns. Some of those could be medium velocity type of blood spatters.
4. Blood-like stains found on the plastic cover of the instrument panel are consistent with medium velocity blood spatters. These blood spatters could have been produced by certain internal or external medium velocity type of forces.

Group D consists of an additional eighty-seven (87) photographs which were taken February 25, 1992 by Detective P. Ferreira. This set of photographs can be divided into the following three sup-groups:

1. Twenty-two (22) of the photographs depict the exterior views of the van. The clearance between the bumper of the van and the ground is approximately fourteen (14) inches.
2. Thirty-one (31) pictures are additional views of the interior of the van. These photographs depict some similar views of blood-like stains described in Group C.
3. Twenty-six (26) of the photographs are views of the under carriage of the van. Blood and tissue-like materials appear to be present at several locations on the passenger side of the under carriage. The clearance between the under carriage appears to be in the range of ten (10) to fourteen (14) inches.
4. Eight (8) of the photographs depict a variety of clothing items and objects. No further interpretation can be made at this time concerning the clothing and objects.

Group E consists of twenty-five (25) autopsy photographs. Various types of facial injures can be seen in these photographs. A tire-like impression can be seen on the left chest area. Other injuries appear to be present on the victim's left hand, left arm, and her head. Detailed description of these injures can be found in the autopsy report issued by Dr. Charles E. Reinhold of Hilo Hospital.

B. Examination of Vehicle

On May 7, 1993, I examined the vehicle involved in the incident at the Hilo Police Department garage. The following information related to the death of Yvonne M. Mathison was found:

The questioned vehicle is a beige colored 1984 Ford van, model Econ E150, VIN #IFTEE14Y9EHB37413, Hawaii vehicle registration plate number HRJ 038, with 92,479 miles on the odometer. The following information concerning the van was found:

1. Photograph #1 depicts the front exterior views of the van. No fresh damage areas can be seen on the exterior surface of the van. No visible bloodstains, tissue-like material, or fabric impressions were noted. A purplish colored stain was observed on the exterior surface of the van, behind the driver's door. Chemical testing for the presence of blood with this stain is negative. This stain appears to be a berry type of fruit stain.

    Some dried vegetation-like materials were noticed on the lower part of the driver door jamb, as depicted in photograph #2.

Photo 2

2. Photograph #3 shows a close-up view of the front lower part of the van under the Hawaii vehicle registration plate. A dented area was noted on the lower portion of the bumper guard. This damage appears to be old.

3. The vehicle was subsequently raised up and the under carriage area was inspected. Several freshly damaged areas were noted. Photographs #4, #5, and #6 depict views of these areas.

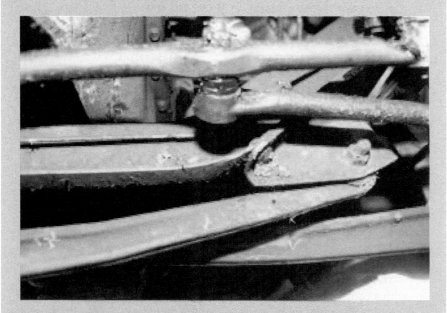

Photo 5

4. Contact transfer types of smears, vegetative matter, soil-like materials and hair-like fibers were found in several areas on the passenger side under carriage of the van. Photographs #7, #8, #9, and #10 are close-up views of those materials.

   Chemical testing for the presence of blood was positive with those areas. The following table summarizes the results of these findings.

Location	Test Result	Trace	Photograph
Front Bumper	–	–	# 3
Wheel Support	–	Grass	# 4
Wheel Support	–	Soil	# 8
Axle	+	Smear	# 6,7
Muffler	+	Smear	# 10

5. Hair/fiber-like materials were noticed on the front right (passenger) side of the axle area. These materials were collected and transferred to the custody of Detective Ferreira.
6. Photograph #11 depicts a view of the front internal portion of the van. A fracture mark was noticed in the windshield. This fracture mark is consistent with a linear, radial fracture mark. Photograph #12 shows a view of the fracture mark on the windshield. No blood or hair-like matter can be seen on this fracture.

7. Reddish-brownish blood-like stains were found on several areas on and around the driver's seat, the roof area of the driver's side, and the driver's door. These stains were tested and showed positive results with a chemical test for the presence of blood. The following table summarizes the testing results:

Location	Test result
Plastic Cover	+
Visor	+
Roof	+
Dome Light	+
Steering Wheel	+
Instrument Panel	+
Door Molding	+
Glass Window	+

8. Photograph #13 depicts a view of the front mid-portion, the area between the driver and passenger seats. A bloodstain was observed on the side of the back support of the driver's seat.

    This bloodstain measured three (3) by five (5) inches and is consistent with a contact transfer type of smear.

    In addition, blood-like stains also were found on the plastic cover in front of the instrument panel. These bloodstains are consistent with medium velocity impact type of spatters.

    Photographs #14 and #15 are close-up views of these blood spatters. The impact direction of these blood spatters is from up to downward, impacting the plastic cover at an angle of approximately ten (10) to twenty (20) degrees.

Photo 14

9. Photographs #16 and #17 show the roof portion of the van near the driver's side. One large bloodstain was observed on the sun visor on the driver's side and another large bloodstain was found on the roof near the dome light.

Photograph #18 is a close-up view of the bloodstain found on the sun visor. This stain measured five (5) by three (3) inches. It is consistent with a contact transfer swipe type of pattern. The direction of the swipe is consistent with that produced in a right to left motion. Photograph #19 is a chemically enhanced pattern of this bloodstain. Hair-like swipe patterns and medium velocity impact blood spatters were also found on this area.

A long and crusty blood stain was noticed on the roof next to the dome light. Photograph #20 shows this bloodstain. This stain is eleven (11) inches long and consists of four (4) distinct but connected blood patterns. This bloodstain is consistent with a typical contact transfer type of pattern.

Hair-like fibers were found in this area. These hair-like fibers were collected and transferred to the custody of Detective Ferreira.

Photo 21

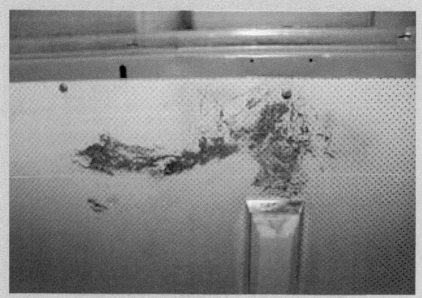

Photograph #21 is a view of the pattern after it has been chemically enhanced. Hair-like swipe patterns were also developed in this area. Several other bloodstains were also found on the roof on the driver's side. These bloodstains are shown in photograph #22 and are also similar to contact transfer types of patterns.

10. Blood-like stains were found on the middle top portion of the metal door frame as depicted in photograph #23. This stain is heavy, crusty and is approximately two (2) by three (3) inches. This bloodstain is consistent

Photo 22

with a combination of direct contact and transfer types of patterns. This pattern indicates that at one point in time, a blood source had direct contact with this metal surface and subsequently moved away from this surface and thus resulted in this type of transfer pattern.

Blood-like crusts are also found on the screw and nut above that bloodstain. Photograph #24 is a close-up view showing those blood crusts. Photograph #25 is a view showing these blood patterns after chemical enhancement.

Hair-like material was found embedded in the bloodstain. This material is consistent with human head hair and it was collected and transferred to the custody of Detective Ferreira.

Photo 24

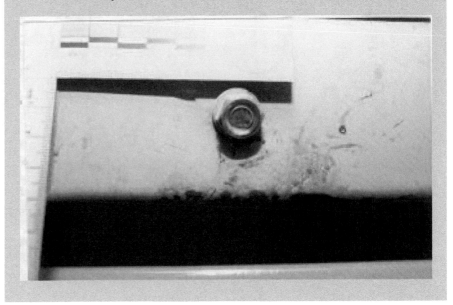

11. Blood-like stains were also observed on the interior surface of the driver's window. These bloodstains consist of a group of approximately thirty (30) individual small blood spatters. The size of these bloodstains is approximately 1–3 mm in diameter. Photograph #26 shows an overall view of these blood spatters.

    Photograph #27 is a close-up view of some of the blood splatters found on the window. The pattern of the stains are consistent with medium velocity impact spatters. This fact suggests that the driver's window was up at the time that these blood spatters were deposited.

12. Photograph #28 shows an overall view of the bloodstain found on the left hand (driver's) door. Approximately fifteen (15) bloodstains were found on the interior surface of the driver's door. Photograph #29 shows an overall view of the lower portion of the door. Bloodstains and soil-like smears can seen on this area. These smears appear to represent a motion from right to left and downward.

    Photograph #30 is a close-up view depicting the bloodstains found on this area. Some of these bloodstains are consistent with vertically deposited blood drops which impacted the surface of the door at an angle of approximately 10 to 20 degrees. Photograph #31 shows these blood patterns with scale.

13. Blood-like stains were also observed on the interior surface of the driver's door frame. Photograph #32 is a view which depicts the upper portion of the right side of the door frame.

    Blood-like stains can be seen in this area. A four (4) inch long blood-stain was located on the upper right corner of the door frame. This stain is consistent with a contact transfer type of pattern. Photograph #33 is view of this blood pattern with scale. Blood spatters and blood smears were also observed on this area. These bloodstain patterns are shown in photographs #34 and #35.

    A bloodstain approximately 2 inches wide and 30 inches long was found on the left side of the door frame. The pattern of this bloodstain is consistent with a contact dripping and running pattern. Photograph #36 is a distance view of this bloodstain pattern. The direction of the blood flow is clearly from the top downward. Photograph #37 is a close-up view of the upper portion of this bloodstain which mainly consists of a contact transfer type of pattern.

14. Photograph #38 depicts a view of the instep area of the driver's door. Dry vegetative materials, a cigarette butt, soil-like debris, hair-like matter, and blood-like stains were found in this area. A close-up view of those materials is shown in photograph #39.

    Photograph #40 is a close-up view depicting those blood splatters. This group consists of twenty (20) small blood spatters (1–3 mm. in size). These bloodstains are consistent with medium velocity blood splatter.

    Photograph #41 shows the middle portion of the instep. Soil-like smears and hair-like matter can be seen in this area. A bundle of hairs was noticed in the corner of the instep, as shown in photograph #42. This

Photo 39

bundle consists of approximately twenty (20) hairs. These hairs are macroscopically similar to human head hair. Blood-like crusts were also noticed on the surface of this bundle of human head hairs. These hairs were subsequently collected and transferred to Detective Ferreira of the Hilo Police Department.

15. Blood-like smears were also observed on the steering wheel of the vehicle. Photograph #43 shows that these smears are multiple deposits. Some of the bloodstains were deposited on top of other bloodstains.

Photo 43

A watch was noticed hanging on the signal light handle on the left side of the steering wheel column, as shown in photograph #44. Blood-like stains were also observed on the plastic surface adjacent to the left side of the steering wheel column, as depicted in the same photograph.

16. Photograph #45 depicts a view of the bloodstains found on the surface of the odometer cover. Approximately 100 or more bloodlike spatters were located predominantly on the right side of the odometer cover.

These bloodstains are consistent with medium velocity impact spatters. The direction of these spatters is from the upper left towards the lower right and impacting the surface at a 10 to 20 degree angle. Photograph #46 is a close-up view of these blood spatters with a scale.

Photo 46

17. A large amount of bloodstains, blood drops, soil-like stains, cigarette packages, and other debris were observed on the sheetrock type of materials in the cargo portion of the van. Photographs #47 and #48 are two views of these stains.

Since the position of the sheetrock type of material has changed and items in the cargo bay have been moved (when compared to the original crime scene photographs described under heading A), no further interpretation and reconstruction were made.

18. Photographs #49 shows an overall interior view of the right side of the van. At the time of this examination, the side door and the back door were both closed. Blood-like stains were noticed on various areas of the back portion of the van.

Photograph #50 depicts a close-up view of the handle portion of the side door. Blood-like stains can be seen in this area and a white colored tissue with small amount blood-like smear on it was also noticed in this area.

Photo 47

19. Photograph #51 shows a distance view of the interior, rear right side of the van. A spare tire is mounted on the wall near the rear of the van. Blood-like stains can be seen in this area.

    Photograph #52 is a close-up view of a portion of the spare tire. A large amount of bloodstains were noticed on the surface of the tire. Some of those bloodstains are consistent with a contact transfer type of pattern. Others are similar to medium velocity blood spatters.

20. Photograph #53 depicts a view of the area adjacent to the left of the spare tire. A large amount of bloodstains were found on this area. The majority of those bloodstains are consistent with transfer smears. Photographs #54, #55, and #56 are close-up views depicting some of those bloodstains.

21. An impression-like pattern was found on the top panel of the area depicted in photograph #51. This impression appears to have been made with blood. Photograph #57 is a close-up view of this impression.

    A chemical reagent for enhancement of blood was applied to the surface containing the impression. Photograph #58 is a distance view showing the enhanced patterns. The top portion of the pattern area appears to consist of two (2) contact imprints. Both imprints were made by an individual's hand with blood.

    Photograph #59 is a close-up view of these bloody hand prints. The imprint on the left appears to have been made with a partial fist in motion. The direction of the motion is from left to right, downward at a forty-five (45) degree angle.

    The imprint on the right was made by a hand with a twisting motion. The direction of the motion is from right to left, downward. This imprint continues moving downward towards the left, as shown in photograph #60.

Photo 58

Photograph #61 shows an overall view of these bloody imprints. These imprints indicate that a person's hand covered with blood had contact with this area of the van and caused such a transfer.

22. A large amount of blood spatters were also found on the roof near the middle portion of the van. The area which contains those blood spatters is shown in photograph #62.

Approximately one hundred (100) blood spatters were found in this area. Photograph #63 depicts a view of those blood spatters. These blood spatters are consistent with medium velocity spatter. Some of those blood spatters appear to be moving from right to left and others appear to be moving from back to front, as depicted in photograph #64. Some of those blood spatters could have made by a cast-off type of action. Others are similar to medium velocity impact types of patterns.

FULL RECONSTRUCTION
(FOCUS POINT: SHOOTING SCENE RECONSTRUCTIONS)

Investigation of shooting scenes can be complex and challenging, and often there are many questions that can be adequately answered only through reconstruction. Reconstruction of shooting scenes involves trajectory determinations, muzzle-to-target distance determinations through analysis of gun shot residue and shotgun pellet distribution patterns, cartridge casing ejection patterns, glass fracture analysis, blood spatter interpretation, and microscopic analysis of trace material recovered from a projectile. As with other types of reconstruction, the final reconstruction report is only as good as the quality of the components upon which it is constructed.

Shooting incidents occur in a variety of criminal cases, from acts of vandalism to homicide, and reconstruction of these scenes is often very helpful to the investigator and court. However, shooting incidents involving police officers are generally such high-profile and highly scrutinized cases that there is an absolute necessity to fully and objectively investigate the incident. This can best be accomplished by conducting a full reconstruction. The following case scenario details a police-involved shooting that ended in the death of the suspect and serious injury of a 13-year-old boy would have been kidnapped by the suspect. As a result of a full reconstruction, which was initiated from the initial crime scene, this case was brought to a successful conclusion and public trust and confidence in the police and criminal justice system was maintained.

On January 11, 1993, Jack Jones, a 42-year-old male, with an extensive criminal history, went to a car dealership along the Connecticut shoreline and asked to test drive a Mustang. A salesman agreed and got into the car with the accused.

Once on Interstate 95, the gunman pulled out a handgun, shot the salesman and fled in the Mustang. Several towns away the Mustang ran out of gas. The accused flagged down a passing motorist and got a ride to a nearby gas station. After filling the Mustang with gas from a can, he drove to the gas station and filled the gas tank. The gas station attendant recognized both the car and individual from news broadcasts and notified the Connecticut State Police. Troopers responding to the area observed the stolen Mustang and engaged the accused in a pursuit. The accused lost control and crashed the Mustang, and fled on foot. State Police Officers set up roadblocks. A woman driving a school van with two special education students, ages 13 and 14, stopped at the roadblock. Before leaving the roadblock, the accused, with gun in hand, entered the van and ordered the school van driver to flee. A 20-mile pursuit began with the gunman shooting at pursuing State Troopers. Almost 45 minutes later, the chase was ended when Troopers used a cement truck and four state police vehicles to force the commandeered school van to a stop. Once stopped he fired several shots through the front and side windows of the van at the approaching Troopers. Four State Troopers surrounding the van returned gun fire, striking the accused several times, fatally injuring him.

In addition, one of the juvenile passengers was suffering from a gunshot wound to the chest. It was unclear as to how that boy was shot. Emergency medical personnel transferred the boy to a hospital. The attending physician examined the boy and concluded that the shot was from front to back, through and through, by a small caliber weapon, similar to a .25 caliber weapon. However, during the crime scene reconstruction it was determined that the shot had a trajectory from back to front. Careful examination of the boy's clothing did not reveal an exit hole for the bullet. This shot was more likely fired by one of the Troopers with a 9 mm weapon. A re-examination in the hospital by a physician revealed that the bullet was still inside the boy, and that it in fact was consistent with a 9 mm bullet.

In the days that followed, a detailed reconstruction process was conducted to address the issues generated during the investigation. The school van and involved police cars were placed in their original positions for the reconstruction.

ISSUES DEVELOPED DURING INVESTIGATION:

1. How many shots were fired during the shooting incident?
2. How many shots were fired by State Troopers and how many shots by the accused?
3. What were the trajectories, directions and angles of each of the shots?
4. Who fired the fatal shots that struck the suspect?
5. Who fired the shot that injured the student?
6. What was the sequence of events of this shooting incident, and was the shooting justified?

The following is a copy of the actual reconstruction report prepared in this investigation. Due to the length of this comprehensive reconstruction, some of the report and included photographs were not reprinted in this section.

RECONSTRUCTION

TOWN OF INCIDENT:	Portland	DATE OF REQUEST:	01-11-93
SUBMITTING AGENCY:	Eastern District Major Crime Squad	DATE OF REPORT:	07-13-93

REPORT TO: Middlesex State's Attorney's Office and
Eastern District Major Crime Squad's Commanding Officer

LOCAL CASE #:	C-93-0528	LABORATORY CASE #:	ID9300117

I. Crime Scene Analysis

On January 11, 1993 at the request of the Eastern District Major Crime Squad and the Middlesex County District Attorney's Office, Dr. Henry C. Lee, Sgt. Robert J. Mills, Supervising Criminalists Elaine Pagliaro and Kenneth Zercie and Lead Criminalist Robert Finkle responded to the scene of a shooting incident. The scene was located on Route 66 West in the Town of Portland.

Photographs #1, #2, and #3 are overall views showing the scene on the night of the incident. The scene had been secured by State Police personnel, as shown in photograph #4. Preliminary scene survey and examination were conducted. The following observations were noted:

1. A white colored Ford Club Wagon with CT Service Bus registration plate #24064 was found on the right side of the westbound lane of Route 66. Photograph #5 shows the location and position of this van.

2. The front windshield of the vehicle appears to be damaged. Eight (8) bullet-like holes were observed in the windshield. Photograph #6 shows an overall view of the front portion of the van.

    These bullet-like holes are randomly distributed on the windshield. Some of these bullet-like holes appear to have been produced from the inside. Photograph #7 is a close-up view of these bullet-like holes.

3. Photograph #8 is an overall view of the driver's side of the van. There are three (3) windows on this side of the van.

    A. The front driver's side window appears to be in a down position, as shown in Photograph #9.

    B. The middle driver's side window was broken. Photograph #10 is a close-up view of this window. As shown in this photograph, the majority of the glass of this window is missing. This damage could have been produced by one or more bullet-type projectiles.

    C. Photograph #11 shows a view of the third driver's side window. This window was also damaged; however, the majority of the glass was still intact. One (1) visible bullet-type hole was observed.

Photo 6

Photo 10

4. Photograph #12 is a distant view of the damaged rear windows. Both rear windows were damaged. The majority of the glass from both mid-portions of the windows was missing. This damage is consistent with typical damage produced by bullet-like projectiles.
5. Two (2) bullet-like holes and one (1) additional defect were noted in the front right portion of the roof of the van. Photograph #13 depicts a view of these damages.

Photo 11

. . .

5. Photograph #46 depicts a close-up view of bullet hole #4 in the front windshield of the van.This hole is located approximately 28 inches from the left side edge of the windshield and 3 inches from the bottom of the windshield. This hole measures approximately 0.5 inches by 0.3 inches.

6. Photograph #47 depicts a close-up view of bullet hole #5 in the front windshield of the van. This hole is located approximately 25 inches from the left side edge of the windshield and 4 inches from the bottom of the windshield. This hole measures approximately 1.0 inch by 0.7 inches.

7. Photograph #48 depicts a close-up view of bullet hole #6 in the front windshield of the van. This hole is located approximately 21 inches from the left side edge of the windshield and 6 inches from the bottom of the windshield. This hole measures approximately 0.5 inches by 0.3 inches.

8. Photograph #49 depicts a close-up view of bullet hole #7 in the front windshield of the van. This hole is located approximately 17 inches from the left side edge of the windshield and 10 inches from the bottom of the windshield. This hole measures approximately 0.5 inches by 0.3 inches.

9. Photograph #50 depicts a close-up view of bullet hole #8 in the front windshield of the van. This hole is located approximately 1.5 inches from the left side edge of the windshield and 15 inches from the bottom of the windshield. This hole measures approximately 0.4 inches by 0.3 inches.

10. The following table summarizes the location and size of the eight (8) bullet holes mentioned in the above paragraphs numbered 2 through 9.

Photo 49

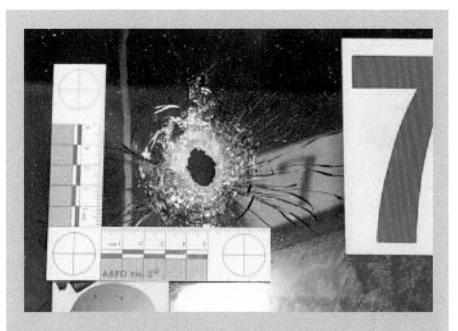

Hole Number*	Distance from driver's edge	Distance from bottom edge	Size
1	41"	11.5"	.9" diameter
2	34"	16"	.9" diameter
3	31"	10"	.9" diameter
4	28"	3"	.5" x .3"
5	25"	4"	1" x .7"
6	21"	6"	.5" x .3"
7	17"	10"	.5" x .3"
8	1.5"	15"	.4" x .3"

* The number of the hole does not necessarily represent the sequence of the shot.

11. The radial and concentric fractures of each bullet hole on the front windshield of the van were studied. In addition, the patterns of the fracture craters were also subjected to macroscopical analysis. Based on these examinations, it was determined that bullet holes #1, #2, and #3 were caused by projectiles that traveled from inside the van through the windshield and exited the van. In addition, it was determined that bullet holes #4, #5, #6, #7 and #8 were caused by projectiles that travelled from the front outside of the van through the windshield entering the van.

12. Bullet hole #9 was located in the front grill of the van adjacent to the "FORD" logo as shown in photograph #51. Photograph #52 is a close-up view of this buller defect. The trajectory of the projectile causing this defect appears to have come from a location in front of the van and

travelling through the front portion of the grill and entering the engine compartment of the van.

13. Photograph #53 depicts an interior view of the front portion of the van. Photograph #54 shows bullet-like holes that were observed on the interior surface of the front windshield and dashboard of the van.

14. Photograph #55 depicts an overall view of a bullet-like defect on the back support of the front passenger seat. This hole is located approximately 26 inches from the floor and 4 inches from the outer edge of the passenger seat. This hole measures approximately 0.25 inches in diameter. Sponge-like material can be seen protruding from the hole as depicted in Photograph #56. Photograph #57 is a close-up view of this hole with scale. This hole is consistent with an exit hole.

15. Photograph #58 depicts bullet hole #9 located on the interior surface of the side cargo door. This hole is located approximately 36 inches from the step-down floor and measures approximately 3/4 inch by 5/8 inch. Photograph #59 is a close-up view of the bullet hole and photograph #60 is a view of this bullet hole with scale. This hole is consistent with a bullet entrance hole.

16. Photograph #61 depcits a view of bullet hole #10. This hole is located on the back side of the front passenger seat approximately 25 inches from the floor and 4 inches from the outer edge of the passenger seat. This hole measures approximately 1/16 inch in diameter. Photograph #62 is a close-up view of this hole with scale. This hole is consistent with a bullet entrance hole.

Photo 62

17. Photograph #63 is an overall view of bullet holes #11, #12, and #13. These holes were located on the right side of the first row bench seat. Photographs #64 and #65 are additional views of these holes. Photograph #66 is a view of hole #11 with scale. This hole is located approxximately 25 inches from the floor and 6 inches from the edge of the arm rest. This hole measures approximately 1/16 inch. Photograph #67 shows a view of hole #12 with scale. This hole is located approximately 25 inches from the floor and 4 inches from the edge of the arm rest. This hole measures approximately 1/4 inch in diameter. Photograph #68 is a close-up view of hole #13 with scale. This hole is located approximately 23 inches from the floor and 5.5 inches from the edge of the arm rest. This hole is a half circle in shape and measures approximately 1/2 inch in diameter. Bullet holes #11, #12, and #13 are consistent with bullet exit holes.

18. Photograph #69 depicts an overall view of hole #14 in the first row bench seat. This hole is located approximately 29 inches from the floor and 20 inches from the edge of the arm rest. This hole caused an approximately 1 inch separation of the seam. Sponge-like material can be seen protruding from this hole. Photograph #70 is a close-up view of this hole. Photograph #71 is a close-up view of the hole with scale. This hole is consistent with a bullet exit hole.

19. Photograph #72 depicts an overall view of hole #15 located on the back of the first row bench seat. This hole is located approximately 31 inches from the floor and 28 inches from the edge of the arm rest. This hole measures approximately 1 inch in diameter and has a slightly elongated appearance. Photograph #73 is a close-up view of this hole. Photograph #74 is a view of the hole with scale. This hole is consistent with a bullet entrance hole.

20. Photograph #75 depicts an overall view of holes #16 and #17. These holes are located on the back right side surface of the first row bench seat. Photograph #76 is a close-up view of hole #16. This hole is located approximately 31 inches from the floor and 4 inches from the edge of the arm rest. This hole measures approximately 1/4 inch in diameter. Photograph #77 is a view of this hole with scale. Photograph #78 is a close-up view of hole #17. This hole is located approximately 31 inches from the floor and 1 inch from the edge of the arm rest. This hole measures approximately 1/4 inch in diameter. Photograph #79 is a close-up view of this hole with scale. These holes are consistent with bullet entrance holes.

21. Photograph #80 depicts an overall view of holes #18 and #19. These holes are located on the upper left region of the second row bench seat. Photograph #81 is a close-up view of hole #18. This hole is located approximately 33 inches from the floor and 50 inches from the edge of the arm rest. This hole consists of a tear that measures approximately 1 inch long. Photograph #82 is a view of this hole with scale. This hole is consistent with a bullet exit hole. Photograph #83 is a view of hole #19. This hole is located approximately 34 inches from the floor and 51 inches from the edge of the arm rest. This hole measures approximately 1/4 inch in

Photo 85

diameter. Photograph #84 is a view of this hole with scale. This hole is consistent with a bullet entrance hole.

22. Photograph #85 depicts an overall view of holes #20, #21, and #22. These holes are located on the front right side of the second row bench seat. Photograph #86 is an overall close-up view of these holes. Photograph #87 is a close-up view of hole #20. This hole is located approximately 33 inches from the floor and 4 inches from the edge of the arm rest. This hole measures approximately 1/4 inch in diameter. Photograph #88 is a close-up view of this hole with scale. This hole is consistent with a bullet exit hole. Photograph #89 is a close-up view of hole #21. This hole is located approximately 31 inches from the floor and 4 inches from the edge of the arm rest. This hole measures approximately 1/4 inch in diameter. Photograph #90 is a view of this hole with scale. This hole is consistent with a bullet exit hole. Photograph #91 is a close-up view of hole #22. This hole is located approximately 30 inches from the floor and 2-1/2 inches from the edge of the arm rest. This hole measures approximately 1/2 inch in daimeter. Photograph #92 is a view of this hole with scale. This hole is consistent with a bullet exit hole.

23. Photograph #93 depcits an overall view of holes #23, #24, #25, and #26. These holes are located on the back right side of the second row bench seat. Photograph #94 is a close-up view of hole #23. This hole is located approximately 28.5 inches from the floor and 10 inches from the edge of the arm rest. This hole measures approximately 1/2 inches in diameter and is consistent with a bullet entrance hole. Photograph #95 is a close-up view of this hole with scale. Photograph #96 is a close-up view of hole #24. This hole is located approximately 31 inches from the floor and 9.5 inches from the edge of the arm rest. This hole measures approximately 3/4 inches in diameter and is consistent with a bullet entrance hole.

Photograph #97 is a close-up view of this hole with scale. Photograph #98 is a close-up view of hole #25. This hole is located approximately 31.5 inches from the floor and 4 inches from the edge of the arm rest. This hole measures approximately 1/4 inch in diameter and is consistent with a bullet entrance hole. Photograph #99 is a close-up view of this hole with scale. Photograph #100 is a close-up view of hole #26. This hole is located approximately 31 inches from the floor and 2 inches from the edge of the seat. This hole measures approximately 1/4 inch in diameter and is consistent with a bullet entrance hole. Photograph #101 is a close-up view of this hole with scale.

24. Photograph #102 depicts a view of hole #27. This hole is located on the right front region of the third row bench seat and measures approximately 31 inches from the floor and seven inches from the edge of the seat. This hole consists of a tear measuring approximately 1.5 inches long. In addition, a 1/4 inch hole is located inside this tear. This hole is consistent with a bullet exit hole. Photograph #103 is a view of this hole with scale.

25. Photograph #104 depicts an overall view of hole #28 located on the back right region of the fourth row bench seat. This hole is located approximately 31 inches from the floor and 6 inches from the edge of the seat. This hole measures approximately 1/4 inch in diameter and is consistent with a bullet entrance hole. Photograph #105 is a close-up view of this hole. Photograph #106 is a view of this hole with scale.

26. Photograph #107 shows defect #29 located on the driver's side of the third row bench seat. This defect is inconsistent with a buller type hole. Macroscopical examination indicates that the defect was produced by cutting with a sharp instrument. Photograph #108 is a close-up view of this cut-like defect.

27. Four (4) bullet-like defects were observed on the door frame and surrounding area of the interior portion of the rear of the van. Photograph #109 is an overall view of some of these bullet-like defects. Photograph #110 is a view of bullet defect #30. This defect is located approximately 48 inches from the floor and 12 inches from the metal side of the van and measures 1/2 inch by 3/4 inch. Photograph #111 is a close-up view of this defect with scale. Photograph #112 is a view of defect #31. This defect is located approximately 47 inches from the floor and 35 inches from the metal side of the van and measures 1 inch by 1/2 inch. Photograph #113 is a close-up view of this defect with scale. Photograph #114 is a view of defect #32. Photograph #115 is a close-up view of this defect. This defect is located approximately 47 inches from the floor and is on the rear right hand corner of the van and measures approximately 2 inches by 1 inch. Photograph #116 is a view of this defect with scale. Photograph #117 is a view of defect #33. This defect is located approximately 38 inches from the floor and 29 inches from the side of the van and measures 1/2 inch in daimeter. Photograph #118 is a view of this defect with scale. Defects #30, #31, #32, and #33 are consistent with bullet entrance holes.

28. Photographs #119 and #120 depict three (3) bullet-like holes in the headliner of the front right portion of the van. These three holes appear to correspond to the three (3) bullet-type holes/defects observed on the front right outer surface of the roof of the van.

29. In addition to the previously mentioned bullet holes, bullet-type defects were also observed on some of the windows of the van. Photograph #121 depicts a reconstructed view of the driver's side windows. Photograph #122 shows a close-up view of a bullet-type hole in the third window of the left side of the van. This hole measures approximately 1-3/4 inches in diameter and is located approximately 6.75 inches from the bottom of the window and 27.25 inches from the left edge of the window. Based on the glass fracture and pattern analysis of this window, it was determined that this bullet hole was produced by an entrance gunshot into the van through the window.

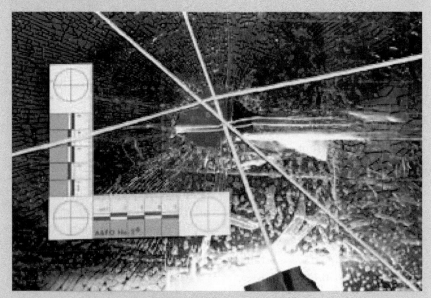

Photo 122

III. Reconstruction of Bullet Trajectories

On January 15, 1993, Dr. Henry C. Lee, Supervising Criminalist Kenneth Zercie, Det. David Gibbs, Lead Criminalist Robert K. O'Brien and Photographer Paul Penders returned to Troop K in Colchester to continue the reconstruction of this shooting incident. The van and the two police vehicles directly involved in the incident were re-positioned according to measurements taken the night of January 11, 1993. These vehicles were re-positioned at the Troop K garage by State Police Eastern Major Crime Squad. The following observations were made:

1. Photographs #123 and #124 show views of the driver's side of the van and the two (2) State Police vehicles after the re-positioning. Photographs #125 and #126 depict the front view of the van after the

Photo 124

re-positioning. Photographs #127 and #128 show a rear view of the van after the re-positioning.

2. Six (6) 9 mm-type cartridge casings were located on the ground by the driver's side of the van. Seven (7) 9 mm-type spent cartridge casings were located in the front of the van. Four (4) 9 mm-type spent cartridge casings were located at the inside rear portion of the van. One (1) 9 mm type spent cartridge casing was located on the ground near the rear of the van.

3. Wooden probes, strings, and laser sighting devices were utilized to aid in the determination of bullet trajectories. Photographs #129, #130, #131, #132 and #133 depict several views of the reconstruction of the front windshield of the van. The trajectory of the eight (8) bullet holes on the front windshield were established. The results of the reconstruction are summarized as follows:

Hole number*	Entrance/ exit	Direction	Distance from left edge	Distance from bottom edge
1	Exit	Outward	41″	11.5″
2	Exit	Outward	34″	16″
3	Exit	Outward	31″	10″
4	Entrance	Inward	28″	3″
5	Entrance	Inward	25″	4″
6	Entrance	Inward	21″	6″
7	Entrance	Inward	17″	10″
8	Entrance	Inward	1.5″	15″

* The number of the hole does not necessarily represent the sequence of the shot.

4. Photographs #134 and #135 show two (2) views after the direction of each shot was established.

5. Photographs #136 and #137 show the bullet hole in the front grill of the van. The direction of this shot was from outside-in. The trajectory is from front to back and at a slight downward angle of approximately ten (10) degrees. The damage to the grill was approximately one and one half inches (1-1/2") in length with the bullet penetrating through to the radiator.

6. Photograph #138 depicts a view of the middle window on the driver's side of the van. The maJority of the glass is missing from the wIndow. Through the study of fracture patterns on the remaining glass on the window, it is clear that shots were fired through this window. However, due to the severe damage of the window glass, it is unclear as to the exact number of shots fired from the outside-in and or any shots were fired from the inside-out. Hole #9 (interior of the passenger side cargo door) and #9A (exterior of the passenger side cargo door), as shown below, were an entry and exit combination for the trajectory of a bullet coming from the direction of the middle window of the driver's side of the van.

7. Photograph #139 is an overall view showing the bullet hole located on the third side window on the driver's side of the van. This bullet hole measures approximately 1-3/4" in diameter and is approximately 5' 6" up from the ground. This hole is located approximately 6-3/4" up from the bottom of the window and approximately 27-1/4" from the left edge of the window.

8. The hole mentioned in paragraph #7 appears to have been produced by a single gunshot. The trajectory of this shot was determined to be from the exterior of the van, from left to right, back to front at a 45 degree angle against the normal. The bullet after entering the window then entered through the second row bench seat at hole marked #19 and exiting through hole marked #18. The bullet then reentered the first row bench seat at hole marked #15 and re-exits through hole marked #14.

9. Photograph #140 shows the condition of the exterior side of the rear door windows. As shown in this photograph, the center portions of the windows are missing. From the fracture patterns of the glass, the possible points of impact were reconstructed.

10. Photographs #141 and #142 depict interior views of the rear doors of the van. White strings were used to reconstruct the possible centers of the impact which caused the fracture pattern on the glass. Additional bullet-like holes were identified on the surrounding areas of the rear doors. The following table summarizes the location and description of each of these bullet-like holes:

Photo 142

	Location		
Hole	Right side	From floor	Size
30	12"	48"	1/2" x 3/4"
31	35"	47"	1" x 1/2"
32	0"	47"	2" x 1"
33	29"	38"	1/2"

11. A total of thirty-three (33) possible bullet-like holes were identified in various locations inside the van. Each of these holes were numbered, identified, measured and studied. The following table shows the results of these examinations.

Number	Location	Entrance/Exit	Evidence recovered
1	roof	entrance	–
2	roof	entrance	–
3	roof	entrance	–
4	dash board	entrance	#124
5	dash board	entrance	#126
6	dash board	entrance	#129
7	dash board	?	–
8	passenger seat	exit	–
9	side cargo door	entrance	#143 & #162
10	passenger seat	entrance	–
11	1st row bench seat	exit	–
12	1st row bench seat	exit	–

Number	Location	Entrance/Exit	Evidence recovered
13	1st row bench seat	exit	–
14	1st row bench seat	exit	–
15	1st row bench seat	entrance	–
16	1st row bench seat	entrance	–
17	1st row bench seat	entrance	–
18	2nd row bench seat	exit	–
19	2nd row bench seat	entrance	#130
20	2nd row bench seat	exit	–
21	2nd row bench seat	exit	–
22	2nd row bench seat	exit	–
23	2nd row bench seat	entrance	9 mm (#153 or #154)
24	2nd row bench seat	entrance	9 mm (#153 or #154)
25	2nd row bench seat	entrance	–
26	2nd row bench seat	entrance	–
27	3rd row bench seat	exit	–
28	3rd row bench seat	entrance	–
29	3rd row bench seat	cut	–
30	rear door	entrance	#53
31	rear door	entrance	#150
32	rear door	entrance	–
33	rear door	entrance	#144

12. The majority of the bullet-like holes were located on the right side of the seats inside the van. The trajectories of these bullet-type holes were studied with the aid of probes, laser sighting devices and strings. It was found that these holes appear to have been produced by five separate trajectories. The following are detailed descriptions of each trajectory:

A. Photographs #143 through #149 show the trajectory of a bullet fired from the rear window which passed up into the inside roof (hole marked #3) near the front of the van and exited out through the roof of the van.

B. Photographs #150 through #157 show the trajectory of another bullet fired from the rear window. This bullet passed through the third row bench seat entering hole marked #28 exiting hole marked #27 and re-entered the second row of seats into hole marked #23 where it lodged inside the seat material of the second row bench seat. This projectile was removed by Major Crime Squad Personnel.

C. Photograph #158 depicts another bullet trajectory from the rear window area into the van. This bullet entered into the second row bench seat through hole marked #24 and remained lodged in this seat material. The projectile was recovered by Major Crime Squad detectives.

D. Another bullet entered the second row bench seat through hole marked #25 and exited through hole marked #21, re-enters the first

Photo 162

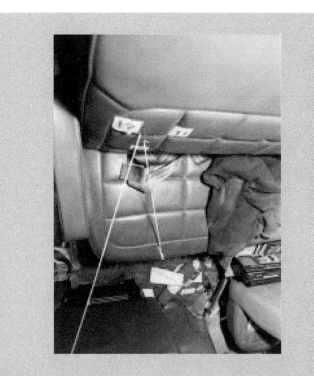

Photo 163

row bench seat through hole marked #16 and re-exits through hole marked #12, re-enters hole marked #10 and re-exits through hole marked #8. This trajectory is shown in photographs #159 through #164.

E. Another bullet trajectory entered the second row bench seat through hole marked #26 and exited through hole marked #22, re-entered the

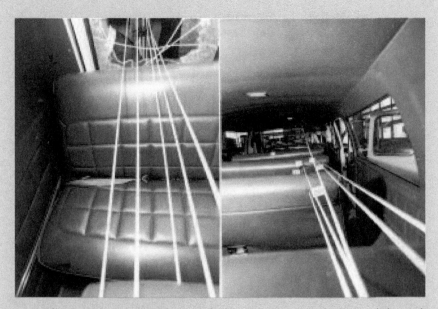

Photo 166

first row bench seat through hole marked #17 and re-exited through hole marked #13. Photographs #165 and #166 show the composite of all the trajectories of the fired shots.

13. Subsequently, the seat covers of the seats were partly cut open to examine the interior part of the seat for further analysis of the trajectories. Photographs #167 through #175 depict the view of the cutting process. Upon cutting the backing of the seat cover of the first row bench seat, the trajectory path hole marked #16 to hole marked #12 was revealed. A bullet hole was located directly in the center of the metal strap as seen in photographs #176 and #177. This bullet hole measured approximately 3/4 inch in length by 1/2 inch wide. The hole was approximately 26 inches up from the floor of the van and 4-1/2 inches away from the side of the seat.

14. The bullet described in the above paragraph is in the center of the path of bullet trajectory (D). This fact suggests that this hole located on the metal bar was produced by the same bullet as the hole marked #16 and hole marked #12.

The backing of the seat cover of the front passenger seat was also cut open. Photographs #178 and #179 show views of this cutting process. A bullet path was located in the thick portion of the sponge material. The path is located in between the hole marked #10 and the hole marked #8. This fact indicates that this bullet path is produced by the same projectile as the hole marked #10 and hole marked #8. The following table summarizes these five trajectories:

Bullet trajectory	Trajectory degrees/direction	Distance from ground
A	5–10 / Upward	5' 4"
B	10 / Downward	5' 3"
C	10–15 / Downward	5' 7"
D	15 / Downward	5' 8"
E	25 / Downward	5' 7"

15. Photographs #180 through #184 depict the use of a mannequin to demonstrate a possible bullet path. This bullet passed through four (4) seats and finally entered the person in the front passenger seat. The mannequin was outfitted with submitted evidence item #59 (shirt) and item #93 (jacket). These photographs illustrate the possible position the person in the front passenger seat could have been in at the time of the shooting.

Photo 182

IV. Results of Physical Evidence
A total of one-hundred-eighteen (118) items of physical evidence were submitted to the Forensic Laboratory for examination. These items were subjected to serological, instrumental, chemical, physical, macroscopical, and microscopical analysis. The results of these analysis are summarized in this section of the report. For complete reports, refer to Appendix A for Latent Prints, Appendix B for Firearms, and Appendix C for Criminalistics.

Num.	Item	Laboratory findings

1. "9mm casing"
   A. This item consisted of a "WIN 9mm LUGER" fired cartridge case.
   B. There were no identifiable latents developed or found on this item.
2. "9mm casing"
   A. This item consisted of a "WIN 9mm LUGER" fired cartridge case.
   B. There were no identifiable latents developed or found on this item.
3. "9mm casing"
   A. This item consisted of a "WIN 9mm LUGER" fired cartridge case.
   B. There were no identifiable latents developed or found on this item.
4. "9mm casing"
   A. This item consisted of a "WIN 9mm LUGER" fired cartridge case.
   B. There were no identifiable latents developed or found on this item.
5. "9mm casing"
   A. This item consisted of a "WIN 9mm LUGER" fired cartridge case.
   B. There were no identifiable latents developed or found on this item.
6. "9mm casing"
   A. This item consisted of a "WIN 9mm LUGER" fired cartridge case.
   B. There were no identifiable latents developed or found on this item.
7. "9mm casing"
   A. This item consisted of a "WIN 9mm LUGER" fired cartridge case.
   B. There were no identifiable latents developed or found on this item.
8. "9mm casing"
   A. This item consisted of a "WIN 9mm LUGER" fired cartridge case.
   B. There were no identifiable latents developed or found on this item.
9. "9mm casing"
   A. This item consisted of a "WIN 9mm LUGER" fired cartridge case.
   B. There were no identifiable latents developed or found on this item.
10. "9mm casing"
    A. This item consisted of a "WIN 9mm LUGER" fired cartridge case.
    B. There were no identifiable latents developed or found on this item.
11. "9mm casing"
    A. This item consisted of a "WIN 9mm LUGER" fired cartridge case.
    B. There were no identifiable latents developed or found on this item.
12. "9mm casing"
    A. This item consisted of a "WIN 9mm LUGER" fired cartridge case.
    B. There were no identifiable latents developed or found on this item.
13. "9mm casing"
    A. This item consisted of a "WIN 9mm LUGER" fired cartridge case.
    B. There were no identifiable latents developed or found on this item.
14. "Copper jacket fragment"
    A. Bullet jacket fragment from Winchester Silvertip Hollow Point bullet, 19.03 grains.
    B. Tests for the presence of blood were negative.
    C. Mineral matter was located on this item.

Num.	Item	Laboratory findings

15. ".22 shell casing"
This item contained one (1) caliber .22 long rifle Winchester "SUPER X" fired cartridge case.

16. "Metal fragment"
A. Bullet jacket fragment from Winchester Silvertip Hollow Point bullet, 16.08 grains.
B. Tests for the presence of blood were negative.
C. Mineral matter was located on this item.

17. "Metal fragment with base"
A. Bullet jacket fragment from Winchester Silvertip Hollow Point bullet, 14.72 grains.
B. Tests for the presence of blood were negative.
C. Mineral matter was located on this item.

18. "Copper jacket fragment with base"
A. Bullet jacket fragment from Winchester Silvertip Hollow Point bullet, 15.31 grains.
B. Aqua-colored, blue-colored, and white-colored fibers were located on this item.

19. ".22 cal. live round"
This item consisted of one (1) caliber .22 long rifle Winchester "SUPER X" lead round nose cartridge.

20. ".22 revolver with six envelopes"
A. This item consists of a Smith & Wesson revolver, model 34-1, caliber .22 long rifle, serial number M76315.
B. Also contained in this item were four (4) caliber .22 long rifle Winchester "SUPER X" fired cartridge cases (#20A and #20D-#20F) and two (2) caliber .22 long rifle Winchester "SUPER X" lead round nose cartridges (#20B and #20C).
C. This weapon was examined and test fired and found to be operable.
D. There were no identifiable latents developed or found on this item.
E. This item was determined to have fired items #15, #20A, #20D-#20F, #21–#24, #26–#30, #33–#40,#47-#49, and #53.

21. ".22 casing spent"
This item contained one (1) caliber .22 long rifle Winchester "SUPER X" fired cartridge case.

22. ".22 casing spent"
This item contained one (1) caliber .22 long rifle Winchester "SUPER X" fired cartridge case.

23. ".22 casing spent"
This item contained one (1) caliber .22 long rifle Winchester "SUPER X" fired cartridge case.

24. ".22 casing spent"
This item contained one (1) caliber .22 long rifle Winchester "SUPER X" fired cartridge case.

Num.	Item	Laboratory findings

25. ".22 live round"
This item consisted of one (1) caliber .22 long rifle Winchester "SUPER X" lead round nose cartridge.

26. ".22 casing spent"
This item contained one (1) caliber .22 long rifle Winchester "SUPER X" fired cartridge case.

27. ".22 casing spent"
This item contained one (1) caliber .22 long rifle Winchester "SUPER X" fired cartridge case.

28. ".22 casing spent"
This item contained one (1) caliber .22 long rifle Winchester "SUPER X" fired cartridge case.

29. ".22 casing spent"
This item contained one (1) caliber .22 long rifle Winchester "SUPER X" fired cartridge case.

30. ".22 casing spent"
This item contained one (1) caliber .22 long rifle Winchester "SUPER X" fired cartridge case.

31. "Lead fragment"
A. Lead fragment, 63.50 grains.
B. Bluish-gray polymer-type material was located on this item.

32. "Lead fragment"
A. Lead fragment, 11.14 grains.
B. Bluish-gray polymer-type material was located on this item.

33. ".22 casing spent"
This item contained one (1) caliber .22 long rifle Winchester "SUPER X" fired cartridge case.

34. ".22 casing spent"
This item contained one (1) caliber .22 long rifle Winchester "SUPER X" fired cartridge case.

35. ".22 casing spent"
This item contained one (1) caliber .22 long rifle Winchester "SUPER X" fired cartridge case.

36. ".22 casing spent"
This item contained one (1) caliber .22 long rifle Winchester "SUPER X" fired cartridge case.

37. ".22 casing spent"
This item contained one (1) caliber .22 long rifle Winchester "SUPER X" fired cartridge case.

38. ".22 casing spent"
This item contained one (1) caliber .22 long rifle Winchester "SUPER X" fired cartridge case.

39. ".22 casing spent"
This item contained one (1) caliber .22 long rifle Winchester "SUPER X" fired cartridge case.

Num.	Item	Laboratory findings

40. ".22 casing spent"
This item contained one (1) caliber .22 long rifle Winchester "SUPER X" fired cartridge case.

42. "9mm casing spent"
A. This item consisted of a "WIN 9mm LUGER" fired cartridge case.
B. There were no identifiable latents developed or found on this item.

43. "9mm casing spent"
A. This item consisted of a "WIN 9mm LUGER" fired cartridge case.
B. There were no identifiable latents developed or found on this item.

44. "Box of Winchester 22 bullets 50ct/empty"
A. This item consisted of an empty 50 round box of Winchester Wildcat High Velocity 22 Long Rifle ammunition.
B. There were no identifiable latents developed or found on this item.

45. "9mm casing spent"
A. This item consisted of a "WIN 9mm LUGER" fired cartridge case.
B. There were no identifiable latents developed or found on this item.

46. "9mm casing spent"
A. This item consisted of a "WIN 9mm LUGER" fired cartridge case.
B. There were no identifiable latents developed or found on this item.

47. ".22 casing spent"
This item contained one (1) caliber .22 long rifle Winchester "SUPER X" fired cartridge case.

48. ".22 casing spent"
This item contained one (1) caliber .22 long rifle Winchester "SUPER X" fired cartridge case.

49. ".22 casing spent"
This item contained one (1) caliber .22 long rifle Winchester "SUPER X" fired cartridge case.

50. "Small lead fragment"
A. Lead fragment, 2.65 grains.
B. Tests for the presence of blood were negative.

51. "Skin like material and hair"
A. Human tissue was found in this item.
B. Caucasian-type hairs were located in this item. These hairs demonstrated microscopical characteristics similar to the known head hairs in item #72.

52. "Skin like material and hair"
A. Human tissue was found in this item. Antigenic substance "A" was detected in this tissue.
B. Caucasian-type hairs were located in this item. These hairs demonstrated microscopical characteristics similar to the known head hairs in item #72.

53. "Lead fragment"
A. Caliber .22 long rifle lead bullet, 30.00 grains.
B. Bluish-gray polymer-type material was located on this item.

Num.	Item	Laboratory findings

59. "Maroon and blue shirt"
A. Bloodstains were located on the front and back of this item.
B. One (1) hole (~1/4" diameter) was located in the central region of this item.

63. "9mm casing spent"
A. This item consisted of a "WIN 9mm LUGER" fired cartridge case.
B. There were no identifiable latents developed or found on this item.

64. "Small metal fragment"
A. Bullet jacket fragment from Winchester Silvertip Hollow Point bullet, 2.67 grains.
B. Test for the presence of blood were negative.

67. "Undershirt – short sleeve"

68. "Sweatshirt – long sleeve"

69. "Jacket"
A. A 16.88 grains caliber 9mm bullet jacket fragment from a Winchester Silvertip Hollow point bullet was located on this item.
B. An irregular piece of metal was located on this item, 0.69 grains.

72. "Pulled head hair – Jack Jones"

86. "Known blood sample of Jack Jones"
This blood sample demonstrated the following genetic markers: "A", "Le(a + b-)".

87. "Bullet fragments from autopsy – brain"
Fragmented Winchester Silvertip Hollow Point bullet, 60.76 grains.

88. "Bullet fragment from autopsy – upper back"
Winchester Silvertip Hollow Point bullet, 105.59 grains.

89. "Bullet fragment from autopsy – back at right scapula"
A. Lead bullet core, 70.15 grains.
B. This lead bullet core is consistent in size to caliber 9mm ammunition.

93. "Giant's jacket"
A total of four (4) holes were located on this item.
(A) Three (3) of these holes were located in the center right of the outside back region of this item. These holes measured approximately 1/4" x 1/8", 3/16" x 1/8", and 3/16".
(B) The fourth hole was located in the inside back lining and measured approximately 1/8" in diameter.

97. "Lead fragment"
Lead bullet fragment, 36.16 grains, of unidentified origin.

98. "Saliva control"
Tests for the presence of blood and antigenic substances were negative with this item.

99. "Swab with blood"
Tests for the presence of human blood were positive.

100. "Lead fragments from van's step at cargo door"

Num.	Item	Laboratory findings

A. Lead fragment, 12.84 grains

B. Screening tests for blood gave weak positive results.

C. Foam rubber-type material was located on this item.

103.   "G.S.R. kit – Jack Jones"

Instrumental analysis of the swabs labeled "left palm", "left back", "right palm" and "right back" revealed the presence of lead, barium and antimony.

105.   "Copper jacket fragments from van's driver's hat"

A. Bullet jacket fragment from Winchester Silvertip Hollow Point bullet, 20.83 grains.

B. Fibers and whitish-colored, paint-like material were found on this item.

109.   "Beretta SB # B73982Z"

A. This item consists of a Beretta semiautomatic pistol, model 92SB, caliber 9mm, serial number B73982Z.

B. Also submitted with this item were one (1) fifteen round capacity magazine containing eight "WIN 9mm LUGER" Silvertip Hollow Point cartridges and one (1) loose "WIN 9mm LUGER" cartridge.

C. This weapon was examined and test fired and found to be operable.

D. This weapon was determined to have fired items #7, #8, #10–#13.

110.   "2 magazines 9mm – full"

111.   "2 magazines 9mm – full"

112.   "Bullet"

Winchester Silvertip Hollow Point bullet, 113.36 grains.

113.   "Beretta SB # D01997Z -12 9mm round and cllp"

A. This item consists of a Beretta semiautomatic pistol, caliber 9mm, serial number D01997Z.

B. Also submitted with this item were one (1) extended twenty round capacity magazine and twelve "WIN 9mm LUGER" Silvertip Hollow Point cartridges.

C. This weapon was examined and test fired and found to be operable.

D. This weapon was determined to have fired items #1–#5, #16 and #18.

114.   "Beretta SB # B74448Z – clip – 12 rounds"

A. This item consists of a Bereffa semiautomatic pistol, model 92SB, caliber 9mm, serial number B74448Z.

B. Also submitted with this item were one (1) fifteen round capacity magazine containing eleven "WIN 9mm LUGER" Silvertip Hollow Point cartridges and one loose "WIN 9mm LUGER" Silvertip Hollow Point cartridge.

C. This weapon was examined and test fired and found to be operable.

D. This weapon was determined to have fired item #6.

115. "2 magazines – 9mm – full"
116. "2 magazines – 30 rounds 9mm"
117. "Beretta SB # B78614Z
    A. This item consists of a Beretta semiautomatic pistol, model 92SB, caliber 9mm, serial number B78614Z.
    B. Also submitted with this item were one (1) fifteen round capacity magazine containing ten "WIN 9mm LUGER" Silvertip Hollow Point cartridges and one loose "WIN 9mm LUGER" Silvertip Hollow Point cartridge.
    C. This weapon was examined and test fired and found to be operable.
    D. This weapon was determined to have fired items #42, #43, #45, #46, #63, #88, #112, and #130,
121. "Metal fragment"
    Lead fragment, 0.83 grains.
122. "Metal fragment"
    Lead fragment, 5.20 grains.
123. "Swab with blood"
    Tests for the presence of human blood were positive. Antigenic substance "H" was detected in this blood.
124. "Metal fragment"
    Lead fragment, 1.14 grains.
125. "Lead fragment"
    Lead fragment, 1.05 grains.
126. "Metal fragment"
    Soft, grayish material was located in this item. Portions of this material demonstrated microscopical characteristics similar to a foam.
127. "Small lead fragment"
    Lead fragment, 2.81 grains.
128. "Metal fragment"
    Lead bullet core fragment, 22.16 grains.
129. "Metal fragment with material substance"
    A. Blue polymer and foam-like material were located in this item. The blue polymer material demonstrated characteristics similar to item #156.
    B. Bullet jacket fragment from Winchester Silvertip Hollow Point bullet, 15.59 grains.
    C. This item was fired from Beretta pistol #109.
130. "Metal fragment"
    A. Red-colored material was located in this item. This material demonstrated microscopical characteristics similar to the red layer of item #157.
    B. Bullet jacket fragment from Winchester Silvertip Hollow Point bullet, 18.41 grains.
    C. This item was fired from Beretta pistol #117.
135. "Metal fragment"
    Lead fragment, 4.71 grains.

Num.	Item	Laboratory findings
136.	"Two (2) metal fragments" Lead fragment, 1.08 grains.	
137.	"Super X shell casings" A. Caliber 22 long rifle Winchester "SUPER X" fired cartridge case. B. This item was fired from the Smith & Wesson revolver #20.	
138.	"Small metal fragment" Lead fragment, 2.64 grains.	
139.	"Metal fragment" Steel fragment, 14.28 grains.	
140.	"Small metal fragment" Lead fragment, 1.13 grains.	
141.	"Metal fragment" Lead fragment, 4.80 grains.	
142.	"Small metal fragment" Lead fragment, 0.48 grains.	
143.	"Copper jacket fragment" Bullet jacket fragment from Winchester Silvertip Hollow Point bullet, 6.45 grains.	
144.	"Three (3) lead fragments" A. Lead fragment, 36.11 grains. B. Insect fragments were also located in this item.	
1 45.	"Paint chips" This paint demonstrated physical characteristics similar to the known paint sample in submitted item #148.	
1 46.	"Metal fragment" Metal fragment, 0.46 grains.	
147.	"Skin-like material and hair fiber" A. Human tissue was found in this item. Antigenic substance "A" was detected in this tissue. B. Caucasian-type hairs were located in this item.	
148.	"Known paint sample – white & gray"	
149.	"Three (3) metal fragments with material" A. Lead fragment, 1.78 grains. B. Fibers, red material, and foam-like material were also located in this item.	
150.	"Lead fragment" Lead fragment, 15.97 grains.	
151.	"Small metal fragment" Metal fragment, 0.29 grains.	
152.	"Small metal fragment" Bullet jacket fragment from Winchester Silvertip Hollow Point bullet, 1.10 grains.	
153.	"Lead fragment" Lead fragment, 38.52 grains.	

Num.	Item	Laboratory findings

154. "Lead fragment"
Lead fragment, 43.10 grains.
156. "Blue vinyl"
157. "Rear foam cushioning"
158. "Netting"
159. "Foam"
160. "Three (3) metal fragments"
A. Lead fragments, 1.33 grains.
B. Foam-like material was also located in this item.
161. "Black paint scrapings"
162. "Metal flakes"
A. Paint chips located in this item were similar to the paint chips in item #148.
B. Metal fragments, 0.42 grains.
164. "Vial of known blood sample – Nick Crump"
This blood sample demonstrated the following genetic markers: "O", "Le(a–b +)".
167. "Lead fragment"
Caliber 22 long rifle lead bullet, 39.15 grains. This bullet was fired from submitted item #20.

V. Summary

Based on the results of direct crime scene observations, study of scene investigation reports, crime scene photographs, laboratory analysis of physical evidence, and the results of the scene reconstruction, the following information related to the shooting incident on January 11, 1993 has been summarized.

1. The shooting incident was located in the west bound lane of Route 66 in Portland, CT. This incident was the result of several continuous incidents that began on North Bridebrook Road, East Lyme on January 11, 1993.
2. The van appears to have been stopped at a slight angle on the right shoulder of the west bound lane of Route 66 by several State Police cruisers. One of these cruisers appears to have had direct contact with the left front area of the van while the second cruiser appears to have had direct contact with the left rear area of the van.
3. At least seventeen (17) recognizable bullet-like holes were observed on the exterior of the van. The following table depicts the bullet holes located on the exterior of the van:

Hole #	Location	Type	Direction
1	Front windshield	Exit	Inside to outside
2	Front windshield	Exit	Inside to outside
3	Front windshield	Exit	Inside to outside

Hole #	Location	Type	Direction
4	Front windshield	Entrance	Front to back
5	Front windshield	Entrance	Front to back
6	Front windshield	Entrance	Front to back
7	Front windshield	Entrance	Front to back
8	Front windshield	Entrance	Front to back
9	Front grill	Entrance	Front to back
10	2nd driver side window	Entrance/Exit	Side to side
11	2nd driver side window	Entrance/Exit	Side to side
12	3rd driver side window	Entrance	Side to side
13	Rear window	Entrance/Exit	Back/front
14	Rear window	Entrance/Exit	Back/front
15	Cargo door	Entrance	Inside to outside
16	Roof	Exit	Back to front
17	Roof	Exit	Back to front

4. A total of eighteen (18) 9mm spent casings were found at three different locations on westbound lanes of Route 66. The following table summarizes the location of the spent casings.

*Casing #	Location	Type
1	Driver's side of van	9mm
2	Driver's side of van	9mm
3	Driver's side of van	9mm
4	Driver's side of van	9mm
5	Driver's side of van	9mm
6	Driver's side of van	9mm
7	Front of van	9mm
8	Front of van	9mm
9	Front of van	9mm
10	Front of van	9mm
11	Front of van	9mm
12	Front of van	9mm
13	Front of van	9mm
42	Inside rear of van	9mm
43	Inside rear of van	9mm
45	Inside rear of van	9mm
46	Inside rear of van	9mm
63	Outside rear of van	9mm

* By State Police evidence tag number

5. These 9mm casings were identified through firing pin impression comparisons to the weapons involved in the shooting incident. The following table summarizes the results of the findings:

Item #	Location with respect to van	Fired from item #
1	Driver's side, ground	113
2	Driver's side, ground	113
3	Driver's side, ground	113
4	Driver's side, ground	113
5	Driver's side, ground	113
6	Driver's side, ground	114
7	Front, ground	109
8	Front, ground	109
9	Front, ground	INC
10	Front, ground	109
11	Front, ground	109
12	Front, ground	109
13	Front, ground	109
42	Rear, inside	117
43	Rear, inside	117
45	Rear, inside	117
46	Rear, inside	117
63	Rear, ground	117

6. The decedent was found outside the van on the ground between the right side of the van and a guardrail. The body was found in a supine position with both arms on the ground adjacent to the body. Based on the Medical Examiner's report, the decedent died of gunshot wounds received during the shooting incident. The following table describes the wounds received by the decedent.

Wound #	Type	Location	Trajectory
1	graze	left forehead	right to left inferior to superior
2	entry	posterior axillary line of left chest	left to right front to back slightly upwards
3	entry	back of neck	left to right back to front slightly upwards
4	entry	right upper back	subcutaneously lodged

7. A .22 caliber weapon was observed under the seat on the right side of the first row bench of the van. Upon examination of this weapon it was revealed that it contained four (4) discharged casings and two (2) bullets in the cylinder. In addition, examination of the interior of the van and surrounding area revealed a total of twenty-one (21) discharged .22

caliber casings and three (3) .22 caliber bullets. The following table shows where these casings and bullets were located in and round the van.

Submitted item	Location
#15	On ground below cargo doors
#19	On cargo door step of van
#21	On seat cushion of first row bench seat
#22	On seat cushion of first row bench seat
#23	On seat cushion of first row bench seat
#24	On floor behind front passenger seat
#25	On floor directly behind passenger seat
#26	On floor between driver's seat and front passenger seat
#27	On floor between driver's seat and front passenger seat
#28	On floor between driver's seat and front passenger seat
#29	On floor between driver's seat and front passenger seat
#30	On floor under accelerator pedal
#33	On floor below driver's seat
#34	On floor below driver's seat
#35	On floor below front passenger seat
#36	On floor below front passenger seat
#37	On floor front passenger side
#38	On floor front passenger side
#39	On floor behind driver's seat
#40	On floor behind driver's seat
#47	On floor behind the rear wheel well, passenger side
#48	On floor rear of the wheel well on the passenger side
#49	On floor under 3rd row bench seat
#137	On floor below the front passenger seat

8. Blood-like stains were observed on the front passenger seat of the van. Serological analysis determined that these blood-like stains were of human origin and consistent with coming from an individual with 'O' type blood. The pattern of this bloodstain is consistent with contact transfer deposit. Photograph #185 depicts this bloodstained area.

9. Blood and tissue-like material were observed on the interior region of the back door of the van. This material is consistent with a high velocity impact type of spatter pattern. This pattern is typically produced by a gunshot type injury. Serological analysis determined that these materials were of human origin and consistent with coming from an individual with 'A' type blood. Photograph #186 depicts the area in the van where this blood and tissue-like material was located.

10. Based on examination of the firearms evidence involved in the shooting incident and the crime scene reconstruction it was concluded that a total of 18 shots were fired by the State Police officers. The following table summarizes the number of shots fired by each weapon:

Weapon	Number of cartridge positively identified
#1 (submitted item #109) (serial #B73982Z)	6
#2 (submitted item #113) (serial #D01997Z)	5
#3 (submitted item #114) (serial #B74448Z)	1
#4 (submitted item #117) (serial #B78614Z)	5

NOTE: One discharged cartridge was unable to be positively identified. However, it was collected with the group of discharged cartridges fired by weapon #1.

11. The weapons described in the above paragraph were submitted to fingerprint section of the laboratory for latent print analysis. The results of the examination of these items revealed that there were no identifiable fingerprints located on these items.
12. Based on macroscopic examination of the bullet holes, trajectory determination, and laser sighting the following table summarizes the path of the projectiles fired during the shooting incident.

Location	Path of Projectile
Front Windshield	Hole #1 inside → outside, bullet not recovered
	Hole #2 inside → outside, bullet not recovered
	Hole #3 inside → outside, bullet not recovered
	Hole #4 → bullet in dashboard
	Hole #5A → #5 → back interior of van
	Hole #6 → bullet in dashboard
	Hole #7 outslde → inside, bullet not recovered
	Hole #8 → #32
	Hole #9 → engine block
Driver's Side 2nd Window	From window → #9 → #9A
Driver's Side 3rd Window	From window → #19 → #18 → #15 → #14, bullet not recovered
Back Window	From window → front interior of van
	From window → #28 → #27 → #23
	From window → #24
	From window → #25 → #21 → #16 → #12 → #10 → #8
	From window → #26 → #22 → #17 → #13

13. Based on the above table, a chart was constructed to represent the locations of the officers during the shooting incident. Please see Appendix D.

14. Eight (8) bullet holes were observed in the front windshield of the van. Examination of these holes revealed that five (5) of these hole came from shots fired into the van and three (3) of these hole came from shots fired out of the van. The following table summarizes these eight bullet holes:

Hole #	Location	Direction
1	Front windshield	Exit
2	Front windshield	Exit
3	Front windshield	Exit
4	Front windshield	Entrance
5	Front windshield	Entrance
6	Front windshield	Entrance
7	Front windshield	Entrance
8	Front windshield	Entrance

15. A review of a video tape produced by channel 8 WTNH indicates that two (2) of the bullet holes in the windshield were produced prior to the final stopping of the van. Photograph #187 is a freeze-frame photograph depicting these two (2) holes. In addition, the video tape also shows that the back window of the van was blown out and the left passenger side window was intact prior to the final stopping of the van as shown in photograph #188.

16. Based on the above information concerning the front windshield of the van, it can be concluded that only six (6) holes out of the eight (8) were produced in the front windshield during the final shooting incident. Furthermore, it can be concluded that one (1) of these six (6) holes was produced by a projectile exiting the van and that five (5) of the holes were produced by projectiles entering the van.

17. The number of casings recovered during the investigation suggest that at least twenty-five (25) rounds were fired by the decedent. However, with the limited information obtained, it can not be accurately determined how many shots were fired through the left window of the van or the rear window of the van and at what point of time these shots were fired.

18. Submitted item #105 consisted of "copper jacket fragments from van driver's hat". Laboratory examination of this item determined it to be a bullet jacket fragment from a Winchester Silvertip Hollow Point bullet (weight 20.83 grains). Due to the lack of individualizing characteristics, it could not be determined from what weapon this copper jacket fragment was fired. Macroscopic and microscopic examination revealed the presence of white colored paint-like material and fibers. Since the hat (item #104) from which this item was recovered was not submitted, no further analysis was conducted.

19. Figure #1 shows a sketch of the vehicle, the location of 3 bullet holes and the possible paths through the front windshield fired by the decedent with submitted item #20.

20. Figure #2 shows a sketch of the vehicle. Overlay shows the path of the bullets fired by submitted item #109, items #113, #114 and item #117.

21. Based on the results of the firearms examination of the weapons and the bullets recovered from the decedent's body, the following can be concluded. Two (2) of the projectile fragments recovered, due to severe damage, could not be identified as coming from which weapon. One (1) of the projectiles was identified to have come from weapon #4. The following table summarizes these results.

Item #	Item	Weight	Results
87	Bullet fragment	60.76 grains	Fragmented Winchester Silvertip Hollow Point bullet
88	Winchester Silvertip Hollow Point bullet	105.59 grains	Fired from weapon #4
89	Lead bullet core	70.15 grains	Consistent to caliber 9mm ammunition

22. Based on reconstruction of the trajectory and the examination of the physical evidence regarding the injured student, N. Crump, in the front passenger seat of the van, it was determined that the bullet was discharged from weapon #4. The trajectory of the projectile was at a slight downward angle from the rear to the front of the van. The trajectory reconstruction results indicate that the bullet did not travel in a straight path. Based on these conclusions, two scenarios are possible.
A. The first scenario is that the bullet was deflected in its path by hitting the material in the seats. This bullet subsequently entered the back of the front passenger seat and struck the student.
B. The second scenario is that the bullet at one point hit Mr. Jones or his clothing or another intermediate target beside the seat and was deflected at an angle by this obstruction. This bullet subsequently entered the back of the seat and struck the student.

23. The decedent (Jones) received four (4) gunshot wounds. The trajectory of the wound track on the left forehead is from front to back and is consistent with a graze. The other three (3) wounds enter his body but do not exit.

24. Macroscopical and microscopical examination of the student's clothing shows three (3) holes in the outer shell of his jacket, one (1) hole in the inner shell of the jacket, and one (1) hole in the shirt. The three (3) holes found in the outer shell of the jacket are consistent with a set of

entrance, exit, and re-entrance combination holes. This information could suggest that the student was in a position near parallel to the plane of the van floor in a slightly downward angle at the time when the bullet entered his jacket producing a set of three holes (entrance/exit/re-entrance). This bullet then entered the inner shell of the jacket and the shirt producing a path parallel to the plane of the floor.

25. Medical reports indicate that the student received a single gunshot wound to the upper body. This information further supports the position of the student at the time of the incident.

26. There is no physical evidence to indicate that any State Police officer's shots were directly aimed at the bus driver or either student at the time of the shooting.

ADDENDUM

On November 10, 1993 a meeting took place at the State Forensic Laboratory regarding this Laboratory Case. Present at this meeting were Dr. Henry C. Lee, Sgt. Robert Mills, Det. Michael Foley, and Daniel Tramontozzi.

During this meeting additional information was provided regarding the shooting incident in this case. In addition, four (4) items of physical evidence (not previously submitted to the Laboratory), were submitted.

Based on this new information and physical evidence, some of the trajectories of the five (5) shots that originated from the back window area of the van, as described in the Forensic Science Report, become uncertain and cannot be positively determined at this time. The reported trajectory D is one of two possible scenarios as stated in the conclusion of this report. Although the exact path of the trajectory cannot be positively determined, the general direction of the projectile remains the same.

LIMITED RECONSTRUCTION (FOCUS POINT: LOCATION OF PHYSICAL EVIDENCE)

At times incomplete crime scene documentation, coupled with insufficient recognition and collection of relevant evidence, result in an inability to conduct a full reconstruction. The basic elements – 6 W's: "Who, What, When, Where, Why, How" in any criminal investigation might never be completely answered. However, if sufficient crime scene documentation is available, a limited reconstruction might be able to be conducted. This type of reconstruction could provide answers for a limited scope of questions and issues related to the scene. The investigation into the deaths of Nicole Brown Simpson and Ronald Goldman was such a case. Thus, while it was not possible to fully reconstruct the case and determine the complete sequence of events or eliminate the event or actions that occurred, a limited reconstruction was still possible. The limited reconstruction can provide valuable answers for some of the questions related to the homicide.

On June 12, 1994, Nicole Brown Simpson and Ronal Goldman were brutally murdered at Nicole's Bundy Drive residence. At 12:10am two individuals, walking by the Bundy estate, observed the body of Nicole Simpson lying at the foot of the steps at the alcove to the residence. Ron Goldman's body was found by responding police officers. Nicole and Ron had been stabbed numerous times. In addition to the pools of blood under and around each of their bodies, blood was running down the walkways. Also, there were numerous bloody footwear impressions on the walkways and around the bodies; most of these visible footwear impressions were documented or preserved.

Unfortunately, chemical enhancement reagents for bloody footwear patterns were not used. Therefore, some of the latent footwear patterns were not documented or preserved.

Early on in the investigation O. J. Simpson, Nicole's ex-husband, became the prime suspect. During the investigation three areas of potential evidence were identified; Nicole Simpson's condo at Bundy which was the primary crime scene, whilst O. J. Simpson's Ford Bronco and Rockingham estate which were secondary crime scenes.

As previously mentioned, the majority of problems identified with the investigation and subsequent criminal trail can be attributed to incomplete crime scene searching, documentation and evidence collection and preservation. There were several of these issues with the Simpson and Goldman murder investigation. There was the failure to recognize, document, and preserve all of the pattern and physical evidence at the scene. In addition, there were bloodstains on O. J. Simpson's socks that were never adequately explained or accounted for during the investigation and trial. Finally, the missing or altered evidence at the scene were never reported and never explained during the trial.

Many of the questions and issues relating to the crime scene investigation were raised during the investigation. Although some of those questions appear trivial at the time of trial, they became important issues. A limited reconstruction was conducted and some of the issues were answered. Other issues will likely never be answered due to the lack of complete scene documentation and videotaping. Following are examples of some of these issues.

1. Whether or not physical evidence were handled or altered during the crime scene search.
2. Whether or not a second type of shoeprint was present at the Bundy crime scene.
3. Whether or not the crime scene at Rockingham was altered prior to documentation.
4. Whether or not the DNA evidence found at the Bundy scene was in fact O. J. Simpson's or due to contamination.
5. What is the mechanism of transfer of Nicole Simpson's DNA to O. J. Simpson's socks.

ISSUE 1

Recognition, collection, and preservation of all pertinent evidence are essential to any investigation – yet investigators failed to identify, or account for, several pieces of key evidence. Ron Goldman went to Nicole Simpson's home to return a pair of eyeglasses belonging to Nicole's mother, Juditha Brown, which was placed in a white envelope. The white envelope was located at the Bundy scene. In addition, the bloodstained envelope that contained the eyeglasses was depicted in two different locations in the series of crime scene photographs. Not knowing which location was the correct original location of the envelope was problematic – as there was pattern evidence, including bloody parallel line transfers on this envelope. Photographs 1 and 2 show two different locations where the bloodstained envelope (containing eyeglasses) were photographed. The locations of this envelope clearly shows that evidence was in fact picked up then re-positioned. Although this is not a critical issue in the investigation it raised some questions concerning the procedures used to search the crime scene.

In addition, one of the lenses was missing. Not only was the missing lens not found, but also there was no mention of efforts to locate the lens – or an

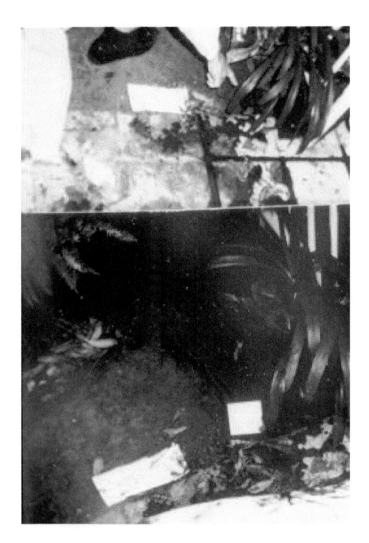

explanation as to its disappearance. Photograph 3 shows the bloodstained envelope, which contains the eyeglass. Photograph 4 is a close-up view of the eyeglasses with only one lens.

ISSUE 2

Crime scene investigators located and documented a bloody footwear imprint, which was later identified as being consistent with a size $12^1/_2$ Bruno Magli shoe. O. J. Simpson was reported to have worn such a pair of shoes. However, investigators never made note of – or documented – a second bloody footwear pattern located at the Bundy scene. During defense examination of the scene they observed these "parallel line" sole patterns of footwear impression on the Bundy walkway. These footwear patterns were consistent with a size 10 sneakers

Photo 3

Photo 4

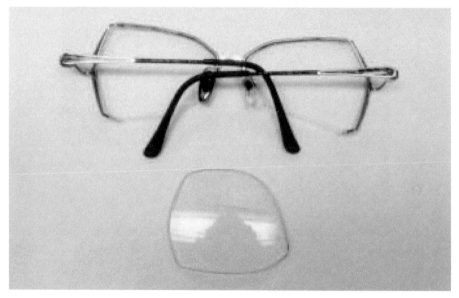

or boat shoe with parallel line sole pattern. A chemical presumptive blood test was performed on a swabbing taken from these bloody imprint patterns, and yielded positive results for presumptive test for the presence of blood. The bloody print enhancement reagent was not available for use by prosecutors. Application of bloody print enhancement reagents at initial crime scene search would have given a more complete picture as to the number of different footwear types, direction of travel associated with these patterns, and whether or not the "parallel line" bloody shoeprints were originally at the scene or

Photo 5

Photo 6

subsequently deposited at the scene of the crime. A partial sequence of events associated with the bloody footwear evidence could have been reconstructed. Photograph 5 shows the overall view of the walkway at Bundy crime scene. Photograph 6 shows a close-up view of one of the Bruno Magli shoe prints found on the Bundy walkway. Photograph 7 shows a "parallel line" type of shoe print found on Bundy walkway. Photograph 8 shows the results of a chemical presumptive test for blood.

Failure to recognize, collect, and preserve this footwear evidence to its fullest

Photo 7

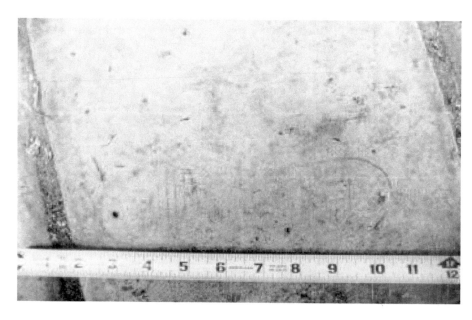

Photo 8

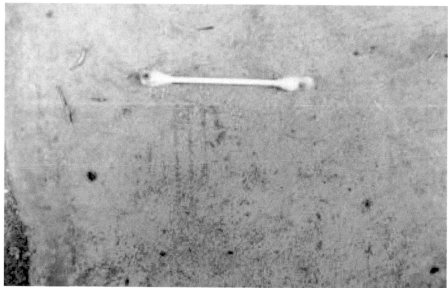

extent prohibited the ability to fully reconstruct the sequence of events and actions that transpired at Bundy, and in fact may have resulted in the failure to identify all parties involved with these brutal murders.

ISSUE 3

In addition to the issues related to the blood stained socks in O. J. Simpson's Rockingham bedroom, there were other discrepancies with the integrity of that

scene. A pair of pant suspenders located in that bedroom was depicted in various locations in different photographs. Also, one of the blood soaked leather gloves was found next to the fence of the breezeway on the side of the guest home at Rockingham.

Photographs 9 and 10 show the crime scene photographs depicting O. J. Simpson's bedroom at Rockingham home. The bottom photo shows the suspenders completely on the bed while the top photograph illustrated that the suspenders were hanging over the end of the bed. Once again, although this issue did not effect the overall investigation it illustrates the importance of crime scene integrity.

ISSUE 4

During the crime scene search investigators located 5 drops of blood on Bundy walkway. These 5 drops of blood were subjected to DNA analysis. Photograph 11

Photo 11

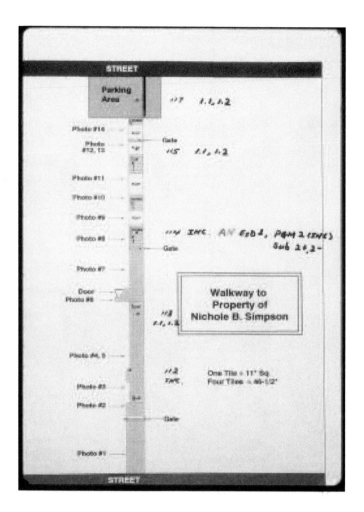

is a diagram showing the 5 drops of blood. Photograph 12 is a close-up view of the pattern.

The results of DNA testing from Los Angeles Crime Laboratory, Cellmark Diagnostic Laboratory and the Department of Justice Laboratory shows that the Bundy scene DNA matches O. J. Simpson's DNA. Defense raised questions concerning the DNA match. Defense experts review of DNA data from these laboratories and other serological and DNA results allowed for a limited reconstruction, concluding that the DNA from Bundy originated from O. J. Simpson. Photograph 13 shows a chart of DNA typing results. Photograph 14 is a news clipping showing defense experts agreeing with DNA results. However, the procedure used to collect bloodstains was questioned. According to investigators, bloodstains (Items 48, 50, 52) were collected on 13th June and dried overnight (as shown in Photo 15). Upon examination of the evidence it was found that the bloodstains were not dried as claimed. Photo 16 shows the wet blood transfer stain on the paper bindle.

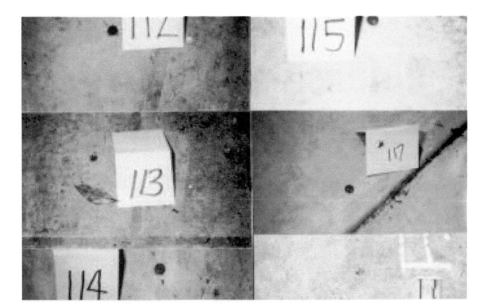

Photo 12

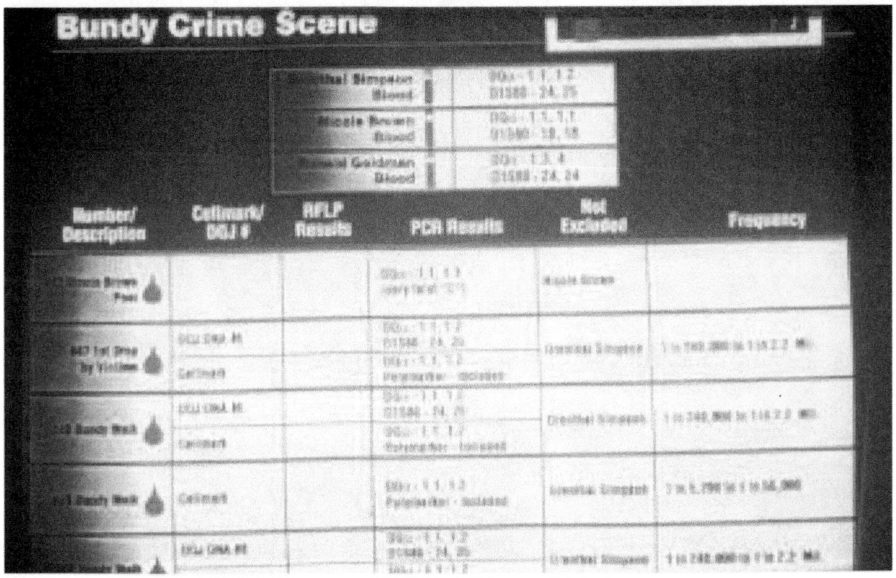

Photo 13

ISSUE 5

Investigators conducted a search at O. J. Simpson's Rockingham residence. Among other items, a pair of socks was seized from O. J. Simpson's bedroom floor. Several months after the search, laboratory personnel noted bloodstains on these socks. Upon review of crime scene documentation to observe exactly where the socks had been located a major discrepancy was noted. Crime scene photographs of the bedroom depicted the collected socks, which were blood stained.

Photo 14

Photo 15

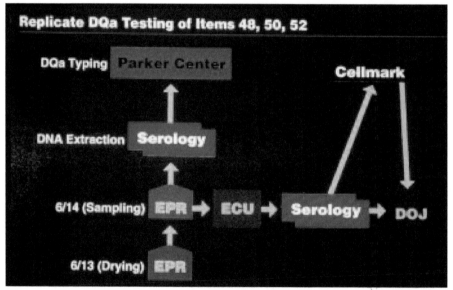

However, a video supposedly taken within 24 hours of the discovery of Nicole and Ron Goldman's bodies failed to show the socks within the bedroom. This issue became even more complicated when it was determined that the bloodstains on the sock contained EDTA, a common preservative for whole blood samples.

Moreover, a closer examination of the blood stained sock showed that the stain soaked through one side of the sock and into the interior, adjacent surface of the other side of the sock. This stain was found to be consistent with a compression transfer stain that could not have occurred if the blood was deposited on the sock when it was on someone's foot. Photograph 17 shows the location of

Photo 16

Photo 17

the socks found on the floor of O. J. Simpson's bedroom, and that there was no
bloodstain transfer on the carpet below were the bloody sock was located.

INDEX

9780124408302